The
Pentagon
Wars

The Pentagon Wars

Reformers
Challenge
the
Old Guard

James G. Burton

Naval Institute Press
Annapolis, Maryland

Frontispiece: The second-floor hallway of the Pentagon dedicated to the NATO alliance. Under the flags of the NATO nations, John Boyd, Chuck Spinney, and the author frequently met in secret to discuss national security matters. *Drawing by James G. Burton, Jr.*

© 1993 James G. Burton

Library of Congress Cataloging-in-Publication Data

Burton, James G., 1937–
    The Pentagon wars : reformers challenge the old guard /
James G. Burton.
        p.   cm.
    Includes bibliographical references and index.
    ISBN 1-55750-081-9 (acid-free)
    1. United States—Armed Forces—Reorganization.
2. United States—Military policy.   I. Title.
UA23.B795   1993
355'.00973'09049—dc20   93-3424
                                                CIP

Printed in the United States of America on acid-free paper ∞
9 8 7 6 5 4 3 2

First printing

Dedication

I dedicate this book to my late wife Nancy Lee, one of the most wonderful people who ever walked the face of this earth. As I wrestled with the decision to fight the system, she told me I had to do what I believed was right no matter what the consequences. "We can always get along," she would say. She insisted that I write this book because she felt the story was part of our history and needed to be recorded.

Throughout the trying times of that journey on the other side of the Rubicon, she was always there with her smile, the ever-present smile that lit up the darkest of days and touched the hearts of everyone who met her. I thank the Lord for the time we had together and for letting her see the completed first draft of this book.

Contents

The
Pentagon
Wars

Prologue

The initial euphoria of victory in the Gulf War has dissipated, but a lingering feeling of pride over a job well done still exists after more than two years. For the first time in almost half a century, the United States won a war, or so it seemed at the time. Although the victory itself was enough reason to celebrate, the manner in which we apparently won—swiftly, decisively, and with unbelievably few casualties—was cause for an even greater celebration. It signaled that a major change had occurred in the thinking of many U.S. military strategists and tacticians.

The "dinosaurs" of the 1960s and 1970s are slowly fading from the scene. A new breed of military thinkers, with totally different operational concepts, has arrived. As the dinosaurs become extinct, so will their philosophy of rushing to meet an opponent head on and slugging it out. The toe-to-toe approach to war can lead to victory, but it also leaves lots of dead bodies on both sides. It is an attrition philosophy where firepower is king, and the number of dead bodies is a measure of

1

2   who is winning. This war-fighting philosophy dominated military thinking during the Vietnam era and immediately thereafter.

In July 1976, the Army published this doctrine in *Field Manual 100-5, Operations,* which told commanders how to use their armored forces. The instructions reveal the mind-set of those officers who had risen through the ranks during the Vietnam War:

> The chief mission of these forces must be to fight with sufficient strength and tenacity to force the enemy to disclose the size and direction of his main attack, and to buy time while defending forces *concentrate in front of the main thrust.* . . . In mounted warfare, armored and mechanized elements (tanks and armored personnel carriers) must be set in motion toward the battle positions *in the path of the enemy thrust.*[1] (Emphasis added)

The philosophy embodied in these instructions was so important to the military thinkers of that time that the entire paragraph was emphasized with a box around it.

The new breed, on the other hand, thinks in terms of feints, deceptions, multiple thrusts, and the use of firepower to tie up the enemy while maneuvering around behind it and capturing its forces. Confusion, chaos, panic, surrender, "being inside the opponent's decision time," collapse, envelopment, hook around behind—this is the language of the new thinkers.

The Gulf War battle plans of the Army and the Marines were well conceived by this new breed. The execution of those plans, however, was bungled by the senior commanders, which suggests that considerable dinosaur blood remains within the upper ranks of the general officer corps—just enough to allow the majority of the elite Iraqi Republican Guard to escape a well-planned trap and continue as the linchpin of Saddam Hussein's power. (See the Epilogue for an expansion of this point.)

The conceptual framework for the Gulf War plans and the theoretical underpinning for the new breed of military thinkers who prepared those plans can be found in the "Green Book," so called because of the book's green cover. This unofficial publication, titled *A Discourse on Winning and Losing,* contains the unique theories of John Boyd, a retired Air Force colonel. During the past fifteen years, Boyd has become one of the premier military theorists in the United States.[2]

Between 1987 and the start of the Gulf War in January 1991, the Marine Corps's Amphibious Warfare School at Quantico, Virginia, printed and distributed one thousand copies of the Green Book.[3] More importantly, the Marine Corps ingested Boyd's theories into its own doctrine. *Fleet Marine Force Manual Number 1,* published by the Marine Corps in March 1989, is not as comprehensive as the Green Book, but its theoretical framework is clearly based on Boyd's work. The same can be said about the Army.

From the late 1970s through the early 1980s, Boyd unmercifully attacked the Army's 1976 edition of *Field Manual 100-5, Operations* and the philosophy it espoused. In countless briefings and lectures throughout the Department of Defense, he openly called the *Field Manual* "a piece of garbage." Boyd offered an alternative philosophy and concepts based on maneuver, rather than attrition. After considerable internal debate, the Army revised the *Field Manual* in 1982 and 1986. In those revisions, the Army threw out most of the dinosaurs' philosophy and embraced the philosophy espoused by Boyd.

Almost single-handedly, yet almost invisibly, Boyd has changed the way our military leaders think about and fight wars. A week before the Gulf hostilities began, Gen. Alfred Gray, commandant of the Marine Corps, acknowledged this in an interview with the *Wall Street Journal.*[4] General Gray had listened to Boyd's marathon briefings (that totaled thirteen hours) on his theories three separate times.

During countless hours in private sessions, Boyd explained his theories to Richard Cheney before Cheney became secretary of defense in March 1989. Cheney has a copy of the Green Book. And, long before the Gulf crisis, two copies of the Green Book were in the White House.[5]

Brig. Gen. Richard Neal, so familiar to millions of Americans as the daily television briefer in Saudi Arabia, studied Boyd's theories.[6] In one broadcast, General Neal stated, "We are inside the opponent's decision time." I nearly fell out of my chair—that phrase came directly from the Green Book. I knew immediately that Boyd's years of hard work finally had paid off. He had infiltrated the minds of many people involved in the Gulf War, and signs of his influence could be seen everywhere.

Even Gen. Norman Schwarzkopf used Boyd's vocabulary, including the unique concept mentioned by Neal. Schwarzkopf's "Jedi Knights," the people to whom he gives credit for planning his operations, studied Boyd's theories. Boyd's work was mandatory reading (at least early on) for the Jedi Knights during their schooling at Fort Leavenworth, Kansas.[7]

Boyd's contributions to the military go far beyond the Green Book. He and his colleague Pierre Sprey were personally responsible for the design, and the mere existence, of most of the combat aircraft used in the Gulf War. They are recognized as the fathers of the Air Force's F-15, F-16, and A-10 and the Navy's F/A-18.[8] The origin of the Stealth Fighter, the F-117, can be traced to the work of another colleague, C. E. "Chuck" Myers, Jr., and his "Harvey" project of the mid-1970s.

4   Boyd and Sprey were the leaders of a small band of mavericks and rebels, no more than a dozen or so people, who set out during the late 1970s to reform the military. Their goal was to change the military's thinking about people, tactics, and strategy; the kinds of weapons the Pentagon bought; the manner in which these weapons were tested; and the budgetary decision-making process associated with buying and fielding those weapons.

The first half of this book deals with the "Reform Movement"—who the reformers were, why they decided to take on the system, and how the system reacted to their criticisms. The second half of the book deals with my own experiences, as one of the hard-core reformers, in trying to get our front-line equipment tested to see how vulnerable it is to enemy fire under actual combat conditions.

Simply put, I wanted the Army to run some realistic tests of the Bradley Fighting Vehicle (BFV) to see what would happen to it and the people inside when it was hit by the kinds of weapons we could expect on the battlefield. The Army did not want to run these tests. We locked horns in a bitter bureaucratic fight lasting more than two years and occasionally spilling out into the public domain, where it became a national story. In the end, the Army tested the Bradley and, as a result of what it learned, changed the Bradley design in the middle of the production run to make it a safer vehicle in combat. The Army then did the same thing with its M-1 and M-1A1 tanks. As a consequence, I believe it is fair to say that many lives were saved in the Gulf War because of the controversial bureaucratic battles we fought during the middle 1980s.

Patriotism, admiration, and respect for the military have returned as a result of the Gulf War. The troops in the field rightfully earned this admiration and respect. Previously, however, a nasty and messy fight had taken place in the halls of the Pentagon for more than a decade. This book tells the ugly truth about the guerrilla warfare waged between the reformers and the establishment during the late 1970s and the 1980s that led to many significant changes in the military.

For years to come, military experts will analyze the Gulf War. Some of these analyses will certainly deal with the validity of many of the reformers' criticisms, as well as the influence the reformers had on the military. They will probably show that the reformers were right about a lot of things and wrong about others, but any competent analyst will show that serious and significant changes occurred in the military over a broad range of subjects as a result of the Reform Movement. My personal belief is that history will also show that, during the past two decades, John Boyd has had more influence on the military than any other single individual.

Prologue

I wrote most of this book before the Gulf War began. I later incorporated comments on the war where appropriate and added an epilogue relating to events just prior to, during, and after the war. Unfortunately, many combat details are not available to the public. Also, as usual, each military service is busy rewriting the history of the war to make its own contributions appear more significant than those of its sister services. By claiming the lion's share of credit for the victory, each hopes to avoid major budget cuts in the post–Cold War period. In many ways, nothing has changed in the Pentagon.

The reader may find unbelievable my description of certain events and actions by people inside the Pentagon. Although I have documented these events as best I can, the reader may still find it difficult to understand how people, especially those in positions of public trust, could behave as I describe. There are many reasons. Occasionally, such behavior results from honest disagreements over the best course of action that, in turn, lead to old-fashioned games of power politics. Quite often, however, the bizarre behavior—and misbehavior—that I describe occurred because people were corrupt, incompetent, blindly ambitious, or a combination of all three.

Careerism is a pervasive force inside the Pentagon. Its symptoms are often subtle, not blatant. As the various events unfold in the following chapters, I ask the reader to think about the motivation behind the actions of the people involved. Why did they do what they did? In each case, I try to present the reasons as part of the story, and the reader can find them. All too often, moral and ethical corruption, incompetence, and blind ambition, in some form, are the main culprits.

1

The Fighter Mafia

During the 1980s, the American public gave the Pentagon not only an unprecedented amount of money, but also its trust that the military would spend the money wisely for a strong national defense. Both the public's money and trust were squandered. In this book, the reader takes a trip inside the Pentagon for a view of what really goes on in the five-sided "puzzle palace." The trip is not pleasant. The business of buying weapons is dirty and corrupt from top to bottom. It will remain that way unless the process changes.

The Pentagon, the largest office building in the world, has more than 6.5 million square feet of floor area. At the height of the war in Southeast Asia, at least thirty thousand people went to work there every day. It is a cold, impersonal, intimidating building with more than seventeen miles of hallways and corridors.[1] One can easily get lost in these never-ending, drab, look-alike halls, in both a literal sense and a figurative sense.

Most career military officers who serve in the Pentagon hate it. They feel inadequate and unable

8   to influence events in the world's largest bureaucracy. They are over-
whelmed by the sheer magnitude of the issues, debates, and bureaucratic
battles. The hours are long, the cost of living is high, the traffic is terrible,
and the rewards are few. Yet, they have to be there at certain points in
their careers to be competitive for the next promotion. They must make
their marks quickly as team players worthy of advancement. Happiness is
defined by many officers as a copy of transfer orders in one hand, an outstanding fitness report in the other, and the Pentagon in the rearview mirror. Many sell their souls for that fitness report.

During twenty-seven years as an Air Force officer, I was assigned to the
Pentagon three times and served a total of fourteen years in the building.
Like everyone else, I reported to the Pentagon the first two times with the
hope of achieving some visibility, catching the eye of a few high-ranking
generals, and getting a few gold stars in my personnel folder that would
give me an edge with the next promotion board. By the third tour, I had
come of age and entered the building with the hope of changing the way
the Pentagon conducted its business. By that time, I had been a witness
to the moral and ethical corruption that was so commonplace at the
senior levels of both the military and civilian leadership. And what I saw
sickened me.

I was not alone in my belief that it was time for serious changes. For an
eight-year period—from the late 1970s to the mid-1980s—a small band of
rebels, who shared this belief, turned the Pentagon upside down and
shook it until its walls rattled. The group came to be known as the "Military Reformers." The establishment gave the rebels other names: traitors,
Luddites, fuzzy-heads, and conspirators who were hell-bent to embarrass
our national defense leaders. An Air Force vice chief of staff even called
them, in all earnestness, the evidence of "dark and satanic forces" at
work.

During these eight years, the reformers and the Defense establishment, civilian and military leaders in the Pentagon, Congress, and the
defense industry were locked in mortal combat. A dirty, nasty guerrilla
war was waged in the halls of Congress, inside the Pentagon itself, and in
headlines across the land. Many battles and skirmishes, some very messy,
took place. The reformers could claim victory in only a few engagements.
(I was personally involved in one of these victories.) The reformers, acting as the public's conscience, caused the senior civilian and military
leadership to work a little harder in making most major decisions that
would shape the future of the armed forces.

The Reform Movement burst on the national scene in October 1979
with the publication of James Fallows's "Muscle-Bound Super Power" in
The Atlantic Monthly.[2] Basically, the article charged that the United States

was investing in overly complex and costly weapons systems and had lost the "military art" and the ability to win. Fallows had been selected by the reformers to fire the first shot in what they anticipated would be a spirited fight. He had much help from John Boyd, Pierre Sprey, and Chuck Spinney.

Newspapers on the eastern seaboard immediately came to the Pentagon's defense and began attacking Fallows, his sources, and his basic theme. A few months later, Congressman Jack Edwards (with the help of a reformer) revealed to the public that Air Force mechanics had to spend money out of their own pockets to buy electronics parts at the local Radio Shack just to keep their sophisticated jet fighters in commission. This was followed by the Desert One fiasco in April 1980 (trouble began with equipment failures), when U.S. forces were embarrassed by their attempt to rescue the hostages in Iran. From that point on, a large portion of the press who covered the defense beat became sympathetic to the reformers and their message. So began the steady drumbeat of criticism aimed at the Pentagon by the reformers.

The Reform Movement was started by a small group of people, some inside and some outside of government, who sensed that something was seriously wrong with the Pentagon. Defeat in Vietnam, disaster at Desert One, unbridled ambition and rampant careerism in the officer corps of all services, the incestuous revolving door between the defense industry and Pentagon officials, the almost daily revelation of horror stories about $600 toilet seats and $400 hammers, a steady stream of weapons systems either inadequately tested or purchased regardless of poor test results, and a regular diet of senior military and civilian officials lying to the public and Congress to cover up embarrassments were only a few of the symptoms of a corrupt business that cried out for reform.

The reformers sought not only revisions in the mechanical procedures and processes of the Pentagon's system of buying weapons but a change in the mind-set of the military and civilian leadership. In their view, the entire Pentagon needed shaking—until the military came to its senses—until it learned how to win wars again—until it learned how to buy weapons that were affordable and actually worked in combat. The small group of reformers attempted to do the shaking.

The driving forces behind the Reform Movement were John Boyd and Pierre Sprey. They are as different as night and day, as different as the left and right hemispheres of the brain. In fact, that is probably the best way to describe these two remarkable men.

Sprey is an analytical genius. He entered Yale University at age fifteen and was graduated with a double major, French literature and mechanical engineering—an interesting combination. By the time he was twenty-one years old, he had a master of engineering degree in mathematical statistics and operations research from Cornell University. Born in Nice, France, Sprey is fluent in French and German; the reformers nicknamed him "the Alsatian." He is a handsome, dashing figure—Gallic features, medium stature, silver-gray hair, and an ever-present scarf around his neck—a dashing personality with a rapier for a tongue.

To Sprey, the world is black and white. To Boyd, the intuitive, creative genius, on the other hand, the world appears in various shades of gray. Pierre thinks in absolutes; Boyd thinks in relative terms. They are so different, yet so alike—two mavericks who have no patience for bureaucrats or incompetence and who love a good fight with the establishment.

From 1966 through 1970, Sprey was a special assistant in the Office of the Secretary of Defense and one of Robert MacNamara's "whiz kids." He studied combat to see how weapons were actually used as opposed to how we thought they would be used. His studies provided insights into weapons system characteristics that were indeed useful in combat.

Sprey's analyses of combat results often provided insights that ran contrary to the claims of high-technology advocates who have slowly, but surely, taken over positions of authority in the Department of Defense. For example, one analysis Sprey published in 1968 showed that pilots delivering precision-guided munitions in Southeast Asia suffered two to three times as many hits from enemy ground fire as did pilots delivering regular, dumb bombs. To the growing crowd of officials enamored of high-tech guided weapons, this was an extremely unwelcome conclusion.

Boyd studied combat and all forms of conflict, for insights into the fundamentals of tactics and strategies as they affect human behavior in conflict. His treatise, "A Discourse on Winning and Losing," will go down in history as the twentieth century's most original thinking in the military arts. No one, not even Karl von Clausewitz, Henri de Jomini, Sun Tzu, or any of the past masters of military theory, shed as much light on the mental and moral aspects of conflict as Boyd. And, he tested his theories during the Reform Movement. Together, Boyd and Sprey are an unbeatable combination, as many high-ranking Pentagon officials have discovered the hard way.

John Boyd is a national asset, but the public does not know him. He prefers it that way. As an Air Force fighter pilot, he laid out the basic tactics used by Air Force, Navy, and Marine pilots in Vietnam. His energy-maneuverability theories revolutionized fighter designs. Boyd conceptualized the relationship of altitude and energy, as expressed in a common term of maneuvering potential. Maneuverability is displayed in chart form for each individual aircraft type. These charts, known as "E-M diagrams," are overlaid, one over another, and plainly show a pilot at what speed-altitude combinations the plane will have a maneuvering advantage, or suffer a disadvantage, in air combat against specific enemy aircraft types. E-M has been a key factor in the development of U.S. Air Force and U.S. Navy air superiority tactics, doctrine, and equipment.

Boyd's trade-off techniques were directly responsible for the superior performance of the Air Force's two frontline fighters, the F-15 and F-16. In fact, the mere existence of these two planes is due largely to Boyd.

After Boyd retired from the Air Force in 1975, his creative genius took him on a journey through the history of conflict from 400 B.C. to the present, and through the disciplines of mathematical logic, physics, thermodynamics, biology, psychology, and anthropology. He was looking for bits and pieces of knowledge that would, in his words, "unveil the character of conflict, survival, and conquest" in a competitive and hostile world. Boyd's great talent is the ability to integrate seemingly unrelated ideas and notions into a synthesis, but he pays a price for his genius.

Boyd is eccentric. His behavior at times can appear irrational, like a wild man's. I say appear, because often that is a calculated move on his part. Madman or genius? His enemies could never quite decide. Slightly over six feet tall and athletic looking, Boyd radiates intensity. He enjoys making people uneasy—it gives him an advantage.

Over the years, Boyd has earned several nicknames: "The Mad Colonel," "The Ayatollah," "Genghis John," and, quite often, "That F___ing Boyd," a term of endearment usually uttered by a general who had just had his clock cleaned by Boyd.

His mind is uncontrollable. You cannot communicate with him unless the window into his mind is open, but there are no visible signs to tell you when it is open. You can talk to him and he will answer you. Twenty minutes later, you may discover that the window had been closed and nothing registered.

Boyd needs other people to use as sounding boards for his ideas. Along with Chuck Spinney, Ray Leopold, Pierre Sprey, and a few others, I have been fortunate to be one of those sounding boards. Our conversations are open-ended and spontaneous. His mind picks the topics and the direction of the discussion. Typically, the telephone rings late at night and Boyd starts by saying, "Let me read you something." For the next hour or two, he reads from a book on quantum physics, mathematical logic, military history, or a host of other disciplines. We then discuss the implications of what he has read or how those ideas fit into his grand synthesis on conflict.

These conversations became a daily part of my life for more than a decade. They also tied up the line so much that my wife bought me a separate telephone with an unlisted number. The "Boyd Phone," as it was

12 called, became the envy of the other reformers. I was forced to read books and study harder than I had in graduate school just so I could keep up my end of the conversations. The price of admission to the club of Boyd confidants was high but well worth the effort. (See Appendix A for a list of Boyd's required reading.)

Although his contributions to the military have been immeasurable, his rewards have been few. When you challenge the system with unconventional ideas and behavior, the system usually reacts violently, especially when you prove it wrong and force it to change. Over and over again, Boyd drummed this into my head. This is one of the key ideas I hope to get across as the story of the Reform Movement unfolds in coming chapters. The hard-core reformers understood this concept, yet they chose to take on the system regardless of the consequences. The system reacted as they expected.

Boyd is a subject worthy of a book in itself. I can only shed a little light on this complex and remarkable man. He was an Air Force fighter pilot during the 1950s and saw combat in Korea.[3] Fighter pilots in those days were wild, aggressive, irreverent, self-confident, and independent—they had to be in order to survive. The training was so aggressive and realistic that pilots killed themselves left and right.

After the war, Boyd was an instructor pilot at the Fighter Weapons School in Nevada, where he earned the nickname "40-second Boyd."[4] As the stories go, he would accept any challenge to "meet me over the green patch and we'll see who's the best"—the terms were forty seconds or $40. Boyd would rendezvous with his opponent high over a green piece of Nevada real estate and, within forty seconds, wind up in firing position on his opponent's tail. If he couldn't whip an opponent in forty seconds, he would pay the $40.

In 1960, Boyd published his *Aerial Attack Study*, the first comprehensive logical exposition of all known (and some hitherto unknown) fighter tactics in terms of moves and countermoves. Previous tactics manuals were just bags of tricks, without the logic of move and countermove. Boyd did not advocate one maneuver over another but presented the options (and the logic for selecting them) available to a pilot to counter any move his opponent made. The study represented the first time that anyone had based fighter tactics on three-dimensional, rather than two-dimensional, maneuvers.

The moves and countermoves laid out in this study formed the basis for all fighter tactics used by Air Force, Navy, and Marine fighter pilots in Southeast Asia. It is still the basis for tactics used in all jet fighter air forces today. Visualizing these moves and countermoves was instinctive to Boyd—this is the way he thinks. According to the Navy Fighter Weapons

School journal, *Top Gun*, since Boyd's 1960 treatise "not even one truly   **13**
new move has been uncovered."[5]

In 1962, the Air Force sent Boyd to Georgia Institute of Technology to get an engineering degree. There, he formulated his famous energy-maneuverability theories, which were to revolutionize fighter aircraft design. He developed a series of equations that, for the first time, tied together in one package the twisting, turning, and accelerating maneuvers required by fighter tactics and linked them to the aerodynamic design parameters of thrust, weight, lift, and drag. For this tremendous scientific achievement, Boyd later received the Harold Brown Award, the highest scientific award given to an Air Force engineer.

When Boyd left Georgia Tech, he reported to Eglin Air Force Base, Florida. There he met and befriended Thomas P. "Tom" Christie, a civilian mathematician. With Christie's help, Boyd's theories were translated into computer programs to compare existing U.S. fighters with enemy fighters in order to develop better tactics.[6] Later, when Boyd was redesigning the F-15, Christie and Boyd wrote new computer programs that permitted engineers quickly and easily to perform aircraft design trade-off studies. (Boyd and Christie would team up again in years to come and cause discomfort to many Pentagon officials.)

With this computer tool, engineers could change a design at will and immediately learn what effect the changes had on a fighter's ability to perform twisting and turning maneuvers. They could then shape a design for the tactics they wanted the plane to use. The tool also indicated to fighter pilots which maneuvers both their planes and their opponents' planes had the potential to perform at any point in their twisting and turning battle. The impact of this work on the aircraft design world, as well as the development of new fighter tactics and the training of fighter pilots, cannot be overstated.

In the mid-1960s, the Air Force decided it wanted a new fighter aircraft of high performance for real air-to-air maneuvering; not an unmaneuverable interceptor, like the F-4, handed down from the Navy or an expensive, sluggish disaster, like the F-111. The Air Force had just come through the unpleasant experience of having to defend the F-111, which was a kluge of technological fads. An 80,000-pound, twin-engine, swing-wing radar bomber masquerading as a fighter, the F-111 was expensive to buy and to operate.

The Air Force's new fighter was designated the F-X. Its initial design looked remarkably like the F-111 and the Navy's F-14. The proposed design was a general-purpose fighter, with a huge weight of 60,000 pounds, many F-111 features, such as twin engines, and variable sweep wings.[7] It did not take a genius to figure out that the secretary of defense

14   and the Congress would never approve a multibillion dollar program to develop a new airplane that looked just like the last one.

By this time, Major Boyd and his theories were known to many senior Air Force officials and he was highly sought after as a lecturer on fighter tactics. Called to the Pentagon from Florida, Boyd received the task of converting a floundering fighter program into an acceptable one. Boyd's new boss, Gen. K.C. "Casey" Dempster gave him two weeks to study the F-X design and then summoned him to his office. Dempster asked, "Well, Major, what do you think of our F-X design?"

He responded in typical Boyd fashion, "Hell, I've never designed an airplane before, but I could f___ up and still do better than this." He was promptly given the chance.

The chief of staff gave Boyd wide freedom. He soon learned, though, that the chief's blessing was not enough. Before Boyd could truly change the proposed design of the F-X, he had to change the minds of people in the various technical communities within the Air Force and the industry. These people and their institutions had wormed their pet technologies into the design. They justified their existence and their continued share of the Air Force budget by the fact that their technological ideas had been actually incorporated into a weapons system headed for the inventory. Once in the design, they would fight tooth and nail to stay there.

Boyd began the difficult task of completely redoing the F-X design and, in the process, bringing discipline to the design process. To do this, either he had to convert many people to the notion that technical features should be the *output* of a disciplined design trade-off process, not the *input*, or he had to simply clean them out by proving that their pet features were of no value to the whole system. In the bureaucratic battles that followed, many were converted but more were cleaned out.

When the smoke cleared, the F-X had changed from a 60,000-pound, swing-wing F-111 look-alike to a 40,000-pound, fixed-wing, twin-engine agile fighter based on Boyd's energy-maneuverability theories.[8] For the first time in history, an Air Force fighter had specific design requirements for maneuvering.

Boyd's reputation as a maverick, an unconventional thinker whose ideas ran counter to the establishment, was firmly established. So, too, was his reputation as a master of bureaucratic infighting.

In the middle of the F-X redesign exercise, Boyd's maverick behavior got him fired (transferred off the job with prejudice). He had irritated his immediate supervisor, an ambitious colonel. Before he could pack his bags and leave the Pentagon for another assignment, several generals realized that Boyd was the only person who understood his design theories well enough to complete the job. To save the F-X, Boyd had to be reinstated. Boyd also knew this. In his typical fashion, he refused to go back to the job until the colonel who had fired him called him in and ceremoniously rehired him—the pound of flesh.

In the spring of 1967, Boyd met Sprey and briefed him on his trade-off techniques and the new F-X design. Boyd had been sent to clean out Sprey, who was viewed as an Air Force enemy, a possible roadblock within the Office of the Secretary of Defense to the success of the Air Force's new fighter.[9] Sprey was already making noises about excessive costs and complexity and inadequate effectiveness.

Sprey immediately recognized the power of Boyd's theories and techniques. In them, he saw the opportunity to develop much more combat-realistic analyses of fighter effectiveness and to use them to design austere, high-performance fighters. Austere meant that each fighter would be better and more effective, and that more fighters could be fielded for the same budget. Sprey was a strong, vocal advocate for larger numbers of weapons with higher effectiveness at lower cost. To him, effectiveness and numbers were more important than technical complexity. Boyd and Sprey were immediately drawn together by common beliefs. Thus began a long and very close friendship. It was also the beginning of the "Fighter Mafia."

The following year, Boyd's 40,000-pound F-X design was formally approved by the secretary of defense. The F-X designation was changed to the F-15, and the plane would replace the F-4Es in the Air Force inventory.[10] Air Force senior leaders were euphoric, for they now had their own design and it would be much hotter than the Navy's competitor, the VFX/F-14. Left to its own devices, the Air Force probably would have made the F-15 a much heavier, variable geometry (swing-wing) aircraft with less capability of high maneuverability and good acceleration for close-in air combat. Given the eventual increase in weight of the F-15, as built, and the delays in fielding higher-performance engines, such an aircraft might have been a disaster without Boyd's contribution.

Boyd and Sprey were not satisfied, however, with the 40,000-pound design. Even before the design was approved, they argued strongly throughout the Pentagon that the weight (along with the cost) could be lowered to 33,000 pounds by stripping a few of the combat-irrelevant design specifications.[11] For example, was it really necessary for the airplane to have a top speed of 2.5 times the speed of sound? Most air combat occurred at subsonic speeds and never occurred above one and a half times (1.5) the speed of sound. A top speed of 2.5 carried with it severe design penalties, such as the need for engine inlets that constantly changed their geometry to meter the proper amount of air into the engine. Boyd called them "talking inlets" and felt that a lower top speed would permit fixed inlets, which were cheaper and simpler. Sprey felt that the fixed inlets would actually give hotter accelerating performance in the critical fighting regime right around the speed of sound. Boyd and Sprey believed that other, similar features were also irrelevant and harmful to high dogfight performance.

A normal Air Force officer who has just saved a major Air Force program would bask in the limelight and soak up all the praise from the generals, but Boyd is not normal. His criticisms of a design that had his own signature on it created quite a stir.

Boyd and Sprey were still rebuked by the Air Force, and the 40,000-pound design was approved.[12] Had the Air Force listened to them and taken the F-15 design down to 33,000 pounds, the Air Force's next fighter, the F-16, probably would not exist today. Because they were rebuked, Boyd and Sprey decided to redouble their efforts. If relaxing a few specifications would drop the weight from 40,000 to 33,000 pounds, what would happen if all specifications were challenged? They set out together to find the answer. Using Boyd's theories, Sprey started with a clean piece of paper and laid out a whole new design.

This design turned out to be a single-engine, fixed-wing fighter weighing 25,000 pounds, with 35,000 pounds of thrust—a fighter of unprecedented maneuvering performance. Pierre called it the "F-XX," a not so subtle dig at the F-X.[13] He gave a copy of his work to two contractor design teams, one at General Dynamics Corporation and the other at Northrop Corporation, for independent validations. These designers confirmed most of Sprey's calculations.

In March 1970, the American Institute for Aeronautics and Astronautics (AIAA) sponsored a large conference of aircraft designers in Saint Louis, the home of the F-15 contractor. The idea was to have designers gather and sing praise to the Air Force's new fighter, the F-15. Sprey was invited to be the keynote speaker. Instead of praising the F-15, he announced, "We can do better," whereupon he revealed the 25,000-pound F-XX concept and called for a competition between two contractors, each building two prototypes and going head to head in a fly-off contest.[14] Needless to say, the speech created quite a stir.

In the meantime, a third musketeer had joined forces with Boyd and Sprey. Col. Everest Riccioni was a fighter pilot and aeronautical engineer serving on the Air Staff. He recognized the power of Boyd's theories and also favored lightweight, low-cost fighters. Boyd and Riccioni had known each other since the 1950s. Together, they refined Boyd's combat task–oriented, trade-off process. They laid out six specific tasks, or maneuvers, that a fighter should accomplish on a typical combat mission.

Riccioni believed that when Boyd's theories were applied to these combat tasks, a superior fighter could be designed in the 17,000- to 20,000-pound class and based on the already paid-for F-15 engine.[15] This was an important step forward in practicality because Sprey's F-XX was based on a completely new fighter-optimized engine.

To prove that such a hot lightweight fighter could be built, Riccioni let a small, innocuous study contract to General Dynamics and Northrop in February 1971.[16] In an effort to keep the study quiet, it was entitled "Study to Validate the Integration of Advanced Energy-Maneuverability Theory with Trade Off Analysis," but, in reality, this was the preliminary design and analysis of three lightweight fighter configurations.

There was a certain sense of urgency in Riccioni's study contracts, for he had learned that the Navy was secretly working on a lightweight fighter design of its own to replace the F-14.[17] Unless the Fighter Mafia beat the Navy to the punch, the Air Force would probably wind up with another Navy airplane. Yet, all this maneuvering had to be kept quiet because the Fighter Mafia's ideas were a threat to the F-15 program. No sensible person could envision the Air Force building two different fighters at the same time. The F-15 was an approved program, and the Air Force would not permit any new proposal that might siphon money and support away from it.

A serious student of guerrilla warfare would do well to study the operations of the Fighter Mafia. Quietly, secretly, it worked the hallways, back doors, and alleys of the Pentagon and the aircraft industry. Its members probed the establishment everywhere and looked for any signs of support for their theme of building a better fighter than the F-15 at half the cost. Slowly but surely, they established a network of sympathetic key officials within the Air Force and the Office of the Secretary of Defense, a network that would be instrumental when it came time to strike in the open. Before that could happen, however, one member of the Fighter Mafia became a casualty.

Riccioni would not be called a shy, bashful wallflower. He loves to talk, and he has a way of embellishing his stories. At a large cocktail party attended by many senior Air Force officials, Riccioni became too vocal and too visible in preaching his Fighter Mafia theme. Gen. John C. Meyer, the vice chief of staff, was not amused by Riccioni's comments. On the contrary, he saw Riccioni as a serious threat to the fledgling F-15 program.

General Meyer reacted like most senior generals in the Air Force when they encounter a dissenting view in their own ranks. Rather than counter that view with convincing arguments, they simply remove the source of the dissent. Ten days after the cocktail party discussions with General Meyer, Riccioni received transfer orders to Korea where he could preach his unconventional views on fighter design to the local citizens until he was blue in the face.[18]

The practice of purging the ranks of "difficult" subordinates—people who question the wisdom of conventional thinking, who challenge their superiors, who do not automatically salute and say, "yes sir, yes sir, six bags full," when their superiors speak—over the years has produced a crop of senior officials long on form and short on substance. The long-term result of stifling dissent and discouraging unconventional views, while rewarding those who conform, is an officer corps that is sterile, stagnant, and predictable. Promoting clones, while purging mavericks, is tantamount to incest. We all know the possible long-term effects of generations of incest—feeblemindedness, debilitation, and insanity.

Another aspect of the Pentagon story relates to the "total package procurement" concept. By 1971, the Pentagon had been widely attacked for this much ballyhooed method of buying weapons systems, by which the government bought weapons primarily based on paper analyses of cost and performance. The contractor was given a large pile of money and left alone to design, build, and deliver the system with little government review, control, or testing. The contractor was responsible for the total package. In 1969, the Air Force's C-5A cargo plane had become famous because of a $2 billion cost overrun incurred under this concept.[19] So, Congress and many Defense officials were looking for another way to buy weapons.

Sprey was very active in his advocacy of building prototypes first and then having head-to-head fly-off competitions to pick the more effective competitor. This was diametrically opposed to the total package approach where the competition was based on paper promises. Many people began to listen to Sprey.

Dr. Alan Simon, head of research and development in the Defense Department, was one who listened. In July 1971, he convinced Deputy Secretary David Packard to put up a $200 million pot and direct the services to put together, for his approval, candidate programs that were suitable for prototype competition funded under the $200 million pot.[20] All of a sudden, everything began to fall into place for the Fighter Mafia. Riccioni's secret seed money was ready to bear fruit, and Packard wanted to see if prototypes were feasible. Of course, the Fighter Mafia had a lot to do with everything falling into place.

Boyd and Sprey developed a program that would allow the Air Force to grab the lion's share of Packard's $200 million pot, and they proposed a lightweight fighter prototype competition. They could move much faster than any other Air Force or non–Air Force team because Riccioni's design study provided all the necessary data and validation. The games entered a new phase, and the plot thickened.

As Boyd began briefing his lightweight fighter proposal up the Air Staff ladder, the senior leaders saw immediately that the proposal could be a serious threat to the F-15 program. Concern was growing about the rising costs of the F-15, and someone might want to drop it for whatever came out of Boyd's proposal.

Boyd received a tip from one of the moles in his information network. The senior leaders' game plan was to let Boyd proceed up the Air Staff and get a positive endorsement at each level until he got to the top, where the three-star generals would shoot him down in flames and disapprove his proposal. This would give the outward appearance that his proposal had received an honest and serious consideration but simply did not make the final cut, so to speak.

Briefing the lowest-level committee on the Air Staff, Boyd got the colonels' endorsement. He then briefed, and received the green light of approval from, the next-highest committee made up of two-star generals. Before going before the three-stars and the vice chief for final approval, Boyd made a telephone call to a member of his underground who had direct access to the deputy secretary of defense. Boyd's proposal fit Packard's agenda. The secretary was immediately convinced to go for the program.[21]

Boyd's next stop was the vice chief and his three-star crew. They were looking forward to the briefing. So was Boyd, but for other reasons. His opening remarks sent them into shock: "Gentlemen, this is not a decision briefing. Since the secretary of defense has already approved this program, today's briefing will be for information only."[22]

The generals were stunned. They were looking forward to sticking it to Boyd; instead, he outwitted them on an end run. There was nothing they could do about it. In the words of one, "That F___ing Boyd struck again."

The rest is history. Two competing designs were picked from a field of six. During the next two and a half years, two prototype aircraft of each design were built and flight-tested in a fly-off competition for a total cost of $86 million, a truly remarkable feat.[23] The "Statement of Work," the contractual document outlining what the government wanted from industry (written by Boyd and Sprey), also reflected the Fighter Mafia's philosophy—short and simple. It was only 25 pages long, and contractor proposal responses were forbidden to be longer than 50 pages, a revolution.[24] Doing this today inside the system would take 10 years, cost billions, and result in contractual documents 25 feet high. I invite anyone who doubts this to examine the B-1B and B-2 bomber programs, as well as a host of others.

The two aircraft, designated the YF-16 and the YF-17, were built by General Dynamics and Northrop, respectively. Both were superior dog-fighting aircraft. They both whipped every aircraft they went up against in the fly-off, but the YF-16 usually won a little quicker than the YF-17. The YF-16 was picked as the winner and became the Air Force's F-16.[25] The Navy took the YF-17 design, modified it somewhat, added a lot of weight and cost, and put it into production as the F-18.

The Fighter Mafia got to a confidant of James Schlesinger as soon as he was sworn in as secretary of defense. Based on the confidant's advice, Schlesinger made the lightweight fighter his top-priority program and enticed the Air Force to accept the F-16 into its inventory. In exchange for its reluctant agreement, he permitted the Air Force to increase the size of its tactical forces from twenty-two to twenty-six wings (a wing is comprised of about one hundred aircraft).[26] The Air Force did not really want the F-16 but could not pass up the opportunity to have four hundred more airplanes.

Meanwhile, with Schlesinger's active encouragement, the United States joined with Belgium, Denmark, the Netherlands, and Norway to form a five-nation consortium to produce the F-16 jointly for the air forces of these countries. Under this agreement, a total of 650 aircraft would be produced for the U.S. Air Force and 348 for the Europeans.

A steering committee was established to manage this large, international program, with the United States as permanent chairman. The job was assigned to the Air Force's assistant secretary for research, development and logistics.[27] The chairman reported directly to the secretary of defense on all matters dealing with F-16 production. Even though he was an Air Force assistant secretary, he could make decisions or take positions contrary to those of the corporate Air Force when the F-16 was involved. He could take his views directly to the secretary of defense without passing through the Air Force filters. This unique arrangement proved quite important a few years later when the F-15 crowd, who had by then risen through the ranks to the highest levels in the leadership, launched a concerted effort to shut down the F-16 production line in favor of more F-15s.

The reader might find an explanation of a few of the differences between the F-15 and F-16 useful at this time. These differences became the main points of contention between the Fighter Mafia and the senior Air Force leadership and led directly to the Reform Movement.

Most importantly, the F-16 was the first and last fighter that cost less than its predecessor.

Both aircraft used the same engine, with two in the F-15 and one in the F-16. The single engine allowed the F-16 to come in at only half the size, half the weight, and half the cost of the F-15. The F-15 could fly 2.5 times the speed of sound; however, history shows that combat never occurred at this speed. The F-16's top speed was intentionally limited to only

1.9 times the speed of sound, thereby allowing it to accelerate much faster.

Both aircraft were designed primarily for dogfighting. The F-16 could pull 9 g's in a tight turn, while the F-15 was limited to 7.33 g's. Even though the F-16 was smaller, it could fly farther than the F-15. When all this became apparent, the F-15 went through several modifications to beef up its wings and add more fuel so it could pull as many g's and fly as far as its little brother. The added weight further increased its maneuvering inferiority to the F-16.

The F-15 carries radar-guided air-to-air missiles for shooting at enemy aircraft at long ranges (beyond visual range). It also carries infrared tracking missiles and a gun, both of which are for short-range (within visual range) dogfights. History shows that, until the Gulf War, long-range kills seldom occurred and the overwhelming majority of air fights were close-range dogfights. Between 1958 and 1982, there were 2,014 trigger squeezes by fighter pilots engaged in air-to-air combat in five wars, but they resulted in only four beyond-visual-range kills.[28] Thus, the F-16 does not carry the expensive, relatively unreliable, and nonlethal radar-guided missile that seldom had been effectively used at long range, as its advocates promised, prior to the Gulf War.*

Both the F-15 and the F-16 are outstanding fighters, but the F-16 is slightly better. Its small size makes it harder to see, it is more maneuverable, and, since it costs less, there are more of them in the sky. Both aircraft saw combat in the 1982 Middle East war. The Israeli Air Force assigned the F-15 only the job of air-to-air combat to gain and maintain control of the skies. The F-16, on the other hand, was given the primary job of dropping bombs on ground targets. Even so, the little F-16 wound up shooting down more enemy aircraft than its big brother. It also suffered fewer hits from enemy fire and had less combat damage to repair.[29]

At the same time the Fighter Mafia was maneuvering the F-16 through the bureaucratic swamps, it was also ushering another combat aircraft,

---

*The Gulf War marked the first time that air forces of any nation achieved a significant number of beyond-visual-range combat kills. According to an unclassified Air Force briefing in March 1991, sixteen of the total thirty-five Iraqi fighters shot down by allied pilots were credited to Air Force F-15s firing radar-guided missiles beyond visual range. (The number of misses and launch failures is not known.) Before launching their missiles, pilots were required to have two independent sources of information that identified the target as an enemy. The nature of the air war, primarily ambushes of Iraqi planes fleeing to Iran as opposed to a large-scale free-for-all, was conducive to the Air Force pilots' obtaining two sources before firing. Because Navy pilots could not communicate with Air Force early-warning radar aircraft, one of the prime sources of identification information, they were never able to obtain a second source. Consequently, there were no Navy beyond-visual-range kills in the war.

the A-10, into the inventory. Like the F-16, the A-10 was the product of a prototype fly-off competition. It defeated both its prototype competitor, the A-9, and, later in another fly-off, a conventional, high-speed attack jet, the A-7.

Throughout U.S. air history, the A-10 was the first and only aircraft designed to attack ground targets and provide direct support to troops on the ground. That means bombing and strafing the enemy in close proximity to U.S. troops, often when they are intertwined. A simple, lethal, extraordinarily survivable, relatively inexpensive airplane devoid of high-tech bells and whistles, the A-10 was designed in true Fighter Mafia fashion.

Under the National Security Act of 1947, the Army Air Corps was separated from the Army and became the U.S. Air Force. The Key West Agreement (so named because the key elements of the military reorganization of the War and Navy departments into the Department of Defense were negotiated at a conference in Key West, Florida) spelled out the terms of this separation. One of the missions assigned to the new Air Force was that of providing close air support to the Army ground forces. The Army, on the other hand, was prevented from purchasing any fixed-wing aircraft that weighed over 10,000 pounds, the kind of aircraft usually involved in a close air-support mission.

Since the Key West Agreement, the Air Force has considered the close air support mission its lowest priority. It has been reluctant to commit a significant portion of its budget solely to this mission. The A-10, designed during the early 1970s and no longer in production, was the only aircraft ever developed by the Air Force specifically for this role. The mission is usually accomplished with aircraft designed initially for other missions, such as air-to-air combat and basic pilot training, or, believe it or not, even 30-year-old cargo planes outfitted with guns.

Between 1950 and 1990, the Air Force produced 15,600 fighter aircraft. Only 707 were designed for close air support. This is the true measure of priority.[30]

The type, nature, and timing of close air support are usually dictated by the Army ground commander. Air support must meet the Army's needs and be a vital part of the ground scheme of maneuver. The ground commander is the only one who can determine how and when close air support fits in. These requirements do not sit well with Air Force generals; they prefer to be the ones picking the targets.

I suppose there always has been a fear on the part of Air Force leaders that sooner or later the close air-support mission would be given back to the Army. If that happened, they would not want to be forced to give up a sizable inventory of special-purpose airplanes, people, and resources.

The Army has tried to fill the void of close air support by developing a large inventory of armed attack helicopters, all perfectly legal under the Key West agreement.

Interdiction, the mission the Air Force much prefers to close support, involves attacking ground targets deep behind enemy lines. It means bombing and strafing "choke" points, such as railroad yards and bridges, in an attempt to prevent enemy forces and supplies from getting to the front lines.

The Air Force claims that our ground forces can probably handle the initial engagement with enemy ground forces; the best way to use airpower is to interdict the flow of enemy reinforcements so that they either do not arrive or arrive at a rate that does not overwhelm friendly forces.

Interdiction targets can be chosen by the Air Force without too much consultation with the Army ground commander. Herein lies the true reason for the Air Force's emphasis on interdiction rather than close air support. Interdiction helps to preserve its independence from the Army, and that, after all, is more important to the Air Force in the broader scheme of things.

Unfortunately, interdiction usually does not work. If anyone doubts this, I suggest they look into the government's attempts to interdict the flow of drugs or illegal aliens into this country.

Interdiction rarely has been a significant factor in the outcome of any major battle, campaign, or war. Interdiction did not work in Italy and France during World War II or in Korea or Vietnam. In Southeast Asia, only four major trails brought troops and supplies from the north. Those well-known trails were bombarded by the Air Force continuously, yet the supplies and troops continued to come. The enemy suffered many losses from the heavy bombing, of course, but the flow was never "interdicted."

During the recent Gulf War, Air Force interdiction failed to prevent the Iraqi Republican Guard's escape down a known path from allied ground force encirclement. How did the Iraqis get out of the trap when we had total command of the air?

In order to attack ground targets behind enemy lines, airplanes must pass through the enemy's defenses. They either have to blast their way through, sneak through undetected (highly unlikely), or employ all sorts of electronic jamming equipment to deceive or blind the enemy's radars. Penetrating the defenses, navigating to the targets (sometimes flying at treetop level, at night, or in bad weather) and delivering precision-guided munitions result in airplanes that are loaded with complex, elaborate, electronically interdependent equipment—extremely expensive to buy and to maintain. All of this is for a mission that historically has had little or no influence on the outcome of campaigns or wars but one that is not likely to be controlled by the local Army commander.

Unfortunately, interdiction airplanes are so expensive that, no matter how large the overall budget, relatively few airplanes—only enough to be little more than a nuisance behind the enemy lines—can be purchased and maintained. Chuck Myers, former World War II pilot and member of the Fighter Mafia, said it best: "Airpower should strike like a violent thunderstorm, not a gentle rain." When interdiction airplanes, such as Mac-Namara's F-111, cost ten to fifteen times as much as close air support airplanes, such as the A-10, the Air Force is lucky if it can generate more than a mere sprinkle.

The threat of the Army's new attack helicopters taking over the close air support mission, along with a significant portion of the Air Force's budget, forced the Air Force to develop its first and only airplane designed solely to support ground troops. During the mid-1960s, the Army began development of its first attack helicopter, the Cheyenne. Its cost and complexity were fairly close to that of a fixed-wing jet. A few senior Air Force leaders, led by Gen. Richard A. Yudkin, saw the handwriting on the wall and reluctantly began to push for a new, special-purpose, close air support airplane to head off the Army's de facto assumption of this mission.[31] This was a gutsy move on Yudkin's part. Almost every three-star general on the Air Staff was against the idea, but Yudkin had the support of Air Force Chief of Staff Gen. John P. McConnell.

With the chief of staff's approval, Yudkin put together a team of experts to lay out the design concept for this new plane. Even though he was still on the defense secretary's staff, Pierre Sprey was invited by the Air Force to help shape that design. Sprey was not yet at the top of the Air Force's hit list, a position of distinction that he would gain a few years later.

In 1970, Air Force Under Secretary John L. McLucas accepted Sprey's novel suggestion that the final design be selected as a result of a prototype fly-off between two competing contractors. The first "fly-before-buy" prototype competition was held between Northrop's A-9 and Fairchild Industries' A-10.[32] The A-10 was selected as the winner in January 1973.

Sprey believes that actual combat results should shape the design of weapons systems. This may sound logical, but it is a novel approach in the Pentagon. The Vietnam War provided many of the insights Sprey needed to shape the A-10. So did the experiences of Col. Hans Rudel.

Rudel was a German Stuka pilot who flew 2,500 close air support sorties on the Eastern Front in World War II. He was shot down seventeen times and credited with destroying more Russian tanks (519) than any other pilot.[33] The Stuka's main weapon was a 37-mm cannon, one mounted on each wing. The cannon could fire only one shell on a pass at a tank, crude by today's standards but effective. (Sprey eventually tracked down Rudel and interviewed him extensively. He also interviewed many of Germany's best field commanders, including Gen. Hermann Balck and Lt. Gen. Heinz Gaedke.)

In Vietnam, the United States lost 5,148 fixed-wing aircraft and helicopters to enemy action.[34] Ground fire, guns of all sorts, accounted for 83.3 percent of the fixed-wing loses and 92 percent of the helicopter losses.[35] Lesson: any aircraft operating in the thick of action in support of ground troops must be designed to take a lot of hits from ground fire. It has to be rugged. Who can forget the vivid picture on the nightly news of a Gulf War A-10 pilot landing his plane full of bullet holes and a large, gaping hole in the right wing, courtesy of an Iraqi missile? He climbed out of his plane, kissed it, and then gave thanks to the guy who designed it to be so rugged. A National Guard pilot flew his plane, with over three hundred bullet holes in it, all the way home to New Orleans from the Middle East.

To be effective, a close air support aircraft must be able to get near the action on the ground so that the pilot can sort out the good guys and the bad guys and find specific targets, such as tanks. An aircraft designed specifically to survive in this environment has features quite different from an air-superiority fighter.

Like the Stuka, the main weapon of the A-10 is a cannon. It has seven barrels that rotate rapidly, in the fashion of a Gatling gun, and fires a depleted uranium-tipped 30-mm shell. Uranium had never been tried before, but Sprey insisted on using it, over the objections of the entire Air Force gun bureaucracy, as the only means of making the 30-mm lethal enough. These shells are very effective at destroying tanks, trucks, bunkers, and most targets of interest on a battlefield. They cost only $13 apiece, a far cry from $100,000 for a Maverick missile.[36] Pilots can visually find the targets and fly a continuous series of jinking maneuvers so that the enemy air-defense weapons cannot track them. The nose of the plane is pointed at the target and a burst of cannon shells squeezed off—simply, quickly, and efficiently.

The 30-mm cannon and the effective, cheap ammunition were developed and produced largely through the efforts of Col. Robert "Bob" Dilger.[37] Dilger was a fighter pilot with one kill in Southeast Asia; he literally ran his opponent into the ground.[38] As you might guess, Dilger was a member of the Fighter Mafia. He was aggressive, irreverent, and always out of step with the establishment. Even though he gave the Air Force its most effective and cheapest antitank weapon, he suffered the same fate as Riccioni because of his association with the Fighter Mafia (see chapter 6).

The A-10 was the first Air Force plane designed solely to provide close air support to the ground forces—and the last. It had Sprey's fingerprints all over it. The cheapest airplane to buy and to operate, it was also the most effective ground support airplane in the world. It was ugly (its appearance matched its unofficial name, the "Warthog") and slow (the butt of many jokes about bird strikes from the rear), but, most importantly, it performed a mission that the Air Force senior leadership has never really embraced. The A-10 is no longer in production, and the Air Force has been reluctant to develop a replacement.

I have explained at length certain features of the A-10 so that the reader might gain an appreciation of the heated debate that raged during the late 1970s and early 1980s between the reformers and the establishment. The reformers favored close air support as a proper use of air power; the establishment favored interdiction. The reformers preferred eyeballs as primary sensors in finding tanks and the use of inexpensive cannon in killing them. The establishment wanted radars and infrared sensors to find tanks and guided missiles, such as the Maverick, to kill them. Unfortunately, the establishment's approach seldom worked in tests, unless the tests were rigged—as sometimes they were.

By the mid-1970s, the Fighter Mafia had greatly influenced the shape, character, and content of the tactical air forces. Its philosophy is easily stated: Technology can be used to produce simpler, hence lower-cost weapons; lower-cost weapons can permit larger forces. The Fighter Mafia could rightfully claim parenthood of all three of the new Air Force combat aircraft, the F-15, F-16, and A-10, as well as the Navy's new F-18. Both the F-16 and A-10 were relatively low-cost, high-performance designs that were strongly resisted by the mainstream of the Air Force establishment. Secretary of Defense Schlesinger overcame that resistance with his bribe of four additional fighter wings (four hundred aircraft). The Air Force could not resist Schlesinger, even though its senior officers did not want to accept these two airplanes or to embrace the Fighter Mafia's philosophy represented in their design.

The establishment eventually ruined the later versions of the F-16 by adding tons of high-tech gadgetry, which increased its weight and cost and significantly degraded its performance. Secretary of the Air Force Edward C. "Pete" Aldridge admitted this embarrassing fact to the press in 1987.[39] The Air Force also retired most of the A-10s prematurely to the scrap heap or sent them to the Air National Guard.

National Guard and Reserve A-10 units, called to active duty during the Gulf War, comprised 20 percent of the combat aircraft used in Desert Storm. Lt. Gen. Charles Horner, commander of the allied air forces in the Gulf, initially opposed sending the A-10s to the Gulf. After hostilities began, General Horner stated in his battle staff meeting on 20 January 1991, "I take back all the bad things I've ever said about the A-10s—I love them. They're saving our asses!" The A-10s flew more combat sorties than any other aircraft and were credited with destroying 1,000 Iraqi tanks and 1,200 artillery, nearly one-fourth of the entire Iraqi arsenal. Unfortunately, the Air Force has gone out of its way to avoid publicizing the A-10's achievements in the war, thus making it the only true "stealth" aircraft in the Air Force inventory. The A-10 is still headed for retirement. The Air Force has no plans to replace it with a similar plane.

The deep-seated philosophical differences between the Fighter Mafia and the senior leadership of the Air Force led to a polarization. The Fighter Mafia had helped the Air Force to develop and buy all those new airplanes, but the senior leadership was not grateful. Rather, the senior officers felt that the Fighter Mafia had somehow outmaneuvered them in the bureaucratic battles and rammed a bunch of cheap, inferior, special-purpose airplanes down their throats. They would have much preferred to spend the same money buying fewer, more technically complex airplanes of their own choosing. They misrepresented the debate that unfolded as a high-tech versus low-tech argument. This was not the case. The reformers were concerned about complexity, cost, and combat usefulness, not "high" or "low" technology.

The Fighter Mafia's interests and influence began to spread to other areas of the Pentagon's business. Because of its track record of success, unmatched in modern times, the leadership of the entire Department of Defense became alarmed—it simply would not do for this philosophy to spread to other areas. The high priests of technology, who had misapplied that technology to give us ever-increasing complexity, held many positions of power and influence. They had other plans in mind, and the Fighter Mafia's philosophy did not fit into those plans.

Nevertheless, membership in this group began to grow quietly and secretly. As the Fighter Mafia of the late 1960s evolved into the reformers of the late 1970s, infighting with the establishment became dirty and nasty, complete with infiltrations, spies, and counterspies. During this period, I became caught up in the web of intrigue.

2

To Be
or to Do

I first met John Boyd in June 1974 when I reported to the Pentagon as his deputy. I had just graduated from the Industrial College of the Armed Forces, a prestigious senior service school for up-and-coming, select officers. I was a young lieutenant colonel rising through the ranks on the fast track.

After graduation from the Air Force Academy as a member of its first graduating class, I attended graduate school in two separate fields. I had been promoted ahead of schedule to the rank of major and then to lieutenant colonel. I was the first Academy graduate to attend the Air Force's three professional schools, Squadron Officers School, Air Command and Staff College, and Industrial College of the Armed Forces.

As a product of the "system," as well as a believer, I was doing quite well. I was five years ahead of my contemporaries in the race to the top of the career ladder, which was my goal. I believed that if I did all the things the system required of me, and did them better than my peers, I would achieve that goal. I was very ambitious, but not to the point of blind ambition. My outlook, background, experiences, education, and personnel folder all reflected the belief that honest, hard work inside the system would get me to the top. I believed that the people at the top were equally honest and the system had rewarded them for believing the same as I did. Then I met Boyd. My life and my view of the world changed dramatically.

I thought Boyd was crazy. He did nothing right, according to what I had been taught since entering the Academy. His uniform was a mess; he never got to work on time; he ignored work deadlines; he even ignored the work itself. When the generals told him to do something, he would do something else. He was uncontrollable. He openly criticized numerous generals as either corrupt or incompetent, some as both. He even called President Richard Nixon a crook. To me, this was blasphemy. How could this guy have such a big reputation for contributing so much to the Air Force when he seemed to be so out of step? I would learn the answer to that question and, in the process, change my mind about what was really important in my "career."

Colonel Boyd, head of a small office on the Air Staff, was charged with developing a plan or, better yet, a way to bring long-range planning into the actual decision process of the Air Staff. Then, as now, long-range planning was an academic exercise only.

There were offices with the word *plans* over their doors and many published documents with this word in their titles, but I was to learn that none of these had anything to do with the actual decisions made to shape the future Air Force. Instead, these activities usually produced unconstrained wish lists of futuristic concepts and weapons—visions of what the Air Force might look like twenty or thirty years down the road if there were no limits on how much money could be spent and no limits on the achievements of science and technology.

No systematic process existed to bring these visions to the budget decision table. There were no fiscal constraints on the visions, and no visions were included in budget decisions. The planning world and the budget-decision world were separate, with no real communication between them.

Budget decisions were based on pragmatic, near-term considerations, such as the degree of political support for a particular program. The ax fell on programs that could not muster strong support from Congress, industry, international allies, or the secretary of defense and his staff. In short, political wheeling and dealing, hidden agendas, and turf battles determined the future Air Force, rather than carefully weighed visions.

Boyd and a couple of bright young captains, Ray Leopold and Franklin C. "Chuck" Spinney, who worked for him, laid out an approach to bring the two worlds of budget and planning together. It was similar in theory to the approach Boyd used in producing superior fighter designs.

The key to this approach was forcing the senior leaders to think about budget contingency plans in a systematic fashion that revealed, in explicit terms, the future consequences of alternative budgets. I would soon discover that the senior leaders did not want to do this. A systematic process that brings such openness and objectivity to the major decisions of corporate leaders discloses, for all to see, the dirty little games and hidden agendas that form the real basis for many decisions.

The Light Weight Fighter Fly-Off competition had just ended, and the process of selecting the winner took up most of Boyd's time and attention. During the last half of 1974, he pored over the competition test results at Wright Patterson Air Force Base. The job of convincing the Air Staff that it needed to change completely its decision-making process would fall on my shoulders.

Chuck Spinney and Ray Leopold were not very happy about working for me on this project. True Boyd disciples, they thought I was a hopeless case, too locked up in the system to be able to do anything meaningful to change the Air Staff. Spinney even suggested to Boyd that he get rid of me because I was so hopeless. Boyd ignored that suggestion; perhaps he saw something the captains had missed.

Ray had a doctorate in electrical engineering, and Chuck was working on an advanced degree in economics. Few people are as mentally quick as Ray. Everything came easy to him. I recall one general introducing him to another general as "the captain who runs the Air Staff." Chuck was a little more reserved, but equally intelligent and maybe a little more competitive. Both had an understanding of the bureaucratic workings of the Pentagon that was far beyond their years.

We could not convince people that they needed to change the way they were doing business unless we could prove that something was seriously wrong with how they were doing it. With Boyd as our teacher, the two young captains and I dove into the subject of how the Air Staff actually made its decisions (as opposed to the official explanations laid out so neatly in the brochures). In the process, we could not help but examine and pass judgment on the quality of decisions being made by the Air Staff, both individual decisions on particular programs and collective decisions on a macro scale that charted the direction of the future Air Force as a whole.

This examination was an eye-opener—the first of many—to all three of us. I suspect that Boyd knew this would occur and that's why he left me alone.

Ray's analysis showed beyond doubt that the Air Force could not afford all the programs it had recently started. Ray coined the expression "procurement bow wave" to describe the tremendous mismatch between the procurement bills that would come due over the next five years and even the most optimistic projection of how much money Congress would give the Air Force. With each passing year, the unpaid bills were pushed farther into the future where they piled up higher and higher—thus the term *bow wave*.

When an individual runs up credit card balances to a point where the bills cannot be paid, all kinds of problems surface and that person's world usually comes unglued. So it was with the Air Force. We foresaw bankruptcy, financial chaos, and a host of other horrible problems. They would be the result of an undisciplined decision-making process and an Air Staff unable or unwilling to match its financial commitments with its expected financial resources. The mismatch between spending plans and expected funding from Congress was in the tens of billions of dollars. (A few years later, Chuck Spinney would document this mismatch for the entire Department of Defense. To the horror of the incoming administration of Ronald Reagan, Chuck would reveal to the public the amount of mismatch at $500 billion—a staggering sum.[1])

Too many new weapons programs had been started. In each case, the advocates of an individual program intentionally understated the costs to make it easier to get the program approved. The real costs began to surface after the program got started, and they were usually higher. The real schedules surfaced, too, and they were usually longer than promised. Finally, the real performance surfaced, and it was most often worse than predicted.

Our look into this whole mess had only scratched the surface, but it was sobering enough for the three of us, especially me. Chuck Spinney would leave the Air Force the next year and pursue the subject in more depth as a civilian analyst on the defense secretary's staff. His analyses, most notably "Defense Facts of Life" and "Plans/Reality Mismatch and Why We Need Realistic Budgeting," later became a centerpiece of the Reform Movement. They would also lead him into violent confrontations with the Reagan administration that exploded onto the public scene, complete with congressional hearings, television cameras, and Chuck's picture on the cover of *Time Magazine*.

The financial havoc caused by cost overruns on top of a pile of procurement bills that could not be paid became evident in December 1974. Word was leaking out of the B-1 program office at Wright Patterson that the cost of this new bomber was growing out of control. The official cost, the one advertised around the Pentagon and Congress, was $25 million per airplane.[2] This was a lot of money in 1974: F-16s were going for $6 million apiece and A-10s for $3 million. Our "bow wave" analysis (which by now we had briefed far and wide across the Air Staff) showed that, even at the $25 million price, the Air Force could not afford the B-1 plus three new fighters and a host of other goodies. If the bomber's cost was actually growing, political support surely would be lost and Secretary Schlesinger or Congress would probably cancel the B-1.

At this time, twelve four-star generals ruled the Air Force. They would gather as a group on rare occasions and only for matters of grave concern. The future of the B-1 bomber was one of those matters. The gathering of the four-stars is called a "Corona." Gen. David Jones, chief of staff, called for a meeting in December—Corona Quest.

Ray, Chuck, and I were given the task of preparing a study of the true cost of the B-1 for the Corona. The true cost was measured in terms of what the Air Force had to give up in order to buy the B-1, since it could not afford to buy everything. We saw this as an excellent opportunity to use the contingency planning principles that we had been preaching around the Air Staff. The deputy chief of staff for research and development, Lt. Gen. William Evans (our three-star boss whose tall, dark, and handsome appearance earned him the nickname "Hollywood Bill"), assigned the study to us, and he would personally brief it to the Corona.

Digging into the B-1 program, we discovered that the costs were indeed growing out of control but also found considerable uncertainty as to the actual costs. The deputy program manager admitted to us that the figure would be about $100 million per airplane, and Wright Patterson had not yet built the first one. We laid out the yearly costs of the program that reflected several prices ranging between $25 and $100 million. These were placed on top of the yearly costs of all the other weapons systems that the Air Force planned to buy over the next five years. The bow wave now looked like Mount Everest.

We next compared this pile of future bills with several estimates of how much money Congress would give the Air Force in each of the next five years. The mismatch between the bills that were due and even the most optimistic projection of congressional funding was mind-boggling. The Air Force would have to cancel all of the new fighter programs, as well as many other weapons, in order to save the B-1.

We laid out various options for program cancellations so that the four-stars could see in explicit, graphic terms the true cost of the B-1. If the senior leaders had been exposed to this type of information on a regular basis, they could have avoided getting into such a financial disaster.

Before showing our results to our three-star boss, General Evans, we had to show everything to his two-star deputy. We were summoned to the latter's office, where we met with him alone.

Generals, like all senior officials in the Pentagon, have very luxurious and spacious offices. Most have plush carpeting, large wooden desks with matching conference tables, various flags draped behind them on stanchions (American, Air Force, and special flags that denote rank or position), paintings on the walls from the Air Force art collection, pictures showing them posed with higher-ranking officials, and the most important badge of distinction in the Pentagon—a window. This setting can appear quite imposing and intimidating to younger officers, the worker bees, who spend their time in small cubicles in overcrowded offices with no carpeting, few creature comforts, little secretarial support, and often inadequate air conditioning.

When the two-star saw our briefing charts, he nearly gagged. He immediately ordered us to change the estimate of future congressional funding to make it higher by billions of dollars. This would give the impression that the Air Force had a better chance of being able to buy everything. We were told to fudge the numbers to save a program on a direct order from a two-star general.

This was the first time I had encountered a situation like this, and I suspect that was also true for Chuck and Ray. Boyd was always telling us about how often this kind of behavior occurred at the senior level, but I had not really believed him until it was right in front of me. The moral dilemma: do what the general ordered, or do what was right and suffer his wrath later down the line? I would encounter this dilemma with increasing frequency as my exposure to the inner workings of the senior levels increased during the coming years.

Any thoughts of fudging figures had never crossed our minds, so we were not prepared to argue with the general on the spot. He talked; we listened. We went back to our office and made the changes that he had ordered. None of us had any question about what we had to do, but there was the matter of how best to treat this sticky situation.

Chuck, Ray, and I made an appointment with General Evans and his deputy to show them our final results. Early in the briefing, we showed General Evans the price tag of $100 million per copy that we had uncovered. He did not seem surprised and commented, "That's a nice round number, easy to remember."

Just then, his phone rang. The B-1 program manager was on the line from Wright Patterson. His mother had died, and he had been out of town for a week. Upon returning, he discovered that his staff had revealed the $100 million figure, which he had been hiding from us. Now that it was out, he could see his reputation, career, and whole world coming apart before his eyes. In an act of desperation, he had called General Evans to disavow the $100 million figure. He said that his staff had acted without his knowledge and approval. Would General Evans please forget he ever heard that number? General Evans thanked him for his call, hung up, and told us, "Keep the $100 million figure in the briefing."

We then came to the part about the expected funding from Congress. Before Chuck started, he told General Evans that there was a great deal of uncertainty in this kind of analysis. Everything depended on the assumptions made, so he was presenting a range of assumptions. These, of course, included our preferred assumptions, as well as the two-star's assumptions.

Evans said, "I can't take all this to the Chief, it's too confusing. Which one do you like?"

Chuck put his finger on our chart. The two-star almost went through the roof. He started to argue, and Evans seemed to understand that he was pressuring us.

General Evans turned to the two-star for an explanation. I had never seen a two-star tap-dance before. It was fascinating to watch. His explanations quickly became transparent, and his real motive began to surface— do anything to save the program.

When the tap dance was over, General Evans calmly announced, "We will go with the Captain's numbers." He gathered up the charts and headed for the Corona. It is interesting to note that the two-star never became a three-star, whereas General Evans moved up to four stars.

The secretary of the Air Force and the chief of staff each have a suite of offices adjoining one another on the "E" ring (the outermost ring), fourth floor, on the eastern side of the Pentagon. Unlike the western side, the afternoon sun does not overheat their offices. At this level of rank, each suite has several windows, so these officials have a magnificent view of the Potomac with its backdrop of the Washington skyline and all of the monuments.

Directly across the hall from these offices is the secretary's conference room. Large wooden tables are arranged in a horseshoe configuration. A second row of chairs outlines the horseshoe; each principal at the table can have a staff aide sitting behind him. The secretary and the chief of staff, who share this room, sit at the top of the horseshoe. This is where the senior leaders gather for their most important meetings. The room holds only about thirty-five or forty people. It is a true measure of a senior official's stature to be allowed in this room for an important meeting. Many egos have been crushed when their owners discovered that they were not on the access list. This room is also where the secretary holds daily staff meetings with civilian political appointees and the most senior generals from the Air Staff, usually led by the vice chief. (In the years to come, I would spend several hours a day in this room as I watched closely the behavior of our senior leaders.)

When General Evans finished his briefing to the Corona, the four-stars asked him to leave the room, but they kept our briefing charts. For the next two days, they secretly deliberated the fate of the B-1. When they emerged, we got our charts back, covered with thumbprints, smudges, and smears. The generals had decided to continue their public support for the B-1. We noticed during the next two years that the official projected costs of the program surprisingly remained at a stable level of about $25 million per copy. Chuck, Ray, and I knew that this projection could not be true—there was some kind of game going on.

Although I have no proof, I believe that the generals decided in that meeting to dump the B-1 by finding someone else to do their dirty work for them—to cancel it over their pro forma objections. Two years later, President Jimmy Carter did just that as one of his first acts on taking office. Four years later, President Reagan resurrected the B-1, bought it for $280 million per copy, accepted it without testing it, and then found out that its electronics did not work.

I noticed no great public outcry by the four-stars when President Carter canceled the B-1. No Air Force general resigned in protest. I think the generals were happy to have this albatross removed from their collective neck. They would welcome the B-1 back when President Reagan later showed up with his moneybags.

This episode was only one of three or four occurring within a year's time that shook my faith in the system. I opened my eyes to the real world of military politics and its domination over so many people in the Pentagon. I didn't like what I saw, but Boyd would not let me close my eyes and retreat to that naive, idealistic world that I had left at the Academy.

As I indicated earlier, I had the job of convincing the Air Staff that it needed to change the way it made decisions so that more financial discipline was brought to the process. The two captains and I briefed our bow-wave horror story all over the Air Staff until finally it was generally agreed that something had to be done.

Another lieutenant colonel, who represented that part of the Air Staff concerned with the operational units in the field, was selected to work with me on specific details for implementing the planning activities across the Air Staff. He was a personal friend of mine, and we seemed to share the same goals. Months went by, and nothing happened. I was getting nowhere. My friend and I would meet and agree on things, but we never made any real progress.

Boyd took me to the blackboard in his office one day and laid out the sequence of events over the past several months. He told me that I was being led down the garden path and that I was blind to that fact because of my friendship. Boyd pointed out that the operations side of the Air Staff clearly did not want to change current arrangements and the way

36   decisions were made. It liked things as they were. If changes were made, the operations officers might lose their power and influence. They talked freely about needing changes but sabotaged every effort in that direction.

I had been misled, even lied to, and I had swallowed it hook, line, and sinker. As Boyd put it: "Your friend is not really a friend. He used you." Boyd was right. I learned a painful, but valuable lesson about dealing with people in the Pentagon—trust no one and judge each person solely on actions, not words.

All of this was going on while, for the first time, I was being exposed to the evils of blind ambition at the general officer level. We worked directly for a two-star general, whom I will call "General Infamous." Boyd referred to him as "that asshole," which was probably a more apt description.

To General Infamous, truth was a foreign concept. The polygraph has not been made that would work on him. He was obsessed with creating and presenting to his superiors an image of knowing everything and being in complete control of his domain. Everything was on track, just like the boss wanted. The party line was safe in his hands. He treated his staff and people like dirt. They existed for the sole purpose of making him look good in front of his superiors. The following excerpts from a memorandum he sent his subordinates illustrate this point:

> On several occasions recently I have been embarrassed by late receipt of information pertaining to events involving systems or projects under development and/or test. The lateness has varied from an hour or so to several days. In each case, the event was of special interest not only to me but, more to the point of this memorandum, to the Chief of Staff and Secretary. . . .
>
> In trying to find out where the choke points lie in the information pipe line, I inevitably come up with one of two stories:
>
> a. The "Regular Crew Chief" wasn't around at the time the information came in and no one else could, would, or was allowed to do anything about it (25%).
>
> b. You and/or your Deputies/Division Chiefs, through prior bronze tablet engravement of the "Chain of Command," caused complete constipation of the pipe line (75%)."

The general was always angry because the chief of staff and the secretary often knew things that he didn't—his image of being on top of everything was tarnished—and it was always his staff's fault. In fact, he didn't want to hear any bad news, so his staff never passed it on to him. Whenever they did, he always shot the messenger. If anyone needed an enema, it was the general, not his staff.

This obsession with looking good in front of the big boss caused the staff to spend 95 percent of its time reacting to events rather than controlling them. General Infamous berated them daily, yelled and screamed at them, and even threw things at them. Staff members cowered before him like the wimps they were, for he controlled their future. He decided which ones would be promoted and which ones would not. Seeking his favor, they routinely falsified data and information to support answers and statements he had previously given to the chief of staff or secretary before the real information was available.

Those who played the game with the general were rewarded with promotions as he progressed to four-star general. Anyone who would not play his game was fired. I watched many people sell their souls, piece by piece, to this man in exchange for one more promotion. They always had the same excuse: "When I get to the top, I'll be in a position to do things right." They never realized that, in the process of compromising their principles so often in order to get there, they would become programmed to continue operating in that same fashion once they arrived at the top.

In the middle of these antics, Boyd gave me his "to be or to do" speech, which I was to hear again and again for the next ten years. It ran something like this: "Jim, you are at a point in your life where you have to make a choice about what kind of a person you are going to be. There are two career paths in front of you, and you have to choose which path you will follow. One path leads to promotions, titles, and positions of distinction. To achieve success down that path, you have to conduct yourself a certain way. You must go along with the system and show that you are a better team player than your competitors. The other path leads to doing things that are truly significant for the Air Force, but the rewards will quite often be a kick in the stomach because you may have to cross swords with the party line on occasion. You can't go down both paths, you have to choose. Do you want *to be* a man of distinction or do you want *to do* things that really influence the shape of the Air Force? To be or to do, that is the question."

I didn't believe Boyd at first, but as time went on it became clear that he was right. He had clearly been a "doer" himself and he certainly did not seek the general's favor. He used the general as an example to make his point. General Infamous was a man of form, not substance. Whenever he stood near a window, the light shone right through him. All the general ever did was get promoted.

Boyd, on the other hand, was a man of substance who cared nothing about form. His work had a lasting effect on the Air Force, but it was always controversial at the time. Boyd's courage and perseverance always got him through the turmoil. Sooner or later, his controversial ideas were accepted by the system and became the system. In the process, however, he upset the world of those people whose ideas represented conventional thinking. Because they were in power, Boyd seldom received the recognition and rewards that normally go with major achievements.

The general sought recognition and rewards, while making no contributions. Boyd made contributions that changed things and received few rewards. That's the way life is in the Pentagon, and it took me a long time to accept it.

Boyd usually ignored the general or treated him with contempt in front of the staff. The two crossed swords several times, and the general learned to leave Boyd alone. He could not intimidate Boyd as he could other people who were afraid of not being promoted. It is a sad commentary, though, that a man of his character could move through the ranks all the way to the four-star level. That, in itself, says something about the system.

Boyd retired on 1 September 1975. The system did not want him promoted to general. He had accomplished about all he could in the Air Force, and his fantastic mind was calling him in a new direction. He was not completely sure where he was heading, but it would prove to be a fascinating journey into the fundamentals of human conflict.

Unlike most military retirees, Boyd chose not to work for the defense industry. His family was concerned about managing on just his retirement pay. In typical Boyd fashion, he bought a copy of Darwin's *Origin of Species* and suggested that his family read it.

Ray Leopold moved on to a new assignment. Chuck Spinney, disillusioned with the Air Force, got out and went to work as an analyst with a local think tank. Years later, he would return to the Pentagon as a civilian analyst with the Office of the Secretary of Defense. Although I continued to preach the need to change the Air Staff's way of doing business, my duties degenerated primarily to preparing speeches, briefings, and congressional testimony for General Infamous. He had now been promoted to three stars, although the Senate had made a half-hearted attempt to deny him the promotion because he was deeply implicated in the illegal bombing of Cambodia.

During 1976, I became, more and more, a "difficult" subordinate. Both the failures in Vietnam and the revelations of Watergate had added to my disillusionment. Cynicism began to rear its ugly head. My conversion from a naive, trusting believer in the system to a skeptical, questioning nonbeliever was becoming more complete each day. I was quite critical and outspoken, not only about the lack of planning and discipline in the Air Staff process but also about specific decisions that were made.

And—more dangerously—I was becoming critical of the conduct and character of many senior leaders, especially my boss.

Time and again, I prepared speeches or briefings containing factual information that ran contrary to the beliefs or views of the boss. The drill was always the same. I was directed to change the data to conform—to fudge the numbers, so to speak. I refused and then had to watch one of his lackeys make the change. I circulated copies of the original versions all around the Air Staff, thereby exposing the lackeys for what they were.

I recall preparing a briefing for the general to give to Secretary of Defense Donald H. Rumsfeld soon after he took office in December 1975. The briefing was supposed to show how wonderful all the new Air Force weapons systems were. I prepared a chart that graphically demonstrated the turning capability of the new fighters and compared them with our older fighters, as well as Soviet planes. At a speed of 350 knots, the little F-16 could complete a 360-degree turn, a full circle, inside the perimeter of the Pentagon building itself. The F-15 completed the turn just outside the boundary of the building but within the confines of the surrounding parking lot. The older F-4 and the Soviet planes were lucky to complete the turn within Arlington County.

This picture was not well received. It implied that the F-16 was a little better than the F-15, which in fact it was. The senior leaders were still smarting over having the F-16 rammed down their throats. Naturally, I was directed to change the chart so that the F-16 and F-15 appeared the same. I refused, but someone seeking the general's favor made the change.

Although not a big deal in itself, this kind of thing happened daily over a wide range of subjects. Truth and fiction became intertwined. Sound decisions cannot be made in an environment where truth is hard to find.

Sooner or later, I knew my rebellious actions would get me into trouble. As a member of the Force Structure Committee, I advocated the cancellation of the B-1 bomber because the Air Force could not afford it and the performance was not measuring up to what had been promised.[3] I recall how the other committee members sat in stunned silence as I spoke. The B-1 was still sacrosanct. This type of speech was not appropriate for young lieutenant colonels to give if they had any thoughts of becoming full colonels.

So it happened that I was soon passed over for promotion to full colonel and then fired—thrown out of the building. In the military, the term *fired* means that you are removed from your job and responsibilities, then transferred to another assignment with prejudice and little or no chance of promotion to higher rank. You remain on active duty with pay, unless you retire or resign your commission.

As my boss put it, I was becoming too much of a problem and was no longer a "team player"—the Boyd influence was beginning to show. It turned out that I was not the only one who heard these words.

At this time, there were six one-star and two-star generals working for General Infamous. They also were becoming disgusted with his behavior. The most vocal was Maj. Gen. John Toomay, a man of intelligence, integrity, and principle, which were rare qualities indeed at that level. (In one of his staff meetings, General Infamous was throwing documents at his general officer deputies. General Toomay reached out and snagged a document in midair with one hand. Toomay then turned to the head of the table and said, "In case you haven't noticed, General, I'm seven for nine this week. I've only dropped two."[4])

In the spring of 1976, these six generals decided to confront General Infamous as a group and ask him to clean up his act. They agreed to meet at his office door and march in together. Toomay was the only one who showed up. True to form, the others had chickened out. Toomay went in and gave the speech anyway. It must have been a really good speech, for he was immediately fired and thrown out of the building. He landed a few miles away at Air Force Systems Command Headquarters at Andrews Air Force Base, Maryland.

Although I had met General Toomay only a few times, we quickly discovered that we shared the same views on a variety of subjects, one of which was the lack of planning on the Air Staff. We had been fired by the same person for basically the same reasons. Before we both had been fired, he had been a strong supporter of the planning initiatives that I had tried to get the Air Staff to adopt. He recognized that the methodology I preached would create an overall picture of the state of affairs within the Air Force and that it could be a powerful tool in debating future directions.

Although he had ripped his knickers with a three-star and had been physically thrown out of the Pentagon, General Toomay was not ready to retire from the Air Force. After accepting an out-of-the-way assignment at Andrews, he hired me. Together, we set out to do the Air Staff's job. Along the way, I became a "hard-core, dyed-in-the-wool reformer."

3

Storm Clouds of Reform

Weapons developers, when given a choice, always go for the complex, elaborate solution at the expense of the simple one. Complexity leads to higher costs—purchase costs, operations costs, and maintenance costs. Higher costs result in fewer weapons, which, in turn, lead to contrived tests and analyses to prove that the relatively few complex systems can overcome the larger numbers of the simpler, less expensive weapons of the enemy. The fewer the weapons, the tighter is the control of these precious assets by a centralized command structure. The elaborate paraphernalia that comes with the centralized command structure only adds to the complexity of the overall system.

The more complex the overall system, the more difficult it is to test the weapons in a realistic fashion. We are therefore asked to trust the high priests of technology and accept their claims of future performance. I found that there was no desire by the senior leaders to find out whether or not such claims were true.

41

I also discovered that often the new high-tech wonder weapons could not stand up to careful examination. Their performance claims were exaggerated, and testing often involved demonstrations designed and staged solely for the purpose of supporting those claims. Unflattering test results were ignored or interpreted to mean that even greater degrees of complexity were needed to solve the problems. This approach became a death spiral of fewer and fewer weapons with ever-tightening control to prevent any waste. Supposedly, the battle could be "managed" so that the superior numbers of the enemy would be defeated by the more technically sophisticated weapons of the Western democracies.

All kinds of battle management schemes surfaced. One Air Force scheme involved equipping every airplane with sensors and data-link systems that transmitted to a central computer the status of every subsystem on the plane; the plane's location, altitude, heading, and fuel supply; every target blip on the radar scope; and even the status of the pilot's bladder—all because it was technically feasible to do so. The central controller would then dictate what targets to attack and how. The Army was also caught up in this philosophy. It had plans to put a beacon on every soldier's back that tied into the central computer—one giant Atari game.

The pilots or the infantrymen at the end of these electronic tentacles could not be trusted to do what was right. They had to be closely controlled in the name of efficiency. In my view, a scheme based on mistrust or presumed incompetence of the people doing the fighting is doomed to failure.

This philosophy dominated senior leaders in the Department of Defense during the middle to late 1970s. It was the philosophy espoused by the growing number of scientists and technocrats who assumed positions of power at the higher levels of the Pentagon. Typical of these people was Under Secretary of Defense for Research and Engineering Dr. William J. Perry, who was in charge of all weapons development in the Pentagon during the Carter administration.

With Perry at the helm, the Pentagon began investing in weapons that, more and more, removed the human element from warfare, weapons that were so loaded with electronic equipment and computer chips that they supposedly could make their own decisions on the battlefield. They were called "smart weapons." Some were even referred to as "brilliant weapons."[1] The electronic battlefield![2]

In this mechanistic view, warfare is simply a contest between the machines of opposing forces on the electronic battlefield. The side with the superior technology prevails, according to the claims of the high priests. Computer analyses of warfare were constructed to compare the killing power of one set of machines (as claimed, but never as tested) against another. The debates, arguments, and decisions on various weapons proposals were all shaped by this mechanistic view of war, which naturally led to proposals of weapons with ever-increasing complexity.

Many high-tech proponents claimed that technology could, in fact, solve all problems and that it was the only solution to the problems. This argument was used to justify even more technically elaborate and complex programs.

I must be fair to Dr. Perry. He was just one of a long line of senior officials who believed in this philosophy. On his watch, however, large numbers of high-tech gadgets masquerading as weapons started down the development road. When the Reagan administration arrived on the scene in 1981 with its bags full of money, many of those weapons programs received extremely large sums.

Once again, John Boyd, by then in retirement, upset the establishment's applecart. While Dr. Perry and his fellow high priests were preaching the gospel of high-tech mechanistic warfare, in which firepower was king and attrition was the objective, Boyd, in a series of profound briefings, began to remind everyone: "Machines don't fight wars. Terrain doesn't fight wars. Humans fight wars. You must get into the minds of humans. That's where the battles are won".[3]

During the late 1970s, Boyd had brought to the table the notion that conflict is fundamentally a human endeavor. If you want to be successful in war or any kind of conflict, he had said, you have to understand what goes on in people's minds when they are locked in mortal combat. This aspect of conflict was totally missing from the current debate in the Pentagon. Boyd forced it back in, and, in the process, rekindled an interest in the "art" of conflict.

In the spring of 1981, Boyd's theories suddenly burst onto the national scene. He had been briefing them around the Defense establishment since the fall of 1976, but it was not until late 1980 and early 1981 that the national press began to take notice. As the press became interested in Boyd's theories, more people in the defense business naturally took notice.

Typical of the headlines that began to appear around the country in early 1981 were "New War Theory Gains Notice" (*Fort Worth Star Telegram,* 23 March 1981), "Dogfight Tacks Can Win Big Wars, Preaches Pilot Turned Tactician" (*The Washington Post,* 4 January 1981), "New War Theory Shoots Down Old War Ideas" (*Atlanta Constitution,* 22 March 1981), and "A New Kind of Reformer" (*The Washington Post,* 13 March 1981).

Once again, Boyd embarrassed the nation's military leaders by showing that there were no real military theorists practicing their craft in this country. They had been replaced by scientists and technologists who thought in terms of bandwidth, gigahertz and computer memory—people who had no idea what the tactical and strategic concepts of Schwerpunkt or Cheng/Ch'i meant or that they even existed. Boyd would change that and would force the military to scramble like mad to catch up with him as he produced theory after theory that was unique and revolutionary in the art of war. The ineptness of the military services was evident by the fact that, initially, the best they could do was to plagiarize his work. Quite often, they got it wrong, especially the Army.

Boyd emerged as the country's most original thinker in the business of figuring out how to whip an opponent at any level of conflict, no matter what the opponent did. This was a natural extension of his fighter tactics work of the late 1950s and 1960s.

War is a terrible thing, and the will to fight is so delicate that it can be strengthened or destroyed in an instant by the strangest things. Boyd revealed historical evidence that, while the physical aspects of war are indeed important, the mental and moral aspects of conflict can be even more important in determining the outcome.

For example, why did the French Army, with more than two million men, suddenly collapse and surrender to the German Blitzkrieg in the summer of 1940? The answer had nothing to do with the technical sophistication of German weapons. Instead, it dealt with what was happening in the minds of the Frenchmen—confusion, chaos, fear, panic, mental paralysis. There were demons loose in their minds. Boyd concentrated his efforts on how to create these demons and set them loose in the opponent's mind.

When Boyd retired from the Air Force in the fall of 1975, he went into seclusion. He concentrated entirely on putting into words the ideas that had been swirling around in his head on the subject of how the mind works. During this time, our friendship really began and the nightly telephone calls became a regular part of my life. My teenage daughter could not understand how someone could talk so long on the telephone every night. Her repeated complaints to her mother led to the "Boyd Phone" with its separate number.

When Boyd gets into a subject, he is consumed by it and so are his friends. Night after night, we talked for hours about the implications of the work of Heisenberg, Godel, Piaget, Polanyi, Skinner, Kuhn, and a host of others from seemingly unrelated fields (see Appendix A). By the spring of 1976, Boyd had written a twelve-page paper titled "Destruction and Creation."

This paper described how the mind goes through the process of analysis and synthesis to form mental concepts that we use to govern our actions as we deal with an ever-changing environment around us. The key to this paper was the notion that, sooner or later, these mental concepts no longer match the observed reality as our surrounding environment changes. Unless we change our mental concepts as the reality around us changes (destroy the old concepts and create new ones), we make decisions and take actions that are out of step with the real world around us. When this happens, we become confused. Our actions are no longer in harmony with our surroundings. If we continue to hold onto our old views of the world, we begin to look inward and eventually become totally out of tune with the real world surrounding us—a system talking to itself. Invariably, confusion and disorder result. When the surrounding environment is menacing and threatening, the confusion and disorder in our minds quickly lead to panic and mental paralysis.

"Destruction and Creation" is heavy stuff. It is also unique. Boyd linked together three famous scientific and mathematical theories that never before had been related to each other—Heisenberg's indeterminacy principle from the world of physics; Godel's incompleteness and consistency theorems from mathematical logic; and the second law of thermodynamics, which deals with order and disorder.

Many of the nation's leading scientists and mathematicians have linked two of these concepts together in various combinations, but only Boyd has linked all three. Within the past decade, the book market has been flooded with works on chaos and chaotic systems, as well as others that show a sudden renewed interest in Godel's 1931 proof. Nobel Prize winner Ilya Prigogine's "Order Out of Chaos," Paul Davies's "The Cosmic Blueprint," and Rudy Rucker's "Mind Tools" are three examples.

Boyd's paper has been reviewed by many of the country's leading physicists, mathematicians, and scientists. Their reactions are usually the same. They do not like his paper. Many of them get very angry because they cannot find anything wrong with it. They get doubly mad when they realize that, although Boyd had no formal training in their fields, he is able to produce rich and unique ideas, often better than theirs.

Typical was the reaction of JASON. Each year, a group of the nation's select nuclear physicists gather at a secluded private school in LaJolla, California, that overlooks the Pacific. The Bishop's School, resembling a monastery, is a beautiful setting that invites deep thought about the nation's defense problems and how the world of physics can solve them.

No one on the outside knows what JASON stands for. Some believe that it is an acronym for July, August, September, October, and November, the months during which these scientists, at government expense, study a problem and report their findings to the secretary of defense. The scientists are sworn to secrecy and refuse to divulge the name.

Dr. Jack Martin, Air Force assistant secretary and former administrator of JASON, asked many of this group to review Boyd's paper. Martin called Boyd into his office. For thirty minutes, Martin went on and on about various aspects of the scientists' critique. Boyd sat quietly until Martin was finished. He then said, "So far, you have told me everything that you don't like about the paper, but you haven't told me what is wrong with the paper. Show me where I have made a mistake or said something that is wrong."

Martin replied, "We can't find anything wrong with what you have done, we just don't like it."

Much of what Boyd does produces this same reaction, whether it is in the realm of new fighter tactics, new aircraft design theories, new concepts for the conduct of land warfare, or whatever. The recognized experts get very upset because his ideas hold together and are usually better than theirs, even though he has no formal training in their fields. This last point really gets to them.

By the summer of 1976, Boyd was beginning to study military history, not because he wanted to but because his mind kept drawing him deeper into this subject. It all began when the National Aeronautics and Space Administration (NASA) asked Boyd to look at air-to-air combat simulators. NASA wanted to know why pilots acted differently in the simulators than they did when flying combat maneuvers in real airplanes. One thing led to another, and soon Boyd was researching human behavior at all levels of conflict. What he found fit within the theme of "Destruction and Creation" and became an extension of the ideas in his paper.

Boyd's research into military history became his most consuming project of all. Since 1976, he has been dissecting the theories and practices of the great military minds of the past and extracting bits and pieces of knowledge from each. He climbed inside the minds of every theoretician and practitioner from 400 B.C. to the present—Sun Tzu, Genghis Khan and the Mongols, Maurice de Saxe, Pierre de Bourcet, Comte de Guibert, Napoleon, Baron Antoine Jomini, Karl von Clausewitz, Thomas J. (Stonewall) Jackson, Robert E. Lee, Ulysses S. Grant, Alfred von Schlieffen, Eric von Ludendorff, J. F. C. Fuller, Heinz Guderian, Eric von Manstein, Hermann Balck, Erwin Rommel, George S. Patton, T. E. Lawrence, and Ramon Magsaysay, to mention a few.

Boyd did not limit himself to military history. He dove into other disciplines, including physics, mathematical logic, science, and engineering, with the same intensity. His effort was truly multidimensional. From these diverse fields, he integrated bits and pieces to form a comprehensive whole that is unique. His briefing, "Patterns of Conflict," is the prod-

uct of Boyd's analysis of historical patterns of conflict and his synthesis of   **47**
scientific theories for successful operations. It is not a formula or a checklist to follow or a set of principles. It is a way of thinking in terms of
actions that will lead to the disintegration and collapse of an opponent's
will to resist.

"Patterns of Conflict" shows how to penetrate an "adversary's moral-
mental-physical being, and sever those interacting bonds that permit him
to exist as an organic whole, as well as subvert or seize those moral-mental-
physical bastions, connections, or activities that he depends upon. . . ."
The aim is to "render adversary powerless by denying him the opportunity
to cope with unfolding circumstances."[4]

Working on their minds, Boyd folds people back into themselves so
they cannot adapt to the surrounding environment. He ensures that the
environment undergoes rapid changes. His antagonists become quivering masses of jelly, ready for the rubber room. One famous Air Force officer, in the process of crossing swords with Boyd, had a nervous break-
down and collapsed on the floor. Pierre Sprey witnessed the collapse;
John Boyd was on the telephone arguing with the officer when it
occurred. (The officer recovered and went on to become chief of staff of
the Air Force.)

In "Patterns of Conflict," Boyd's theories deal with all types of conflict,
not just war. An argument with a neighbor, a bureaucratic turf battle, a
political campaign, guerrilla warfare, corporate competition—every kind
of conflict fits his "Patterns."

All over Washington and across the country, people lined up to listen
to Boyd's briefing. Captains, majors, colonels, generals, most of the Pentagon press corps, congressional aides, congressmen, and senators asked
for the brief.

Wyoming Congressman Richard "Dick" Cheney was one of those who
asked to hear Boyd's briefing. He and Boyd spent hours together discussing the fundamentals of Boyd's theories and the importance of strategy. These meetings gave Cheney a fundamental understanding of the
concept of strategy. Cheney was one of the original founders of the Military Reform Caucus on Capitol Hill. When Cheney was nominated to
become secretary of defense, he quietly made the rounds on Capitol Hill
to assure his reformer colleagues that he would take the reformers' philosophy to the Pentagon. His unprecedented decision in 1991 to cancel
the Navy's $57 billion stealth fighter-bomber program, because he was
misled about cost overruns, schedule slippage, and performance that was
less than promised, indicates that he has not forgotten his reformer
roots. (See the case study, "The Navy Runs Aground," at the end of the
book for details of the Navy's A-12 program.)

Boyd did not go out and sell his briefing; rather, news of it spread by word of mouth. People asked him to brief them, so Boyd felt no obligation to alter the briefing to fit their schedules. When his briefing got to be several hours long, many high-ranking generals asked for a condensed version: "Just concentrate on the bottom line." His response was always the same, "Full brief or no brief," which infuriated the generals. They would then ask for a copy of his briefing charts instead of the full briefing. Again, he would respond, "No charts until after you hear the briefing."

Those who sat through the briefing usually learned something. Those who did not take the time were left in the dark as their peers and subordinates alike began to talk about Boyd's theories.

In the early days, the briefing was an hour long. By 1980, it had grown to four hours. During the mid 1980s, it was thirteen hours long—yes, *thirteen* hours. I know people who have sat through the briefing numerous times and learned something new each time. It grew and grew in richness, breadth, and depth. As of this writing, Boyd lists 317 sources in his research bibliography. Those of us on the telephone net had to read most of them, some more than once.

I recall introducing Boyd to General Toomay in 1976 when Boyd's briefing was only one hour long. Toomay, an intelligent man, was highly respected around the Air Force for his analytical skills. He was greatly impressed with Boyd's work, but he was also frustrated by it. As an analyst, he was looking for that checklist or formula he could apply. As I indicated before, Boyd does not give formulas and recipes for one to follow but teaches people how to think.

In years to come, I would introduce Boyd to many military and civilian leaders higher up in the chain of command. Their reactions were usually similar to Toomay's. They were impressed, even intimidated, by the power and scope of Boyd's ideas but incapable of converting the ideas into actions. I interpreted this as an indication of how rigid and unimaginative our leaders were. The younger officers, the ones not yet totally programmed by the system, were more able to grasp Boyd's ideas. As these officers progressed through the ranks over the years, however, Boyd's theories became entrenched and somewhat institutionalized for them.

Freeman Dyson and Alfred Gray were among those who sat through Boyd's marathon briefing several times. Dyson, a physicist, mathematician, and one of the world's great thinkers, was then a professor at Princeton University's Institute for Advanced Study. His work with Hans Bethe and Robert Oppenheimer is marvelously told in his book *Disturbing the Universe.*

Alfred Gray first listened to Boyd in the late 1970s, when he was a Marine colonel. He was so struck by Boyd's work that he sat through the briefing twice after he became a Marine general. Later, as commandant of the Marine Corps, he had several private sessions with Boyd to discuss the implications of Boyd's theories. He arranged for Boyd to lecture at the Marine Infantry School at Quantico, Virginia. In a further attempt to rekindle an interest in the "art of war," he mailed a copy of Sun Tzu's *The Art of War* to the home of every Marine officer.

Gray's two predecessors as commandant, Generals Robert H. Barrow and P. X. Kelly, also sat through Boyd's briefing and had numerous private sessions with him to discuss his theories. In an interview with *The Washington Post* in January 1981, Kelly stated: "An hour with John is of inestimable value. He has become well accepted by field-grade officers in the military. We need officers who think about war and how to defeat the enemy."[5]

Boyd's "Patterns" became a symbol and a cornerstone of the Reform Movement.[6] When Boyd began briefing in 1976, there were few officers in any service who could intelligently discuss his theories or any of the concepts of the past masters of the art of war. The military education system either ignored the military art or gave it only lip service. It was more important for an officer to study management principles than guerrilla warfare. More Air Force officers could quote Peter Drucker than Clausewitz; few could even spell Clausewitz. Perhaps this is why we had not won a war since the 1940s.

Boyd single-handedly educated a large portion of the Department of Defense, Congress, the press corps, and defense industry on the concepts of blitzkrieg and guerrilla war and how to counter blitzkriegs and guerrilla wars. His theories embarrassed the services, for they had nothing that compared with them.

It is important to recall that, in the mid-1970s, this nation had just lost the Vietnam War. A lot of soul-searching was taking place in the military. People were looking for excuses and reasons. Younger officers were openly questioning the philosophy and approaches of the senior officers who had prosecuted the war. This explains why, as General Kelly said, Boyd was so accepted by the field-grade officers, the younger ones. The more senior military leaders were desperately clinging to their old theories and trying to find scapegoats for their failures.

Boyd did not make the leadership feel any better by pointing out that we were losers because our leaders did not understand the nature of the Vietnam War. Anyone who had sat through Boyd's briefing came to that conclusion unequivocally. Boyd did not have to say it. It was all there in his explanation of how successful guerrilla wars have been fought and how they are successfully countered.

The conventional military thinkers had become locked into the physical aspects of conflict. Who can forget the nightly newscast giving body counts as an indication of who was winning? The leaders did not under-

50   stand, or appreciate, the leverage available in the mental and moral aspects of war. Many had become enamored with computer models of combat. The most popular models were known as piston-action-FEBA-movement models. The FEBA (forward edge of the battle area) is a line drawn on the map that separates the opposing forces: good guys on one side, bad guys on the other. In the models, the opposing forces lined up along the FEBA and shot at each other. Using the number of weapons on each side and their relative effectiveness, the models calculated which side suffered the greatest losses. When the losses on one side relative to the other reached some arbitrary level, such as 15 percent, the force on that side retreated, which caused the FEBA to move as if some giant piston were pushing it—and the enemy—across the battlefield. Infiltrations, flanking movements, encirclements, surrender, or any aspects dealing with the mental and moral elements of conflict were ignored because the models could not handle these concepts. This is the essence of the mechanistic view of warfare that dominated the thinking of the Army's doctrinaires during and immediately following the Vietnam War.

To the conventional military thinkers of our time, the Vietnam War should have been a cakewalk for our forces, but we lost to a bunch of guys in black pajamas and sandals. Why? The answer most commonly given is that our forces lost the moral support of the public back home. Moral support collapsed. Why? Boyd's treatise explains why it collapsed in very graphic terms.

The Vietnamese understood the mental and moral aspects of the war far better than our leaders. We blew it because our military and civilian leaders did not understand the nature of the war, whereas the other side did. Arguments that our forces were not allowed to do what was required to win are not persuasive. For anyone who doubts these statements, I recommend Frances Fitzgerald's best-seller, *Fire in the Lake,* and Bruce Palmer's *25 Year War.* Palmer was Gen. William Westmoreland's four-star deputy in Vietnam. The following excerpts from Palmer[7] suggest that the senior U.S. leadership did not understand the nature of war in Vietnam or otherwise:

> The United States was overconfident in believing that superior U.S. technology, Yankee ingenuity, industrial and military might, modern military organizations, tactics, and techniques, and a tradition of crises solving in peace and war would surely bring success where the French had failed. One of our handicaps was that few Americans understood the true nature of the war—the devilishly clever mixture of conventional warfare fought somewhat unconventionally and guerrilla warfare fought in the classical manner. (p. 176)

> The employment of military force—in peace, cold war, or actual conflict—is an art, not an exact science. It is supremely important that our national leaders, civilian and military, have a fundamental understanding of the capabilities and limitations of military power. Vietnam demonstrated how the lack of such understanding can lead to disastrous failure. (p. 193)

Our military had a blank check until the Tet offensive of 1968 revealed to the American public that we were losing when it had been led to believe we were winning. The mismatch between what was actually occurring and what was being claimed shattered the moral bonds between the military and the public. The destruction of moral bonds by exploiting the differences between what actually happened and what is claimed to have happened is a key part of Boyd's theories.

Embarrassed by the attention and commotion stirred up by Boyd's briefing, the services tried to show that they, too, could think about the "art" of war, but they lacked the ability because doctrine had become dogma and managers had replaced warriors. Their initial efforts to mimic Boyd were feeble.

On 5 February 1982, Air Force Chief of Staff Gen. Lew Allen announced the formation of Project Warrior, a program to "encourage increased familiarity with war-fighting theories."[8] About all Project Warrior ever did was to publish suggested reading lists of books and articles dealing with warriors and heroes (many taken directly from Boyd's source list). Oh yes, there were also "Warrior of the Month" awards. The Air Force did the least to change its thinking.

The Army was a little more inventive. It tried to copy Boyd's work. One of the key elements of Boyd's theories is the notion that every individual or organization goes through a four-part cycle of (1) observing its surrounding environment, (2) orienting itself mentally to those observations, (3) deciding on a course of action, and (4) acting. Observation, Orientation, Decision, Action—the OODA loop, Boyd called it.

Boyd's theories are based on the premise that if you observe, orient, decide, and act at a quicker tempo than your adversaries, you could get inside their "time-mind-space" and drive them into confusion and chaos. Everything your adversaries do would always be a half-count behind what is unfolding before them, and this would cause panic in their minds.

Five years after Boyd began briefing his "Patterns" with their OODA loops, the Army made an attempt to catch up with him. In the fall of 1981, Brig. Gen. Donald Morelli, the Army's chief doctrine specialist, began briefing around Washington the Army's plan to establish a doctrine based on maneuver and deception that would replace its current doctrine of firepower and attrition. This new doctrine was called "Air

Land Battle."[9] Its central idea was to have the Army operate at a quicker tempo than its adversary by going through the steps of "see, analyze, decide, synchronize, and act" faster than an opponent. This is almost identical to Boyd's OODA loop theory, except for the synchronized step.

I arranged for Morelli to brief this so-called new concept to several senior Air Force leaders in the Pentagon. During the course of the briefing, I commented to General Morelli that his ideas bore a remarkable similarity to Boyd's theories. Morelli, exploding into a tirade, claimed that the ideas were all original and not taken from Boyd's work. His reaction was so emotional and defensive that I presumed he had run into this same criticism before. Morelli did not know that most people in the room had heard Boyd's briefing years before and recognized his work for what it was.

Of this, there can be no question. Four years before Morelli's doctrine came along, Boyd had briefed Gen. William DePuy, commander of the Army's Training and Doctrine Command (TRADOC) and the recognized father of the much maligned 1976 *Field Manual*, which Morelli's work would replace. TRADOC still had many copies of Boyd's work when Morelli came to work there and started putting together the Air Land Battle package.

General DePuy had been enamored with systems analysis and surrounded himself with officers who had a background in operations research. DePuy wrote much of the 1976 *Field Manual* himself with the details filled in by a small team from his staff known as the "boat house gang" because the team's office was in a building once used as a yacht club. The manual, and the doctrine it represented, reflected DePuy's mechanistic mind-set. Then, as now, systems analysts could quantify only portions of the physical aspects of combat, such as weapons systems characteristics. Winners and losers were determined by comparing the numbers and relative lethalities of opposing weapons systems. The mental, moral, and human aspects of combat, which Boyd emphasized in stark contrast, were ignored by DePuy and his followers because they could not be quantified. Reflecting DePuy's view of the battlefield, the 1976 *Field Manual* contained an entire chapter on weapons systems and less than one page on leadership. Emphasizing force ratios as the determining factor in battle, the *Field Manual* declared that an attacking force could not be successful unless it outnumbered the defender by a ratio of at least six to one. As DePuy instructed his staff, "We have to stick to fundamentals, stick to the arithmetic of the battlefield."[10] Force ratios, superior firepower, attrition, and toe-to-toe slugfests characterized Depuy's *Field Manual.*

Boyd's work had also penetrated another Army institution, as Maj. Gen. Jack Merrit, commandant of the Army War College, acknowledged in the 4 January 1981 edition of *The Washington Post*, some nine months before Morelli surfaced. Speaking of Boyd's work, Merrit said: "It's a real tour de force. He is really one of the most innovative and original guys I've ever had anything to do with, and he created a lot of excitement up here among strategists and historians on the college staff." Merrit announced plans to incorporate Boyd's theories in the War College curriculum.[11]

At the same time, Boyd was infiltrating yet another Army school, the Army Command and General Staff College at Fort Leavenworth, Kansas. Army Lt. Col. Huba Wass de Czege, a Hungarian-born, Harvard-educated instructor there, was one of many Vietnam veterans who were beginning to question the doctrinal thinking of the senior leaders. Wass de Czege heard Boyd's briefing and immediately invited him to lecture his students on a regular basis.

Boyd and his colleague, Bill Lind, became regular lecturers. They stirred the pot by openly attacking the Army's 1976 *Field Manual* as a "piece of garbage" that could lead only to excessive casualties on both sides of a conflict. Lind, an aide to Senator Gary Hart and a frequent author of articles in trade journals, advocated "maneuver warfare" based on Boyd's theories. His articles and lectures were particularly aimed at the Marine Corps, but he never passed up the opportunity to accompany Boyd on a lecture tour to Air Force or Army installations. Lind was brash, cocky, and quick to criticize the Marines for adhering to war-fighting philosophies of the Vietnam era. Although he made a lot of enemies in the defense business, his efforts served a valuable purpose by helping to stir the pot of reform.

Boyd not only attacked the Army's doctrine when he lectured Army audiences, but he went out of his way to attack it in the open press and when he lectured the Air Force, Navy, industry, congressmen, and everyone who would listen. That way, his comments would surely get back to senior Army leaders, who would then have to either respond to his criticisms or change their doctrine. They decided to change it.

Boyd's constant pounding on the Army, coupled with a growing chorus of criticism from officers like Wass de Czege, caused the Army to decide in 1982 to rewrite completely its *Field Manual*, throw out the firepower and attrition philosophy of the Vietnam era, and embrace a philosophy espoused by Boyd. Colonel Wass de Czege was chosen to head up the effort, which culminated in a totally new version of *Field Manual 100-5, Operations* that was published in September 1982. The manual was revised again in 1986 to clear up many, but not all, inconsistencies in the first version. Unfortunately, even with the two major revisions, the Army never did get things quite right.

As I indicate in the Prologue, the 1976 Army doctrine advocated maneuver of our friendly forces in order to get in front of the enemy to slug it out—maneuver in order to shoot at the enemy. Boyd preached the opposite—shoot in order to create opportunities to maneuver—and maneuver in order to create chaos, panic, and collapse and get behind the enemy to capture its forces. "Fighter pilots always come in the back door, not the front," he stated over and over.

The Army's new doctrine of 1982 reflected most of this view. It centered around the four ideas of depth, initiative, agility, and synchronization. The first three ideas were consistent with Boyd's teaching. He openly congratulated the Army for throwing out the failed doctrine of the Vietnam era, but he continued to criticize it unmercifully for hanging on to the idea of synchronization. He felt that it was a giant step backward past World War II all the way to World War I.

"How can the Army advocate initiative at the lower levels, agility of fast moving armored forces, and then insist upon everyone remaining synchronized? Synchronized forces can only advance at the pace of the slowest unit. Everyone has to stay in formation and advance together. This is wrong and flies in the face of the other three notions," Boyd said. Over and over he preached this point, but his criticisms fell on deaf ears. Synchronization became a key element of the Army's new war-fighting doctrine. (It appears that Boyd's criticisms were well founded. Strong evidence indicates that the Army's obsession with remaining synchronized permitted the Iraqi Republican Guard to escape entrapment by allied forces during the Gulf War. This is discussed in the Epilogue.)

While Wass de Czege was revising the Army's *Field Manual* in 1982, he also established the School of Advanced Studies at Leavenworth. A few of the best and brightest graduates of the Army Command and General Staff College were asked to stay on for an additional year of advanced study of military history and theories. These students dubbed themselves the "Jedi Knights."[12] Boyd's work was mandatory study when the school was first established; however, when Wass de Czege left the school for another assignment, the lecture invitations to Boyd stopped. I suppose his lectures were too controversial and irreverent.

While this revolution in thinking was occurring in the Army, a similar change was unfolding within the Marine Corps. Again, John Boyd was the catalyst. Bill Lind introduced Boyd to Marine Lt. Col. Mike Wyly, an instructor at the Marine Corps Infantry School at Quantico, Virginia. Wyly, like Wass de Czege in the Army, was one of many officers trying to shed the yoke of Vietnam. Struggling with this legacy, Wyly knew there was a better way of thinking about how to fight wars, but he had not found anything of substance to replace the old theories. Boyd provided the answers.

Wyly describes the first Boyd briefing to his students as "electrifying."[13] Normally, his young Marine officers could not wait to get out of class and off to the golf course or officers club for a round of cheer. When Boyd finished his first lecture, the students were mesmerized. A dozen or so stayed after class, long into the night, to discuss Boyd's theories with him. Wyly had never seen such excitement in his classes. He immediately knew that here was the answer he had been seeking—a replacement for the old paradigm.

Boyd became a regular lecturer at Quantico. As his briefing grew in content and length, Wyly became his unofficial publisher. Copies of Boyd's lectures were bound in booklet form and printed with a green cover, hence its name, the Green Book. As the Gulf War approached, the demand for copies of the Green Book outstripped the Marines' ability to print enough of them. Between 1987 and the start of the Gulf War, Wyly's school distributed one thousand copies, not just to Marines but to Army, Navy, and Air Force officers and many other people in the defense business. As the storm clouds of war darkened, Wyly was deluged by requests for the Green Book.

When the Army published the revised *Field Manual*, Marine Corps Commandant Gen. Alfred Gray decided that the Marines Corps should have its own war-fighting manual, something like the Army's. He turned to the school at Quantico. Gray, like Wyly, was thoroughly familiar with Boyd's work, having sat through his marathon briefing three times. It was no surprise to any student of military doctrine that the first Marine Corps doctrine manual (*Fleet Marine Force Manual Number 1*, published in March 1989) was based largely on Boyd's theories.

For fifteen years, Boyd has briefed his theories throughout the defense world. As previously indicated, the initial responses by many of the senior leaders demonstrated their lack of understanding or appreciation of the fundamentals of conflict. Over the years, however, Boyd infiltrated the minds of literally hundreds of younger officers in all of the services. Slowly, his ideas and theories took hold in those officers, who were beginning to assume positions of higher rank and authority. By the end of the 1980s, real change had occurred in the military's thinking about war fighting. Many people were involved in that change. Any competent historical analysis will show that John Boyd was one of the key movers and shakers. The Army and Marine Corps did not influence his thinking or his theories, but he certainly influenced theirs.

In 1977, when Boyd and his "Patterns" were starting to raise eyebrows around Washington, the unofficial headquarters for the Reform Movement was established. It just sort of happened, as a group of people with the same views came together and reached a critical mass.

Tom Christie, Boyd's friend from Eglin Air Force Base, Florida, was now an intermediate-level civilian on the staff of the secretary of defense. He was in charge of the office that performed analyses of the effectiveness of the tactical air forces of the Air Force, Navy, and Marine Corps, the fighters and fighter-bombers of all U.S. forces. Christie's office was referred to as the "TAC Air Shop." It quickly became the watering hole and gathering place of the old Fighter Mafia. It also would become the target of concerted spy operations by the establishment.

Christie hired Chuck Spinney. He also hired John Boyd as a part-time consultant—"Christmas help," as Boyd put it. This gave Boyd an official excuse to be in the Pentagon every day where he could work on his "Patterns" and "do the Lord's work" (a code expression for activities that furthered the cause of reform). Boyd was the magnet that drew the skeptics and dissidents to this den of iniquity. The TAC Air Shop became the base of operations for the reformers.

Boyd's expanding "Patterns" pointed clearly to the need for the military establishment to change its way of thinking, to get back to the business of learning how to win wars. Spinney's work soon became another cornerstone in the reformers' argument that serious changes were needed. My own work, in its small way, began to add to the Reform Movement.

By the spring of 1978, I was convinced that the Air Force was headed for complete disaster. Not only was I disillusioned by the conduct of many people in positions of authority, but I was now openly questioning their competence. For two years, I had examined in great detail the promises of every new weapons system that was planned for the next ten years. Three factors were evident to me:

1. The process of deciding which weapons to develop and buy was undisciplined. It contained few real checks and balances because no one at the top wanted any.

2. The investment philosophy of the Air Force would lead to a hollow force, one that would become smaller, more expensive, and less capable.

3. A deep-seated military mind-set existed that considered warfare only in terms of bombing an opponent back to the Stone Age. This Neanderthal approach was totally devoid of any understanding or appreciation of the art of war.

General Toomay became concerned about my attitude. Although he agreed with my assessment of the situation, he warned that if I continued to offer only criticism, I would become a nihilist, someone who believed in nothing. As he put it, "Critics are obliged to assume the role of author on occasion." In other words, if you don't like what's going on, you have to offer a better alternative. So I did.

Meanwhile, the intelligence community was claiming that the Soviets had adopted the German blitzkrieg tactics from World War II and would swiftly and easily "blitz" western Europe if war broke out. (It is no coincidence that the intelligence community began using the term blitzkrieg after Boyd's briefing became popular.) The Soviets, according to the intelligence reports, had a tremendous advantage in numbers of tanks and infantrymen at their disposal. When these superior numbers were combined with the blitzkrieg tactics, the Soviets were being portrayed as almost unbeatable. Exaggerating a threat to justify new wonder weapons was, and still is, a common practice.

The Air Force's answer to this bloated Soviet threat was a new fighter-bomber called the Enhanced Tactical Fighter, a proposed night all-weather interdiction aircraft. In the view of the Air Force, the word enhanced referred to the new technologies planned for the plane. In my view, it referred to their costs. This plane was being designed to attack Soviet tank forces deep behind enemy lines and destroy them before they could get to the front and exploit any breakthroughs that would occur (night, all weather interdiction). The price was a mere $50 million per airplane.

As it happened, I was putting together a proposal for a new airplane at that time (March 1978). My proposal was exactly the opposite of the $50 million plane. I prepared an advocacy briefing that called for the development of a small, simple, lethal, and relatively cheap airplane that would be designed solely for close support of the ground troops who would be engaged with Soviet tanks and armor. Because the intelligence community was making such a big deal about how difficult it would be to stop the Soviet blitzkrieg, I named this airplane the "Blitzfighter." Rather catchy, I thought.

Everything about my proposal, including how the plane would be used, was diametrically opposed to the prevailing philosophy relating to the new wonder weapons of the Air Force. I wanted an airplane in the 5,000- to 10,000-pound class (one-tenth the weight of the Enhanced Tactical Fighter), one smaller than any combat airplane in the inventory (one-fourth the size of the A-10), and one that cost less than $2 million. At this price, we could flood the battlefield with swarms of airplanes.

The airplane would be designed around a four-barrel version of the same cannon that was in production on the A-10, which used a seven-barrel cannon that fired shells costing only $13 apiece. This was a far cry

58   from the guided missiles on the Enhanced Tactical Fighter that cost several hundred thousand apiece. The Blitzfighter would have no high-tech bells and whistles and no wonder weapons. Essentially, it would contain an engine (an existing commercial one), a pilot, a titanium-armored bathtub for the pilot to sit in, a few flight instruments, a radio for the pilot to talk to the ground troops, and a cannon for killing tanks. Nothing more—no radars, infrared sensors, guided missiles, or any of that high-priced junk being installed on every other airplane—was needed.

With the ability to operate from grass fields, the Blitzfighter did not demand fixed, expensive airfields that probably would cease to exist ten minutes after a war started. Squadrons of Blitzfighters would pack up, move from pasture to pasture overnight and follow the flow of battle. Pilots would receive only verbal orders that identified the main points of their effort and left the details of execution to them, a notion that was consistent with Boyd's theories. The plan was in direct contrast to the standard practice of using excruciatingly detailed orders published by higher headquarters for each mission. The orders dictated how much fuel went on board, which weapons were loaded on which wing, the exact route that would be flown to the exact target that had been assigned, and even when the pilot would be allowed to relieve himself. Such rigid orders did not always match up to what was happening in a fast-moving situation.

Finally, the Blitzfighter would be operated at treetop level so that pilots could use their eyeballs to find tanks that were trying to hide. To survive at this level, the plane had to be extremely agile and dart, twist, turn, accelerate, and decelerate far better than any airplane we had.

I presented this advocacy briefing to General Toomay and asked his permission to make a formal request to our design bureau at Wright Patterson Air Force Base for design studies. He nearly gagged. He was a high-tech advocate. Everything I was proposing was anti–high-tech. Naturally, we got into an argument.

He said, "You have to put a radar on the plane; you can't find tanks without a radar."

I responded, "You can't find tanks with radars; radars can't see through trees, over hills, and when they do see something, you don't know whether the blob on the scope is a friendly tank, an enemy tank, or a Volkswagen full of refugees; no sir, you can't find tanks with radars."

He said, "Yes, you can."

I said, "No, you can't," my voice rising.

Then, standing up, he raised his voice, "Yes, you can." General Toomay was a large man, over 6 feet 8 inches tall. (His son, Pat Toomay, who took after his father, was a defensive end for the Dallas Cowboys at the time.) At this point, the argument was over. We had been through this routine many times.

Even though he disagreed with me, General Toomay permitted me to proceed without making any changes. That's the kind of man he was. He knew that my proposal was going to stir up a hornet's nest once the word got out, and he really enjoyed making the system react to unconventional ideas.

I immediately fired off a teletype message to John Chuprin, chief of our design bureau at Wright Patterson. John had performed thousands of design trade-off studies on the lightweight fighters for Boyd a few years before. He and his staff went to work and, within a month, reported back that it was entirely feasible to build the airplane I wanted—like I wanted it. He even gave me preliminary designs for three possible configurations.

Armed with this information, I hit the briefing trail. My intent was to quietly build a network of support at various key agencies within the Air Force and within the Office of the Secretary of Defense before the establishment could react and kill the idea—much the same way the lightweight fighter program had been ushered in.

One of the first places I went with my briefing was the A-10 program office at Wright Patterson, where Boyd arranged for me to meet Col. Bob Dilger. Dilger was in charge of producing the 30-mm cannon and the ammunition used on the A-10. Because that equipment was such a key part of my proposal, I was anxious to get his reaction.

Dilger is an eccentric character. He was a fighter pilot in Vietnam and was credited with one MIG kill. After firing his radar-guided missiles at his opponent and watching them all miss, he literally ran his opponent into the ground. Bob can be quite aggressive, and he loves a good fight. I liked his style. We quickly became friends. We would join forces a few years later, to the discomfort of the army.

Dilger was very excited about my proposal and pledged his support. While I was there, he also briefed me on an unusual test program he was running. The normal way to test ammunition coming off the production line is to select samples at random and fire them in a laboratory environment to measure muzzle velocity, trajectory, and other factors to determine if they meet the specifications of the production contract.

Dilger did it differently. He put some realism into the tests. He scrounged up a bunch of old Army tanks and about a half dozen Soviet tanks (T-55s and T-62s), loaded them up with fuel and live ammunition as though they were in combat, and deployed them in typical Soviet tank formations on the Nevada desert. He then talked operational A-10 fighter units into attacking the tanks. Using their combat tactics, they fired Dilger's production line samples of ammunition.

These tests gave pilots valuable training experience. They also revealed, for the first time, major inconsistencies in the computer models that were used to predict the lethality of U.S. weapons. It seems that the test results differed by a factor of two from the model predictions on the lethality of the ammunition. The Soviet tanks were easier to kill than predicted, and the old U.S. tanks were more difficult to kill than predicted. The models were not only in error by a factor of two, but they were off in two different directions. This really caught my attention, and I would pursue this subject with great vigor in the years to come.

I next slipped into the Pentagon and quietly briefed Boyd, Spinney, Christie, and the other rebels in the TAC Air Shop. It was like preaching to the choir, for this whole crowd had become disenchanted with the direction things were headed in the tactical air forces of all three services.

Boyd arranged for me to meet and brief Pierre Sprey. I had heard much about Pierre and was anxious to meet him. He became extremely excited over the Blitzfighter concept, not just the airplane itself but the whole philosophy and concept of operation. He offered suggestions to improve my briefing and put a little more bite into it. Pierre is very good with the editing pen, as I would learn in the years to come. He would become my chief editor during my running battle with the Army over the Bradley. His pens are shaped like fangs, and his finished product drips with blood, usually Army blood.

Christie then ushered me into a secret meeting with Russell "Russ" Murray II, director of Program Analysis and Evaluation (PA&E). Murray was the defense secretary's chief analyst. Over the years, this position has been one of great power and influence—one that the secretary has turned to for advice on the weapons systems to buy. That advice, in the past, usually was contrary to the wishes of the services and led to a longstanding adversarial relationship between the director and the various services. In my view, that relationship was healthy, for it sharpened the debate over the appropriate choice of weapons. Under the Reagan administration, unfortunately, the position was completely neutered so that it was no longer a force to be reckoned with.

Russ Murray was receptive and pledged his support if my Blitzfighter proposal ever officially got to his level, but he doubted that would ever happen. In his view, the Air Force senior leaders would kill the idea as soon as they heard about it. "The airplane doesn't cost enough," he said. "They might buy it if you jack the price up two or three times." It turned out that he was correct.

My career suddenly took on new life. For some strange reason, the Air Force promoted me to full colonel after passing me over for two straight years. Historically, the chances of promotion after being passed over twice is less than 3 percent. General Toomay surprised me one night when he called my home to give me the news. This promotion meant that I would be able to stay in the Air Force for many years to come, rather than have to leave the service within the next year. (This is known as the "up or out" policy. Any officer who is passed over three times must leave the service.)

Another promotion was important to my future. My favorite three-star, General Infamous, who had so kindly asked me to leave the Pentagon two years earlier, was promoted to four stars. You guessed it—he was immediately assigned to Air Force Systems Command Headquarters at Andrews. He would again become my boss and General Toomay's. I will never forget the day he arrived. He came to Toomay's office to greet us. In front of the staff, he actually wrapped his arms around me and greeted me like a long-lost brother. I thought to myself, "What's wrong with this picture?" I soon found out—within weeks, I was shipped out again.

Meanwhile, unknown to me, Pierre was busy spreading the Blitzfighter story throughout the defense industry and on Capitol Hill. The concept was stirring up a lot of excitement in the design bureaus of various companies. Early in June 1978, a large group of designers and newfound advocates met in a hotel conference room in Springfield, Virginia, about 10 miles south of the Pentagon, to explore the concept in some detail and trade ideas on design approaches. Unfortunately, the press also was there.

Aviation Week ran a two-page story about the conference and treated the Blitzfighter like it was an officially sanctioned Air Force program. The story cited the design studies that I had asked Wright Patterson to do and even showed sketches of the designs. The Air Force senior leaders were shocked and horrified. The story broke about two weeks after my favorite four-star, General Infamous, had arrived on the scene, and he immediately went ballistic.

Undoubtedly, he got many calls from his fellow four-stars. Like many of them, he was an Enhanced Tactical Fighter advocate, and he was not going to let this Blitzfighter nonsense continue. He directed that I stop briefing. I was not allowed even to show him the briefing or explain the concept to him in any fashion. His closed mind had all the answers, and the Blitzfighter was not one of them. He pronounced to the world that the Blitzfighter idea was dead, by fiat, and then he arranged for me to be transferred out of his hair—again.

But the Blitzfighter was not dead. It would raise its ugly head numerous times during the next few years as one of several symbols of the Reform Movement. Each time it surfaced, the senior leadership went berserk.

The Air Force made a big mistake with my transfer. I was sent back into the Pentagon and directed toward the smoke-filled rooms of the "E" ring. There, I would witness most of the decisions made by the highest levels of the Air Force leadership. All of my suspicions were to be confirmed.

Four years previously, when I had first entered the Pentagon as a naive, gung-ho believer in the system, I was a young officer with complete faith in the senior leaders. Now, as I headed back there, my viewpoint had changed. I was convinced that the Air Force was being led down the garden path by people who didn't know what they were doing or didn't have the best interests of the Air Force at heart. I was not alone in these views. The storm clouds of reform were gathering.

4

Meet Me at the Flags

The Constitution establishes civilian rule over the military. Our founding fathers set things up this way because they were afraid of "the man on horseback" arriving on the scene and taking over the government. Accordingly, each president appoints, and the Senate confirms, a handful of civilians to serve in various positions of authority in the Department of Defense. The secretary of defense, deputy secretary, and a few under secretaries and assistant secretaries comprise the Office of the Secretary of Defense (OSD). The civilians are physically located on the third floor of the Pentagon. In Pentagon language, the *third floor* is synonymous with the secretary of defense and the OSD staff.

Each one of the services, the Army, Navy, and Air Force, has a civilian secretary, under secretary (No. 2 position) and three or four assistant secretaries. Most of these political appointees are located on the fourth floor, "E" ring, directly above the OSD principals. Altogether, about three dozen presidential appointees preside over the military.

Each presidential appointee is personally assigned a military officer who serves as the appointee's military assistant. For the secretary and deputy secretary of defense, the military assistant is a two-star general. (Colin Powell, before he became chairman of the Joint Chiefs of Staff, served as Secretary Caspar Weinberger's military assistant.) The secretary of each service has a one-star general, and each remaining appointee has a full colonel.

As the title implies, the official job of a military assistant is to provide assistance to the civilian appointee in that individual's dealings with the uniformed military. The military assistant schedules and sits in on all meetings, takes notes, ensures that the civilian receives all the information needed to exercise his or her responsibilities, and makes sure that his or her directions are followed. As an aide and confidant, the military assistant often gives advice on issues and, most importantly, screens and controls all correspondence, telephone calls, and visitors.

Military assistants act as liaisons between the civilian rulers and the uniformed military. They are often referred to as the "Palace Guard." In the Pentagon, information is power. Most people think that rank, title, and position constitute power, but these things only determine whether you sit at the head of the table or near the foot. The people who know things—who have access to information that others do not—are the ones who really influence events and decisions. The military assistants, to a large extent, control the flow of information inside the Pentagon. Therefore, they are very powerful, regardless of rank.

The military does not enjoy having civilian masters. Military officers publicly support the Constitution, but privately they wish that the civilians would just go away. The generals view the civilians as transients who come in, mess things up, and then move on. For good reasons, general mistrust exists between the two camps. Each spends a lot of time keeping track of what people in the other camp are doing, what they think, who they talk to, what information they are privy to, and what they are up to. These become the questions that are asked and answered dozens of times a day, by both sides, on a broad range of issues and topics. The military assistant is in the middle of this constant tug of war.

The real job of military assistants is to "capture" the civilian officials so that their views, actions, and decisions are consistent with and agreeable to the wishes of the generals. If the generals cannot capture the civilians and turn them into fully committed members of the team, they must neutralize the civilians so that they cannot interfere too much with the generals' plans.

The generals have many methods to neutralize civilians. One convenient method is to exclude civilians from certain key strategy sessions.

For this reason, most officials, both civilian and military, study the daily calendars of every key official with whom they deal. Other methods include withholding critical information, such as latest test results or cost figures, from civilians; creating special classified categories, not for the purpose of keeping secrets from foreign powers but to prevent civilians from gaining access to military plans; asking civilians to represent the Air Force in far-off lands at just the time they might be persuasive in internal debates at home; or simply ignoring civilians until they demonstrate resolve—the military is always testing the civilians' backbones for stiffness. The list could go on.

Some civilians are content to be captured. They do not mind being nothing more than puppets or mouthpieces for the generals. They enjoy being wined and dined and treated like royalty in exchange for their services. Other civilians exercise their independence on occasion; sooner or later, however, the constant and subtle pressures from the generals wear them down. Few civilian appointees are able to maintain their independence for any length of time.

Some military assistants cast their lots entirely with their general officer sponsors and act as blatant spies in the civilian camp. Others develop close relationships with their civilian bosses and are loyal to them. They spend more time with them than they do with their families. The hours are long, and the pace of activity is often frantic.

Daily, contentious issues create friction between various factions in the building. At times, bureaucratic battles become almost bloody. No one likes to lose a battle. Winning the battle is sometimes more important than the subject at hand, and this leads to all kinds of dirty games. The players of these games are truly masters at winning, no matter how underhandedly. Machiavelli himself would be considered a rank amateur in many of these contests.

When the military assistants cast their lots with civilian bosses, they make career enemies in the general officer corps—serious, big-time enemies. Few military assistants are able to walk the fine line between their civilian and military masters without incurring the wrath of one or the other, or both. I speak from experience. From June 1978 to June 1982, I served as military assistant to three consecutive Air Force assistant secretaries during two administrations, one Democratic and one Republican.

Throughout this period, Boyd's advice on loyalty guided my actions. Loyalty must be earned, not commanded. In my view, I had three options: (1) if my boss demanded that I be loyal to him, I responded with integrity; (2) if my boss acted with integrity and insisted that I act the same way, he earned my loyalty; and (3) if my boss acted like a scoundrel, he was fair game—boss or not.

While serving as a military assistant, I was fortunate or unfortunate (take your pick) to witness directly the day-to-day behavior of the senior Air Force military and civilian leadership, as well as the senior civilian staff members of the Office of the Secretary of Defense. The power politics, wheeling and dealing, and the games that go on at this level are a sight to behold.

Coalitions form and dissolve overnight between the strangest bedfellows. Dire enemies momentarily join forces to battle someone else, then resume their old fight as if nothing had happened. The only way to get a decision to stand is to "shoot the losers"—line up everyone who opposes the decision and shoot them down. Otherwise, they begin to undermine the decision before the ink is dry on the paper. Quite often, the real debate begins only after a major decision has been made. Time and again, I have listened to senior officials express total frustration when issues that they thought were settled suddenly reappeared.

I have seen countless civilian Pentagon officials, who had been appointed from the ranks of defense contractors, conduct themselves as if they were still working for the defense industry instead of the troops in the field. I have seen military and civilian officials leave government service and go to work for defense contractors, who benefited from actions they took before leaving. This is legally permissible; however, in my view, it is morally wrong. There have been many attempts to legislate ethics and slow down this revolving door, but clever people can always find ways around legislation, especially when large sums of money are involved.

I have been in meetings where there were more hidden agendas than people in the room. Sadly, I have seen program managers lie to high-level review boards, generals lie to civilians, civilians lie to generals, and both lie to the Congress and the American public. Seldom is anyone held accountable. On the contrary, many are rewarded for their behavior. These rewards are duly noted by the legions of lower-level subordinates who look to their superiors for examples of acceptable and expected behavior at the top. Integrity and principle are strangers in this arena. In short, the business of buying weapons in the Pentagon is a dirty business that, at times, has little or nothing to do with national defense. Neither changes in procurement rules and procedures nor organizational realignments will eliminate the corruption. As long as people in positions of authority behave like scoundrels and are not held accountable for their actions, we will continue to have scandals such as those that plagued the Pentagon throughout the 1980s.

In my job as a military assistant, I believed that the secretary should have the benefit of both sides of an argument before he made up his mind. The strengths and weaknesses of proposed weapons systems

should be represented with equal vigor. Above all, the information presented to him should be truthful. The "system" was geared to presenting
a "cooked" solution, where the briefings, analyses, and information were
all shaped to support a preferred decision. The secretary was expected to
be a rubber stamp of approval. Occasionally, there would be pro forma
attempts at objective debate, but usually these were only for show.

Personally, I could not stomach this charade, this orchestrated dance
of deception. Boyd's words about "to be or to do" kept ringing in my ears
every time one of these situations arose, which was far too often. I tried
"to do" what little I could to bring some semblance of honest objectivity
to the decision-making process, but I knew full well the reaction I would
get from anyone embarrassed or challenged in the process. As Boyd
would remind me constantly on the phone, "Jim, you may not win, but
you can't give the bastards a free ride. Make them work for it." And so I
did.

My first attempt to "make them work for it" came shortly after I
returned to the Pentagon in June 1978 as military assistant to Air Force
Assistant Secretary for Research, Development, and Logistics Dr. Jack
Martin. By law, the Air Force cannot negotiate and sign a contract to
develop or produce a weapons system unless it has its civilian master's signature on a document that permits it to do so. Called a Secretarial Deter-
mination and Finding (D&F), that document represents the instrument
of control over the military's plans to buy new weapons—no signature,
no program.

Dr. Martin, as the acquisition executive of the Air Force, would sign literally hundreds of D&Fs a year. My job was to make sure he knew the
implications of what he was signing. Once he had signed, he became an
equal partner to the venture (or crime).

I shall never forget that summer day in 1978 when Brig. Gen. Richard
"Dick" Phillips and his team of briefers marched into Dr. Martin's office
to seek his signature on the D&F for the Air Force's new fighter, the
Enhanced Tactical Fighter. The rationale for developing this new airplane was so full of holes and the arguments presented by Phillips were
so misleading that I could not remain silent, as I was expected to do. I
must admit that as a newcomer to this arena, I was apprehensive about
speaking up, but I did. In the middle of the briefing, I interrupted
Phillips and blurted out three questions:

"What is the mission of this airplane?"

"Night, all-weather deep interdiction," the answer came back.

"General, could you give Dr. Martin an example or two from history
where deep interdiction has actually influenced the outcome of a battle
or campaign?"

The silence was deafening. Phillips scowled at me, but there was no answer. So I quickly moved on to my last question.

"Is this airplane going to cost $2 million apiece or $50 million?"

Answer: "Well, we really don't know because we haven't gotten that far in the program yet."

I knew this to be untrue, for I had talked to the cost analysts at Wright Patterson Air Force Base the day before in anticipation of this meeting, which is why I used the figure of $50 million. The $2 million figure was a subtle reference to the Blitzfighter, which was at the other end of the spectrum in both cost and mission.

The meeting broke up in disarray. Dr. Martin asked me to remain as the others filed out. He asked me what was going on since this was the first time I had become an active participant in his meetings. I explained to him that the Air Force was intentionally misleading him on this proposed program, and I gave him names and telephone numbers he could call to confirm if he had any doubt.

Dr. Martin picked up the phone, called Vice Chief of Staff Gen. James Hill, and asked for an immediate private meeting. He then walked next door and handed the unsigned D&F to the vice chief, and told him to forget about the program. Who says there is no justice in this world? The mighty Enhanced Tactical Fighter had been shot down in flames by the Blitzfighter. (During the Reagan administration, the Enhanced Tactical Fighter was resurrected and placed in production.)

Needless to say, General Phillips was not happy with me. I was soon braced up against the wall in the hall of the "E" ring. With his forefinger pounding on my breastbone like a jackhammer and his nose about one inch from mine, he let me know that I was dog meat and that he and several other generals would have a feast when I came back into the "blue suit" Air Force.

Then the paranoia surfaced: "You are not going to ram that f___ing Blitzfighter down our throats like your friends did the F-16!" They were still smarting over that coup.

General Phillips and I would cross paths and cross swords on many occasions during the next eight years. The confrontations would always take the same form. He would try to slip a questionable weapons system through the decision makers by suppressing unflattering data, and I would go out of my way to make sure everyone knew the whole story.

This incident became the model for the performance of my duties over the next four years as I served three consecutive presidential appointees, Dr. Martin, Dr. Robert Hermann, and Dr. Alton Keel. On most topics that were to come before them, I tapped my information network beforehand. Then, privately, I presented my boss with the damaging data (conveniently missing from the Air Staff's briefing or analysis), countering arguments, and, in many cases, physical evidence of outright lies that were being perpetrated for the purpose of getting him to agree to one of the high-tech tinker toys the generals were selling.

As time progressed, I developed a sixth sense for detecting con games, lies of omission and commission, and intentionally biased arguments. I took particular delight in tracking down the evidence that exposed these things for what they were. My civilian bosses must have appreciated my efforts (Dr. Hermann often referred to me as his "hair shirt"). As each one left the government, his replacement asked me to stay on and provide the same service to him. Normal procedure was to select a fresh team for each new assistant secretary.

The list of generals whose little games were being exposed began to grow like topsy. Most of them were generals in the research and development field who were trying to usher questionable weapons systems into the process. The word was soon out that I was not a team player and that certain generals were to be informed whenever I placed a call seeking data or information to the Air Force—anywhere. Anyone seen talking to me was duly reported to one general or another. While this discouraged some people from talking to me, it actually encouraged others. In fact, my information network began to expand. The more the generals tried to "interdict" the flow of information, more sources and paths appeared. Apparently, there was a growing body of concerned people, both military and civilian, at the grass-roots level who were sick of the corruption and dirty games in the weapons bureaucracy. They began to seek out anyone who could help change the way things were.

A. Ernest "Ernie" Fitzgerald, a civilian analyst, referred to these people as "closet patriots," people who wanted to expose wrongdoing but were afraid of losing their jobs if they raised an issue through normal channels. Ernie was instrumental in setting up an outside channel where the closet patriots could funnel information to the public and Congress and still remain anonymous. In 1969, Fitzgerald had been a civilian financial analyst on the staff of the secretary of the Air Force. He committed the cardinal sin of telling Congress the truth about the costs of the C-5 cargo plane. It seems that the costs were $2 billion more than Congress had been led to believe. For this dastardly deed of telling the truth, Fitzgerald was fired. He did not take it lying down. After he fought through 12 years of legal battles, the courts finally ruled in his favor and ordered the Air Force to reinstate him in his old job.[1]

Along the way, there were several suits, including one against President Richard Nixon. The first time Fitzgerald sued the government to get his job back, the courts rule that the Air Force had to reinstate him.

At 0001 on 10 December 1973, the Air Force, in fact, reinstated Fitzgerald in his old job. One minute later, at 0002 it transferred him to another job, one that had no duties.[2] So, Fitzgerald sued again. He also sued Nixon for giving the orders to go after him. His suit against Nixon went all the way to the Supreme Court, which decided in July 1982 that the president could not be sued. This case is interesting because it went to the Supreme Court without ever having been tried. A lot of maneuvering was needed to keep the case out of the lower courts. The prospect of Nixon as a defendant before a jury of Washington, D.C., citizens during the mid-1970s is absolutely mind-boggling. In any event, before the final ruling by the Supreme Court, Nixon paid Fitzgerald $140,000 in penalties, all of which Fitzgerald donated to charity.[3]

In June 1982, the courts finally ruled in Fitzgerald's favor on his second suit to be reinstated in his original job. I recall the staff meeting on the morning that Secretary of the Air Force Verne Orr learned of the final court decision. Orr directed the Air Force to accept Fitzgerald back into his old job and to put aside its animosity. He even instructed the Air Force to pay Ernie's legal fees. The generals in the staff meeting were not happy with this, but there was nothing else they could do. I recall the pained expressions on their faces when the secretary rubbed salt in their wounds by ordering them to pay the legal fees, which they eventually did. Fitzgerald is currently serving in his old job, but the courts have kept the case open to make sure the Air Force continues to honor the 1982 decision.

Secretary Orr, an honest man and a true gentleman, came to the Air Force with an open mind and a commitment to do what was right. Ironically, the most honest member of President Reagan's first Pentagon team was a California automobile dealer. Even Orr was eventually "captured" by the generals, however, and was reading from their scripts by the end of his term. Sadly, I personally watched his slow but steady conversion.

While Ernie Fitzgerald was fighting to get his job back, he maintained his personal contacts in the Pentagon. He was continually approached by frustrated closet patriots seeking advice on what to do about scandalous situations to which they were privy. Fitzgerald referred them to two staffers at the National Taxpayers' Union. Dina Rasor and David Keating translated the information they received into plain and simple language that the taxpayers could understand and then passed it on to the press and Congress. Quite often, the information was in the form of documents written in "Pentagonese," a strange language that resembles English but is almost undecipherable by the average American. Pierre Sprey was one of Dina's principal interpreters.

By the late 1970s, the press was becoming more and more critical of the Pentagon. Dina's business grew by leaps and bounds; in 1980, the

Project on Military Procurement was established, with Dina as director.[4] The Project became a conduit, or clearinghouse, for unclassified information from closet patriots concerned about waste, fraud, and abuse and "cheap hawks," people who thought a better defense could be built for less money. The sources of information were always protected, and Dina would not accept classified information under any circumstances.

Dina rapidly moved to the top of the Pentagon's most hated list. In essence, she became the press agent for the Reform Movement. Her business grew for one reason—she filled a need. As the number of critical or unflattering stories in the press began to increase and as interest in Pentagon reform began to grow on Capitol Hill, so did the Pentagon witch hunts.

By 1979, it became very apparent that I should be discreet about my relationships with Boyd, Spinney, and Sprey. They were becoming quite visible as ringleaders in the budding Reform Movement. I had reason to deal with each of them on a daily basis. They were sources of valuable information that I needed in my own battles with the system, and I was a valuable source to them. I was physically present in the inner circles of the senior Air Force leadership and was privy to its plans to counter the reformers.

I was rapidly moving up the generals' hit list because of my own reputation. I did not need a boost in my rating simply from my association with the movers and shakers of the Reform Movement.

All of my telephone calls were taken by a battery of secretaries and Air Force personnel who performed administrative duties for my boss, the assistant secretary. I could not afford to have a secretary routinely announce in the open that Boyd, Sprey, or Spinney was on the phone or leave notes of phone messages from them. It is a common bureaucratic intelligence practice to take note of telephone messages on people's desks when you visit their offices. (It is also common practice to leave fake messages lying around so they will be noticed.) Our outer office was almost always packed with Air Force briefing teams waiting to give their dog and pony shows to my boss.

To solve the message problem, Boyd, Sprey, and Spinney adopted code names for their telephone calls to me. For the next seven years, Pierre Sprey was "Mr. Grau." John Boyd became "Mr. Arbuthnott," a name Chuck Spinney also used. When I placed calls to them, I used the same names.

Now Arbuthnott is not exactly a household name, so I asked Boyd, "Where in the hell did you get that name?"

"I don't know," he replied, "It just came to me."

Months later, I was once again reading Anthony Cave Brown's wonderful book, *Bodyguard of Lies*, a fascinating description of Allied intelligence activities in World War II. I had read the book a few years before because it was on Boyd's mandatory reading list. On page 277 was a picture of "the secret organization formed by Churchill to plan the stratagems that would leave Hitler 'puzzled as well as beaten.'" One of the nine members of this organization was a British Intelligence officer, Comdr. James Arbuthnott. I nearly fell out of my chair when I saw this—that strange Boyd mind at work again.

Fearing that our telephones were tapped, and there were indications at times that this was the case, we needed places where we could meet and talk privately. My office, which was next to the vice chief's, and the TAC Air Shop were obviously out of the question.

The "A" ring hallway on the second floor of the Pentagon, between the 10th and 1st corridors, is dedicated to the NATO Alliance. The entire hallway is lined with displays from each nation on one side and the flags of each member on the other side. The U.S. flag is in the center of this impressive and patriotic exhibit. What better place for people to meet and discuss important matters that dealt with preserving the strength of the Alliance and the national security of this country? So began the almost daily routine of placing or receiving the telephone message, "Arbuthnott calling, meet me at the flags." Amidst all this intrigue, I began to realize what it must have been like to be a member of the Schwarze Kapelle in Berlin in the early 1940s. (The Schwarze Kapelle, or Black Orchestra, was a conspiracy by German military officers to overthrow Adolf Hitler. Their second bungled attempt to assassinate him in the bunker on 20 July 1944 led to the execution of most of them.)

In telling the ugly truth about the behavior of many people in the Pentagon, I am aware of the danger that the reader may conclude that I believed almost everyone near the top to be despicable. This is not the case. I have encountered many good and honest people along the way, some of whom the reader has already met. Others appear in later chapters, but I must admit that they are in the minority. Although a lot of basically good people worked in the Pentagon and wanted to do what was right, most of them were insecure. They were not willing to take the grief dished out by the system to anyone who gets out of step. Those who had the courage of their convictions stand out in this book.

This said, the saga of Chuck Spinney now may be in order. The Pentagon, by trying to suppress his work, actually catapulted Chuck into the national limelight and onto the cover of *Time Magazine*. In the process, the Pentagon fueled the Reform Movement. Chuck's story clearly indicates why we had to resort to code names and meetings at the flags.

Soon after Chuck joined the TAC Air Shop in 1977, he began work on an analysis of the tactical air forces of the U.S. Air Force. His study took the form of a briefing titled *Defense Facts of Life*. It was an exhaustive analysis of the various factors required for an overall judgment of the state of affairs in the tactical forces.

In the early days of the Reform Movement, Chuck's briefing became the instrument for stimulating debate on the need for change inside the Pentagon. Chuck was the first reformer openly to challenge the system from within and call for sweeping changes. Of course, he had a lot of help from the hard-core gang putting his study together, but he was the one who stepped forward and took the initial heat from the system.

Using the Air Force's own data (in true Boyd fashion—always stuff the other guy with his own data or logic), Chuck presented the following facts: The Air Force was decreasing in size, pilots were leaving the service in droves (not for pay reasons), flying hours were decreasing, actual training was being replaced by simulation, spare parts were not available, skill levels required by mechanics were so high that contractors had to be hired to maintain the equipment, readiness (the ability of the force to fly and fight on a daily basis) was at an all-time low, the cost of that low readiness was steadily increasing, the supplies of preferred munitions would last only a couple of days in an all-out war, and the actual performance of many of the frontline systems was seriously questioned.

The most damning revelation was that this state of affairs did not result from a lack of money. In Chuck's words: "Budget constraints are not the source of the problem."[5] The Defense budget increased by small amounts each year during the middle and late 1970s. Because of the high inflation rate, however, the real buying power of the Defense budget actually decreased slightly each year under the Carter administration. This became a major campaign issue for the 1980 election. Ronald Reagan promised to "re-arm America" by raising the peacetime Defense budget to unprecedented levels.

It was not commonly known until Chuck began briefing that the Air Force, throughout the 1970s, had allocated large sums of its budget to its tactical air forces at the expense of other areas. In fact, the budget for the tactical air forces (fighters and fighter-bombers) increased more than 11 percent each year, even after subtracting the effects of inflation.[6] This enormous growth rate actually exceeded the Reagan administration's plans for funding the whole Pentagon budget. Unfortunately, too much of the money had been spent on overly complex weapons that were extremely costly to operate and maintain. Not enough money was left over to pay support costs.

The Air Force's budgetary actions in building up its tactical air forces represented a preview of what to expect when the Reagan administration arrived on the scene and simply threw money at the Pentagon. The Air

Force's obsession with overly complex weapons systems, coupled with an undisciplined decision-making process, had produced a hollow force.

When the senior Air Force leadership learned of Chuck's briefing, it came unglued. As spokesman for the Reform Movement, Chuck was saying that, unless the Pentagon changed the way it did business, more money would make things worse, not better. He held up the Air Force as living proof.

In his study, Chuck cited the F-15 fighter and the F-111D fighter-bomber (used for night, all-weather interdiction) to prove beyond a doubt that the promises of the high priests of technology had been false. He pointed out that the high-tech systems designed to make these airplanes more reliable and cheaper to maintain than the older airplanes in the inventory had an exactly opposite effect. The systems failed more often than predicted, and the time and costs to repair the failures were far greater than predicted. The net result, in Chuck's words, was that "current AF budget data indicate that the F-15 costs about twice as much as the (older) F-4 per flying hour to support."[7] It cost more than even the aging B-52.

The situation was worse with the F-111D. In 1979, the average maintenance hours per sortie, or the average time spent fixing things that broke during a flight, was twenty-three times greater than predicted. Failure rates and the lack of spare parts were so bad that mechanics daily had to take parts off one airplane to get another one ready to fly.[8]

Chuck produced combat data from F-111 bombing missions in Southeast Asia that showed the radar bombing accuracy to have been so poor that the bombs could not have hit the targets anyway, even when the equipment worked. According to the Air Force's own data, the average distance that the F-111's bombs missed the target was four times greater in combat than it was in peacetime training flights. The Air Force, of course, always used the peacetime training numbers in all of its advocacy briefings and computerized war games.

I dwell on these two examples because Air Force Vice Chief of Staff Gen. Robert Mathis, had been the program manager for both the F-15 and the F-111 earlier in his career. He was among those who had made such glowing promises about the two systems, promises that Chuck now exposed as false.

With General Mathis at the helm, the Air Force declared war on Chuck Spinney and anyone who showed signs of agreeing with him. The general put together a team of analysts and experts to prove Chuck wrong. I was invited to participate in the strategy sessions when Mathis met with his team. He ordered an F-111 crew to fly a radar bombing mission against an old aircraft hulk on a desert runway in Nevada. Naturally, the results were impressive.

At one of Mathis's meetings, I pointed out that this was a large metal target on a flat desert floor with nothing around it to cause clutter on the radarscope and no defenses for the crew to worry about. The glowing results could not be compared with the actual combat data Chuck had cited. I suggested that demonstrations like this and computer model analyses, on which Mathis relied for his data, were not persuasive arguments against Chuck's briefing. The general stopped inviting me to his meetings.

Chuck gave his briefing far and wide throughout the Pentagon for about two years. He briefed low-, intermediate-, and high-level officials (including my boss) and also lectured the student body at the Industrial College of the Armed Forces on a regular basis. His briefing always created a stir and certainly stimulated the debate, which, after all, were his intentions.

By the spring of 1980, Senator Sam Nunn got wind of Chuck's briefing. He asked the Pentagon to send Chuck over to brief his Readiness, Sustainability, and Support Subcommittee of the Senate Armed Services Committee. Naturally, the Pentagon said no. For the next six months, a real tug of war took place between Senator Nunn and the Pentagon. Following Ronald Reagan's election to the presidency that November, there was considerable confusion in the Pentagon. As one transition team set up shop, it was suddenly replaced overnight by a totally new team. In all of the confusion, someone gave permission for Chuck to brief Senator Nunn's subcommittee, which he did in early December 1980.

Senator Nunn immediately recognized the explosive nature of Chuck's briefing. The Republicans were coming into office with a plan to throw large sums of money at the Pentagon. Chuck pointed out that, unless the Pentagon changed the way it did business, more money would make things worse, not better. This was political dynamite. Senator Nunn directed Chuck to prepare an unclassified version of his briefing and submit it to him in report form within two weeks.[9] Chuck worked hard over the Christmas holidays and submitted a report through channels so that it was officially cleared for public release.

A few weeks later, Caspar Weinberger appeared before the Senate Armed Services Committee for his confirmation hearing as the new secretary of defense. At this hearing, Senator Nunn raised the issue of Chuck's report and caught Weinberger completely by surprise. Apparently, he knew nothing of Chuck's report or the controversy surrounding it. Senator Nunn charged that Chuck was being muzzled by the Pentagon because of the substance of his message.

Copies of Chuck's report were then distributed to the press. Over two hundred copies had been printed.[10] Naturally, the report was a gold mine for the press corps, which had been growing more critical of the Pentagon. Chuck quickly became nationally known.

How did Weinberger react to all this? Did he look into the issues that Chuck had raised? No, he did not. Instead, the muzzle around Chuck's mouth tightened.

Weinberger chose David Chu to replace Russ Murray as the head of Program Analysis and Evaluation (PA&E). One of Chu's first official acts was to direct Chuck to stop briefing *Defense Facts of Life*—no more briefs to anyone, anywhere, anytime. In fact, Chuck was ordered to stop working on the subject altogether and go find something else to do.[11] So he did, and it turned out to be even more controversial.

Chuck spent a year, beginning in the latter half of 1981, examining the accuracy of the projected production costs of all the weapons systems listed in the Department of Defense budget. Each year, the Pentagon constructs a five-year defense program projecting the number of weapons that will be produced and the annual costs of producing each weapon during that period. For each of 150 weapons systems, Chuck compared the projected costs of the previous ten years with the actual cost figures for the same years. (What a nasty thing to do!) His study covered every weapons system that the Pentagon had included in its production plans during the ten-year period.

Chuck found that the Pentagon systematically underestimated the cost of weapons entering production. For whatever reason, the actual costs incurred were always much higher than those projected when decisions were made to move into production. This is called "buying in." Once the camel gets his nose into the tent, you cannot keep him out. The reformers had suspected this was true, but now Chuck had proved it beyond a doubt.

Chuck's conclusions meant that the proposed Reagan defense buildup was going to cost about $500 billion more than Congress and the public had been told. The administration was having a hard time maintaining a national consensus to spend unprecedented amounts of money on defense at the expense of social programs and a skyrocketing national debt. The last thing it wanted to hear was, "Oh, by the way, it's going to cost you another $500 billion to pay for all those new weapons programs you have started." So began yet another attempt to squelch, and squash, Chuck Spinney.

In June 1982, Chuck presented his findings to David Chu, who immediately recognized the implications. Chu reacted, "You're right, Chuck. We've got a problem. I'm going to Carlucci with this."[12] Frank Carlucci was Weinberger's deputy secretary. There were only two ways to fix the immediate problem: raise the Defense budget even more to cover the true costs or eliminate some of the new programs that had been started. Neither option was politically attractive. Chuck argued the necessity to fix the fundamental problems that permitted such an outrageous cost discrepancy, which meant reforming many aspects of the decision-making process.

A couple of weeks passed, and there was no word from Chu. Finally, Chuck and his boss, Tom Christie, called on Chu to ask him about Carlucci's instructions. They quickly discovered that Chu had lost his enthusiasm for solving this problem. He hemmed and hawed and tap-danced all around the subject but gave no instructions on what to do. As they left the meeting, Chuck told Christie, "It's obvious Chu isn't going to do anything. I'm going to start a grass-roots operation and see if I can light a fire under them."[13]

Chuck quickly put his study into briefing form and began to brief around the building. Ironically, he began with the Air Force. He called up a colonel he knew on the Air Staff and invited him down to see his brief, which he called "Plans/Reality Mismatch." Strangely, his briefing literally exploded throughout the Air Staff.

Within two weeks, Chuck had briefed almost every general of any importance on the Air Staff. For some reason, the Air Force seemed extremely interested in his work. This was very puzzling, for Chuck was hated and feared by the Air Force general officer corps. He also began briefing senior civilian officials on the OSD staff. Chuck's phone was ringing off the hook as more and more senior people called to schedule his brief. (Naturally, I arranged for him to quietly brief my boss.)

Chuck and his immediate supervisor, Robert "Bob" Croteau, decided they probably should let David Chu know what was happening. Croteau sent Chu a memorandum telling him who had been briefed thus far, as well as who was scheduled to hear the brief in the near future. Chu directed Chuck, via memorandum, to stop briefing. Chu never explained to Chuck his reasons for this.[14]

Chu now raised the issue of whether or not Chuck's work was technically correct. He put a hold on any more briefings until Milt Margolis, the head of Chu's cost shop, could do an independent study of Chuck's study. This was fair; it should have been done two months earlier when Chuck first raised the issues with Chu. Chuck sat back and waited for Margolis to finish his review.

Months passed, with no Margolis study. Meanwhile, the list of people who wanted to hear Chuck's brief was growing by leaps and bounds. Chuck made sure that everyone who asked for the brief called Chu and put the pressure on him to turn Chuck loose again. Chu got a lot of calls. It was clear that Chu and Margolis were stalling and hoping that the subject would go away, but it didn't. Pressure continued to mount. Finally, Margolis reluctantly finished his work in the late fall of 1982.[15]

Margolis's report to Chu was unclassified and confirmed that Chuck's work was correct. Chu called a meeting with Chuck, Christie, and Margolis to discuss what to do about fixing the overall problem, now that it had been confirmed. Concentrating on solutions to the secondary and tertiary aspects of the problem, Chu intentionally avoided the main issues during the meeting. Chuck realized that the old stall was at work again. He lost his patience and temper. Some heated exchanges followed, and the meeting broke up acrimoniously.

Because Margolis's study confirmed Chuck's work, Chuck decided that everyone in the Pentagon who had heard his briefing and everyone who wanted to hear it should have a copy of Margolis's work. Chuck and his allies hit the Xerox machines and papered the building with copies. Not surprisingly, a copy leaked to the press. Margolis's report mentioned Chuck's study by name. Chuck was known to the press because of his earlier episode with Senator Nunn, and reporters descended on the Pentagon like sharks in a feeding frenzy.

On the morning of December 7, Chu was summoned to an impromptu press conference. He denied that a Spinney report existed. When asked why he would not release Chuck's report, he responded, "The simple reason is there isn't a study to release. There's a set of people's scribblings and other conversations and that's about it which have been scarfed up by somebody and stapled together and given out."[16]

The reporters did not buy this. They had a copy of the Margolis report that mentioned Chuck's report by name, so they knew they were being misled. When Chu lied, they smelled blood.

Chuck was concerned that he might be ordered to destroy all copies of his work. He asked me to act as a "safe house" and store a complete copy of everything, including the mountains of raw data computer printouts. I gladly agreed.

At about this time, a second study leaked to the press. The Air Force generals had been secretly conducting their own study of the same subject and had come to the same conclusion as Chuck. This explained why they had been so interested in his work and eager to hear his briefing, even though he was one of their most hated enemies. On top of this, a third study with similar results surfaced from the Heritage Foundation, a conservative think tank.

Naturally, all this commotion got the attention of Capitol Hill. Senator Charles Grassley, a conservative Republican from Iowa, called Weinberger and asked to meet Chuck Spinney and see his analysis. To Grassley's surprise, Weinberger refused.

Senator Grassley was angry. He got into his car, drove himself to the Pentagon, and marched into Weinberger's office, where he was met by

David Chu.[17] Chu stood firm and told the senator that he could not meet Spinney. Absolutely furious by now, Senator Grassley returned to his office and called for Senate hearings on the matter. As a member of the Senate Budget Committee, he found more than enough support for a hearing. Grassley and his supporters threatened to subpoena Spinney if they had to.

As expected, the Pentagon and its allies on Capitol Hill resisted. Senator John Tower, Republican chairman of the Armed Services Committee and Pentagon supporter, tried to prevent the hearing by claiming that his committee had jurisdiction over the subject.[18] Because the Senate Armed Services Committee under Tower was viewed by the reformers as a wholly-owned subsidiary of the Pentagon, a whitewash could be expected. Grassley was able to muster enough support from members of both committees to force a joint hearing.

Tower took charge of the agenda and arrangements. He scheduled the hearing for a Friday afternoon when most senators are usually out of town. Also, Friday hearings often get light press coverage over the weekend. In Washington, Friday's news is old news by Monday and soon forgotten. Tower scheduled the hearing for a small room and tried to ban television cameras. His colleagues would have none of this.

On 4 March 1983, Chuck Spinney presented his briefing to a joint session of the Senate Armed Service and Budget committees before a packed house of reporters and eight television cameras. For two hours, Spinney saturated the hearing room with indisputable evidence that because the Pentagon intentionally underestimates the costs of weapons, the President's defense plan was going to cost $500 billion more than anticipated. This additional $500 billion was fiscal suicide. Shocked and dismayed, the senators turned to David Chu for some answers.

Chu was sitting next to Chuck at the witness table. He did not challenge the accuracy of Chuck's work. Instead, he argued that Chuck's analysis was historical in nature and therefore did not apply to the Reagan administration. Somehow the Reagan team was different, and the historical patterns pointed out by Chuck would certainly not repeat themselves under its administration. In other words: Trust us, we won't let this happen to *our* budgets, so don't get excited and do something rash that might jeopardize our plans.

As expected, the weekend and Monday morning press coverage was relatively light compared with what it might have been. Weinberger and his staff were feeling fairly confident on Monday morning that they had avoided a major catastrophe. By midmorning, Weinberger's public affairs spokesman, Henry Cato, was on the phone to a Reform Movement sympathizer and actually gloated over their apparent success. As he was speaking, his secretary placed before him a copy of *Time Magazine* that had just hit the newsstands. On the cover, Chuck Spinney's picture appeared under the headline, "U.S. Defense Spending—Are Billions Being Wasted?" A series of strange noises led the man on the other end of the line to fear that Cato was having a heart attack.

Time's eighteen-page article was a real bombshell. In addition to its coverage of the congressional hearing, eleven pages of the article were devoted to the Reform Movement, who was involved in it, and why it existed. *Time* even presented comparisons between the gold-plated weapons systems and simpler, less expensive alternatives advocated by the reformers. The magazine captured and presented the reformers' philosophy and perspective in a powerful manner. John Boyd and Pierre Sprey were identified as the "architects" of the Reform Movement.[19]

Senior Pentagon leaders went into shock when the *Time* thunderbolt hit them. The article also stirred up additional press and congressional interest in the Pentagon. The House and Senate called for more hearings. During the next six months, Chuck Spinney and David Chu appeared before every House and Senate committee of any importance in what became known as the "Chucki-Chu Show." The script was always the same. Chuck gave his devastating briefing. Chu offered his only defense—that Chuck's work was historical and therefore irrelevant.

In September, the House Budget Committee wrote to Secretary Weinberger. The committee requested that Chuck update his analysis to include data from the Reagan administration and present the results in October. When the hearing convened, Chuck announced in his opening remarks that his analysis contained no new data. Chairman James R. "Jim" Jones and the committee were stunned.[20]

Angered, Chairman Jones tore into Chu. In a heated exchange, Chu admitted that he had forbidden Chuck to update his analysis. This infuriated the committee.

Congressman Thomas J. "Tom" Downey's reaction was typical: "Mr. Chairman, this is simply an outrage. The fact is that Mr. Spinney's analysis embarrassed the Department of Defense when it was first done, and rather than suffer any further embarrassment, they are not going to give him the leeway to give us an opportunity to understand if this problem has been corrected. . . . I think it is an outrage and I hope this Committee takes strong actions, Mr. Chairman, and sends another letter to the Secretary of Defense expressing our outrage, because I think it is an outrage."[21]

Similar comments followed from other members. Chu lost his composure and knocked over a water glass. Completely frustrated by the committee's support for Chuck, he blurted out to the chairman, "If you are offering him [Chuck] a position on your staff, Mr. Jones, I am not standing in your way." [22] This comment did little to help his case.

In the end, Chuck was ordered to update his briefing and return to the committee.

Four months later, in February 1984, Chuck reappeared before the House and the Senate Budget committees with his updated analysis that included three years of data under the Reagan administration. The title of his new briefing was "Is History Repeating Itself?" The answer was a resounding "yes." David Chu's original (and only) defense, that the new team had things under control, was proved false. For obvious reasons, David Chu did not accompany Chuck to these last two hearings.

At this time, the spare-parts horror stories were beginning to surface. Almost daily, the American taxpayers learned that they were paying for $400 hammers, $600 toilet seats, and other outrageous rip-offs. By now, Ernie Fitzgerald was well established in his old job with the secretary of the Air Force. This entire area of corruption and mismanagement in the contracting and pricing business came to light largely through his efforts.

By the summer of 1984, the focus and spotlight had shifted from Chuck and his message to the outright waste, fraud, and abuse scandals of the procurement contracting world. Since Chuck was no longer in the national limelight, it was now time for the administration to reward him properly for all the good work he had done.

If a civil servant's annual performance ratings show a trend toward lower performance over a period of a few years, he or she can be fired with little recourse. This tactic was used to try to fire Chuck. Chuck's annual rating was prepared by his immediate supervisor, Bob Croteau, and endorsed by Tom Christie, next in line in the chain of command. It was then forwarded to David Chu. Croteau was pressured to give Chuck a lower rating than the previous year. This would be the first step in establishing a trend of deteriorating performance.

When Chuck saw his new rating, he immediately sought legal advice. The rating appeared to be retribution against Chuck for his testimony before Congress, and, if so, it was illegal. A battery of lawyers who specialized in First Amendment rights offered free legal services to Chuck. They began to prepare a case to charge David Chu with conspiracy to deny Chuck his First Amendment rights. They were prepared to have a judge order U.S. marshals to seal David Chu's office and seize his records.

Spinney's lawyers scheduled a press conference for a Friday morning to announce these charges. Two days before the press conference, George Wilson of *The Washington Post* broke the story. All hell broke loose inside the Pentagon.

David O. "Doc" Cooke, Secretary Weinberger's director of administration, conducted an investigation. He called in Bob Croteau and asked if he had been pressured to lower Chuck's rating. Croteau answered, "Yes."[23] Whereupon Doc Cooke threw his hands up in the air and pronounced, "The ball game is over." Cooke and Chu called Christie, who was vacationing in Florida. They told him to prepare a new rating, a good one this time.

The press conference and legal actions were canceled when Chuck's low rating was reversed.

What happened to David Chu? For his loyalty to the administration team, he remained the president's choice to head up PA&E through Reagan's first and second terms. George Bush reappointed Chu to this position when he became president. Chu served in the same job through the end of the Bush administration. There must be a lesson in all of this.

5

The Wheel of Conspiracy

A slightly different aspect of the bitter struggle between the reformers in the TAC Air Shop and the senior Air Force leadership had unfolded during the late 1970s. This story also concerns lies, spies, and subterfuge.

The F-111D was a relatively new fighter-bomber packed with the latest state-of-the-art electronics known as MARK II Avionics. This system permitted the F-111D to fly at treetop level, at night, and in all kinds of weather deep behind enemy lines and attack targets with the use of its on-board radar. Unfortunately, MARK II Avionics was an electronic disaster. It did not work long or often enough to be useful, and downtime for repairs was twenty-three times longer than predicted.[1] The F-111Ds had few flight hours on them simply because they were never in commission long enough to acquire much flight time. In May 1978, the Air Force informed the secretary of defense that it was removing the F-111D fleet from its inventory because it could no longer afford to maintain the planes. The Air Force had arrived at this decision on its own. Chuck Spinney used the F-111D horror story in his *Defense Facts of Life* as an example of the pitfalls of overly complex equipment.

In the fall of 1978, the Air Force informally notified Congress of its decision and sought permission to develop the Enhanced Tactical Fighter, a new fighter-bomber to replace the canceled F-111D. Congress refused to allow a new, *more* complex, and costly airplane to replace one that the Air Force admitted was too complex to keep in its inventory. On top of this, the Air Force senior civilian leadership (namely, my boss, Dr. Martin) would not agree to the new airplane, either. The Air Force was now between a rock and a hard place. In its view, night, all-weather interdiction was its primary air-to-ground mission, and it no longer had an airplane for the role. The games now began.

Rather than shell out the money needed to fix the F-111D electronics system, the Air Force decided to convince everyone that the system was not so bad after all. In the spring of 1979, Air Force Vice Chief of Staff Gen. James Hill put the F-111D back into the budget. This action led to a big fight with the TAC Air Shop, which argued that the airplane should not come back into the inventory unless the electronics system was fixed.[2]

Tactical Air Command (TAC), the user command that operated the F-111Ds, did not want them back because the F-111Ds were driving TAC into bankruptcy. The chief, vice chief, and Air Staff had spoken, however. By fiat, the F-111Ds were now reliable, affordable, and effective and did not need to be overhauled. Everyone knew that this was not true. The ensuing battle royal lasted for a year.

On one side were the Air Force's chief and vice chief and the Air Staff generals. On the other side were Chuck Spinney; his cohorts in the TAC Air Shop, supported by their bosses, Tom Christie and Russ Murray; and a lot of people of various rank within the Air Force who were so opposed to the F-111D that they constantly fed Chuck and the gang the information that was needed to carry on the fight. This fight eventually led to a major confrontation between the deputy secretary of defense and the Air Force chief of staff.

The commander of Tactical Air Command, Gen. William "Bill" Creech, and his deputy, Gen. Lawrence "Larry" Welch, pleaded privately with Russ Murray and Tom Christie of PA&E to do what they could to keep the F-111D out of their inventory.[3] Creech's staff became a prime source of inside information for Chuck Spinney. Whenever the Air Staff ordered Creech and his staff to prepare a rebuttal of Chuck's work, they always slipped Chuck a bootleg copy of their rebuttal, with all the raw data they used. Chuck usually had his copy before the senior Air Staff generals did, so he was ready to counter immediately when they made their move. This always left the Air Staff generals somewhat bewildered. What strange bedfellows, for Creech and Welch were vocal in their opposition to the whole philosophy of the reformers, in general, and Chuck Spinney and the TAC Air Shop, in particular. Yet, they aided and abetted each other to undermine the Air Staff.

To prove that the F-111D was now miraculously reliable and effective, the Air Force decided to deploy some of the planes from their home base in New Mexico to Australia, where they would fly in simulated combat missions around the outback. Six F-111Ds actually arrived in Australia. Their pilots set up shop and flew some missions, just as though they were deployed to an overseas base in wartime. Air Force officials were quite proud of this achievement. They boasted all around the Pentagon that this exercise proved Spinney and the TAC Air Shop to be wrong in their claims that the airplane was not reliable enough for wartime missions.

Unfortunately for the Air Force, another civilian analyst in the TAC Air Shop, Frank McDonald, watched this exercise firsthand. As the Air Force took its bows around the Pentagon, McDonald published a trip report that included the following three statements:

> 1. The rest of the F-111D fleet, which was not involved in the deployment to Australia, had to be grounded for a month because the planes had been stripped of parts to supply the six planes that made it to Australia.
>
> 2. Twelve Australia-bound airplanes had actually departed New Mexico. Six broke down on the way and never made it there. Two did not get as far as Hawaii, and four broke down in Hawaii.
>
> 3. The planes that did make it to Australia were maintained by civilian contractor mechanics, rather than by regular Air Force enlisted personnel.[4]

Air Force Under Secretary Antonia Cheyes admitted these facts in a letter to Russ Murray.[5] A strong critic of the F-111D, Murray often referred to the "D" in F-111D as standing for "Dog," a very derogatory term in airplane language. Realizing that Cheyes's admission was embarrassing, an ambitious, lower-level "captured civilian" official, Willard Mitchell, sent a follow-up letter the same day trying to change the story.[6] His efforts were futile and only made things worse.

The argument over the reliability of the electronics system in the F-111D reached a peak in October 1979. On October 30, Air Force Chief of Staff Gen. Lew Allen briefed Secretary of Defense Harold Brown on the F-111D and how great it was doing. Brown had been a real champion of the F-111D when he was secretary of the Air Force in the late 1960s. General Allen's presentation included a briefing chart showing that the reliability of the electronics system was improving over time; things were getting better, and Spinney's criticisms were unfounded. When General Allen finished, Russ Murray spoke.

Murray produced earlier copies of General Allen's briefing chart. These copies showed that the reliability numbers had been altered, not once but twice, in preparation for the meeting with Secretary Brown.[7] The alterations were intended to make things look better than they were. The numbers on the original chart showed clearly that the reliability was getting worse, not better, over time. Close examination of General Allen's own briefing chart revealed clear signs of the alterations. Whoever had erased the original numbers and typed in the new ones had been very sloppy. General Allen was embarrassed, as well he should have been.

This episode was a double embarrassment for the Air Force. First, the Air Force had been exposed as trying to mislead Secretary Brown. Second, the briefing was viewed as an informal, internal rebuttal to James Fallows's "Muscle-Bound Super Power" (*Atlantic Monthly,* October 1979) that had hit the newsstands three weeks before. Fallows's article was the first major news story to articulate the theme of the Reform Movement. The Pentagon, in general, and the Air Force, in particular, were criticized for fielding excessively complex equipment.

Fallows was the talk of the town. His article had a definite "Alsatian flavor" (a reformer's expression denoting Sprey's editorial touch) that was recognized by the senior Air Force leadership. The article hit like a thunderbolt, and the senior leadership began scrambling to refute Fallows and the reformers' theme. Unfortunately, its attempts resembled a Keystone Kops operation, and the F-111D briefing to Secretary Brown was a typical fiasco.

This is but one example of a long series of events in late 1979 and early 1980 through which the Air Force tried to prove to the world that the F-111D was something that it was not, only to have the TAC Air Shop immediately trump it by pointing out the truth. The information that Chuck Spinney and the rest of the reformers in the TAC Air Shop used to outmaneuver the generals always came from deep within the ranks of the Air Force itself.

In early 1980, Chuck published a study that dealt with the accuracy of radar bombing in general. He used a lot of the data Pierre Sprey had collected when he was an analyst on the staff of the secretary of defense during the late 1960s. Chuck's study was not a direct attack on the F-111D. It was a good piece of work that laid out all of the factors that contribute to the poor combat accuracy of radar bombing. Chuck published this study to build the case for canceling the F-111D outright because it was a radar bomber. Naturally, the Air Force responded. Once again, its response was inept, and its leadership was trumped and embarrassed.

Dr. Walter LeBerge was the No. 2 ranking OSD civilian in charge of developing new weapons. His military assistant, an Air Force colonel, talked him into sending a rather nasty letter to Russ Murray that claimed to refute Chuck's radar bombing study. LeBerge's letter was attached to an Air Force analysis of F-111 bombing results in Vietnam. Films of the radarscopes showed where the bombardier placed the crosshairs in relation to the blobs that represented the targets. The Air Force claimed that the small distance between the crosshairs and a blob was the combat accuracy of radar bombing. Unfortunately, where the crosshairs and the blob were on the scope had little to do with where the bombs actually hit the ground in relation to the target.

Chuck was well aware of this Air Force study and its failings. The people who had actually performed the work had already fed Chuck a copy, along with all the data that went into their work. Those data included reconnaissance photos that showed clearly where the bombs actually hit. Measuring the distance between the holes in the ground and the target gave the true accuracy of the F-111D bombing system—four times worse than what the Air Force was claiming.

The day after he received a copy of LeBerge's letter, Chuck published a rebuttal that was extremely embarrassing to LeBerge and the Air Force. In it, Chuck pointed out that the Air Force had intentionally ignored the real accuracy data. Chuck's rebuttal found its way far and wide throughout the Pentagon; everyone remotely interested in the topic got copies. Chagrined, LeBerge withdrew from the battleground.

The Air Force senior leaders were not only embarrassed on many such occasions, but they were becoming very angry because Chuck and the TAC Air Shop had so much accurate information. General Allen began to question his staff regularly about how these bad guys on the second floor could get so much information that was obviously coming from deep within the Air Force.

The bombing accuracy fiasco occurred during the spring of 1980, shortly after Gen. Robert Mathis became vice chief of staff. He was the No. 2 ranking general behind Allen. Earlier in his career, Mathis had been the program manager for both the F-15 and the F-111D, the two airplanes that were the subject of so much controversy in Chuck Spinney's work. By now, Chuck's *Defense Facts of Life* briefing had become a hot item around the Pentagon and the senior professional military schools. Senator Nunn and the Senate Armed Services Committee were beginning to make noises about bringing Chuck over to Capitol Hill for a briefing. This was the last thing the Air Force wanted to happen. The tension was mounting; it was no coincidence that the relationship between the TAC Air Shop and the Air Force senior leadership deteriorated with Mathis's arrival.

General Mathis viewed the reformers, in general, and Chuck Spinney, in particular, as serious threats to the national security—conspirators who were antidefense and hell-bent to destroy the military establishment. Mathis believed that highly complex weapons, such as his beloved F-15 and F-111D, were the only things that could save us from the Soviet hordes, and anyone who disagreed with him was somehow unpatriotic and evil. He publicly referred to the reformers as "dark and satanic forces." (I personally heard such statements many times during Air Staff meetings in the Pentagon.)

By criticizing the overly complex and costly weapons systems with which General Mathis had been associated during his rise through the ranks, the reformers were, in effect, calling into question his judgment. Mathis's reputation was at stake. He had moved beyond the realm of advocate for these systems to the realm of surrogate. A criticism of the F-111D was viewed as a criticism of General Mathis.

Mathis was later joined in his public attacks on the reformers by Gen. Jack Chain, who had been Air Force Secretary John C. Stetson's military assistant in 1979. As such, Chain had been instrumental in making Stetson an ineffective secretary, strictly a figurehead. With Chain guarding the door, nothing but the "blue suit party line" got in to see Stetson. Chain was completely in character when he became a party line defender in the early 1980s and went on the offensive with Mathis against the reformers. His public speeches spewed venom. He would get so worked up in his speeches that he reminded me of a television evangelist. I have watched him stand before audiences and rant and rave at the top of his lungs. (General Chain went on to reach the rank of four-star general and became commander of the Strategic Air Command, where he had his finger on the nuclear button—a rather sobering thought.)

Chain and Mathis often referred to the reformers as "Luddites" and a host of other uncomplimentary names just short of traitor. In an interview with *The New York Times* that was reported in its 24 October 1982 issue, Chain called the reformers "fuzzy heads" who were "doing a disservice to the country" by foisting "plain vanilla airplanes" onto the Air Force.[8] I mention General Chain only because his attitude toward the reformers was typical of many generals. The feelings of animosity and pure hatred ran very strong throughout the senior Air Force leadership. When Chief of Staff Gen. Lew Allen began to wonder out loud where the reformers were getting all their accurate information, the situation was ripe for a spy operation.

As mentioned before, the TAC Air Shop was informal headquarters for the reformers. It was a relatively small office with four or five civilian analysts, like Chuck Spinney, as well as about four military officers, one from each service with an air power mission. The officers were there for "career-broadening" assignments to learn how OSD and the services work with each other. Their real jobs were to look out for their respective services' interests.

The Air Force officer assigned to the TAC Air Shop was a young man who desperately wanted to be promoted to the rank of full colonel. I shall refer to him as Lieutenant Colonel "Sleez." Although he worked in the TAC Air Shop, his annual effectiveness report was endorsed by the vice chief of staff. A good effectiveness report signed by the vice chief would guarantee promotion; a poor report meant early retirement. So, the stage was set to put the squeeze on Sleez.

The TAC Air Shop was a beehive of activity. A steady stream of visitors came to listen to Boyd's "Patterns of Conflict" briefing or Spinney's *Defense Facts of Life*. Nameless and faceless people slipped in, dropped off a stack of documents, and slipped out without saying a word. In a sense, the place resembled a Lisbon café in 1939.

Almost every afternoon at around 1500, the hard-core reformers (except me) would gather and exchange horror stories about the latest Pentagon fiasco. They would openly criticize policies, specific weapons system decisions, and even question the competence of certain military and civilian leaders. Irreverence for the system was the only price of admission for these sessions. Pierre Sprey, Chuck Myers, Bob Dilger, Ernie Fitzgerald, Tom Amlie (who worked for Ernie), and others were regular visitors.

On Wednesday evenings, the whole gang adjourned to Happy Hour at the Fort Meyer Officers Club just north of the Pentagon. They were often joined by other Pentagon closet patriots, critics, sympathetic members of the press, and an occasional congressional staffer. A few drinks would loosen tongues, and the Pentagon bashing would get very lively. Of course, the military services knew about these gatherings, and the reformers knew that the services were always observing the festivities.

One particular Wednesday evening, a large group of Navy observers joined the party. A stranger to the group was introduced as Captain Black, a Navy officer passing through Washington on his way to his next assignment. Captain Black began criticizing the Pentagon, in general, and the Navy, in particular. After a few drinks, the Navy observers were playing "Can you top this?" and a whole string of embarrassing Navy stories emerged. Only the hard-core reformers knew that Captain Black was, in fact, George Wilson of *The Washington Post*.* This kind of cat-and-mouse game was commonplace, good-natured fun and not really harmful to anyone. But Sleez's activities were another matter.

Sleez began reporting back to the vice chief on the daily activities of almost everyone in the TAC Air Shop. He pressured the secretaries to inform him of the names of people calling Chuck Spinney and the other dark and satanic forces. He kept track of all visitors and even rifled people's safes and desks as he looked for God knows what. Sleez was not a very good spy, however, either in the quality of the information he reported to the vice chief or in the manner in which he conducted his undercover activities.

By the spring of 1980, relations between the senior Air Force generals and the TAC Air Shop were about as bad as they could be. Brig. Gen. Robert A. Rosenberg was the assistant chief of staff for Studies and Analysis, an office that performed the same kind of work for the chief of staff that PA&E did for the secretary of defense. Approaching Tom Christie in March 1980 with a peace offering,[9] Rosenberg indicated that he was acting on behalf of the chief. According to Rosenberg, General Allen wanted to "open up the lines of communication" with the TAC Air Shop. Rosenberg therefore suggested that some of his staff begin meeting with Chuck Spinney and exchange views on various topics of disagreement. Rosenberg also asked that these meetings be kept secret. Christie welcomed the suggestion and agreed to Rosenberg's request to be discreet until there was some indication that the meetings would be helpful in reducing the tension.

Col. Mac Bolton of Rosenberg's staff began meeting regularly with Chuck to talk about issues and points of disagreement. Bolton knew that Chuck was persona non grata with the Air Force, and he asked Chuck to keep their meetings secret. Chuck agreed.

Well, the Keystone Kops struck again. A few weeks after the meetings began, Rosenberg burst into Christie's office and announced that he had just been chewed out by a three-star general for letting his people consort with the enemy. Rosenberg claimed that Christie had violated their agreement to keep their meetings secret. Christie denied the accusation, but he now suspected that there was a spy in the organization.

While Rosenberg was ranting and raving in Christie's office, Mac Bolton was doing the same in Chuck's office. Bolton was furious because

---

*Several years after I retired, I learned that I was not the only person who had a secret code-name rendezvous. Captain Black regularly met reformers at the Hall of Heroes, a magnificent display, on the second floor of the Pentagon, dedicated to the Congressional Medal of Honor winners. The display has a small plaque on the wall for each recipient since the medal was introduced some two hundred years ago.

he thought Chuck had broken his word and blabbed all over the building about their meetings. As a result, Bolton was in a lot of hot water with many Air Staff generals. Chuck assured him that he had kept his word, but the damage was done and the lines of communication were shut down.

Someone had reported these meetings to senior Air Force generals, who either did not agree with the chief's desire to "open the lines of communication" or did not know about his initiative. I suspect the former, not the latter. This is another classic case where the chief erroneously thought he was in charge of his own troops. In any event, the dark and satanic forces were now alert to a spy in their midst. All eyes turned to Lieutenant Colonel Sleez.

Soon after, Sleez was caught red-handed rifling desks and safes. Confronted about his spying activities, he confessed. He admitted that he was being pressured by the senior leaders to report the daily activities of the hard-core reformers, including contacts with possible sympathizers. The pressures came from, and the reports went back to, the chief's group.

The chief and the vice chief had a personal staff of five lieutenant colonels known formally as "The Chief's Group." These young officers were the cream of the crop, the best and brightest lieutenant colonels on the Air Staff. They worked directly for the two senior leaders. They wrote their speeches, helped smooth over contentious issues with various agencies in the building, and were the chief and vice chief's eyes and ears throughout the Air Staff and the rest of the building.

Boyd, Spinney, and I referred to these five young men as "The Five Disciples," or "The Five D's" in our list of code names. The Five D's preached the party line gospel according to the chief and vice chief, hence their code name. As I have pointed out, just because the chief of staff was the chief did not mean that he was really in charge.

The Air Staff was not a monolithic organization. Many power centers competed for positions of influence and control. One of the primary jobs of The Five D's was to roam the lower levels of the Air Staff to see that the chief's views, instructions, and policies actually were being implemented. Quite often, they were altered by people who had different agendas in mind. On the other hand, The Five D's had direct access to the chief. They could be used as funnels to get information to the Chief quietly, without the information passing through many filters. So The Five D's served many purposes, and we had to know what we were dealing with.

I had daily contact with The Five D's as we tried to coordinate and reconcile the different views of the senior military and civilian leaders. As individuals, they were fiercely loyal to the chief and vice chief personally because their own careers depended on how well they spread the chief's gospel and how well they kept the chief informed. They were very clever and extremely ambitious people. It was no surprise to me that they were the chief's and vice chief's spymasters in putting the pressure on Sleez.

Boyd, Spinney, McDonald, and the rest of the gang in the TAC Air Shop were furious when Sleez confessed. They wanted him removed and were prepared to move his desk and belongings out of the office and into the hall if he was not fired. There was never any question about his being fired because Russ Murray, head of PA&E, was equally upset. Murray was ready to throw every Air Force officer out of PA&E.

On Friday afternoon in the first week of May 1980, Tom Christie delivered a message to the vice chief of staff, General Mathis.[10] Sleez was to be out by Monday morning. Sleez, however, was not finished with his mischief.

After returning to the Air Staff, Sleez prepared an affidavit charging Tom Christie, Chuck Spinney, and all the reformers with conspiracy to embarrass the Air Force.[11] This was his final report, so to speak, as a spy, and he addressed it to the secretary of defense. He gave the affidavit to an Air Force officer, who worked in the secretary's outer office, and he was to slip it to the secretary. A civilian member of the secretary's legal staff intercepted the affidavit and gave it to Russ Murray. The secretary never saw it.

In the affidavit, Sleez attacked Boyd, Spinney, Sprey, and Chuck Myers. According to Sleez, Tom Christie was the brains behind the Reform Movement. Sleez was not a very good spy. This mistaken assessment of Christie's role would show up again in a formal Air Force briefing to the incoming Reagan administration. (I was not mentioned in the affidavit. "Arbuthnott and the Flags" was apparently a successful stratagem.)

Boyd insisted that the Air Force be made to pay for this outrageous incident. At his suggestion, the Air Force was informed that the TAC Air Shop, not the Air Force, would select Sleez's replacement. Its selection was Maj. Ray Leopold, a professor of electrical engineering at the Air Force Academy.

As Ray headed for Washington, the chief and the vice chief learned of Ray's prior relationship with Boyd. Like Chuck and me, Ray was a Boyd protégé. Ray's assignment was canceled, and he was diverted to a new assignment in Europe. This action led to a confrontation between Deputy Secretary of Defense W. Graham Claytor and Air Force Chief of Staff Gen. Lew Allen.

General Allen was summoned to Secretary Claytor's office where he was reminded that, according to the Constitution, the civilians ruled the military. General Allen was then tacitly informed that if he wished to remain chief of staff, he would reverse his decision to divert Leopold to Europe. He was given until 1630 that day to make up his mind. Allen apparently enjoyed being chief. He returned to his office and immediately reinstated Leopold's assignment to the TAC Air Shop.

As a passing note: Sleez was promoted to full colonel on the next promotion list—he did his job.

There was no question that the relationship between the reformers and the senior Air Force leadership was now damaged beyond repair. It was all-out war. I had to be even more cautious in my meetings and conversations with "Mr. Arbuthnott" and "Mr. Grau."

In the midst of the Sleez spy drama, I was quietly arranging meetings between Boyd and Sprey and my boss, Bob Hermann (see chapter 4). Hermann wanted to understand the reformers' arguments, views, and philosophy. We had several sessions in Hermann's office, which was next door to General Mathis's office. Progress was being made, and a good relationship was developing. Unfortunately, the 1980 presidential election ended this experiment. (These meetings apparently went undetected because I didn't make the cast of the Sleez affidavit.)

In January 1981, James Fallows's book *National Defense* was published. It was an extension of Fallows's "Muscle-Bound Super Power" article in the October 1979 issue of *The Atlantic Monthly*, which thrust the Reform Movement into the national spotlight. Boyd and Sprey were instrumental in shaping the contents of the book, and Fallows gave them full credit for their assistance. Fallows now moved to the top of the Air Force's "hate the press" list. More fuel was added to the fires of controversy.

Early in 1981, the Reform Movement was gathering steam on Capitol Hill. The Military Reform Caucus, now forming as a loosely knit organization, was a bipartisan House and Senate group initially chaired by Representative G. William Whitehurst of Virginia. The executive committee included Representatives Norman D. "Norm" Dicks of Washington and Newt Gingrich of Georgia and Senators Sam Nunn of Georgia, Gary Hart of Colorado, and William S. "Bill" Cohen of Maine.[12]

No one (neither the caucus members nor the hard-core reformers in the Pentagon) knew for sure if so many diverse politicians from each party and each chamber could work together. Just the thought of that prospect, however, struck fear in the hearts of the senior Air Force leaders.

As the Reagan Defense team began to come on board, the Air Force put together an antireformer briefing and quietly presented it to the new civilian leaders. David Chu replaced Russ Murray as the head of PA&E. In May 1981, the Air Force gave him his "Welcome to the Pentagon" briefing.[13]

The Air Force tried to convince Chu that the dark and satanic forces hanging out in his TAC Air Shop were responsible for all of the anti-Defense press that now surfaced on a daily basis. To the Air Force senior leaders, anyone who disagreed with their views was, by definition, "anti-Defense." Although truly absurd, this notion prevailed. The whole theme of the Air Force presentation was that Chu was inheriting an organization that harbored conspirators who were hell-bent on undermining our nation's defenses and the president's plans to "rearm America." (The reformers believed that sending lots of money to the Pentagon was not the same thing as rearming America, a distinction that the Air Force senior leaders never understood or acknowledged.)

Chu received a three-ring notebook full of critical magazine and newspaper articles that the senior leaders claimed had been the work of these evil reformers. Somehow, a handful of reformers had totally captured the entire press corps and was manipulating the press in a fashion that would have made Nazi propagandist Joseph Goebbels proud—a rather flattering claim, perhaps, when one stops to think about it. The notebook was approximately six inches thick, and the first article was Fallows's "Muscle-Bound Super Power" piece from *The Atlantic Monthly*. (If this briefing had occurred two years later, the notebook would have been several feet thick.)

The Air Force senior leaders believed that the reformers were so anti-Defense that they would go to any lengths to prevent the Reagan Defense buildup. This was their true concern—the prospect of not getting all that money promised during the election campaign.

I do not know how Chu reacted to his Air Force briefing, but it is interesting to note that, shortly thereafter, he directed Chuck Spinney to stop briefing his *Defense Facts of Life*. Chuck was directed not only to stop briefing this controversial study but to stop working on the subject altogether. Apparently, the new administration agreed with the Air Force senior leaders that there was no room for dissenting points of view at this level of government.

As a final note, the centerpiece of the Air Force briefing to Chu was a chart titled "The Wheel of Conspiracy." It resembled a wagon wheel with spokes emanating from the hub. Tom Christie's name was printed on the hub; he was identified as the leader of the conspiracy.[14] One of the spokes identified conspirators inside the Pentagon, such as Spinney and Boyd. Another spoke dealt with members of Congress and listed Senator Nunn and Congressman Gingrich, among others. A third spoke listed congressional staffers. A consultant spoke identified Pierre Sprey and Chuck Myers. The first name on the press spoke, naturally, was that of James Fallows. I was pleased to learn that my name did not appear on the wheel. The names Arbuthnott and Grau were also missing.

The author with his wife, Nancy.

Pierre Sprey (*left*) and John Boyd pose in front of a painting of the F-16 that hangs in the office of the secretary of the Air Force. Boyd and Sprey, recognized as the fathers of the F-16 and the architects of the Reform Movement, are laughing because an unwitting Air Force public affairs officer permitted this hated duo inside the secretary's office. (U.S. Air Force photo)

Air Force Academy Cadet James G. Burton with President and Mrs. Dwight D. Eisenhower after dinner at the White House on 19 December 1958.

Reformers (*left to right*) **Winslow Wheeler, former aide to Senators Nancy Kassebaum and David Pryor; Lt. Col. David Evans, USMC (Ret.); Pierre Sprey; Tom Amlie; Jim Burton; Bill Lind; John Boyd; Chuck Myers; and Chuck Spinney in June 1992.**

Top left: Air Force Assistant Secretary Dr. Alton Keel, Jr., the author's wife Nancy, and the author in Keel's office, June 1982. The occasion was a going-away party for the author hosted by the assistant secretary.

Bottom left: The author and his wife Nancy enjoy a Sunday afternoon drive in their pumpkin-orange VW convertible. The author drove this car 30,000 miles in one year during his many trips between the Pentagon and Aberdeen Proving Ground to observe the Bradley live-fire tests.

John Boyd, "the mad colonel." (U.S. Air Force photo)

MAJOR BOYD

Caricature of Maj. John Boyd, when he was called to the Pentagon to save the foundering F-15 program. The only thing wrong with this drawing is that Boyd was usually sticking his disgusting cigar in someone's face. (drawing by Tom Bond)

The F-16—the Fighter Mafia's "child." (U.S. Air Force photo)

Top left: **Dr. Jack Martin, Air Force Assistant Secretary for Research, Development, and Logistics, presents the author with the Legion of Merit. (U.S. Air Force photo)**

Bottom left: **The F-15. In the mid-1960s, Major Boyd redesigned the Air Force's troubled F-X fighter and converted it into the F-15. He based the new design on his energy-maneuverability theories. (U.S. Air Force photo)**

Franklin C. "Chuck" Spinney. (Department of Defense photo)

The Bradley Fighting Vehicle, *left*, with two versions of its Soviet counterpart, the BMP. These are some of the actual vehicles tested during the live-fire tests. (Ballistic Research Laboratory photo)

A TOW antitank missile warhead placed at the exact location that the scientists at the Ballistic Research Laboratory (BRL) wanted for testing its effect against the Bradley's armor. The warhead was detonated at this spot with an electrical charge. BRL tested the armor in this manner until the author forced the testers to shoot the missile at the armor. When they did, the damage caused by the dynamic impact was orders of magnitude larger. (Ballistic Research Laboratory photo)

This is the neat hole caused by the static detonation of the TOW warhead shown in the previous photo. The later dynamic impact testing caused a hole so large that a person could almost crawl through it. (Ballistic Research Laboratory photo)

EXTERNAL FUEL
25MM AMMO COMPARTMENTS
EXTERNAL TOW STOWAGE
IMPROVED 30MM PROTECTION
SPALL LINER

The Minimum Casualty Baseline Vehicle. The author asked the Army to test this Bradley design in the second phase of the live-fire tests. Specific design features to reduce Bradley casualties are external fuel tanks, 25-mm ammunition compartments, external TOW stowage, improved 30-mm protection, and a spall liner. Dubbed by the Army "Burton's F___ing Vehicle," this is the actual vehicle that was tested. (Ballistic Research Laboratory photo)

Top left: At lunch with Air Force Secretary John Stetson in his private dining room in 1979. *Left to right,* the author; Brig. Gen. Jack Chain, USAF, who later became an extremely vocal critic of the reformers; Secretary Stetson; Assistant Secretary Jack Martin; Assistant Secretary Antonia Cheyes; and General Counsel Dan Richart.

Bottom left: Lt. Col. Tom Carter, USMC, who almost single-handedly forced the Army to test the DIVAD air defense gun. When Secretary of Defense Caspar Weinberger saw the test results, he canceled the program. Carter was jousting with the Army at the same time that the author was fighting the Bradley wars. Carter and Burton became close friends. (courtesy Tom Carter)

The A-10 Thunderbolt II. Since its inception, the "Warthog," as it is affectionately called, has been praised by the reformers and disdained by the senior Air Force leadership. While flying only one-third of all combat sorties during the Gulf War, the A-10 was officially credited with destroying more enemy targets than all other combat aircraft combined. (U.S. Air Force photo by SRA Chris Putman)

6

The Dickey Bird Shuffle

he "Yellow Bird management system," to a large extent, dictates the daily activities of most civilian and military officials inside the Pentagon. This system operates on the principle that sunlight is one of the best disinfectants around. In the wee hours of every morning, a small staff of Pentagon civilians peruses the major newspapers, wire services, magazines, and television scripts for stories about defense. The articles are clipped out, pasted together, and reprinted in a publication titled *Current News*. Two versions are printed each day. The first one, distributed before dawn to every official of any importance, is known as the "Early Bird" or the "Yellow Bird" because of the yellow front page. The Yellow Bird is relatively short, a few pages, and contains the most important articles that will be appearing that day in various publications around the nation.

The second edition, distributed in the early afternoon, has a white cover sheet and is often referred to as the "White Bird." It is much longer and contains stories deemed not important enough for the Yellow Bird, as well as additional stories on the same subjects that appeared in the Yellow Bird. When a particular weapons system is in serious trouble, both the Yellow Bird and the White Bird can be saturated with stories, from all across the land, that shine the spotlight on the trouble.

The Yellow Bird is the most widely read publication in the defense business. It is distributed throughout Washington, from Capitol Hill to every defense contractor's Washington office. Copies are even sent to military bases around the world. Harry Zubkoff founded the Yellow Bird and was its editor until he retired in 1986. Zubkoff understood the influence of his publication on the daily business of the Pentagon. He was steadfast in his commitment that the Yellow Bird contain a true representation of press coverage of the military throughout the country. If the stories were critical or embarrassing, so was the Yellow Bird. Bad news and good news were treated equally.

In previous chapters, I explain how the flow of information from the military institutions to the senior leaders at the top is filtered, massaged, manipulated, and shaped to pump up the good news and suppress the bad news. If senior leaders really want to know what is happening in their domain, they must develop outside sources of information, that is, sources that are outside the normal chain of command. Otherwise, they can become "prisoners of the Pentagon," or captives of the very institutions that they think they are leading.

For the majority of the senior leaders in the Pentagon, the Yellow Bird is the primary outside source of information. Almost every staff meeting, beginning with the staff of the secretary of defense down to the lowest echelon in the building, starts with a review of the Yellow Bird. Everyone knows that the Yellow Bird dictates the agenda for the morning staff meetings. There is always a scramble to get a copy first and track down the information necessary to explain any embarrassing stories on the front page. It is one of the real pleasures of Pentagon life to sit in at a high-level staff meeting and watch people squirm as they try to pawn off incredible explanations for the latest disaster.

According to aides, Secretary Caspar Weinberger was always asking, "Why didn't I know about this before? Why did I have to learn about this in the Yellow Bird?" These questions set in motion the Yellow Bird management system. (Weinberger probably didn't want to know beforehand; if he had, he would have been obligated to do something about the situation.) The questions would be repeated and expanded at each level below the secretary.

Pleading ignorance is a weak excuse, but it is often done at the top simply to buy time until a better story can be concocted. The prospect of having to answer to an angry or outraged boss in the presence of one's peers and competitors can create a lot of anxiety. If that boss knows that he or she will have to do a lot of explaining up the line, things can get rather dicey. The Pentagon drugstore sells a lot of antacids.

Still, there is an art to what I call the "Dickey Bird Shuffle." For four years (1978–1982), I sat in on the Air Force secretary's daily staff meeting. Each secretary's staff meeting was preceded by an assistant secretary's staff meeting, and so on down the line. One of the most embarrassing things that can happen to ambitious Pentagon bureaucrats, military or civilian, is to be confronted with a situation where they must confess to the boss, in front of their colleagues, that they do not know everything going on in their specialty areas. Ambitious careerists simply do not like to say, "I don't know. I'll have to get the answer for you." Instead, they must always give the impression of being on top of everything. When they are caught unprepared or if the truth is as embarrassing as the apparent disaster they are asked to explain, they make up stories and excuses that sound plausible. In other words, they do the Dickey Bird Shuffle.

I am constantly amazed at how clever and resourceful people can be in explaining away disaster after disaster for which they were responsible without suffering any personal career damage. The Dickey Bird Shuffle is true art. For those who cannot remember the 1940s, a dickey bird is a plastic toy bird that sits on the edge of a water glass. Constantly bobbing its head up and down, the dickey bird dips its bill down into the water every so often. The water passes into the body of the bird and causes it to continue the constant head bobbing—up and down, up and down.

A Pentagon dickey bird is simply someone who always agrees with the boss or with the party line. Neither a plastic dickey bird nor a Pentagon dickey bird can swivel its head from side to side, but only up and down. A Pentagon dickey bird, however, unlike its plastic cousin, can move its feet and dance. The dance is rather strange. If vaguely resembles the Mexican hat dance. Instead of dancing around a hat, however, the dickey bird dances around the truth.

By 1980, the Pentagon was a caldron of underground activity. The building was seething and bubbling with unrest. Signs of dissent were everywhere. Institutions were challenged like never before, and they were not handling the challenges very well. Many things, each a story in itself, were going on at once, yet they were all intertwined with each other so that they formed the fabric of the revolution taking place. Most of the activity was centered in the Air Force, or at least it appeared that way to the Air Force.

The tone of the press covering the Pentagon began to change dramatically. Slowly but surely, an entire generation of reporters was being educated about the true nature of the Pentagon's business. No longer did the press take as gospel the official explanations and party line so smoothly articulated by Pentagon spokesmen. The probes and questions became more penetrating and the articles more critical. The Pentagon's responses were treated with more and more skepticism, for good reason. The reformers continually made available to this new generation of reporters the physical evidence of outright lies pouring out of the mouths of the Pentagon leaders. As time passed, the reformers' credibility grew and the establishment's credibility disappeared. The reformers understood and used the power and leverage of the Yellow Bird. Consequently, the Pentagon was always in a state of reaction.

At the same time, several congressmen and senators were beginning to express publicly the same concerns as the reformers. Not through coincidence, their numbers increased and their voices grew louder. Soon, Democrats and Republicans, liberals and conservatives banded together and formed the Military Reform Caucus. The loosely knit organization had many areas of disagreement, but there was a common feeling that changes were needed in the Pentagon. At the time of the first big Spinney hearing in the spring of 1983, the caucus numbered about fifty. By 1985, membership had grown to more than one hundred. In numbers alone, the Military Reform Caucus represented a political force that could not be ignored.

Bringing this diverse group together to agree on philosophy and procedures was no easy task. Most of the credit belongs to John Boyd and Pierre Sprey. They were everywhere "doing the Lord's work." The *Armed Forces Journal,* about the only defense publication still loyal to the Pentagon party line, called Pierre "the ubiquitous consultant." The Heritage Foundation, in its 1981 publication *Reforming the Military,* referred to Boyd as the "grey eminence" of the movement.[1] Boyd's and Sprey's ideas, philosophy, spin, or fingerprints (whatever one chooses to call it) could be seen by the astute observer in almost everything occurring throughout official Washington that deals with affairs of the Pentagon.

By the middle 1980s, Boyd and Sprey were two of the most influential men in Washington, yet neither held title or position in government. Both sought anonymity and, unlike most powerful people in Washington, did not use their influence for personal gain. Boyd lived on his Air Force pension, and Sprey did most of his consulting in nondefense areas. Both preferred spartan life-styles, and that is what they preached for the military. (Pierre considered it extravagant to spend more than $100 for an automobile. He drove a 1964 Chevy, which he still drives today.) It is no coincidence that the Reform Movement faded later in the 1980s when "Genghis John" and the "Alsatian" lost interest in military reform and shifted their energies to other pursuits. After Boyd moved to Florida and

Sprey took up music recording, the Military Reform Caucus became little
more than another logo on congressional stationery. Until then, however, excitement shook the Pentagon as the reformers forced the military
to revise its policies and procedures.

Recounting a few events that occurred during 1980 may help the
reader to feel the intensity of the struggle between those in authority and
those of us who felt that our defense institutions were led by people who
were corrupt, incompetent, or both. Although this is a strong statement,
it represents our view at that time, a view that evolved as the evidence of
corruption and incompetence piled up in a compelling fashion.

Although the Blitzfighter never got off the drawing board, either as a
weapons system or as a concept, it continually haunted the Air Force
senior leadership. As a symbol of the Reform Movement, it would not go
away no matter what the generals did. Every time the Blitzfighter surfaced, the generals went to "red alert."

Someone on the OSD staff (whose identity is still a mystery to me) had
inserted in the Air Force's Fiscal Year 1980 budget the funds and direction for the purchase of four hundred F-5E fighters. The F-5 is a small,
low-cost fighter version of the T-38 trainer, the plane in which Air Force
pilots learn to fly. Thousands of F-5s have been sold to Third World countries because they are relatively inexpensive. The U.S. Air Force, however, considered it a second-rate fighter; it was beneath the dignity of the
Air Force to have the plane in its own inventory. This is the same fighter
that had embarrassed the Air Force and Navy in the mock combat tests in
1977, when it fought the vaunted F-15 and F-14 to a virtual draw.

When the Air Force senior leaders saw the F-5E entry in the budget
plan, they came unglued. The vice chief of staff called a special meeting
with the secretary of the Air Force and all of the civilian and military leaders. (I attended the meeting. The conversations of the participants are
related below in accordance with the best of my memory.)

At the special meeting, the vice chief explained to Secretary of the Air
Force Dr. Hans Mark that the OSD action was a ruse and the money was
secretly going to pay for the development and production of Blitzfighters, not F-5Es. The vice chief added that this evil deception was being perpetrated by the reformers and it had to be stopped.

Dr. Mark asked, "Who are these reformers?"

Gen. Jasper Welch, the No. 2 man in charge of research and development on the Air Staff, then gave a long speech about this gang of rebels
and mavericks that gathered every afternoon at the TAC Air Shop. He
quickly reviewed the reformers' philosophy and their preference for simple, low-cost weapons instead of the more technically advanced weapons
the Air Force preferred. The other generals began their customary

round of snide remarks aimed at the reformers and openly chuckled and laughed at the stupidity of the reformers' ideas.

As General Welch began to reel off the names of John Boyd, Pierre Sprey, Chuck Spinney, Chuck Myers, and other reformers, Dr. Mark interrupted him: "Wait a minute, I know these guys and they are very smart people. Maybe we should listen to them."

This was not what the generals wanted to hear. Suddenly, they were no longer interested in getting Dr. Mark involved in stamping out the secret Blitzfighter raid on their budget. Dr. Mark was a strong-willed, hands-on secretary. When he became involved, things were done his way. Before coming to the Air Force, he had been director of one of NASA's laboratories.

Dr. Mark had a vision of manned space travel, and the space shuttle was key to his vision. At that time (1979–1980), the shuttle was in serious trouble at NASA. Development costs were out of control, the schedule was slipping, and few agencies were willing to commit to the shuttle as the vehicle for launching their satellites. The old solid-booster rockets were cheaper. The shuttle program was in danger of being canceled by Congress. NASA could not afford to build the shuttle and operate it on its budget alone. Realizing this, Dr. Mark forced the Air Force and the intelligence community to shut down the production lines for solid-booster rockets and commit totally to the shuttle for launching satellites. He also sent the Air Force's most successful program salesman, Gen. James "Jim" Abramson (F-16 program manager), to NASA to take over the management of the shuttle program. These two actions saved the shuttle.

Both the Air Force and the intelligence community had fought Dr. Mark because they were afraid of placing all of their launch eggs in the shuttle basket. (Their concerns were well founded. The Challenger disaster of 28 January 1986 would interrupt all intelligence satellite launches for two years.) The shuttle was well established, however, and in no real danger of being canceled. In my view, Dr. Mark was responsible, more than any other individual, for getting the shuttle into space. His will and vision prevailed.

The Air Force generals were well aware of Dr. Mark's strength and power. They certainly did not want him talking to the reformers—he might become contaminated by their ideas, and that would spell nothing but trouble. The generals decided to handle this little Blitzfighter crisis on their own and quickly went to another subject with Dr. Mark. Because it was obvious that the generals did not want Dr. Mark involved, I naturally arranged for one of the reformers to meet with him privately and talk about the Blitzfighter in some detail. Dr. Mark was intrigued and interested, but, unfortunately, he and the rest of the Carter administration departed the scene shortly thereafter.

It turns out that the generals were all excited over a tempest in a teapot. The reformers had nothing to do with the F-5E showing up in the Air Force budget. In fact, they were more surprised than the generals. Someone else on the OSD staff had placed it there as a lark, simply to make the Air Force mad—which it certainly did. The next time the Blitzfighter surfaced was for real.

The National Guard is a vital part of the overall defense of the nation. The peacetime relationship between National Guard units, who work for their respective state governors, and the regular forces, who work for the president, is somewhat fuzzy. National Guard units receive their equipment from the regular forces, that is, the units do not buy their own airplanes. When the Air Force buys new airplanes, it puts them into the active force and sends its older planes to either National Guard units or the boneyard at Tucson. Whether the boneyard or the National Guard gets the better deal is not clear. Therein lies the rub.

In early 1982, a committee of Army and Air National Guard officers, mostly generals, published a report titled *VISTA 1999*. This report, which had a definite flavor of "Alsatian cuisine," called for two unprecedented actions. First, because the Air Force had, in essence, turned its back on the concept of close air support, the National Guard wanted to assume the responsibility of that mission for the Department of Defense. Second, the National Guard did not want any more worn-out, hand-me-down aircraft from the Air Force. The repair costs for these old planes were much too high. The National Guard wanted Congress to give it permission and the funds to buy its own airplanes—and the airplanes it wanted were Blitzfighters!

This was an act of open rebellion. The National Guard was asking for its own budget and permission to spend the money as it saw fit. Charles Mohr, in an article for *The New York Times*, stated, "The report angered and stunned many regular officers and Pentagon officials because of the degree to which the committee accepted major arguments of the 'military reformers.' "[2]

When Vice Chief of Staff Mathis learned of *VISTA 1999*, he virtually exploded. The National Guard Bureau, located on the second floor of the Pentagon, was the headquarters for all of the guard units. The bureau was run by a two-star National Guard general. According to an aide, when Mathis saw a copy of *VISTA 1999*, he jumped up from his desk and shouted, "I'm going down there [to the Bureau] and punch that general's lights out." He had to be physically restrained by his aides. The battle lines were drawn.

Even though they had old, tired equipment, Air National Guard units almost always performed better than regular Air Force units. At every turn, the National Guard units and their individual pilots were winning fighter competitions against the regular forces. Of course, such victories stuck in the Air Staff's collective craw. These victories were also added ammunition for the reformers, who publicly argued that pilots' and mechanics' skills were more important than the technological sophistication of a weapons system. With motivated and skilled people, National Guard units produced superior performance, even though their equipment came from local Air Force thrift shops. Imagine what they could do with equipment of their own choosing.

When the National Guard stood up and said it was tired of being treated like a poor country cousin, Congress had to listen. Hearings were called. The Air Force scrambled to call in all of its markers to fight off this unusual and unprecedented request by the National Guard to buy its own airplane. After a heated debate on Capitol Hill, the Air Force prevailed.

The National Guard, however, did produce some good results through its efforts. The Air Force began to send the National Guard better equipment, including F-16s and A-10s, instead of worn-out F-4s that were difficult to maintain. Of course, Air Force senior leaders were glad to get rid of some of what they considered low-end-of-the-spectrum systems. They felt that they were "purifying" the regular force because of the reformers' favoritism for the F-16s and A-10s.

By 1980, the end of the F-16 production line was in sight. That fall, the Air Force and the four European countries who were members of the F-16 production consortium—Belgium, Norway, the Netherlands, and Denmark—had to make a major decision. Should they go beyond the total of 998 aircraft (650 F-16s for the United States and 348 for the four European countries) that they had agreed on back in the early 1970s, or should they switch to some other airplane, perhaps even a new one? This decision naturally got wrapped up in the "quantity versus quality" debate between the Air Force generals and the reformers.

The majority of the general officer corps favored switching from the F-16 to the more sophisticated F-15. General Mathis, the vice chief, and General Creech, commander of the Tactical Air Command, were among the most vocal advocates of this switch. In leading a concerted effort in the Pentagon to terminate production of the F-16, Mathis was opposed primarily by my boss, Bob Hermann. Although a few Air Force generals favored the F-16, they were intimidated by the more senior generals and stood quietly in the shadows during the contest between Hermann and Mathis. Naturally, I helped Dr. Hermann as much as I could, which did not please General Mathis at all.

There were lots of maneuvers and countermaneuvers on both sides. Hermann and Mathis both worked Capitol Hill and OSD for support. Dr. Hermann concluded that if he could convince other countries to buy more F-16s, international political pressure would all but guarantee that the production line would continue beyond the original program for 998 aircraft. In the end, he was correct. He had served many years in Europe in the intelligence business and was an internationalist at heart. He had a special rapport with the Europeans that worked to his favor.

Dr. Hermann sent emissaries all around the world to seek potential buyers. The carrot he offered was his "worldwide co-production plan." If a country agreed to buy a dozen or two F-16s, it would be allowed to produce a particular part of the F-16, say the landing gear, for all of the F-16s. The more airplanes that country bought, the more parts it could produce, which would offset the purchase price of the airplanes.

The F-16 contractor, General Dynamics, was given the job of integrating the worldwide co-production plan to ensure that the F-16 did not wind up with too many landing gears and wings. General Dynamics was not particularly happy about giving up part of the production pie, so it put the squeeze on Hermann just to sell airplanes without the co-production offset. James Beck, who later became the head of NASA, was the General Dynamics squeezer. Hermann did not like being the squeezee and became even more determined. He argued with Beck, "If there is no international co-production, then there will be no production at all. We will switch over to F-15s like General Mathis wants." Faced with this alternative, General Dynamics suddenly became very enthusiastic about Hermann's plan.

Meanwhile, General Mathis sent a steady stream of F-15 advocates to see Dr. Hermann, and I made sure that these people were challenged on every claim they made. I recall one officer who presented a cost-effectiveness study with the conclusion that it was better to have a few F-15s than a lot of F-16s. I noticed that he had conveniently left out some of the F-15 costs, so I pulled him aside and asked why. He said, "I had to. If I included those costs, it might have changed the answer. And I was given the answer to begin with." Dickey birds were everywhere.

Dr. Hermann won the battle, and the F-16 production line was extended. Unfortunately, he lost the war. By now, the institution was well on its way to ruining the F-16 design. A long list of so-called enhancements and improvements were added to convert the airplane to a night, all-weather fighter-bomber and an all-weather interceptor. This beautiful little aircraft, which had been the best dogfighter in the world, was now just another overpriced, overweight, underperforming monument to high technology. The Air Force deliberately made the airplane worse so it would not be much cheaper or hotter than the F-15.

In side-by-side tests, the new version could not hold a candle to the old model. The 3,000-plus pounds of extra weight significantly harmed the acceleration and turn capability and wrecked the transient maneuverability. The latter refers to the ability of the plane to switch from one maneuver to another—the very feature that made the YF-16 whip its opponents quicker than the YF-17 in the competitive fly-off. The Air Force's own test report admitted that the new model was not as good as the old model in dogfighting. This admission alone indicated the extent of the difference between the two models.

I became very vocal about how the Air Force had ruined the F-16, and I was not alone. Concerned individuals in two of the four European countries in the F-16 consortium felt the same. The senior national representatives from Belgium and Norway both gave scathing speeches to that effect at their respective retirement ceremonies. I recall that the Belgium representative, standing at the podium, turned to the U.S. party and asked, "Whatever happened to the lightweight, low-cost fighter we signed up to buy?" Of course, there were no answers, and I was accused of writing his speech.

Dr. Hermann served only during the last eighteen months of the Carter administration. In that time, however, he saw enough of the Air Force's decision making to cause him much frustration and discouragement. A constant stream of program managers came to him with wild-eyed promises and claims about costs, performance, and schedules. Almost inevitably, he would learn later that they were lying. Dr. Hermann and I spent countless hours talking about how to bring some honesty and objectivity to the business. I gave him two suggestions. He thought the first suggestion a little too extreme, but he accepted the second one.

My first suggestion was to set up bleachers in the inner courtyard of the Pentagon and call together all program managers, along with their immediate civilian and general officer supervisors. As the Air Force band played a drum roll, the secretary of the Air Force would step to the microphone and call forward the program manager and his two superiors who had lied the most during the year. Without any speech, the secretary would then take out a big pair of scissors or a razor blade and cut off all the medals, ribbons, buttons, and epaulets on all three men and throw their asses out the door. Finally, the secretary would announce to the assembled group, "Gentlemen, we shall all meet here again next year, same time."

I told Dr. Hermann that I would be more than glad to provide the secretary with a list of the biggest liars. Although he agreed that a public defrocking once in a while might be in order, Hermann was not willing to pursue my first suggestion. He then asked, "What's your second idea?"

My second suggestion was to put some real checks and balances in the decision-making process by establishing a formal "devil's advocacy group" to make an independent examination and recommendation to Dr. Hermann on every program that came before him. In the normal situation, he was expected to review ceremoniously and agree with the recommendations of the blue-suit Air Staff. He received only information that was filtered, manipulated, and massaged to support any decision preferred by the Air Staff. I suggested that an opposing point of view be presented formally at each program decision meeting. That would certainly lead to a more lively debate at the top on the proper course of action. To my surprise, Dr. Hermann accepted the suggestion.

Dr. Hermann presented the plan to General Mathis and asked for his support. Hermann wanted about four mid-level generals to serve with the devil's advocacy group, in addition to his principal deputy, Gene Kopf, and me. Mathis did not really like the idea because it was a slap in his face—and he knew who had put Hermann up to it. Forming such a group implied that something was wrong with the way Mathis was running the Air Staff. Hermann persisted, however, and we organized the group that Kopf would chair.

The four generals we picked to serve with us were not very happy with the assignment. They were being asked to take a stand in opposition to decisions made by their bosses. This was something totally new to them. The first couple of times around the block, Kopf and I had to carry the generals, but then something strange began to happen. I was working my tail off to get information that was not accessible to the generals in their normal duties on the Air Staff. With all of this new information now available to them, the generals began to open their eyes and to become believers in this "independent look at things." By the third or fourth program review, they had developed a good set of fangs and were starting to use such unheard-of phrases as "Maybe we ought to cancel this program."

The program reviews suddenly became the scene of serious debate. When Dr. Hermann and Mathis gathered, along with all the military and civilian leaders that formed the weapons acquisition community, the program manager stood up, gave his standard "everything is beautiful" briefing, and recommended moving into production. Kopf then rose and said, "Oh, by the way, here are some things the program manager forgot to mention, things that suggest his program is not ready for production yet." After that, everything started to get lively. This is the way it should have been done in the past—an honest-to-goodness debate at the top with opposing points of view put on the table with equal vigor. A lot of people were embarrassed by this process because information was revealed that they had tried to keep under the rug.

By the end of Dr. Hermann's term in office, the devil's advocacy group had significantly changed and severely constrained several programs expected to breeze through the system with rubber-stamp approvals. Sadly, after Dr. Hermann and I left the scene, the group was disbanded and the Air Staff went back to business as usual.

One day in 1980, Dr. Hermann came out of a meeting with a program manager. Hermann had just learned that the program's costs were still out of control, the schedule was slipping again, and the performance was not measuring up to expectations—a typical meeting that happened all too often. He turned to me in frustration and asked, "Jim, aren't there any good programs in the Air Force, any at all?"

I replied, "Yes, I know one or two; in fact, I know a program where the product turned out to be better than predicted and the costs were far cheaper than planned. The program manager even gave $144 million back to the Air Staff."

This really got his attention. He wanted to meet the program manager and hear more about it. So I called Col. Bob Dilger and scheduled an appointment for him to meet with Dr. Hermann and brief his 30-mm cannon ammunition program. Dilger had done something no other program manager could match. He had introduced competition at the production level. (Note the Alsatian touch; Dilger and Sprey were good friends.) Dilger had two contractors producing the same cannon shell. As they competed each year for the lion's share of the production run, the price went down and the performance went up. I wanted Hermann to hear this.

The day of the scheduled meeting arrived, and Bob Dilger was nowhere in sight. At the appointed hour, I asked Dr. Hermann's secretary, "Where's Dilger?"

"The meeting has been moved down the hall to the secretary's conference room, but you can't start yet because all the generals have not arrived."

I said, "What do you mean, all the generals? This was supposed to be just me, Dilger, and Hermann."

"I don't know about that, sir, but you can't start yet. I'll tell you when."

When we received word that everyone was ready, Hermann and I walked down the hall to the secretary's conference room. The place was packed—standing room only. There were so many stars in the room that it looked like the northern skies on a clear night. Dilger was standing at the podium with a funny look on his face.

Hermann was cool. He and I had been in many surprising situations before, and we could communicate without talking. I gave him the look

that said I did not know what was going on. He acknowledged it and proceeded with the briefing.

It was a good briefing. Dilger had never attended any of the formal Air
Force schools to learn how to be a program manager. Consequently, he
did things differently, and the results spoke for themselves. The Air Force
estimated that the cannon shells would cost $83 apiece under normal
procurement procedures. By specifying the desired performance,
instead of the design, and by having two contractors in constant competition for the bulk of each year's production run, Dilger got the price
down to just below $13 and actually returned production funds to the Air
Staff.

Hermann was impressed with what he heard. He thanked Dilger for
coming and congratulated him for his good work. The meeting broke up
and I grabbed Dilger and pulled him aside.

"What in the hell is going on, Robert? Why are all the generals here?"
I asked.

"Jim, you won't believe what I've been through. I had to give my briefing all through the Air Staff and at TAC Headquarters because they all
thought this was going to be a Blitzfighter meeting! They were not about
to let you and me talk to Hermann alone. That's why they are all here, to
keep you and me from talking Blitzfighters." I never cease to be amazed
at how paranoid the Air Force can be.

The story was not over. Dilger had another surprise coming. That
afternoon, when he got back to his office at Wright Patterson in Ohio, he
found a message on his desk from Air Force personnel. He was given
seven days to accept a transfer to an out-of-the-way desk job or retire. He
chose to retire and take up farming.[3]

When he called to tell me about the ultimatum, I was shocked. Once
again, Boyd was right. When you do good work, the system often rewards
you with a kick in the stomach. Or, as Clare Boothe Luce is reported to
have said, "No good deed goes unpunished."

Early in 1981, Verne Orr and Dr. Alton Keel replaced Dr. Mark and
Dr. Hermann as Air Force secretary and assistant secretary, respectively.
The Reagan administration had arrived. Dr. Keel, like Dr. Hermann
before him, asked me to stay on as his military assistant, and I agreed.

One of the first major decisions facing the new secretary was the selection of a new chief of staff. The current chief, Gen. Lew Allen, was scheduled to retire in the spring of 1982, and his successor would be chosen by
the new administration.

Secretary Orr turned to his most trusted civilian appointee, Dr. Keel,
for advice on how to go about selecting a new chief. Dr. Keel, in turn,
asked me how they should proceed. I pointed out to Dr. Keel that this
decision was probably the most important one that Secretary Orr would

make in his term. Not only would his choice send a message to the outside world—the public, Congress, our allies, and adversaries alike—but it would also send a message to the people inside the Air Force. That message would deal with the expected qualities and character traits of the person selected to serve in the highest position of Air Force leadership. To me, that message was more important than any signals sent to the Soviets.

About twelve four-star generals were candidates for the job. Like politicians running for election, many of them were actively lobbying and campaigning. I offered to prepare a set of criteria for Secretary Orr to use in evaluating the candidates and selecting the best one. Keel said, "Go to it."

For the next several nights, Boyd and I were on the telephone until the wee hours putting together a list of qualities and characteristics that we felt were the most important in a chief of staff. The criteria we developed dealt not only with professional experience and qualities but also with personal character traits. (One of these was the willingness to seek out and consider opposing or dissenting points of view.) Boyd and I even worked up a list of questions that Secretary Orr could use when he interviewed the candidates. The questions were designed to draw out these important character traits.

I had all of this typed up and gave it to Dr. Keel. He immediately took it to Secretary Orr, who was very pleased. Orr asked Keel to evaluate the candidates and rank them in order of preference according to our criteria. Because Dr. Keel, like Secretary Orr, did not know all of the candidates personally, he once again turned to me.

Again, Boyd and I were on the phone long into the night. Between us, we knew the candidates well enough to apply the criteria. Gen. Charles Gabriel emerged from this exercise as the top choice. This choice, along with the individual evaluations, was given to Orr, and General Gabriel was, in fact, chosen as the new chief of staff.

Another general had stood out during our evaluation. Jerome F. O'Malley was a man of character, charisma, and savvy, but he was only a three-star general at the time. It is possible for a three-star to jump over all the four-stars to become chief, but this could be very unsettling to everyone. Boyd and I decided that probably O'Malley should wait for the next time. In our evaluation of the four-stars that Dr. Keel passed on to Secretary Orr, I included a separate treatment of O'Malley. There was no question in my mind that he would be the next chief after Gabriel. Unfortunately, General O'Malley and his wife perished in a tragic airplane accident a couple of years later. The country and the Air Force suffered a great loss.

By the spring of 1982, it was time for me to move on to a new assignment. Dr. Keel and the Reagan administration had been in office just over a year, but I had been military assistant to the assistant secretary for four years. A special office in Air Force personnel, called the Colonels' Group, deals strictly with colonels. In routine fashion, the group contacted me and began negotiating my next tour. Colonels normally have some say in their assignments, unless they are on a hit list. Then, they are treated like Dilger and given a take-it-or-retire option.

One of the assignments suggested by the Colonels' Group sounded interesting. The job was in the testing office, part of the staff of the secretary of defense, and involved overseeing the adequacy of testing various weapons systems for the Air Force and other services. The office personnel consisted of a few civil servants plus several colonels from each service. I indicated that I was interested, so the Colonels' Group arranged an interview. Along with several other Air Force colonels, I was interviewed in early April by Army Gen. Gene Fox, who selected me for the assignment.

The Colonels' Group made the assignment official and published orders directing me to report in early June. This was worked out with personnel as if I were any colonel going through a regular reassignment. Dr. Keel was not involved in any fashion; in fact, I did not tell him about it until the paperwork was completed. Had I wanted to, I could have asked him to place me in any job I wanted, but that is not my style.

Vice Chief of Staff General Mathis was also nearing the end of his tour and his career. He was scheduled to retire on 31 May. Three days before he retired, he learned of my new assignment. His reaction, according to an aide, was: "Not while I am still in the Air Force."

Apparently, Mathis was afraid I would be in a position to adversely influence Air Force decisions in my new job on the OSD staff. He thought the Air Force had seen enough of that. As one of his last official acts on active duty, he canceled my assignment. On the afternoon of 28 May, the Air Force sent a letter to OSD that stated: "We have found it necessary to divert Colonel James G. Burton from assignment to the Office of the Secretary of Defense."[4] I was being sent to Wright Patterson Air Force Base, where I would be in charge of parachutes and oxygen masks. (Fitting!)

Naturally, I was disappointed, but I had made my bed and was prepared to lie in it. I did not tell Dr. Keel about this, but someone else in the office did. Dr. Keel was furious. Although I did not ask him to intervene, he chose to do so on his own.

Dr. Keel called in Gen. Andrew Iosue, who was the deputy chief of staff for personnel, and told him to reinstate my assignment to OSD. General

Iosue refused, which did not set well with Dr. Keel. Several closed-door meetings followed. The Air Force produced a list of generals, totaling eighteen stars, who formally opposed my assignment to OSD. The Air Force stood fast. This was real hardball, but Dr. Keel knew how to play.

Dr. Keel informed Iosue that if the Air Force did not reverse its decision and reinstate my assignment, *he would resign in public* (that is, at a press conference). In doing so, he would raise the issue of civilian rule over the military. Faced with the prospect of a messy public confrontation over a constitutional issue, the Air Force backed down. I was very grateful to Dr. Keel and felt that he valued the service I had given him.

So, I headed for the OSD staff. I was no stranger to controversy, but what lay ahead would make my recent experience seem like a Sunday school picnic.

7

Hollow Victory

The majority of daily activities inside the Pentagon deal with weapons system acquisition. Although the public believes the business of the Pentagon is defending the nation, its real business is buying weapons. The acquisition community within the Office of the Secretary of Defense, each service, and Capitol Hill dominates the system. The entire process of acquisition, in turn, is dominated by unchecked advocacy. Many incentives exist for people to usher new weapons successfully into the system. The rewards include promotions, career advancements, and the possibility of high-salaried jobs with the defense industry after retirement.

Programs for the acquisition of weapons systems are spawned and nurtured within this community. Because the incentives and rewards favor successful advocacy, there is seldom a serious attempt by the acquisition community to cancel its own programs. Tests are constructed, analyses are performed, and briefings are shaped to make weapons systems look good, rather than to find

111

out what the systems can actually do. As a result of unchecked advocacy, a steady stream of weapons of unknown or questionable performance passes into the military inventory.

Testing is the only way to determine the validity of the theories and promises that came from the technical community. If conducted properly, testing provides a natural set of checks and balances to the acquisition process. Unfortunately, strong resistance to realistic testing exists because such testing inevitably produces unflattering data that often inconvenience the military's senior leaders. They prefer to overlook or ignore unflattering data and, indeed, often suppress it. Many do not take kindly to giving equal weight to positive and negative data and have no desire for true checks and balances in the decision process.

There are basically two types of tests in the life of a weapons system, developmental tests and operational tests. They are distinct and separate, conducted by different agencies, and serve different purposes. Developmental tests are highly controlled, engineering-oriented tests designed to determine whether a new weapon meets technical requirements and formal contract specifications. The tests are conducted by the development community itself and are controlled by the program manager of the weapons system being developed. Program managers are rewarded for moving a new weapon through the developmental stage and into production. They are not rewarded for contributing to the demise of their programs. Therefore, developmental tests are usually oriented toward success.

Operational tests are designed to stress the weapon in as realistic an operational environment as possible in order to determine its combat effectiveness. Operational tests are conducted by a testing agency within the service that is independent of the development community and the program manager. These tests are usually performed under combatlike situations and are less engineering oriented than developmental tests. Operational tests usually occur near the end of the developmental phase, and the weapons are representative of those that will come off the production line and go into the inventory.

Because developmental tests are controlled by the program manager, it is not surprising that the results are often quite impressive on the surface. Close examination, however, may reveal that they are not really tests but more like staged demonstrations. For example, the Air Force's sensor fuzed weapon concept of the early 1980s was advertised as a new, high-tech antiarmor weapon that would home in on the heat of a Soviet tank engine. The program manager presented an impressive briefing throughout the Pentagon. Showing videotapes of the weapons striking and destroying tanks on the test range, he argued that the prototype weapon was now ready for full-scale development, the final developmental stage prior to production.

Unfortunately for the program manager, a mole in his organization had alerted me to the fact that these tests were rigged. Fourteen tanks had been arranged in a tight circle, nose to tail like a wagon train in an old western movie. The antiarmor weapons were suspended on a tall crane high above the circle of tanks. When dropped from the crane, the weapons could hit a tank even without the high-tech sensors guiding them. To make matters worse, the weapons did not home in on the heat from the tank engines because the tanks did not have their engines running. In fact, the weapons had homed in on electric hot plates that the program manager had placed on top of each tank. The hot plates were heated to a temperature four times the threshold temperature for the infrared sensors in the weapons, thereby guaranteeing success of the test.

In the program manager's briefing of the test results, he conveniently forgot to mention how the test was conducted and gave Pentagon officials the impression that the new wonder weapon had worked as advertised. Chuck Spinney and I decided to expose this charade in a meeting where the program manager was briefing his impressive test results to the OSD staff. We carefully constructed a series of questions designed to force the program manager to reveal the conditions under which the tests had actually occurred. In that way, we could get the facts on the table without letting on that there was a mole in the program manager's office. When the smoke cleared, the program manager and the Air Force were both embarrassed by this attempted deception. The program was sent back to square one.

The above example is not unique. Rather, it is typical of the lengths to which program managers will go in order to get new weapons approved. Normally, a new weapon demonstrates outstanding developmental test results that are followed by disastrous operational test results. The acquisition community then averages the two together and argues that the overall results justify going into production. Any lingering problems discovered in the operational tests "will be fixed before the weapon gets to the inventory—trust us." Everyone votes yes, and we have another questionable weapons system skating through the process.

The Air Force's third-generation laser-guided bomb, PAVEWAY III, scored fourteen direct hits out of sixteen launches in developmental tests conducted by the program manager.* During the operational tests,

---

*PAVEWAY III was one of many laser-guided weapons used in the Gulf War. Nightly newscasts showed many impressive direct hits, always against high-contrast targets that stood out prominently against their backgrounds but never against any low-contrast targets. The

thirty-nine launches yielded only twenty hits and nineteen failures. Operational testing was suspended seven times because the system did not work well enough to run a test. When it worked, it usually hit the target. When it did not work exactly right (which was half the time), the average miss distance was five miles.[1] Yet, PAVEWAY III was approved for production largely on the recommendation of the new commander of the Operational Test and Evaluation Command. It was his view that the "bugs had been worked out," and he expressed this same view after each of the seven interruptions. This may sound strange, but the new commander was General Richard Phillips, whose former position was that of advocate for Air Force weapons systems, including PAVEWAY III.

Phillips also had been an advocate for the Maverick antitank missile, which had scored twelve direct hits out of fourteen launches in developmental tests, also a very impressive record. The operational test plans called for ten launches. Unfortunately, four of them were failures, including the last two.[2] The operational test results were supposed to be the major factor in the pending decision to enter production. Dick Phillips, in his new position as commander of operational testing, ordered two additional tests following the final two failures. Many times, I heard Phillips remark, "All those failures left a bad taste in everyone's mouth."

The two additional launches were set up to guarantee success. The pilots flew long, straight-in approaches (over seven miles with wings level), while the contractor's engineers in the control room gave them constant advice on whether the instrument readings were right for a good launch. (This is hardly what would occur in combat.) Naturally, the two add-on launches were successful. Production was approved, although there were constraints put on the production rate because of concerns over the objectivity of the testing. More tests were ordered before the production line could ramp up to the maximum production rate. General Phillips controlled these additional tests, and again we saw a success-oriented test program restructured by an admitted advocate. Full production was eventually approved. The Maverick antitank missile headed

---

actual success of guided weapons in the war is unknown and in question. No data on damage caused by the weapons are available. A large amount of input data in the form of television tapes exists, but there are no output data in terms of bomb damage assessment (BDA). There is reason to suspect, however, that all guided munitions did not perform as well as the ones selected for the nightly news. In an article titled "U.S. Success Is Immediate, Victory Is Not," Paul Taylor of *The Washington Post* reported on 31 January 1991 that "allied planes have flown 790 sorties against 33 bridges, Schwarzkopf said, a ratio that suggests that direct-hit videos of yesterday may not be entirely representative of the bridge campaign."

for the inventory, despite the fact that it had demonstrated only a 50 percent success rate in all of the tests conducted over the years.*

I use these examples to show how the acquisition community can easily corrupt the decision process. Many more examples could be listed, but I believe that these adequately demonstrate the point. In theory, operational testing is independent of the acquisition community and should produce objective, cold, hard evidence of whether or not a weapons system actually works, as claimed, under combat conditions. General Phillips, the official Air Staff advocate for all new tactical weapons concepts from 1978 through 1980, had been part of the acquisition community. During those years, it was his job to convince the Air Staff, OSD, and Congress that the Maverick, PAVEWAY III, Enhanced Tactical Fighter, and a host of other systems should be developed and produced. His success was measured by how many of these new weapons he could usher through the process. In 1982, when he became commander of the Operational Test and Evaluation Command, he held the only job in the Air Force that was designed to counter the claims that he had made during his years as an advocate for new weapons.

It should come as no surprise that, under his reign, operational testing in the Air Force became another tool of advocacy for the acquisition community. Consequently, Air Force operational tests and test reports lost all credibility in the eyes of the OSD staff and those members of Congress who were concerned about the quality of weapons systems entering the inventory. Operational tests took on the characteristics of staged firepower demonstrations, and test reports began to read like contractors' brochures.

In the spring of 1982, the retiring commander of the Operational Test and Evaluation Command, who was leaving the testing business as I was entering it, came to me privately. He expressed grave concern that this very thing would happen when General Phillips replaced him. He urged me to do everything I could from my position on the OSD staff to "keep Phillips and his advocates honest." I promised to try as hard as I could, but keeping that promise led me into one nasty bureaucratic fight after another. In three of those fights, involving the Air Force's AMRAAM missile, ALQ-131 jamming pod, and alternate fighter engine, senior Air

*In the Gulf War, Mavericks were launched from relatively high altitudes. The success rate, that is, the percentage of launch attempts that resulted in destroyed enemy targets, is not known. We do know, however, that many Mavericks were mistakenly launched against allied vehicles and caused casualties among many of our own ground forces. Apparently, launching Mavericks at targets too far away to identify as friend or foe is another chapter in the age-old story of death by friendly fire.

Force officials in the acquisition community demanded that I be removed from my job because I was revealing test results and drawing conclusions from them that ran contrary to their plans for the programs. In the end, however, these fights were useful training for my later major league battle with the Army over testing the Bradley Fighting Vehicle.

I must be fair to General Phillips. He was simply doing what the leadership wanted him to do. He was not alone; the same thing was happening in the other services. By 1982, it was clear that the Reagan administration was interested only in throwing money at the Pentagon and not the least bit concerned about how the acquisition community spent the money. Tough, realistic testing of new weapons could very well interrupt the money flow. To prevent this, the natural checks and balances provided by good testing were compromised by carefully placing "team players" from the acquisition community in positions of authority.

At the same time, the press was becoming saturated with stories about weapons that did not work but were making their way through the procurement system. In early 1983, Dina Rasor gathered together thirty-one of these newspaper and magazine articles and reprinted them as a book: *More Bucks, Less Bang: How the Pentagon Buys Ineffective Weapons.* The basic theme of the book was that new systems either were not tested rigorously or were bought despite poor test results. Dina had literally hundreds of articles from which to choose. The articles she chose were a fairly even representation of all three services. They clearly indicated a need to reform the testing business throughout the Department of Defense, not just in any one service. This is exactly what the reformers were attempting to do.

Back in 1970, President Nixon's Blue Ribbon Panel on Defense had recommended that the operational testing function be separated from the acquisition community so that independent testing and evaluation of the new weapons could produce a more objective view. This separation occurred in each of the three services but not at the level of the secretary of defense. The secretary's chief tester continued to be subordinate to and work directly for the chief developer. Under this arrangement, the chief tester's views on the adequacy of testing and the implications of test results were stifled by the chief developer.

The chief developer met daily with the secretary of defense, whereas the chief tester may have been in the same room as the secretary once or twice a year. The chief developer's views, usually to press on with a program regardless of its problems, were constantly fed to the secretary. These views frequently prevailed, especially when no one with different arguments was in the room. This was generally the case.

This lack of checks and balances at the top had been pointed out by

Russ Murray, former head of PA&E, in a Senate Government Affairs Committee hearing in October 1981. The hearing had been called to examine the acquisition process in the Pentagon, but Murray's comments had shifted the focus from acquisition to testing. He had suggested that one of the reasons why so many weapons did not work when they got to the inventory was that operational testing was being neglected, ignored, and subordinated to the more success-oriented developmental testing conducted by the developers.

"Leaving operational test and evaluation in the hands of the Under Secretary for Research and Engineering (the developer) faces him with an unavoidable conflict of interest. In effect, it puts him in the position of grading his own final exams."[3]

Murray had recommended that responsibility for operational testing and evaluation be transferred to an office independent of the chief developer. His testimony had struck a note with Arkansas Senator David Pryor. Senator Pryor was rapidly becoming a convert to the Reform Movement. Working with the reformers, Senator Pryor began to draft legislation that would do exactly what Murray had suggested.

In the spring and fall of 1982, Senator Pryor introduced legislation to create a director of operational testing as a coequal with the secretary's chief developer. The new director would report directly to the secretary of defense on the adequacy of testing, as well as on the implications of test results related to production decisions. More importantly, the director also would report directly to Congress on these matters; the director's views would not be edited by the secretary or anyone else. In other words, the director would work for two bosses, the secretary of defense and the Congress—a unique arrangement.

Naturally, Senator Pryor's proposed legislation was not well received in the Pentagon. If the chief tester could speak freely and often to the secretary and Congress, the real basis for decisions on new weapons would become apparent to all. The acquisition community could not afford to have this happen, so it fought the legislation tooth and nail.

Senator Pryor's bill did not get far when he first introduced it in May 1982. Senators William Roth and Carl Levin joined him as cosponsors when he reintroduced the bill in October.[4] Again, the attempt failed, largely due to the combined efforts of the senior Pentagon leadership and Senator John Tower, a Pentagon supporter and the chairman of the Armed Services Committee. Senators Pryor and Roth, however, steadily gained supporters. The reformers were busy "working the halls of Congress," while the Pentagon itself was inadvertently providing the ammunition that convinced many of the new supporters.

With the help of Dina Rasor's Project on Military Procurement (see chapter 4), the press kept up its constant barrage of stories criticizing the new weapons programs. The press focused on test results and costs. On 13 February 1983, Senator Pryor and Russ Murray appeared on a CBS *60 Minutes* program dealing with the Air Force's controversial Maverick missile. (It seems inevitable that every investigative story about Pentagon procurement practices sooner or later focuses on the Maverick program.) The call for reform was getting louder.

This was the time when the Reform Movement was catapulting onto the national scene. Chuck Spinney presented his controversial briefing to a joint meeting of the Senate Budget and Armed Services committees on 4 March in front of eight television cameras and a roomful of reporters; Chuck and the reformers were then featured in *Time Magazine* on 7 March (see chapter 4). Legislation to reform the Pentagon's testing practices was a natural product of the growing dissatisfaction with the Pentagon's method of conducting business. The timing was perfect for the reformers to strike.

Senators Pryor and Roth announced on 24 March that they would again introduce their legislation to reform and strengthen operational testing.[5] Senator Tower and his Pentagon pals had just lost their battle to prevent Spinney from testifying and to keep the Reform Movement out of the public eye. Now, they had another fight on their hands. They would lose this one, also.

A month later, Dina Rasor's book (*More Bucks, Less Bang*) hit the streets and added fuel to the fire. At the same time, Senators Pryor and Roth formally introduced their testing reform bill.[6] Thirteen other senators joined them as cosponsors, which was an ominous sign for the Pentagon. Shortly thereafter, Congressman Jim Courter, House chairman of the Military Reform Caucus, introduced the same bill in the House. The battle was on!

Dr. Richard DeLauer was Secretary Weinberger's chief developer, the acquisition executive of the Department of Defense. He was given the job of defeating the testing reform bill. The formal title of DeLauer's position, which has been changed many times over the years, was then Under Secretary of Defense for Research and Engineering. Like so many of his predecessors, DeLauer came to the Pentagon from the defense industry, where he had been an executive with TRW Inc., and brought a defense industry perspective to the table.

DeLauer felt that operational testing was a waste of time and unnecessarily stretched out the program schedule. He planned to shorten the required time to get a new weapon into the inventory by either eliminating steps or permitting steps that normally occur sequentially to take place concurrently. For example, he favored development, testing, and production activities taking place simultaneously. (Testing invariably reveals design flaws and failure modes that were unexpected. If the production line is spitting out systems when flaws are discovered, the time saved by having concurrent development and production is a false savings. The whole thing has to be done over to fix the flaws.)

If a contractor did a thorough job of factory testing the components and bits and pieces of a new system as they were made, DeLauer believed that the overall system would work when the components were assembled. In theory, this sounds reasonable. In actuality, it does not work. With DeLauer at the helm of research and engineering, this approach was tried on a major weapons system, the Army's DIVAD air defense gun.

In the spring of 1982, DeLauer approved the production of the DIVAD air defense gun with a unique acquisition approach. There would be little or no government involvement (read: interference or oversight) in the program. No operational tests of production versions were planned or wanted. The Pentagon simply would give the contractor, Ford Aerospace, a lot of money and trust that it would deliver a finished product, which worked as advertised, to the Army inventory.

At the production decision meeting chaired by DeLauer in May 1982, the Army was represented by its second highest-ranking civilian official, Army Under Secretary James Ambrose.[7] As the most powerful man in the Army, civilian or military, Ambrose ran the Army. John Marsh was secretary of the Army, but there were few reported sightings of Marsh. Many members of the acquisition community questioned whether Marsh actually existed, but they had no reason to question the existence of Ambrose or the extent of his power.

Like DeLauer, Ambrose had recently come to the Pentagon from the defense industry. As an executive with Ford Aerospace, Ambrose had been in charge of developing DIVAD. Needless to say, he was pleased with DeLauer's decision to start up DIVAD production without the usual steps of government testing. Problems began to surface, however, as the program proceeded. These problems led my colleague, Marine Lt. Col. Thomas "Tom" Carter, to suspect that the DIVAD would not work in an operational environment. Tom and I worked for DeLauer in the chief tester's office. Tom's job was to monitor testing of DIVAD and certain other programs. Under the terms of DeLauer's 1982 production decision, Carter was not supposed to be watching that closely. The situation was getting so bad, however, that he could not help but notice. He began to call attention to this growing disaster called DIVAD.

During the next two years (1982–1984), Carter produced mountains of physical evidence that all was not well in DIVAD land. Finally, over the Army's strong objections, he convinced DeLauer of this, although

DeLauer was still reluctant to order an operational test. Naturally, the Army resisted this change. Army leaders directed most of their anger at Tom Carter. (Tom was summoned to Marine Corps Headquarters and advised that, if he wanted to continue in a successful career, he should stop giving the Army a hard time. Fortunately for the country, Tom could not be intimidated. When Tom returned to the office from this "come to Jesus meeting," I told him that he must be doing something right; otherwise, the Army would not be so upset with him. He continued his fight until the DIVAD met its demise and then retired as a lieutenant colonel.)

The operational test occurred in early 1985. DIVAD failed the test miserably, and Secretary Weinberger was forced to cancel the program. This was the first and last major program that Weinberger canceled because of poor test results, even though others should have been canceled. The DIVAD story is told marvelously in Hedrick Smith's best-seller, *The Power Game: How Washington Works.*[8]

Meanwhile, during the summer of 1983, DeLauer continued his efforts to fight off the Pryor-Roth operational testing bill. DeLauer was an outspoken, excitable, and confrontational character and left no question as to who was in charge of the acquisition community. Senator Roth and Dina Rasor appeared with DeLauer on ABC's *Good Morning America* to talk about the need for testing reform in the Pentagon. During a commercial break, DeLauer grabbed the senator by his coat lapels and shook him while he shouted at Roth, "Stop listening to those reformers, listen to me!"[9] His argument was not persuasive.

The press loved DeLauer because he was always good for an outrageous quote. When he left the Reagan administration, he was quoted in numerous papers as saying, "When we took office, the contractors showed up at the Pentagon's doorstep with their money bags and we filled them." True.

On the other hand, the secretary's chief tester, Sam Linder, was a quiet, soft-spoken, scholarly gentleman who did not enjoy confrontations. He was constantly overshadowed by his boss, DeLauer. A retired Navy admiral, Linder served as a civilian in his job of chief tester. He was criticized by many reformers on Capitol Hill as being soft on the weapons passing through the decision process. Many reformers thought Admiral Linder was a willing partner in the crimes being committed by the acquisition community. I did not share that view then, nor do I now in retrospect.

Linder was not a voting member of the Acquisition Review Council chaired by DeLauer. (Pryor's legislation would change that.) He was only an adviser, and Delauer and the secretary of defense constantly chose to ignore his advice. Typically, Linder's advice was that a weapons system either had not been adequately tested or the test results did not warrant proceeding as planned. Time and again, I saw Linder present the objective, factual evidence of this to DeLauer and Weinberger on program after program. Yet, the decision was always the same: proceed as planned. The rationale for ignoring Linder's advice was standard: "There are other factors bearing on the decision besides test results" (read: maintain the money flow to industry).

If Linder could be faulted, it would be that he was too much of a gentleman and did not press the issue when DeLauer and the secretary decided to proceed with a program, despite terrible test results. The argument that there is no place for a gentleman in the Pentagon may have some validity.

On Capitol Hill, the prevailing view was that testing needed to play a more significant role in the weapons decisions. Pryor's legislation was gathering supporters left and right. Senator Tower attempted to derail the legislation by claiming that his committee had jurisdiction. He had used this ploy to defuse partially the Spinney hearings earlier in the spring, but his present efforts failed.

Senator Roth's Government Affairs Committee scheduled for 23 June its own hearing on operational testing, a subject normally reserved for Tower's Armed Services Committee. This time, Tower was not invited to play.

Admiral Linder was called as the primary witness for the Department of Defense. He was instructed by DeLauer to present the Pentagon's party line, namely, that there was no need to make the chief tester separate and independent from the chief developer. From private conversations, I knew that Admiral Linder personally agreed with and supported Pryor's legislation, but he had his marching orders for the hearing. He defended the party line, but he did it in such a way that any competent analyst of Pentagon politics could see that he did not believe in the bottom line he was mouthing.

In his prepared statement, Linder went to great lengths to point out the need to separate the tester from the developer (he made this point no fewer than eight times on the first page alone), yet he concluded his testimony with a restatement of DeLauer's party line.[10] This is as close as Linder could come to rebellion. When the hearing adjourned, Linder walked up to Dina Rasor, who was sitting in the audience, and told her that he supported the reformers' efforts and hoped that the Congress would approve Pryor's bill.

DeLauer and Tower were beginning to see that the tide was running against them. In a letter to Tower four days after Roth's hearing, DeLauer urged Tower to continue to resist Pryor's bill.[11] To help Tower fight off the reform legislation, DeLauer proposed a list of "new initiatives" designed to strengthen the testing business and make the tester a more powerful and important player in the decision process.

I must confess a bit of devilishment on my part at this time. Throughout the controversy, Tom Carter and I were DeLauer's action officers in his fight against the unwanted legislation. (Talk about the fox in the hen house!) When he instructed us to prepare his list of new initiatives, we simply pulled out a copy of Pryor's proposed legislation (which had been drafted by Sprey) and restated all of its provisions as initiatives. DeLauer bought all of them except the one that separated the tester from DeLauer's rule. He changed that one to preserve the status quo. On the morning of 27 June, DeLauer met with Senator Tower and proudly revealed his new initiatives. Tower immediately spread copies all over Capitol Hill. When members of the Military Reform Caucus saw these new initiatives, they knew they were on the right track with their reform legislation. Instead of diluting support for the new bill, DeLauer's initiatives had the opposite effect of strengthening its support.

Finally, in an act of desperation, Senator Tower went to see Senator Nancy Kassebaum, who was the Senate chairman of the Reform Caucus. Tower said to her, in essence, "If you will only remove the provision that makes the tester separate from the developer, I will lend my support to the bill and we can get it passed."

Senator Kassebaum replied, "Johnny, we don't need your support. We already have the votes."[12]

So they did. On 24 September 1983, the bill passed the Senate with a 91-5 vote. The companion House bill, as an amendment to the Department of Defense Fiscal 1984 Authorization Bill, passed by a unanimous voice vote. The fight was over. The reformers had won their first major victory. The chief tester would be independent of the chief developer and would have guaranteed access to all test data required from the services (rather than having to fight for them constantly). The operating budget of the chief tester would be determined by Congress, not DeLauer. The chief tester would be a voting member of the Acquisition Review Council and would *report test results directly to the secretary of defense and Congress simultaneously, without anyone editing them.*

It is difficult to imagine Congress giving the Pentagon a stronger mandate to clean up its act. This was a truly significant reform. The reformers could be proud of their victory, but their celebrations were short-lived.

When the legislation was passed, everyone—reformers, OSD staff, press observers—expected the existing testing office, headed by Admiral Linder, to be separated from DeLauer and to operate under the provisions of the new law. After all, Congress had spoken loudly, but DeLauer

and Weinberger had other plans. DeLauer decided that he would keep **123**
his own testing office and make the new one start from scratch, with its
own office space, personnel, and equipment. (Other than an honest
man, there is nothing more difficult to find in the Pentagon than spare
office space.) DeLauer even prepared the charter under which the new
testing office would operate. Naturally, he wrote in provisions that would
curtail the powers given the chief tester by Congress.

More importantly, Secretary Weinberger refused to select a person to
fill the position of director of operational testing. Rather than comply
with the new law, Weinberger and DeLauer chose to ignore it. To the dismay of the reformers and Congress, in general (even the nonreformers),
the stonewalling continued into the spring of 1984.

Meanwhile, Admiral Linder continued to act as the secretary's chief
tester until the new director could be appointed. Even Linder's patience
ran out. At the end of February 1984, DeLauer chaired an Acquisition
Review Council decision meeting on yet another questionable system,
the SINGARS radio. This high-tech radio was designed to allow soldiers
on the battlefield to communicate with each other in the presence of
enemy electronic jammers. DeLauer and the acquisition decision makers
for the secretary of defense and the Army gathered to determine if the
SINGARS should enter full production.

Recent operational tests had shown that the radio did not work. Its
demonstrated reliability was 30 percent of the minimum acceptable value,
even after the contractor had redesigned it several times. The enemy did
not have to jam the radio because it jammed itself. When one radio net
was in the same general area of another, they jammed each other. The
Army's operational test commander reported that the radio was marginal
or unsatisfactory in ten out of thirteen critical areas of evaluation; even
specially trained units were not able to communicate with each other. He
concluded that the radio would not help the troops in the field.[13]

Admiral Linder presented the SINGARS test results at the production
decision meeting on February 23. He argued that the radio should not
enter full production until tests proved that it actually worked. (The
problems identified by Linder still persist. During the Gulf War, the
SINGARS radio demonstrated all of the previous jamming problems and
would not work in the frequency hopping mode that is required to avoid
interference from enemy jammers.) Despite the overwhelming evidence
that the radio did not work, the Army had already signed the production
contract. DeLauer was now in the process of ratifying its decision to proceed with production at top speed.

In the course of the meeting, Admiral Linder, completely out of character, got into a heated argument with Dr. DeLauer over the proper

course of action. The meeting broke up with Linder and DeLauer standing up and shouting at each other while everyone at the meeting table watched in dismay. The quiet, reserved, scholarly gentleman had never before behaved like this.

Army Under Secretary Ambrose, fearing that Secretary Weinberger might be swayed by Linder's arguments, immediately fired off a memorandum to Weinberger, in which he objected to Linder's "silly notion that we should not field equipment until tests showed that it really worked." His comments in that memo pretty well summed up the views of the top people at this time: "If the approach advocated by Adm. Linder is allowed to prevail, even after full consideration of the highest Army levels and the DSARC [Defense Systems Acquisition Review Council], the consequences will be serious delay and substantially increased cost in fielding badly needed equipment. It is conceivable that this approach can even operate to preclude fielding equipment at all before it becomes technically obsolete."[14] (Pogo was right when he said, "I have met the enemy and he are us.")

Shortly thereafter, Admiral Linder resigned from government service. It is my feeling that he resigned in disgust over the administration's decision to stonewall the congressional mandate and continue business as usual by blindly waving questionable weapons through the process.

April came, and Weinberger had not yet found a candidate to nominate for chief tester. Every candidate who volunteered was interviewed by Dr. DeLauer. Weinberger's final choice had to be acceptable to him, and, so far, no one was acceptable. (This was a strange requirement for an independent director of operational testing.)

By now, Congress also was losing patience. As Senate chairman of the Military Reform Caucus, Senator Nancy Kassebaum began personally to pressure Weinberger. His response to her: "I can't find anyone who is willing to take the job. You are asking me to find someone who will wear a black hat and bring mostly bad news to the table. No one wants to do that. If you think you can do better, why don't you nominate a candidate?"

As a result, the Military Reform Caucus approached me through John Boyd and asked whether I would be willing to be nominated as a candidate. I was quite flattered because I strongly believed that the new legislation was good for the military (as well as the taxpayer), provided it was implemented in the same spirit in which it had been conceived. My reputation around the Pentagon indicated that I was not afraid to wear the black hat and bring the bad news to the table. Also well known was my belief that the decision process needed more discipline and checks and balances. I had to consider a few things, however, before I could give the caucus an answer.

The law stated that the new director would be a civilian appointed by the president and confirmed by the Senate. To serve in that capacity, I would have to retire from the military. I was willing to retire, if selected, but what would happen if I were nominated by the Military Reform Caucus and then not selected? That was the key question. The answer was obvious. I would be left hanging out in the breeze. As a marked man formally linked to the hated and despised reformers, I would be unable to function in my job.

After careful consideration, I agreed to allow my name to be submitted to Secretary Weinberger under one condition: Weinberger's assurance of no retribution against me personally if he chose not to select me. Senator Kassebaum called Weinberger and obtained his agreement to my condition.[15] His promise would play an important role in events that unfolded over the next few months.

On 24 April 1984, Senator Kassebaum, in her capacity as Senate chairman of the Military Reform Caucus, sent a letter to Secretary Weinberger that stated: "In response to your request for nominees for Director of the new Office of Operational Testing and Evaluation, I wish to recommend Colonel James G. Burton."[16] Many eyebrows were raised when that letter arrived.

Shortly thereafter, I was interviewed separately by Secretary Weinberger, Deputy Secretary William H. Taft IV, and Dr. DeLauer. The interview with DeLauer was by far the most interesting. The term "fifth columnist" came up several times during the course of our conversation.

These three interviews left me with the clear impression that the most senior leaders of the Pentagon had no intention of reforming the weapons acquisition business. They did not agree with the need for testing reform, and they certainly were not looking for someone who would seriously challenge each weapons program that came down the pike. It was no surprise to me when Weinberger chose not to select me as his new chief tester. Instead, he chose a rather nondescript candidate and forwarded his name to the White House. Conveniently, that candidate failed to pass muster at the White House—something about an irregularity in his financial statement. The whole selection process started over, and almost another year passed before the first director was appointed. He would come from the defense industry and turn out to be nothing more than another industry spokesman. By then, I was embroiled in one of the biggest controversies that the Pentagon had seen in decades.

8

Crossing the Rubicon

The Rubicon is a small river that separated Julius Caesar's province of Gaul from Italy. The story goes that when Caesar crossed the river with his army, he committed himself to civil war with the Roman government, which was then controlled by his rival, Pompey. When Caesar's army got to the other side of the Rubicon, Caesar instructed his lieutenants to burn all the boats. There could be no turning back. His decision to invade was now irrevocable. The expression "crossing the Rubicon" has come to mean a decisive moment, a decision from which there is no retreat.

On 14 June 1984, I crossed the Rubicon on a Bradley Fighting Vehicle. For on that day, I made a conscious choice to engage the U.S. Army senior leadership in a Class A, major league battle. I wanted the Army to run some honest, realistic tests on the Bradley. It did not want to. We argued at first; then we fought.

For two years, we fought like cats and dogs—no rules and no referees. The fight spilled out into the public domain on several occasions. I found that, once the fight started, I could not disengage even if I had wanted to do so. As the public watched, we bit, scratched, and clawed. When the fight was over, I had won. On 17 December 1987, to the Army's credit, it confirmed my victory to the Congress, to the public, and to me.

What is it like on the other side of the Rubicon? It is a hostile land—full of swamps, jungles, dragons, and demons. But, I learned how to survive and prevail.

Almost from the day I first arrived at the OSD testing office in June 1982, Pierre Sprey began working on me to do something about the need for honest, realistic tests to determine how vulnerable our tanks and planes were to actual Soviet weapons and how lethal our weapons were against Soviet vehicles. Pierre was giving a briefing around town titled, "The Terrible Cost of Not Testing with Real Weapons Shooting at Real Targets." He opened with an excerpt from James M. Gavin's *On to Berlin*.

In this book, General Gavin recounted how he had to bury fifty young men near the village of Gela, Sicily, in 1943.[1] The men had pieces of their own bazookas ground into their bodies by the German tanks they had been trying to stop. Their new bazookas had failed to stop the tanks. General Gavin condemned the Ordnance Corps for not testing the bazookas against German tanks that had been captured in North Africa. There had been considerable controversy back in the States over the development of the bazookas. At least one prominent scientist on the project had resigned because of his conviction that the warhead was too small to stop a tank. Sadly, he was proved correct. General Gavin was angry that the Ordnance Corps bureaucracy had given his troops an untested weapon. Too many men had paid the ultimate price for the Army to learn what it should have determined on a test range, not a battlefield.

Pierre claimed that nothing had changed since World War II. None of our current frontline vehicles, none of our tanks or airplanes had ever been tested for vulnerability to actual Soviet weapons. None of our weapons had ever been tested by shooting them at real Soviet vehicles in combat configurations and with live ammunition and fuel on board. According to Pierre, the ordnance community had not changed since 1943. The terrible cost would be more lives unnecessarily lost if our troops had to use any of our frontline equipment in combat.

I did not believe Pierre. I thought he was exaggerating, but I began to check for myself. During the next year, I dug into the subject. I read almost every test report written about the performance of tanks, antitank weapons, airplanes, antiaircraft weapons, and missiles; medical reports on casualties in wars and how casualties are predicted; and, most importantly, reports that analyzed actual combat results from any war, any-where, as far back as World War II. The more I dug, the more convinced I became that Pierre was right. His briefing only scratched the surface.

I found the old Ordnance Corps had been replaced by a small, closed technical community that was seldom challenged. Although its views were accepted as gospel, its methods of determining lethality of weapons and vulnerability of vehicles were questionable.

Fire and explosion inside a tank are the most deadly and dreaded results when a tank is hit by an enemy round. Historically, most casualties in tanks are caused by ammunition fires and explosions. The American Sherman tanks of World War II were nicknamed "Ronson" because they would light up every time they were hit. More than 60 percent of Sher-man tank crew casualties resulted from fuel or ammunition fires inside the tank. To reduce the incidence of fire, the later version of the Sher-man stored the ammunition in water baths.[2]

Israel suffered tremendous burn casualties in its tank corps during the 1973 war. Most of these casualties occurred in American-made tanks. The casualties were so severe, and so unnecessary in Israel's view, that it decided to design and build its own tank, the Merkava, with specific design features to reduce or eliminate casualties from the dreaded ammunition fires and explosions. Israel's efforts were rewarded during the 1982 Middle East War, in which ammunition-related casualties were nonexistent.[3]

Even though fire and explosion were the most deadly results of a hit, they were the least understood and most ignored aspects of vulnerability testing. I learned that the technical community, over the years, had been moving farther away from realism and closer to simulation and computer modeling as the means for determining whether a bazooka would blow up a tank. Vehicles, including tanks, were tested empty or with water in the fuel tanks to prevent fires. Fuel and live ammunition were never pres-ent together in a vehicle. Fires made it difficult to collect precise scien-tific data inside the vehicles. These data were needed as input to com-puter models, which were then used to calculate the vulnerability of the tank. Yet, the models could not handle fire and explosion, the most dominant aspects.

To my surprise, I discovered that these computer models had never been verified. Every time someone had tried to compare the models' pre-dictions of damage or casualties with actual combat results or even test results against empty vehicles, the models failed miserably. Sometimes they predicted a tank was harder to kill than it really was and sometimes just the opposite. I came to the conclusion that reading a goat's entrails was probably a more accurate method of predicting combat damage.

A single concerted effort was made in 1970 to verify the computer models. In an exercise called MEXPO, captured Russian tanks from the 1967 Middle East War were tested.[4] As usual, the tanks were empty and only the physical damage of the penetrating round was documented. No fires or explosions were permitted. The models were run before each test shot, and the predictions of damage were then compared with the actual test result after the shot.

To the surprise of everyone involved in the testing, there was a tremendous mismatch between the predicted damage and the actual damage. No consistent pattern to the mismatch could be determined; the differences were all over the place. The models were changed and the process repeated. The mismatch got worse, not better. Once again, the models were revised and a third comparison made. Unbelievably, the mismatch between model predictions and reality was even worse. At this point, the vulnerability community gave up. The computer models have never been verified to this day.

The models continued to be (and still continue to be) the primary tools for assessing overall vulnerabilities. As such, they have had a tremendous influence on major decisions about which weapons to buy and which design features to incorporate. More often than not, real weapons were not used in the tests that were structured to feed the models. Instead, laboratory devices were constructed to simulate weapon warheads. These devices were often literally Scotch-taped to the vehicles at specific locations and detonated. The dynamic effects of a real weapon slamming into a tank were ignored. These effects could not be controlled precisely enough to satisfy the hordes of technicians primarily interested in gathering only certain kinds of data to feed their computer models. The technicians should have been more interested in whether or not a weapon could actually blow up a tank under realistic conditions.

The purpose of the game was to feed the models, rather than to find out what really happens. The models could then be adjusted or fine-tuned to produce an answer that supported a preferred decision on a particular weapons system—this was their real value. Their output could be controlled, whereas realistic test results could not be controlled. The events surrounding the Army's choice of a new bazooka in 1983 brought this distinction home to me. For years, the Army had been developing a new bazooka called the Viper. When the bazooka was proposed in 1976, the advertised cost was $78 apiece. At that price, every infantryman, cook, and baker could have one. By the time the Viper entered production, the cost had risen to $787, a modest increase by Pentagon standards.[5]

Considerable controversy existed about the ability of the Viper to stop a Russian tank. Many people thought that its warhead was too small. It was only 10 percent larger than the warhead on the bazooka that had sent so many of General Gavin's troops to their graves forty years earlier in Sicily. Of course, the Russian tank armor of the 1980s was far more than 10 percent thicker than the old German armor of World War II.

Led by Senator Warren Rudman, Congress forced the Army to stop production and conduct a competitive shoot-off between the Viper and several European bazookas that already existed.[6] Now, the sole purpose of a bazooka is to kill tanks. It is not a walking stick or a baseball bat; it is a tank killer. The competition was supposed to determine which of these bazookas was the best tank killer, and the winner would be produced in large numbers.

Six candidates competed. A total of 420 rounds was fired in the shoot-off. Not one single round was fired at a tank—any kind of a tank, not even an empty tank, much less a tank loaded with fuel and ammunition. Instead of shooting the bazookas at tanks, the testers placed the warheads on top of a block of steel and detonated them. The size of each hole resulting from the detonation was measured very precisely and entered into the computer model. The model then pronounced a winner. Everyone—the Army, the OSD staff, and Congress—accepted it without question.

In total dismay, I listened to the Army brief these so-called test results to Dr. DeLauer and his famous Acquisition Review Council. I thought to myself, "These people are crazy. They don't really know whether this winner will actually stop a tank or not. I can just see some future General Gavin burying his troops with pieces of these new bazookas ground into them. It's 1943 all over again."

It was my view then, and still is, that the Department of Defense should make no decisions and take no actions that are based on the results of unverified computer models. There is simply no place for these things in our business, especially when soldiers' lives are at stake.

With Pierre's help, I put together a proposal for a large joint test program that would bring some realism back to testing. I called it the Joint Live-Fire Test Program. "Joint" meant that more than one service would be involved. "Live-Fire" meant that we would shoot real weapons, not laboratory devices, at real targets in combat configuration, with all of the dangerous ingredients present inside the vehicles. Mother Nature, not some unverified computer program, would determine how fuel, ammunition, and hot hydraulic fluid reacted together after a hit.

To me, the most important data to collect would deal with what happened to the people inside the vehicle. First, how many casualties would result from the hit? Second, what would be the primary sources of those casualties—burns, explosions, shrapnel wounds, toxic gases, blast waves from overpressures, or what? Terrible things happen inside a tank or personnel carrier after a hit. There are many ways for a soldier to die.

The armored envelope of a tank protects the crew to a point, then the armor turns on the crew. When an antitank round penetrates the armor, metal slivers, called spall fragments, ricocheting inside the crew compartment kill and wound the crew and cut fuel lines, hydraulic lines, and electrical cables. Fires start from ruptured fuel or hydraulic lines. Ammunition burns and explodes to produce more fragments, as well as overpressures high enough to disintegrate a lightly armored vehicle or blow the turret off the top of a heavier tank. As choking fumes fill the vehicle, any crew members, who are still able, usually scramble out. Although the environment inside the vehicle after a hit is grim, certain design features can reduce the severity of this environment, especially the dreaded fires and explosions from ammunition, fuel, and hydraulic fluid.

My hope was to find out what caused the most casualties under what conditions and to let the test results point toward design changes that would reduce those kinds of casualties. Simply put, I wanted realistic tests that focused first on what happened to the people inside the vehicle; what happened to the vehicle itself was secondary to me—people first, vehicle second, and computer models a distant last. This perspective was different from the one dominating the Army acquisition community at the time. Its order of priorities was the exact opposite.

The proposal was revolutionary. Nothing like it had ever been done before. Bob Dilger's 30-mm ammo tests in the Nevada desert in the mid-1970s were the closest thing to it. I expected opposition from the old Ordnance Corps. After all, my proposal was a criticism of its work. To my surprise, the corps technicians agreed that something like this was overdue. They jumped on the bandwagon. When they discovered that I was serious about this, they not only jumped off the bandwagon but did their best to blow it up.

In the spring of 1983, I began briefing the Joint Live-Fire Test Program at the lower levels of the technical communities and worked my way up through the ranks in order to build support from the bottom up. Revolutions or major changes in the behavior of large organizations usually have a better chance of succeeding if they come from the bottom up, instead of being imposed from the top down.

Pierre and I had counted the total number of soldiers, sailors, and airmen who would be actually involved in direct combat with the enemy if we went to war. There were 2 million men and women in the armed forces and another 1 million civilian employees in the Department of Defense. Of these 3 million people, only 300,000 would be actually engaged in direct combat, or 1 out of 10. The other 9 would perform support and management functions behind the lines. I could find no clearer testimony of how top-heavy and bloated we had become and how complex our systems were. My live-fire test program was geared to save as many of those 300,000 lives as possible.[7]

I spent almost a year briefing and advocating this revolutionary test program throughout the Department of Defense. By the spring of 1984, I had built a consensus of support in the Army, Navy, Air Force, Marine Corps, Joint Chiefs of Staff, and the OSD staff. The support ranged from lower-level scientists to senior-level civilian and military leaders.

With unanimous agreement, the Joint Live-Fire Test Program was formally approved and chartered by OSD on 27 March 1984.[8] The charter identified, for testing purposes, specific tanks, personnel carriers, and airplanes from both the United States and the Soviet Union. The intelligence community had its job cut out in locating and acquiring Soviet equipment. I had tried to include naval vessels in the program but was unable to attract enough support from the Navy. Navy officials became horrified at the prospect of testing real Soviet weapons against their vessels. I also wanted to test the Navy's new torpedoes against double-hulled submarines, which had never been done, but I ran into a solid stone wall. Finally, I had to stop trying to convince the Navy to participate as I headed toward my Spring 1984 deadline.

As soon as the charter was signed by Admiral Linder, I began making plans for the first series of tests. Now the games began. I had decided on the Army's Bradley Fighting Vehicle as the first system to go through the test program. I had selected the Bradley for two reasons. First, in the event of war, between 50,000 and 70,000 infantrymen would ride into combat in Bradleys. A lot of lives were at stake. Second, the Bradley was early in its production phase. It would be relatively easy to make design changes if the live-fire testing revealed serious flaws. This kind of testing, of course, should have been done in the development phase.

I would like to explain what a Bradley Fighting Vehicle is, but that is not an easy task. The Army has been trying to explain it for twenty years, without much success. The Bradley is an armored vehicle that looks like a tank, sounds like a tank, travels in the company of tanks, and carries offensive weapons with which to shoot at enemy tanks, but the Bradley is not a tank. Tanks have big cannons to shoot at other tanks, and they have thick, heavy armor to provide protection against antitank weapons. The Bradley's armor is very thin compared with the armor of a tank; it is more like that of a personnel carrier. The Bradley is not exactly a personnel carrier either, although that is what it started out to be. This attempt to define a Bradley reveals the root of most of its problems.

What is the Bradley, and what is it supposed to do? These questions have plagued the Bradley for twenty years. To this day, they have not been fully answered.

In the early 1960s, the Army began to develop a simple, inexpensive replacement for its M-113 Armored Personnel Carrier. The M-113 was, and still is, a "battlefield taxi," a vehicle that simply transports troops to and from the battle. An infantry squad of eleven men rides inside. The armor is thick enough to protect the squad only from small arms fire (rifles and machine guns). Anything larger than small arms will pass through the M-113, or any lightly armored vehicle, like a hot knife through butter. For this reason, troops over the years have refused to ride inside the M-113 when encountering enemy fire larger than small arms is a possibility. Instead, they ride on top.

The Bradley began as the M-113 replacement. Its job would be to transport an eleven-man infantry squad to the battlefield—a simple, straightforward task.[9] The Bradley was in development for seventeen years, however; during that time, the Army kept changing its mind about what it wanted the Bradley to do. The notion of having the Bradley engage other vehicles crept into the picture. The Bradley would team up with the new M-1 tanks, and together they would engage enemy armored forces. In this situation, the Bradley would take return fire from enemy vehicles, which meant taking hits from weapons far larger than small arms, but the Bradley's armor was not beefed up accordingly. Then, someone came up with the idea that the troops inside should be able to stick their rifles out through little portholes to shoot at the enemy. Long after the Bradley had entered production, this feature proved to be useless and the portholes were sealed up.

During the Bradley's development, several committees were formed to review the program and decide on its mission and features. These included the Casey Board, Larkin Committee, and others. Each time a committee met, the mission changed and new design features were added.[10] By the time production was approved in 1980, the Bradley had three missions. It confirmed the old adage that a camel is a horse designed by a committee.

I cannot help but compare the Bradley to the Air Force F-16. Thanks to the Fighter Mafia, the F-16 was the product of a highly disciplined design process. The combat tasks were decided first and were not allowed to vary during the design phase. This produced a superior design that was tailored to those specific tasks. The combat tasks of the Bradley, on the other hand, kept changing. Each change brought a new design feature that was simply added to the picture. The resulting product is a vehicle that performs a variety of tasks but does no task very well.

For example, as a personnel carrier, the Bradley can carry a squad of only six, not eleven. As an armored scout vehicle, it is supposed to seek out the enemy, probe its defenses, and sneak around behind the lines to see what is going on—all without being noticed (sneak, peek, and tell mission). Unfortunately, the Bradley is the largest vehicle on the battlefield and stands out like a sore thumb. It stands 10 feet tall, some 3 feet taller than its Soviet counterpart. It is hard to be inconspicuous when you are the largest guy at the party. Army Gen. Edwin Burba, commandant of the Infantry School, claimed on CBS's *60 Minutes* (15 February 1987) that the added height was an advantage. He could see farther from up there!

A 1976 decision to give the Bradley an antiarmor mission, in my view, was the key decision in the history of the program.[11] A two-man turret was added to the vehicle so that TOW antitank missiles and a 25-mm cannon could be fired at enemy armored personnel carriers (APCs) as the Bradley fought alongside our M-1 tanks. This decision guaranteed that the Bradley would be subject to return fire from antitank weapons, yet its armor would provide little or no protection against any antitank weapons, whether of small, medium, or large caliber.

The turret decision also guaranteed that the troop compartment of the Bradley would be stuffed with dangerous ammunition and TOW missiles and that the compartment could hold only six riflemen instead of eleven, as in its smaller predecessor APC, the M-113.[12]

The inside of the Bradley troop compartment was now packed to the gills with ammunition, fuel, and people, a dangerous combination. The Bradley carried more ammunition than any vehicle on the battlefield, friend or foe. An enemy gunner looking at a Bradley through a gunsight saw two to three times as much ammunition-presented area (percentage of cross section taken up by ammo) as its Soviet counterpart.[13] The troops sat on, leaned up against, and had wrapped around their ears literally thousands of rounds of rifle and machine gun ammunition, up to 1,500 cannon shells, TOW missiles, bazookas, mines, incendiary grenades, flares, and fuel tanks. All of the Bradley's deadly contents were surrounded by thin armor that would keep out only small arms fire.

To make matters worse, the Army refused to conduct tests on the Bradley to see what would happen when it was hit by enemy fire—any kind of fire, even small arms. By the time of the 1980 decision to start production, no vulnerability tests of any kind had been conducted against a Bradley vehicle. A few small arms tests against pieces of Bradley armor had been performed, and the armor plates had failed the tests. This was one of the main issues debated at the production decision meeting.

The Army's attitude was clearly evident in a letter to OSD from Army

Assistant Secretary Percy Pierre dated 17 March 1980: "The key factor here is the relative importance of various kinds of testing. . . . We feel it is counterproductive to conduct destructive testing on such a precious asset when more valuable information can be gained."[14] (Maybe Pierre meant doing something else, like driving the Bradley around a track to determine its gas mileage.)

Reluctantly, the Army agreed to conduct some vulnerability tests in late 1980. True to form, however, these tests were of little value. Because the production contract specified that the armor was required to protect only against small arms fire, that is all that was tested. Rifles and machine guns were fired at an empty Bradley vehicle. There was no ammunition inside, and the fuel tanks were full of water, not fuel. Even if penetrations had occurred, no one knew whether those penetrations would have started fuel or ammunition fires inside the vehicle.

As the Bradleys began rolling off the assembly line, no one had any idea what would happen in combat to the thousands of 18-year-old kids who would ride in these vehicles. The tragedy was compounded because no one seemed to care. By refusing to conduct realistic tests against a vehicle fully loaded with fuel and live ammunition, the Army senior leadership, in my opinion, demonstrated that it had a callous disregard for the lives of the troops in the field. I could arrive at no other conclusion.

It should now be obvious why I picked the Bradley as the first system to be tested in the Joint Live-Fire Test Program. I began making plans to start testing the Bradley immediately, preferably that summer (1984). Suddenly, however, the Army leaders realized that I was serious, and there was a good chance that a few Bradleys might blow up on the test range. They foresaw the whole Bradley concept and program blowing up along with the vehicles. They could not afford to let this happen, so they began to resist, politely and subtly at first. As I kept pushing for tests that summer, the resistance got stronger and not so subtle. The more the Army resisted, the more determined I became. By early June, the Rubicon was looming directly in front of me.

Before entering its waters, I must go back to the previous year. In May 1983, I had traveled to Aberdeen Proving Ground, Maryland, to introduce myself to the Army's vulnerability community and to seek its assistance in putting together my live-fire test program. Aberdeen, about an hour's drive north of Washington, is the home of most of the Army's technical experts in armor, weapons, and just about all aspects of vulnerability. Several agencies, including a testing command, an analytical agency, and the Ballistic Research Laboratory (BRL), are located at Aberdeen. BRL is the center of the Army's technical expertise and the keeper of the computer models.

While I was soliciting BRL's support for my test program, it was looking for help from me. In February 1983, *California Magazine* had published "The $13 Billion Dud," by William Boly, that was extremely critical of the Bradley Fighting Vehicle.[15] *Reader's Digest* reprinted a condensed version of the article under the title "The Army's $11-Billion Deathtrap" and distributed 31 million copies around the world in seventeen languages.[16]

Among his other criticisms, Boly claimed that the Bradley's aluminum armor was more dangerous to the soldiers inside than regular steel armor: "In combat the Bradley Fighting Vehicle will be a rolling death trap for the squad it carries. The vehicle's armor is made of aluminum, a metal whose chemical energy when oxidized is ten times greater than TNT."

Boly cited British experiments in 1980 that compared equivalent aluminum and steel armors subjected to attacks by the same shaped-charge chemical energy antitank weapons. (Some antitank weapons are *solid* cannon shells that penetrate armor. *Shaped-charge* warheads explode on impact and create a small, thin jet of high-energy particles that bore holes through armor. This action is similar to a stream of water coming out of a hose and boring holes in mud.) The British experiments showed that the aluminum armor caused more casualties than steel from burns, flash blindness, shrapnel wounds, blast overpressures, and toxic gases. Boly further claimed that the Army and the Bradley contractor, FMC Corporation, had conducted secret tests of their own and had confirmed the British results. Yet, they continued to produce the Bradley with aluminum armor.

These were very serious charges, and a storm of controversy followed. Army Under Secretary James Ambrose gave BRL the task of repeating the British experiments, but the Army did not give BRL any money to conduct the experiments. I entered the picture here. I had read Boly's article and tracked down a copy of the British test report.[17] It was clear to me that we had to know whether or not Boly's claims were true.

Richard Vitali, chief of the Vulnerability/Survivability Division at BRL, asked me if I could provide funding for his staff to conduct a set of experiments. I returned to Washington and discussed this proposal with my boss, Admiral Linder. When he agreed, I sent BRL $500,000, but I attached a few strings to the money.

Because the Army had not provided its own money, I suspected that it really did not want the answers that the experiments might give. I was also skeptical that BRL could conduct these experiments in a realistic fashion and publish results that might contain bad news for the Bradley program. Therefore, I wanted some approval authority on how the money was spent. I also saw this as an opportunity to get inside the BRL system and to learn firsthand how its engineers and scientists operated and how they thought. This was important because they would be key players later during the full-up live-fire test program. (The term *full-up* refers to vehicles that are fully loaded with live ammunition and fuels.)

Specifically, I wanted more realism than BRL was accustomed to providing, such as using real weapons, instead of laboratory devices, and actually shooting the weapons at the target, instead of taping the warheads to the target and detonating them. I wanted a copy of all raw data, and I wanted the right to have an independent observer present for all tests. I also intended to publish an independent report of the results. BRL had the reputation of not publishing its test results. Its engineers preferred to keep the knowledge to themselves; this tended to preserve their status as technical experts. Who could challenge them if there were no published data around that contradicted their views?

Vitali nearly gagged at these conditions. BRL was not used to being treated this way, but Vitali agreed. The aluminum vaporifics experiments began in November 1983. BRL constructed a large metal box about the size of the Bradley troop compartment. The box was instrumented to measure all the terrible things that would happen inside.

When a shaped-charge warhead penetrates armor, the metal particles vaporize and form a large fireball that fills the troop compartment, hence the term *vaporifics*. This fireball is larger and hotter and lasts about twice as long with aluminum as with steel armor.[18] Bradley aluminum armor was attached to the side of the box. After a test shot, the aluminum armor was replaced by a comparable steel armor just as the British had done. This gave direct comparisons to the differences between aluminum and steel. The environment inside the box after a shot was very grim, but the claim was that the mere presence of aluminum made it even grimmer.

As the data started coming in, I could see the tests heading toward a conclusion that would not be favorable to the aluminum Bradley. I could not be present at Aberdeen for all of the tests, so I hired my old friend, Bob Dilger, as my independent observer. Bob climbed down off his tractor in Ohio and headed his old Dodge pickup truck for Aberdeen. At first, the BRL people resented someone watching them, but they got used to it.

By the spring of 1984, the vaporifics tests had moved into their second phase, which involved taking measurements inside an actual Bradley vehicle. But the vehicle was empty! I could not talk BRL into putting live ammunition and fuel inside to determine if the fireball and hot aluminum particles would start an ammunition or fuel fire. Vitali had agreed in writing to test for fuel fires, but he refused when it was time for the tests.[19]

Now, the games really began. The tests suddenly began to lose their objectivity and realism. A series of events occurred that caused me to doubt that we would ever get the real answers.

Without my knowledge or approval, Rumanian weapons with considerably smaller warheads were substituted for Soviet weapons.[20] I was led to believe that BRL was using Soviet rounds when it was not. The first few tests on a Bradley produced fires inside the troop compartment. Uniforms on the dummies caught fire, as did sleeping bags and other stowage. The dummies were stripped naked.[21] Still, there were more fires. BRL took a fire hose and watered down everything inside the vehicle just before a test.[22] I immediately put a stop to that nonsense because we were trying to find out what happened inside the vehicle—and if fires occurred when it was hit, we needed to know that. (I learned of these games only by having Bob Dilger there as an independent observer. He called me every day with a report.)

Large doses of toxic gases were detected, larger than anticipated. BRL stopped taking measurements. The Army Surgeon General placed pigs and sheep inside the vehicle to test the effects of the choking fumes following a hit. Over my objection, the animals were sacrificed within minutes after each test. No tests for flash blindness were conducted, even though we had agreed there would be. No one was permitted to observe the autopsies, and no animals were allowed to live long enough to determine if complications developed from breathing the terrible fumes. The Surgeon General's action officer reported that no serious aftereffects were noticed, but I did not believe him.

I had conducted a literature search on all similar experiments on other vehicles in the past, and I knew that many animals had died a week after the tests as the result of complications in the respiratory tract.[23] The Surgeon General's officer was an admitted Bradley advocate and an extremely ambitious young man who was not going to produce any data that endangered the Bradley program.

Dilger and I watched as one of the veterinarians went into the Bradley five minutes after a test to retrieve the animals. He staggered out, choking and gagging, and collapsed. He was unable to breathe. I honestly thought we were going to lose him right there, but he revived. After that experience, the vets wore self-contained oxygen masks when they entered the Bradley to retrieve the animals.

It was clear to me that the atmosphere inside the vehicle after a hit was intolerable, and no one could stay in there and continue to fight. Yet, the Surgeon General's report on these experiments gave a rosy picture that indicated no real problems. This report became a major point of contention between the Army and me. (Two years later, the whole set of toxic gas experiments were repeated before a number of independent observers. The later results supported my conclusions.[24])

These are only a few of the events that occurred during the spring of 1984 to convince me that I could not trust BRL to conduct any tests that might challenge the status of our frontline armored vehicles, such as the Bradley and M-1 tank. My Joint Live-Fire Test Program had just been approved and chartered in March. One of the conditions of the charter was that BRL would be the agency to conduct the actual full-up tests, that is, tests of a Bradley fully loaded with fuel and live ammunition. BRL's procedures in the vaporifics tests, which constituted a rather narrow aspect of the Bradley's overall vulnerability, raised real concerns in my mind.

These concerns were magnified as I tried to get Vitali to move directly into full-scale live-fire tests on the Bradley immediately after the vaporifics experiments were concluded in June. He would first agree, then refuse. He began talking about delaying the start of any live-fire tests until 1986, some two years down the road. By the time those tests were over, the production contract would be near completion and all that money would be safely in the contractor's bank account in San Jose, California. The relationship between Vitali and me soured quite rapidly. I began to realize that BRL had no intention of testing the Bradley or any other vehicle in combat configuration with live ammunition and fuel on board.

Was this an issue worth fighting over? The Rubicon loomed large in front of me. I was getting nowhere with Vitali. He was obviously acting under the instructions of people higher up in the chain of command. In my mind, the issue was whether or not the Department of Defense, in general, and the Army, in particular, would ever conduct realistic tests that might save soldiers' lives. The Bradley was merely the case in point. In the Army's collective mind, the issue was the future of the Bradley program. We were on a collision course.

By now, Admiral Linder had resigned and left government service. One of his civilian deputies, Charles Watt, took his place in an acting capacity. Watt would not raise the live-fire testing issue with the Army because doing so might jeopardize his chances of getting Linder's job permanently. Mike Hall, a new Air Force brigadier general, was my immediate supervisor. As the real possibility of a serious confrontation between the Army and me became apparent, both Watt and Hall dove for the nearest exit. Although both agreed with me in principle, I sensed that neither wanted to get involved in something that could get very messy and be detrimental to their careers.

I began to seek help from various high-level officials in OSD to force the Army to begin testing. Those officials who agreed with my concern made many phone calls, but they gave up when negative answers came back. They were content that they had made token efforts.

It was now time to decide how far I was willing to push this issue. If the Army did not test the Bradley, I felt that many young men would die unnecessarily. The Rubicon lapped at my feet. Sitting down with my wife Nancy and our two children, I told them that I wanted to raise the issue to the highest levels but that it could lead to personal and professional retribution. I might be out of a job and even blacklisted. I had to consider the possibility that we could very well wind up on the streets. The system would come back at me with a vengeance. This I knew, although I wasn't sure exactly how it would happen. The decision was not an easy one to make, and I did not want to make it alone.

Both children were in college, with out-of-state tuition costs. The prospect of having their education interrupted was frightening to them, as well as to Nancy and me. The children did not say much. They just sat there and listened, probably without really understanding the significance of what Nancy and I were talking about. In the end, Nancy made the decision. She had watched the whole issue build up and knew that it was eating away at me. She understood that I could not live with myself if I walked away from it. "We can always get along somehow," she said.

On 14 June 1984, I wrote a memorandum to the Principal Deputy Under Secretary of Defense for Research and Engineering James P. Wade, Jr. Dr. Wade was Dr. DeLauer's deputy and had been following my running battle with the Army. He supported me and agreed with what I was trying to do. My "Rubicon Memo" laid out the history of the vaporifics experiments and the Joint Live-Fire Test Program. The memo specified the following charges against BRL:

> Over the course of the past 6–8 months, BRL has made decisions and taken actions in the conduct of this program that, when viewed as a whole, have resulted in less realism than we requested as a condition of funding the test, less realism than was easily achievable under the circumstances, and less realism than is needed if meaningful conclusions are to be drawn with respect to aluminum vaporifics, infantry casualties and the overall combat vulnerabilities of the [Bradley]. In many cases BRL's decisions and actions selectively reduced the severity of the behind armor effects noticed. As a result, BRL analyses and inferences on the meaning of the test results (meaning in terms of combat vulnerabilities) will necessarily be suspect because the final "proof of the pudding" tests—that is, tests of fully combat configured vehicles—were deliberately avoided. This is truly unfortunate for at stake are the lives of some 50,000–70,000 U.S.

infantrymen who may have to ride into combat in Bradley vehicles.[25]

My memo then asked Dr. Wade to direct the Army to test the Bradley immediately and further asked that he support "my effort to install a new management team, one that will conduct tests to save infantrymen's lives, not tests that defend the current configuration of frontline equipment.[26]

I went to Dr. Wade's office, handed him the memo, and left without discussing it. Attached to the memo was a six-page listing of eighteen specific BRL actions to which I had referred. I then gave a copy of the memo to an Army colonel who worked in my office and asked him to give it to the senior Army leadership. He did. The fat was in the fire.

As I expected, the Army exploded. From top senior leadership down to lower-level commands, the Army was outraged at my charges. The next day, I was summoned to a meeting in Dr. Wade's office. There sat Army Assistant Secretary Jay Sculley, Deputy Under Secretary Walt Hollis, and a host of generals and civilian officials from the Army Staff and Aberdeen. They were very unhappy with me (if looks could kill . . .).

Dr. Wade began the meeting by holding up a copy of my memo and proclaiming, "Gentlemen, if Dina Rasor ever gets her hands on a copy of this, we are all dead!" Many in the room wished that I was already dead.

I defended my charges and the Army defended BRL. We argued. The Army had no intentions of testing the Bradley; that became very clear. Lt. Gen. Robert Moore, who was sitting next to me, stated, "We don't want to test it because we know what will happen. It will just blow up and people will get all excited over that and want to cancel the Bradley."

"If you know that it is unsafe, then why don't you do something about it?" I asked.

General Moore responded, "We plan to make a few design changes at the next block change two years from now."

I jumped on that immediately. "No! I don't believe you. I think you will forget all about it once the spotlight is off the subject. This time, we are going to run some real tests and if a few Bradleys blow up in the process, then you will have to do something about changing the design."

The fundamental issue was now on the table. Dr. Wade supported me and ended the meeting by directing the Army to lay out a plan to conduct full-up tests against a combat-configured Bradley as soon as possible.

Walt Hollis, Army Under Secretary Ambrose's righthand man, was a career civil servant with an operations research background and, as such, very protective of the vulnerability modeling community. He had strong personal and professional ties to Aberdeen. Rather than fire BRL, as I had requested, he tried to work out a truce. He invited me to meet with

Vitali in his office on 6 July to discuss a plan that would be responsive to Dr. Wade's direction.

I wanted tests to start immediately. Vitali wanted another fifteen months of preliminary tests before shooting at a full-up vehicle. Naturally, we argued. Hollis ended the meeting by directing Vitali to prepare a plan that completed full-up testing, to be performed as I wanted it, by October 1985. I thought we could do the tests earlier, but at least this was now a firm commitment, or so I thought. Hollis's directive was documented in two separate memoranda for the record, one written by Vitali himself and one written by Hollis's executive officer, Lt. Col. Chaunchy McKearn.[27]

A month later, on 21 August, BRL submitted the live-fire plan to Dr. Wade. Unbelievably, the plan called for testing the Bradley in late 1986, rather than 1985, as we had agreed. BRL made no commitment to test the Bradley fully loaded with live ammunition and fuel. In fact, page 19 of the plan stated: "In general, tests will be conducted against targets configured in an inert fashion, that is, with water in the fuel cells and dummy ammunition (propellent and warheads replaced with sand). This will conserve resources and prevent damage signatures from being effaced by fire and explosion."[28] (Business as usual!)

Dr. Wade immediately fired off an angry letter in response.[29] He also made more telephone calls to Jay Sculley and Walt Hollis. The stonewalling continued. Dr. Wade did not appreciate all of this controversy, but I would not let him off the hook. I kept the pressure on him to force the Army to agree to test. Meanwhile, my two immediate supervisors, General Hall and Charles Watt, stood in the wings and watched as the situation became more explosive.

On 5 September I prepared a strongly worded letter for Dr. Wade to send to the Army, once again laying out the events that had occurred since the June meeting in Wade's office.[30] He did not want to sign it, but he picked up the telephone, called Dr. Sculley, and read it to him in as stern a voice as he could muster. Wade then threatened to sign the letter if the Army did not honor its agreement. Sculley knew that the Army could not afford to have a letter like that floating around the Pentagon.

Wade instructed me to carry a copy of the letter directly to Dr. Sculley and give it to him personally. As I walked into Sculley's office, his only comment was: "You certainly are causing me a lot of trouble, young man." I did not respond.

The atmosphere now was extremely tense. The Army's senior leaders knew that I was not going to fold up and quit. Slowly, but surely, they were being forced to do something that they did not want to do. The confrontation was the talk of the Pentagon. No one knew how it was going to end, but I could see that events were converging toward the right solution.

Then it happened.

General Hall called me into his office and informed me that my position on the staff had just been eliminated. As part of a 5 percent reduction in force (RIF), Watt had decided to eliminate my job. I would be allowed to hang around while waiting for my next assignment. I immediately confronted Watt and asked why he had selected my position when there were two empty positions in the office, either one of which would have sufficed. With two empty slots available, why did he choose to get rid of mine? His answer was not very persuasive. Once again, I had encountered the Dickey Bird Shuffle.

When I told Dr. Wade about my meeting with Hall, his first comment was, "I wonder if this is related to the Bradley." I was not certain of the answer, but it could put a whole new light on the subject.

I documented the RIF action in a memorandum for the record that I distributed throughout the Pentagon on 19 September.[31] At the same time, I made sure that every office in OSD and on the Army staff that was concerned with the Bradley program received copies of all the memos and letters in my files that dealt with the Bradley controversy. This really got the Army's attention. My files were filled with dynamite. Within minutes, the Xerox machines around the building were humming like mad as they spit out copies—"lots of little brothers and sisters," as Boyd puts it.

I had no intention of leaking any information to the press. By pumping the Pentagon full of copies, however, I was telling the Army leadership that I was still in the fight and was quite willing to raise the stakes. All of those copies floating around meant that the possibility of a leak had just increased. I knew that, and the Army knew it. The Army was suddenly eager to resolve the dispute. Two days later, we were back at the bargaining table.

On Friday, 21 September, the major players again gathered in Wade's office. Dr. Sculley announced that the Army wanted to withdraw the Bradley from my Joint Live-Fire Test Program and conduct the full-up tests on its own. The Army promised to complete the tests, including at least ten shots at a combat-configured Bradley, by October 1985. Further, it promised to make design changes based upon those test results and repeat the test in the spring of 1986 to see whether the changes had made the vehicle safer.[32]

This was truly a momentous occasion. The Army had been dragged to this table, kicking and screaming all the way. It was now promising to do exactly what I had asked.

In an effort to smooth over relations, Dr. Sculley invited me to personally participate in the Army tests. He asked me to help with the preparation of the test plan and to observe each test shot.[33] At this point, an Army official from Aberdeen, who was seated behind Sculley, invited me to sit in the Bradley when they shot at it. I declined that invitation, but I accepted Sculley's willingly.

By permitting the Army to run the tests itself, I was giving up some control over how the tests would be conducted. By now, however, I was fairly certain that the tests would actually occur and that changes to the design would be the inevitable result. I would be allowed to influence the process in some fashion, and I could ask for nothing more.

Dr. Wade instructed me to work with Dr. Sculley to draw up the terms of the agreement in a formal document for his signature. I spent the better part of the next week doing just that. Suddenly, Dr. Wade started pressing me to finish the agreement and get the Army's signature so that he could make it an official, completed act. I did not understand why he was pushing me to hurry up.

The reason did not become clear until I learned much later that word of the controversy had leaked out of the building to Capitol Hill. On Thursday, 27 September, a letter was delivered to Secretary Weinberger that had been signed by the four cochairmen of the Military Reform Caucus, Senators David Pryor and Charles Grassley and Congressmen Denny Smith and Mel Levine.[34]

As described in chapter 7, a few months prior to this time Congress had nominated me to Secretary Weinberger as a candidate for the new position of director of operational testing under the condition that there would be no retribution if I were not selected. The Military Reform Caucus believed that eliminating my job was an act of retribution by Weinberger. In addition, it had been more than a year since Congress had passed its testing reform legislation, and Weinberger had done nothing to implement the legislation. Naturally, the caucus members were angry and frustrated on both counts.

On Friday morning, 28 September, Dr. Wade began calling me every thirty minutes to get the agreement to him for signature. He did not tell me about the letter from Congress, but he said he was starting to get feelers from the press about my termination and the whole Bradley situation. He was sure that something was going to break in the newspapers, and he felt that he could minimize the damage by pointing to a signed, sealed, and delivered agreement to test the Bradley.

That afternoon, I delivered the formal agreement, with Sculley's concurring signature, to Wade. He immediately signed it. This was a tremendous accomplishment. I had forced the Army to agree to do something that it did not want to do. I had made it happen by working inside the system, and I was quite proud of this fact.

That weekend, I spent many hours on the telephone with John Boyd. We went over everything that had happened. Boyd was very adamant in his advice to me. I had won this bureaucratic battle with the Army by working inside the system. If the story broke in the press, I should not talk to any reporters under any circumstances. If I did, Boyd said, I could be accused of being another whistleblower looking for someone else to fight my battles, and I was certainly not one of those. When I had started this fight back in June, I was prepared to accept the consequences. That is why I had discussed it with my family first. (During the next two years, I followed Boyd's advice to the letter. I also decided not to talk to members of Congress or congressional staffers, to their dismay and sometimes anger.)

The following Monday morning, 1 October, Dr. Wade was sure something would be in the papers. I thought he was probably correct, but I had no idea what to expect. When I arrived in my office just in time for our 0800 staff meeting, I sensed a certain electricity in the air. No one wanted to sit next to me as the staff meeting began.

General Hall had this strange look on his face. Without saying a word, he reached into his briefcase, grabbed a newspaper, and threw it across the table at me. There on the front page of the *Washington Times* was the whole sordid story going all the way back to June.[35] Similar stories appeared in every major newspaper across the country, including *The Wall Street Journal*, *Washington Post*, *Boston Globe*, *New York Times*, *Chicago Tribune*, and *Los Angeles Times*.

Typical headlines read "Tough Pentagon Tester May Soon Move Out" (*National Journal*), "Colonel a Casualty of Arms-Test Fight (*Chicago Tribune*); "Memos Cite Army Rigging of Tank Tests" (*Boston Globe*), "Critic of New Army Vehicle to Lose Position at Pentagon" (*Philadelphia Inquirer*), and "Army Is Faulted on Its Testing of New Vehicle" (*The Wall Street Journal*).[36]

I was now definitely on the far side of the Rubicon. No boats were in sight.

9

Off to Alaska?

How strongly the Yellow Bird influences the daily activities of most Pentagon officials is described in chapter 6. The morning of 1 October 1984 is a classic example of its part in the workings of the Pentagon. Acute shock permeated the building. The Yellow Bird was full of Bradley stories, all very uncomplimentary. The revelations caught both the Army and the Air Force completely by surprise. They began scrambling to recover. Naturally, the leaders of both services denied that my job elimination had anything to do with the disagreements between the Army and me over the Bradley tests, but the denials had a hollow ring to them.

The stories kept up throughout the week, as Bradley critics began coming out of the woodwork. Reporters were digging everywhere, and they uncovered lots of newsworthy items. Practically every critical or embarrassing document that existed found its way into the hands of one reporter or another.

As the stories finally began to taper off by week's end, the editorials began. Pentagon officials had to read everything all over again, but now the language was saturated with gratuitous remarks. Nicholas Wade, nicknamed the "Hammer of God," struck on Monday, 8 October. The lead editorial of *The New York Times* was headlined "Tests the Army Should Not Shirk."[1] This scathing editorial strongly endorsed my live-fire test program and severely criticized the Army for resisting the Bradley tests. *The New York Times* and *The Washington Post* are the two newspapers most feared in the Pentagon. So when the Hammer of God came down so hard on the Army, the Bradley, and the Pentagon's "personnel policies," the leadership knew that a rough time lay ahead.

Three days later (11 October), Deputy Secretary of Defense William H. Taft IV sent a letter to the four cochairmen of the Military Reform Caucus. By then, the military leadership had measured the public and congressional reaction to the stories. The Yellow Bird discomfort meter registered very high. Weinberger and Taft knew that they had some fence-mending to do. Taft assured Congress that there had been no retribution against me and that the whole flap was a misunderstanding. Although it was true that my job had been eliminated, he saw no relationship between that and the Bradley.

According to Taft, the senior Pentagon leadership strongly endorsed my efforts to have the Army test the Bradley, evidenced by the fact that an agreement had been signed on 28 September. The deputy secretary's wording of the letter made it sound like I had a lot of enthusiastic supporters at the top: "As you are aware, Colonel Burton's recommendations regarding realistic testing have continually been endorsed by my senior staff. . . ."[2]

Then came the key commitment. To convince Congress that there were no ill feelings toward me, Taft announced that I would remain in my job and be involved in the Bradley tests until they were completed. "Colonel Burton will participate in the planning and execution of the tests."[3] It was a rather explicit commitment, one that would come back to haunt Taft a few months later.

The Military Reform Caucus appeared satisfied with Taft's response. The Pentagon settled down, and I went about my business of preparing for the tests that would start in the spring of 1985. My life could never return to normal, however; nothing could be like it was before the explosion in the press. I was now living in a fishbowl. Everything I did or said was watched closely by a lot of people both inside and outside the Pentagon.

My peers and superiors alike did not know exactly how to treat me, so they kept their distance for a while. When it became apparent that I was going to survive the notoriety, my peers began drifting back to a normal relationship with me. Before getting too close, they had wanted to be sure there would not be another explosion because they did not want to get hit by any fallout. My superiors, on the other hand, drifted in the opposite direction. Looking at me rather cross-eyed, they continued to be unsure of how to treat me. I could read in their faces a little respect, some fear, and a lot of dislike. No one called me in to sit down and talk about what had happened. Cool but civil best describes our relationships.

I cannot recall the exact moment when I discovered that the Army was spying on me, but this might be a good place to explain that operation. Spying is a common response when an individual or organization becomes a problem or a threat to another agency in the Pentagon, as the "Sleez" affair in the TAC Air Shop (see chapter 5). There are always so many power struggles going on that the building is awash with spies. When an individual is involved in any kind of serious controversy, he or she can count on skulduggery, so it pays to be alert.

My experience as the subject of a spy operation began shortly after the Rubicon Memo in June 1984. The spying intensified greatly after the stories broke in the press in October. It became the most convoluted operation I have ever seen, with games inside of games on both sides.

My office consisted of colonels from each service. I was the only Air Force officer. I served with one Marine, one Navy, and three Army officers. (This might raise a question about why the only Air Force slot in the office had been chosen for elimination, but I will drop that subject for now because the deputy secretary of defense had said it was all a misunderstanding.)

One of the Army colonels, Dale Brudvig, became my watchdog. Either on his own initiative or at the request of the Army, he began reporting my activities to the senior Army leadership—who I talked to, met with, received telephone calls from, and, especially, everything I wrote that was important to the Army. During the next two years, every piece of correspondence I wrote that dealt with the Army or the Bradley was reproduced by Brudvig and hand delivered to the senior Army leadership. I mean everything—letters and memos to my superiors, trip reports, memos for the record, and sometimes even my handwritten notes.

Dale Brudvig was about as subtle as a bull in a china shop. A large man with a short temper, he was extremely loyal to the Army. He stood 6 feet 5 inches tall and weighed 240 pounds. A former tanker, that is, commander of tank units and armored forces, he was very protective of the Army's M-1 tanks and the Bradley.

Dale thought that his spying activities began in secret. He would sneak a copy of something I had written, Xerox twenty-one copies, and personally deliver them to the Army secretary, under secretary, three assistant secretaries, the chief of staff, the vice chief, all of the three-star generals, and several lower-level two-stars. He made twenty-one stops on his rounds. The recipients, in turn, would make more copies and send them throughout various Army agencies. Within hours after I had written something, the Army would be saturated with copies all the way down to the technician level at BRL. I detected almost immediately that Dale was doing this, but I did not say anything. I had developed my own secret network of informers within the Army. When copies of my correspondence began showing up at the lower echelons of the Army, my network showed them to me.

Knowing that the senior Army leaders were reading my mail, I began to structure my correspondence to influence them. Although I addressed the memos and letters to my superiors, my real audience was the senior Army leadership. The Army thought it was getting secret, inside information about my views, while all the time I was feeding it what I wanted it to have. John Boyd had dubbed this time-honored intelligence strategy the "reverse pump."

The spy game went on for more than a year. Soon after the Bradley full-up tests began in September 1985, Secretary of Defense Weinberger sent me a handwritten note asking me to keep him personally informed on the test results as they occurred. Weinberger's military assistant was Army Gen. Colin Powell, and I suspected that the Army leadership had a copy of Weinberger's note as soon as I did.

Dale Brudvig approached me on behalf of the Army vice chief and asked if he could give the Army a copy of anything I sent to Weinberger. I suspected the Army would get a copy from Powell anyway, so I gladly agreed. This was Brudvig's way of getting his mail run activities out in the open so that they were no longer a secret. I never let on that I knew he had been doing this all along. Asking me helped to clear the air between us, and we became cautious friends. Although never completely trusting each other, we were able to work together at times when we both wanted to influence the Army in the same direction.

What began in secret was now an open line of communication. I had access to the Army's highest leaders. They paid attention to what I said, sometimes out of fear that others would learn of what I was saying and sometimes because I revealed things to them that their staffs had kept hidden. I had to use this communication link in a very judicious manner and be absolutely correct in everything I said that could be perceived as controversial. Before I committed any subject to writing, I checked and

150   cross-checked from many different directions to make sure that I made no mistakes. I knew that legions of Army experts studied my comments carefully and looked for mistakes that could be used to discredit me. I would no longer be a threat if I were discredited, but it never happened during the two years of the spy operation.

Some Army leaders began to look forward to my "cards and letters." In fact, Brudvig brought me a back-channel message from Army Vice Chief of Staff Gen. Max Thurman that said, "Keep the cards and letters coming. It's the only way I can find out what is really going on in my service."

By the fall of 1984, when the Bradley controversy first broke in the press, the Reform Movement was a strong force on Capitol Hill and the Pentagon was locked in mortal combat with the reformers. It was more important than ever that my relationship with Boyd, Sprey, and Spinney be kept secret. We continued to use code names for telephone calls and to meet in out-of-the-way places. I regularly met the "Arbuthnott" brothers, Boyd and Spinney, in front of the NATO flags on the second floor of the Pentagon, but "Mr. Grau" and I had to find a new meeting place.

Pierre Sprey was persona non grata with the Army. He was an outspoken critic of the Army's M-1 tank, among other systems. In plain and simple language, the Army hated Pierre. Weinberger had changed the rules about outsiders coming into the Pentagon. Anyone who did not actually work in the building had to be met at the entrance and escorted by someone who did work inside, so Pierre and I shifted our meeting place to lane 8 of the Pentagon's south parking lot. (Pierre worked in Roslyn, a Washington suburb just north of the Pentagon.)

By the end of October 1984, the newspaper stories had died down, and the Army was ready to discuss details about how the Bradley would be tested. It was decided that the tests would be conducted by BRL at Aberdeen Proving Ground. I was invited to meet with BRL and discuss the plans for the test.

I had not been to BRL since I had so severely criticized the agency in my Rubicon Memo back in June. Now I was going to have to meet with the BRL staff in the laboratory at Aberdeen. I did not look forward to this trip. I had to face a bunch of people who had suffered a great deal of personal and professional grief because of me. A root canal would have been more fun than this trip. I never did get used to walking into a roomful of Army officials who hated my guts, but I learned to grit my teeth and just do it. If I had a dollar for every time it happened, I would be a rich man.

The Army brought in new blood to BRL to run the Bradley tests. Gary Holloway had been an analyst in another Aberdeen organization. He was an intelligent, likable young man who was pleasant to deal with. Perhaps that is why the Army selected him. We met in the conference room at

BRL on 1 November, exactly one month after the explosion in the press. The room was full of representatives from various Army agencies, including the Bradley program office. It was obvious that everyone had been instructed to be nice to me, even though some people in the room had a hard time doing it.

Holloway announced his philosophy for the tests, or rather, the instructions under which he was operating. Back in September, the Army had agreed to at least ten shots with Soviet antitank weapons against a Bradley fully loaded with fuel and live ammunition on board. Holloway announced that the Army would not permit any of the ten shots intentionally to hit the ammunition stored inside the vehicle. He would hand-pick the aim points so that the penetrating round would intentionally miss the stored ammo and thereby avoid a catastrophic loss of a Bradley.

Holloway claimed that the test experts knew for certain what would happen if any ammo inside was hit. A fire or explosion would completely destroy the vehicle. They were not going to permit that because it could lead to all kinds of adverse publicity. I argued strongly that they could not know for certain what would happen; a fully loaded vehicle had never been tested.*

I pointed out to Holloway and everyone else in the room that the ten shots had to be conducted in a credible, realistic fashion. Intentionally avoiding possible catastrophic events did not fit that description. I argued that the aim points should be selected by a random method, so that the Army could not be criticized for picking shots that intentionally avoided catastrophic results. To me, its credibility was at stake. I could just see the Army experts running around town with the news that the current Bradley design was safe because the vehicle did not routinely blow up when they shot at it ten times. In fact, this is exactly what happened a year later. I had to run around town behind the Army experts to remind everyone that because they had intentionally avoided hitting the ammo inside, the results were naturally biased toward making the Bradley look good.

We argued and argued, but the Army would not budge. Now I understood why it had withdrawn the Bradley from my Joint Live-Fire Test Program. Because the Army would pay for and perform the tests, it was dictating how the tests would be done. Had I retained control, we would

---

*Ten months later (September 1985), on the first test shot fired at a fully loaded Bradley, Holloway and his experts were proved wrong on this very point. The gunner missed the aim point by about 8 inches and accidentally struck several boxes of cannon ammunition stored in the troop compartment. The results were a small explosion and an ammunition fire that surprisingly self-extinguished, even though conventional wisdom indicated that the fire should have continued until the vehicle was consumed.

have fired at the Bradley in a more random fashion and might have blown up several vehicles.

After hours of arguing, I finally agreed to let Holloway handpick the ten impact points but only under one condition. If no Bradleys were destroyed by those ten shots, the Army would immediately conduct a separate series of shots (this came to be known as the "Burton tests"). In that series, we would shoot at the fully loaded vehicle in a more random fashion so that no one could claim bias. We would take data after each shot and continue the random shots until at least one Bradley was completely destroyed.[4] Reluctantly, Holloway agreed.

I was not happy with this whole arrangement, but that was the best compromise I could negotiate. It was clear to me that the Army was going to do everything in its power to protect the Bradley's reputation, which meant structuring tests to minimize the damage to the vehicle. I was going to have to be on my toes every minute to ensure that we had a realistic set of tests by which to determine the results, rather than the ideas of some loyal Army technocrat.

The Army leadership apparently was not too happy with the compromise, either. In the first week of December, Holloway and the Bradley program manager traveled to the Pentagon to meet with Army Under Secretary Ambrose. Ambrose was the most powerful person in the Army, civilian or military. He called the shots. Following the meeting with Holloway, Ambrose announced that the Army was not going to honor the 28 September test agreement or test the current Bradley design at all. Instead, it would run a few tests on some changes to the fuel system and on a few other minor design changes when they were ready a few years down the road.[5] In Ambrose's view, nothing else was needed. In my view, it was just another game the Army was playing.

When Dale Brudvig informed me of this decision, I was flabbergasted. The Army never gives up. Clearly, this was another delaying tactic: wait a few years until I was gone or the spotlight was off the Bradley, then cancel any tests that might be embarrassing. I had seen that game many times before and immediately asked for an audience with Ambrose. As I walked toward his office, I kept telling myself, "Be firm, be firm. Don't agree to this, no matter what he says."

I had never met Ambrose and did not know what to expect. His Bradley maneuver was typical of how the most powerful man in the Army operated. He quite often let his deputies, such as Walt Hollis, negotiate the best agreement they could for the Army, then he would step in later and pronounce the agreement void because he personally had not been involved. I had decided that he was going to be personally involved this time.

Ambrose's office, like those of all officials at this level, was plush. We sat down opposite each other. Ambrose was in an overstuffed chair, and I sat on a luxurious couch. For some strange reason, the lights in his office were very dim; perhaps bright lights hurt his eyes. The room seemed more like a dimly lit living room than a Pentagon office. My boss, Charlie Watt, had come with me, but he did not have anything to say. He was still trying to get the word *acting* removed from his title, so I knew that he would not argue strongly with Ambrose.

Ambrose went through his line of reasoning for canceling the tests—I had heard the same old line a thousand times. The Army already knew all the answers, so there was no reason to test. It would wait a few years until a couple of improvements were ready and then test only those.

When he was finished, I countered with an argument that Ambrose had never heard before: "If you do not test the current Bradley design to estab-lish a baseline of knowledge, then how do you know that your so-called improvements will actually make things better? They may make things worse, not better. I have seen this happen on several systems before."

I then rattled off a series of examples where that very thing happened. I followed up with the credibility argument: The Army had told Congress and the public that it would test the Bradley, and now it was going back on its word.

Presenting my arguments in as strong a voice and manner that I could muster, I was calm and collected, yet firm. I went out of my way to avoid appearing emotional or combative, but I told Ambrose that his decision would not go unchallenged. Surprisingly, Ambrose offered no counter-ing arguments. Perhaps he was not used to someone disagreeing with him, or perhaps this had been a "gut check" to see how persistent I was. In any event, he changed his mind again. Following our meeting, an Army staff teletype message announced to field units that Under Secre-tary Ambrose had reversed his previous decision and the original tests would now proceed as agreed on in September.[6]

Constant vigilance became my watchword. I planned to watch those guys like a hawk every minute until this whole thing was over.

During the winter, BRL put together the detailed test plan and began assembling the equipment and supplies for the tests. Phase I dealt with testing the current Bradley design, and it would culminate with the ten full-up shots in September 1985. Phase II involved testing modifications to a prototype Bradley based on the Phase I test results. These modifica-tions would be designed to make the vehicle safer. The Phase II tests were scheduled for April 1986.

Phase I called for about six months of preliminary tests against Bradleys loaded with inert ammunition, that is, dummy ammo with the explosives and propellants removed. These tests would begin in the first week of March 1985 and continue until September, when we would finally get to the full-up tests.[7]

Old habits die hard. I could not wean BRL from shooting at empty vehicles. It would use the preliminary tests to fill out its data base and calibrate the computer models. (I called this BRL foreplay.) I was willing to tolerate this nonsense so that we could get to the real tests in September. Then, we would not only test the Bradley fully loaded but also run the same ten shots against the old M-113 troop carrier and a Soviet BMP. The BMP was the Soviet counterpart to the Bradley, and the M-113 was the vehicle to be replaced by the Bradley. These tests would provide some interesting comparisons—a total of thirty shots against fully loaded vehicles.

Everything was quiet on the Bradley front during the winter. Meanwhile, the administration still had not appointed a director of operational testing. January 1985 marked fifteen months since Congress had passed the testing reform legislation. By then, the entire Congress, not just the Military Reform Caucus, was angry at Weinberger's stonewalling. The administration sent out another call to the reformers for nominations; this time the request came directly from the White House. Again, I was nominated by the reformers in a letter to the White House that was signed by Denny Smith, cochairman of the Military Reform Caucus.[8] I am sure that Mr. Weinberger and various Air Force and Army leaders were extremely excited to see my name in the hopper again. This second nomination was reported in the press.[9] I am sure that many Pentagon officials went to "full red alert." They quickly said, "No, thanks," and became suddenly quite serious about finding their own candidate.

The Phase I Bradley tests began at Aberdeen during the first week of March, as scheduled. Although the tests involved empty vehicles, they marked the beginning of a monumental program. I was going to be there to watch, or so I thought.

On Friday afternoon, 8 March 1985, I received a telephone call from the Colonels' Group at Air Force personnel headquarters. The colonel on the other end of the line informed me that I was being transferred to Alaska and that I had exactly seven days from this official notification to accept the transfer or retire. I was stunned. I chose not to argue with the colonel on the phone, as he told me there would be no negotiating. It was a done deal, and I either went to Alaska or retired. He seemed pleased that he had been chosen to give me the message.

A year later, I would learn that the Alaskan Air Command did not want me. In fact, it had formally objected to Air Force Headquarters that I had no qualifications to serve in the command. They were told to shut up and take what was being given them.[10]

The Bradley tests had just begun that week and Phases I and II would not be over until April 1986. I thought to myself, "Here we go again." I quickly called up Arbuthnott and asked him to meet me at the flags. Boyd could not believe it when I told him what had happened. He actually started laughing; so did everyone else that I told. As Boyd put it, "This was about as dumb a thing the Air Force could do. Whoever dreamed up this one was truly general officer material."

Word of my transfer spread throughout the Pentagon like wildfire. It could not be kept a secret, and it was only a matter of time before it would leak out of the building.

Ernie Fitzgerald thought it "looked like a little chief-to-chief pillow talk," implying that the Army chief of staff had asked the Air Force chief of staff to get me out of the Army's hair. All kinds of similar speculation floated around the Pentagon. Spinney thought the Air Force leaders were doing this themselves because I had caused them problems on some of their sacred cows, such as the Advanced Medium Range Air-to-Air Missile (AMRAAM) and the Maverick. He reasoned that the Air Force probably felt the Army would get the blame. I refused to speculate.

On Monday morning, 11 March, the Pentagon personnel office gave me a copy of the official written notification.[11] I had to sign a statement indicating that my seven-day clock had started. I made numerous copies of these papers and freely passed them out around the building. Again, the Xerox machines started humming, as they created lots of "brothers and sisters." The building was soon flooded with copies.

General Hall called me into his office on Wednesday morning to ask for my decision. He seemed anxious to know. I told him that I still had four days to make up my mind and I did not know how this would all play out. Before the next day was over, it was all settled. On Thursday morning, word of the Alaskan transfer found its way to Capitol Hill. I was surprised it took so long, but then all hell broke loose.

By now, the Military Reform Caucus had more than one hundred members. They included congressmen and senators, Democrats and Republicans, who were furious with Weinberger and Taft. They all had copies of Taft's letter from just a few months before, the one that stated explicitly that "Colonel Burton will participate in the planning and execution of the tests." For the second time in six months, it appeared that Weinberger and Taft were going back on their word.

The telephone lines from Capitol Hill to the Pentagon were buzzing.

Congressman Mel Levine called Dr. Wade from National Airport. He told Wade, "I am getting on the airplane for California. When I get off five hours from now, I will call you again. You had better tell me that the Alaska assignment has been canceled or we will consider this a bipartisan slap in the face."

Wade responded, "Our position as of now is that he is going to Alaska—unless you turn up the heat."[12] This was Dr. Wade's way of saying he could not help me on his own. He needed to be pushed. By now, Dr. DeLauer had left government service, and Wade was acting in DeLauer's job. It was no secret that he wanted a permanent appointment as DeLauer's successor. Getting embroiled in another Burton-Bradley controversy would surely kill his chances. He wanted to help me, but he did not want to—another one of those moral dilemmas, Pentagon-style.

The heat in the Pentagon was turned up—way up. (It is interesting to note that, as in the first controversy, Senator Nancy Kassebaum chose not to participate. Weinberger's pledge to the senator had originally brought the Military Reform Caucus into the fray.) The press corps descended on the Pentagon like sharks in a feeding frenzy. When reporters asked the Air Force to confirm the rumor that I was headed for Alaska, the public affairs office denied the transfer. Within the hour, reporters had uncovered copies of the official transfer notification and were incensed that they had been lied to. This turned the press against the Pentagon even more.

My telephone did not stop ringing. Reporters came barging into my office and demanded a statement. I refused to talk to any of them. At about 1300, I threw my hands up in the air and announced that I was going home. When I arrived home an hour later, it was all over.

At 1330, Dr. Wade had met with Deputy Secretary of Defense Taft and Secretary of the Air Force Orr in Taft's office. After a quick huddle, Secretary Orr concluded that he should cancel my assignment to Alaska. "Gentlemen, we have no choice," as he put it.[13] The press was getting ready to crucify them. All sorts of demons were now working on their minds.

Taft's military assistant, an Air Force two-star general, called Congressman Denny Smith and said, "It's over. You win. We are throwing in the towel. Call off the dogs."[14]

A Pentagon press conference was quickly held, and Dr. Wade announced that I would not go to Alaska. Ironically, the press announcement had been prepared by Dr. Wade's military assistant, Army Col. Ken Hollander, who had been all smiles the day before the press conference. The day after the announcement, Hollander accosted me in the hall. Frowns had replaced the smiles. He called me all kinds of names and

claimed that I was "not fit to wear the uniform" because of the controversy I had caused. Hollander was a true defender of the establishment.

The episode was over in a flash, but the press could not put it to rest.
The major papers were full of Alaska stories the next day.[15] The smaller
papers throughout the country followed suit. Their basic theme was that
Congress had intervened to prevent the Pentagon from banishing me to
the "American equivalent of Siberia." Senator Pryor was quoted by
United Press as saying, "We more or less shamed them into taking this
action."[16]

Most of the stories linked my transfer to the Bradley controversy that
had grabbed attention the previous fall. Again, Pentagon insiders had to
put up with the instant replays—testing controversy, job elimination,
watered-down dummy uniforms, the blocking and interference. Now,
Siberia represented another fumble. Before the next year was over, the
game would move to the Super Bowl.

The roar subsided rather quickly, and I resumed my duties. Whether I
liked it or not, I became a nationally known figure. In a sense, this notoriety was my best protection. Testing reform was now the prime focus of
the Reform Movement. I had become the symbol of that effort, but I had
no control over its direction. I suppose I could have just walked away
from everything, but it never entered my mind. I was committed to do my
part in bringing real reform to the Pentagon, and I was willing to run my
tail off to get to that goal.

The hard-core reformers had been excited when Chuck Spinney first
put the national spotlight on the need for reform; but we were equally as
disappointed when nothing happened to change the way the Pentagon
actually conducted its affairs. The publicity and controversy were followed by business as usual. Now, the spotlight had shifted to me and the
testing operation. If we did not take this opportunity to force reform,
there probably would not be a third chance to make significant changes
in the system.

The preliminary tests against empty Bradleys proceeded throughout
the spring and summer of 1985. I traveled to Aberdeen for most of them.
I put 30,000 miles on my pumpkin-orange VW convertible in twelve
months. About the only thing learned from preliminary tests was that the
computer models were in bad shape.

The models were run before each test shot to check their ability to
predict what would happen. Time and again, what actually happened
bore no relation to what was predicted. Before the summer was over, the
models were revised at least three times—major revisions, not just fine-
tune changes. Revisions were constantly needed just to make the models
account for what had already happened. After each revision, BRL

proudly announced the models were in good shape. Then, another major surprise showed up. Every time that happened, naturally, I rubbed BRL's collective nose in it by writing one of my "reverse pump" memos.

It was my view, and still is, that the environment inside a vehicle after a hit is too complex to be captured completely by a computer model. The best the model can do is to build a description of what happened in the past on various shots. This is not the same as the ability to predict what will happen in the future.

Years later, I would come across a description of "chaotic systems" by Paul Davies in his 1988 book, *The Cosmic Blueprint*. His comments fit these vulnerability models to a tee:

> For a chaotic system, however, simulation is pointless, because we only get the same amount of information out as we put in. More and more computing power is needed to tell us less and less. In other words, we are not predicting anything, merely describing the system to a certain limited level of accuracy as it evolves in real time.[17]

I wish Davies had published his book before 1985. I would have had a lot of fun reading it to the people at BRL.

Following the big Alaska flap, the entire Congress, not just the Military Reform Caucus, became interested in the Bradley tests. On 5 June 1985, I was asked by the House Armed Services Committee to provide a written description of the total Bradley test program, Phases I and II. The committee wanted to have in writing any agreements that had been made between the Army and me. I advised my superiors of this contact by memorandum, as Dr. Wade had instructed me to do in such circumstances. Of course, twenty-one copies of my memo went to the Army.[18]

I laid out in detail the test program that the Army had agreed to and the schedule of events. Phase I would be completed by October 1985, and Phase II (tests of design modifications) would be completed the following April. The House Armed Services Committee converted this description into formal legislation, which mandated that all actions covered by my agreements with the Army must actually occur. The tests were to be conducted according to the test plan that I had negotiated with the Army. A formal report on Phase I results was due to Congress by 1 December 1985 and Phase II results by 1 June 1986.

Apparently, Congress wanted to make sure that the Army did not try to wiggle out of its agreements, so it made the agreements law. The legislation passed the House and Senate without resistance. Congressman Denny Smith's new part-time aide, Bob Dilger, assisted the Armed Services Committee in drafting the legislation. With full knowledge of my superiors, I spent a lot of time on the telephone with Bob to help him with his task. The Army leaders were not too happy about this, but they could do nothing about it.

Over the summer, Secretary Weinberger announced that Dr. Donald Hicks of the Northrop Corporation, not Dr. Wade, would succeed Dr. DeLauer as the under secretary of defense for research and engineering. Consequently, Dr. Wade resigned and left government service. I am certain that his support of me and being in the middle of those two big public explosions had a bearing on his not getting the job.

Another personnel change at that time would greatly influence my future. My immediate supervisor, Air Force Gen. Michael "Mike" Hall, left before his tour was up. He transferred somewhere else in the building and no longer would be involved with my office. Before the Air Force could pick a replacement for him, Army Vice Chief of Staff Gen. Max Thurman called my next highest boss, Charlie Watt, and offered an Army general to replace Hall. Watt still had the word *acting* in front of his title, so he accepted General Thurman's offer.

General Thurman had a bright and upcoming Army general in mind who had never worked in weapons system acquisition or testing. Here was an opportunity for him to broaden his experience, so Brig. Gen. Donald P. Jones arrived to become my immediate supervisor. General Jones's entire career until then had been in Army personnel. It was clear to me that he was there to practice his personnel skills, not to learn the testing business. Over the next nine months, General Jones did what he was sent to do. He later became a three-star general in charge of Army personnel.

10

More Dirty Games

During the summer of 1985, I established a close relationship with the technicians, mechanics, and manual laborers who did most of the actual work at the Aberdeen test site. These were the people who set up the instrumentation, recorded the raw data, fired the weapons at the vehicle, and repaired the damage caused by each shot. I got to know them really well. I went out of my way to seek their opinions and views on everything that happened on each test.

Many of them had seen combat as GIs in previous wars. They understood the importance of the tests. As I showed a genuine interest in their views, they began to feel that they could influence the redesign of the Bradley and help to make it safer in combat.

They had little respect for BRL, or "management," and shared my concerns that the bureaucracy would try its best to make these tests minimize the Bradley's problems. Because they wanted to help, they became my eyes and ears inside the system. They made sure that I knew everything

160

taking place behind the scenes. I had private viewings of the damages from each shot so that I could compare them with the formal documented results prepared by BRL. They called me long distance at home to tell me when they had been instructed to do anything out of the ordinary that might influence the test results. I received several of these calls and then arranged to stumble on the new setup or conditions as if by accident in order to protect my sources. It was a real cat-and-mouse game. I know I drove the BRL and Aberdeen management crazy, for I always seemed to know exactly what they were doing.

It was precisely a 220-mile round-trip from my house to Aberdeen. My little VW made the trip so many times that it seemed to know the route as well as I did. These trips were worth the effort. By observing the tests directly and writing trip reports that documented my observations, I brought checks and balances to the process. Many times, my reports differed from those written by Army observers on the scene. In any test program, there is always the opportunity to interpret results in a manner that favors the reputation of the system being tested. When those interpretations are further edited to protect the program at the intermediate levels of management, the final report for senior management often bears little resemblance to what actually happened.

While BRL ran its series of preliminary tests against empty Bradleys that summer, the pattern of checks and balances was firmly established. My trip reports became best-sellers around the Pentagon. Because they often contained interpretations of test results and implications of far more serious consequences than the official reports received through the Army chain of command, they led to spirited debate at the top.

Finally, in September, it was time for the real tests—one year after the formal agreement. Ten shots of small-, medium-, and large-caliber anti-tank weapons would be fired against the fully loaded Bradley. The standard load inside the vehicle, mostly in the troop compartment, consisted of the following ordnance:

10 TOW (antitank) missiles
3 LAW missiles (bazookas)
1,500 rounds of 25-mm cannon shells
4,400 rounds of 7.62-mm machine-gun ammunition
2 M18 Claymore antipersonnel mines
8 M67 fragmentation grenades
4 TH3 incendiary grenades
4 smoke grenades
10 M49 surface trip flares

Ten shots each would be fired against a Soviet BMP and the older M-113 troop carrier; both also fully loaded. BRL would pick the specific aim points to avoid intentionally striking any ammunition stored inside the vehicles. Because the shots were being fired dynamically, however, there was some uncertainty as to whether the shots would actually strike a vehicle at the specified aim points. Under the highly controlled conditions of the test range, gunners could hit within 6 to 8 inches of their aim points. This was enough variance to place the outcome of each shot in doubt.

BRL chose aim points to avoid hitting ammunition inside the vehicle because the testers believed that striking the ammunition would result in a catastrophic loss of the vehicle. This decision was made in accordance with the conventional wisdom at the time, and it represented the programming in the computer model. The first test shot proved BRL wrong. The gunner missed the aim point by about 8 inches. The penetrating round struck several boxes of cannon shells inside the troop compartment. There was a small explosion inside, followed by an ammunition fire. To everyone's surprise, the ammunition fire self-extinguished after a few rounds had burned. According to conventional wisdom, the ammunition fire should have continued until all of the ammo and the vehicle itself were consumed. This was the first of many major surprises that occurred before the test program was over.

The computer models had to be revised to account for what actually happened. I took particular delight in reporting this unusual event on the very first shot. The physical evidence indicated that the state of knowledge was not what the technical experts had claimed. If they were wrong about this, then they were probably wrong about many other claims.

The second shot confirmed the Army's worst fears. Again, the gunner missed the aim point by a few inches and struck ammo inside the troop compartment. (Knowing the gunner, I would not be surprised if he had aimed a little low.) This time, the ammo fire did not self-extinguish. We sat in the bunker long into the night and watched the Bradley as it was consumed by fire. Every few seconds, the Bradley was rocked by an explosion when the fire caused a missile, bazooka, or mine in the troop compartment to "cook off." These low-order explosions were not strong enough to disintegrate the vehicle. It was eerie to watch the Bradley slowly melt from a 10-foot tall vehicle into a puddle of molten aluminum.

The shot occurred late in the afternoon, but it was close to midnight before we could leave the safety of the bunker a few hundred yards from the fire. There was little conversation that evening as everyone sat staring at this awesome sight. Flames leaped high into the night sky, and explosions sent burning cannon shells flying through the air like fireworks.

Although the vehicle was made of aluminum, the large cannon in the turret was steel. As the aluminum structure weakened from the heat, we watched the steel cannon slowly sink into the vehicle—the silhouette of the barrel pointing up into the night sky like the bow of a ship going down at sea. The sobering sight made a lasting impression on everyone in the bunker. They had never seen anything like this before, but they would see it again.

Sadly, the sight of a Bradley burning would be repeated many times in combat during the Gulf War. Steve Vogel gave a heart-rending account of the "Battle of Norfolk" in *The Washington Post*. Many Bradleys were hit during the night of 26 February 1991 by both friendly and enemy fire. Four Bradleys and five tanks were destroyed, with six U.S. GIs killed and thirty wounded. The following are a few passages from Vogel's story that vividly depict the horrors of war when Bradleys are hit:

> A round from a U.S. tank came in at a low angle underneath Kidd's seat, ripped off his feet, tore out the bottom half of the turret and exploded out the rear end. "It just tore hell out of the Bradley," said Dienstag. "The whole back was burned to a crisp." . . .
>
> Dienstag became aware of a noise coming from below. "The guys in the back are screaming, 'Let us out! Let us out!'" said Dienstag. Up front, Skaggs, not seriously hurt but with hands numbed by the blast, was unable to work the controls to lower the ramp and open the rear compartment. Desperate, he jumped out of his driver's hatch onto the desert floor, grabbed a sledgehammer and started beating on the troop door until he forced it open.
>
> "We thought at first they were more scared than anything else, but when we opened up the door, this big puff of smoke came out the back, and you could smell the burning," said Dienstag. "These guys were just pouring out of the Bradley." . . .
>
> Sedgwick rushed back to check the Bradley that Crumby and the others were in. "I was hesitant about what I was going to see," he said. "I was not mentally prepared."
>
> What he found was devastation, the Bradley consumed by fire, horribly wounded soldiers on the ground. "Flames were coming out everywhere, and TOW missile rounds [inside the Bradley] were starting to pop," he said. . . .
>
> Crumby was critically wounded, Sedgwick knew. A case of ammunition had blown up into his head and back, and he had a huge piece of shrapnel in his skull. . . .
>
> With daylight approaching, Dienstag and Skaggs walked back to the Bradley in which their friends Crumby, Davila and Kramer

had been riding. "It was burned to the ground," said Dienstag. "All you could see was the barrel pointing up in the air."[1]

As we watched the fire that night at Aberdeen, Gary Holloway, the BRL test director, turned to me and said, "We have met our obligation to you—one destroyed Bradley." I agreed, and the Burton tests (the series of random shots that would continue until at least one Bradley was destroyed) were canceled on the spot.

I expected the whole test series of ten shots to stop also, but the Army decided to continue. The aim points for three of the remaining eight shots were altered to lessen the chances of destroying another Bradley. Even that precaution was not enough for some Army officials. They had more games in store.

For obvious reasons, I openly referred to this Bradley shot as the "Meltdown." Future shots would be even more dramatic. They were also labeled with equally descriptive terms. One Bradley shot was intended to come close to, but not hit, the stack of TOW antitank missiles stored on the right side of the troop compartment. The penetrating round miraculously passed between two warheads without touching either one. It was as if some unseen force had parted the warheads and allowed the round to pass through. Naturally, I dubbed this the "Red Sea Shot."

When the same shot was attempted against the M-113, which also had TOW missiles in the troop compartment, the unseen protective force was not present. That result became known as the "Houdini Shot." One instant, the M-113 was there; the next, it literally disappeared. When the smoke cleared, the test pad was empty, with nothing in sight. The next morning, I toured the area. The test pad looked like ground zero. Pieces of the M-113 were spread out over a radius of a kilometer in all directions. The engine was found a kilometer to the east, the rear door a kilometer to the west. This would have been the Bradley's fate had not some unseen force intervened on the earlier shot that resembled the parting of the Red Sea.

Following the meltdown, Holloway went into a huddle with his confidants in the Army and changed three of the remaining eight shots against the Bradley. Politically, the Army could not afford to lose another vehicle. The day the Bradley shots resumed, I called Holloway before leaving the Pentagon for Aberdeen, just to make sure the shot was on for the day. The moment Holloway answered the phone, I knew something was wrong. His voice was quivering and he sounded very nervous. He was about to tell me something that he did not want to. He knew how I would react, and he would be caught in the middle of a cross fire.

The test for the day had been canceled—not postponed but canceled—by the order of Richard Vitali, the BRL official who had tried so hard the previous summer to delay or avoid these tests. Vitali had ordered BRL to run three secret tests, using the same aim point, the night before. The Bradley had been loaded with inert ammunition. The penetrating round struck the dummy ammunition on one of the tests. Vitali, fearing that the same thing would happen with real ammo, unilaterally decided to cancel the actual test permanently. It was time to cancel Vitali.

I had no objections to calling off the test shot, provided a catastrophic event and all casualties were logged and counted in the final tabulations as if they had occurred. In fact, I recommended this as the best way to handle aim points selected on a random basis; however, Vitali was simply canceling the test because he alone was afraid of the outcome. He would not allow BRL to count it as if it had occurred. Vitali was still trying to protect the Bradley image, even though he did not work at BRL anymore. He had been promoted to a higher headquarters and had no business sticking his nose into the Bradley tests.

I was furious, as Holloway had feared. In as serious a tone as I could muster, I said, "Mr. Holloway, I want you to know that there is nothing personal in whatever happens next." These words had already gained a certain reputation at BRL, for I had used them in the past as a signal for serious trouble to come. I wanted the people at BRL to worry about what might happen—create a few demons in their minds.

I hung up and stormed into Dale Brudvig's office. "Go tell your Army friends that I am writing another one of my famous memos, and this one is going to be a barn burner."

Brudvig was horrified when he heard what Vitali had done. He made a beeline for Gen. Max Thurman's office.

I sat down at my desk and started writing the strongest memo I could about Vitali and his interference. Suddenly, an Army colonel appeared in my doorway. "The vice chief wants a copy of your memo."

"I haven't finished it yet. As soon as I finish writing it and get it typed, you can have a copy."

He responded, "You don't understand, the vice chief wants it now!"

So we made a copy of my incomplete scribbling and off the colonel went. A few minutes later, he reappeared. "General Thurman can't read your handwriting. What does this sentence say?" I read it to him and off he went again.

A couple of hours later, I saw Vitali in the halls. He was coming from the area of the senior Army leadership. His face was drawn, and he looked unhappy. We did not speak. No words were necessary.

Later, Brudvig told me that the Army vice chief waved my incomplete memo around in front of Vitali and his four-star boss, Gen. Richard H. Thompson, and said something along the lines of, "Do you guys enjoy reading these memos in *The Washington Post?*" He then figuratively beat them both badly about the head and shoulders for doing something very stupid. Vitali was then told to stay out of the Bradley test program for good. I believe he did, although I am not absolutely certain.

The canceled test was reinstated and nothing eventful happened. Vitali's concerns were not warranted.

While the full-up tests (with everything in the Bradley) were occurring on one test range at Aberdeen, another set of extremely important tests were taking place in parallel at another range, but with little fanfare. These tests became known as the off-line ammunition tests. A couple of Aberdeen engineers got their hands on an old beat-up shell of a Bradley and began shooting small-caliber, shaped-charge antitank warheads directly through the walls of the troop compartment into various amounts of ammunition inside. They began by shooting through the side armor directly into a single cannon shell mounted inside. They measured the violence of the reaction inside the troop compartment when the cannon shell was hit.

Step by step, the engineers increased the number of cannon shells inside to three, then six, then nine, and so on until they worked their way up to a full box of twenty-five shells. A Bradley carries more than forty of these boxes in the troop compartment. The violence of the explosions inside was unbelievable. We now had good documentation in living color on hours of videotape and reams of temperature and pressure measurements.

Armed with these data, the engineers then designed and built some ammunition storage compartments that would vent to the outside atmosphere if a penetrating round caused the stowed ammo to burn or explode. Here was a way to modify the Bradley so that the ammo in the troop compartment would not kill the troops when it exploded.

The concept of compartments vented to the outside atmosphere already had been proved, and they had been used in the Israeli Merkava tank, as well as in our own Army's M-1 tank. In the M-1, the extra ammo is stored in a compartment behind the turret. The crew simply opens a sliding door to get shells when they are needed. If the compartment is struck by an attacking round, the explosion goes outward to the atmosphere with no harm to the crew inside the tank. Why this concept had never been applied to the Bradley was completely beyond me. Incorporating it into the M-1 design and not into the Bradley design, in my view, was unconscionable. I would never get an answer as to why this happened.

I was now determined to test these compartments in a modified Bradley during the Phase II tests the following spring. The physical evidence was overwhelming and undeniable that the ammo stored inside the troop compartment was the single largest hazard to troops riding in the vehicle. Vented ammunition compartments obviously would save many lives. Unbelievably, the Army and the Bradley contractor would later fight bitterly to avoid testing the ammo compartments.

When the Phase I tests were completed in November, it was time to prepare the report on their results. The report was due to Congress on 1 December 1985. A whole new set of games and maneuvers designed to protect the Bradley program, its reputation, and, above all, the flow of money to the contractor began to emerge.

I must momentarily digress to fried chicken and computer models. At my insistence, the computer models were run before every test shot to determine their accuracy in predicting what would happen to the Bradley, as well as the M-113 and the Soviet BMP. The test shots always occurred late in the afternoon. If there was an explosion or a fire, the observers had to remain in the bunker, for obvious safety reasons, until all signs of the fire had disappeared. It would be foolhardy to come out of the bunker just as another missile exploded.

I learned on the very first shot that we could be in that bunker until all hours of the night. From then on, I stopped at the fried chicken carryout just outside the Aberdeen gate and bought a box of chicken when I thought the shot could result in a fire or explosion. Naturally, the Army noticed this pattern and began to keep track of how often I showed up at the test site with a box of chicken under my arm. Although no official records were published, my instincts for chicken turned out to be a more accurate prediction of what was going to happen than the computer models.

In chapter 8, I indicate that BRL had the reputation of seldom publishing reports of its work. When results were published, BRL usually presented only its interpretation of the data it had generated, rather than the actual data. Without a record of the raw data, no one could challenge BRL's interpretation. I was determined to correct this as we prepared to send a report to Congress.

From the outset, I insisted that the report contain a factual summary of every shot, including number of casualties and damage to the vehicle. With this information anyone could examine the data and make his or her own conclusions and inferences. After a short debate, the Army agreed to do this, but it was about the only thing it did agree to do.

In late November, BRL began drafting the Phase I report for Congress. Its first draft was reviewed and edited by various Army agencies as it traveled up the chain of command. By the time the draft reached the top, it gave the impression that the Bradley was invincible in combat. This was a classic case of pumping up the good news, while suppressing the bad news. The Army simply could not be trusted to report the results in a balanced fashion.

The battle now shifted from forcing the Army to perform the actual tests to getting it to report the results in an objective, straightforward manner free of program advocacy. Quickly realizing that this was a losing battle, I announced that I would write an independent report to make sure that checks and balances were brought to bear. I knew that this could lead to major controversies and perhaps again put the Army, the Bradley, and me in the public spotlight, but it had to be done. The draft test reports coming up through the Army were so slanted that I could not allow them to be the only views put on the table.

Before my announcement, I had discussed the matter with my immediate supervisor, Army Gen. Donald P. Jones. Jones agreed that I should write an independent report and, in fact, directed me to do so. He was concerned that the Army might not be able to get its act together in time to meet the 1 December deadline. I point this out because, six months later, General Jones would deny to the Inspector General that we had this conversation. Once my report was written, he would do everything in his power to hide its existence.

Following BRL's disastrous first attempt at a report, Walt Hollis, Secretary Ambrose's right-hand man, took charge of the Army's effort to write a report. He formed a formal "Red Team" of about a dozen Army officials who would be the final authority on the Army's report. BRL continued to do the writing, but only the Red Team could critique the product. Hollis invited me to be an official member of the Army's Red Team.[2] I accepted.

The Army's report was rewritten five times during the next several weeks. As the final product began to emerge, I could see clear lines of disagreement forming between the rest of the Red Team and me over how best to interpret the basic data. One of the reasons BRL had to rewrite the report five times was because important aspects were being left out. When the Red Team saw that I was covering a topic that had been omitted, it was to return again to the drawing boards.

BRL decided, for example, that it would not report any test results from the off-line ammunition tests that measured the violence of the reaction inside the Bradley when ammunition was intentionally hit. When this omission was coupled with the Army's downplaying of the controlled nature of the ten full-up shots, in which the aim points had been intentionally selected to avoid hitting ammunition, the overall impression was that the Bradley would seldom burn or blow up in combat. To counter this clearly misleading impression, I included the off-line ammunition test results in my report and made a special point of explaining how the ten full-up shots had been highly controlled to avoid catastrophic events. The Army then decided to include the off-line results in its report but still downplayed the controlled full-up shots.

There are two versions of the Bradley. More than 90 percent of the Bradleys produced are each configured to carry a six-man infantry squad plus a crew of three. This version is known as the Infantry Fighting Vehicle. The other version is the Cavalry Fighting Vehicle, and it performs the armored scout mission. It does not transport an infantry squad and carries a little more ammunition than the other type. Its only personnel consist of the five-man crew to operate the vehicle and to shoot the weapons.

The Army used the Cavalry Fighting Vehicle in the Bradley ten-shot live-fire tests. It argued that the cavalry version was more dangerous because it carried more ammunition. This argument was bogus. The ammunition was stowed differently in each version. In fact, the infantry vehicle actually presented a larger ammunition profile to an enemy gunner. To prove this, I included in my report front, side, and rear views of each vehicle, with outlines of the stowed ammunition. The infantry version of the Bradley had the largest ammunition-presented area of all vehicles in the test, including the Soviet vehicles.[3] Thus, in combat we could expect more casualties in the infantry version of the Bradley than in the cavalry version. In addition, because the ten test shots were aimed to avoid hitting ammo inside the vehicle, the Army's argument for using the cavalry vehicle did not make sense. The Army, however, obviously had a reason for using that version.

Both the M-113 and the Soviet BMP used in the tests carried an eleven-man infantry squad, more than twice as many people as the cavalry version of the Bradley. Each vehicle in the tests contained wooden mannequins dressed in battle fatigues to represent the troops who would be inside. After each test shot, the mannequins were checked for puncture wounds and burns to determine the number of casualties. Naturally, the raw test data showed about twice as many casualties in the M-113 and the Soviet BMP as in the Bradley. I viewed this as a clever and subtle attempt to mislead the casual reader (Congress and the secretary of defense) into thinking that the Bradley was safer than its predecessor or the enemy's vehicle. A quick glance at every table of data, chart, and graph in the Army report showed stark differences between the Bradley casualty results and those in the other two vehicles.[4]

To counter this misleading impression, I calculated the casualties that would have occurred for each shot had the Army been using the infantry version of the Bradley, with the infantry squad riding in back. My report had four columns of data, unlike the three columns in the Army's report. The fourth column was labeled as an extrapolation of the cavalry version results to the infantry version, so that the reader could get a more objective comparison of similar versions of the Bradley, M-113, and BMP. This forced the Army to include an innocuous statement, buried deep in its report, that the Bradley and BMP casualty results were "comparable" when the differences in the sizes of the crews were considered.[5]

This gives some indication of the kinds of games played by top-level military leadership when big bucks, big programs, and big reputations are at stake. It is a constant, never-ending struggle to get objective pros and cons, strengths and weaknesses on the table for an honest debate. The advocates never quit, and, sooner or later, the watchdogs get tired. I was not yet tired, but that day was coming.

Through the end of November and into the first two weeks of December, the Army and I worked hard to finish our reports. The Army rewrote its report five times, and I went through two drafts on mine. I critiqued the Army's report, and it critiqued mine. I also gave copies of my report to every OSD office that had even a remote interest in the Bradley and asked them to critique it. I accepted several suggestions from both Army and OSD reviewers. Probably one hundred copies of my report were floating around the Pentagon and the Army. I suspect the reader can guess what is coming.

Congress was growing impatient and began to ask for a report. Secretary Weinberger sent Congress a letter saying that the report would be a little late, but it would be there before December 20. Pressures were now beginning to mount. Empirical evidence of serious shortcomings in the Bradley was soon going to be quite visible. The intensity of the struggle between the Army and me to get all of the relevant information out on the table went up about six notches.

In my mind, the reason for conducting the live-fire tests was to reduce casualties in the Bradley should it ever see combat. The point of the tests was to find the primary sources of casualties, so that the vehicle could be modified to make it safer for the guys who rode inside. My report interpreted the test results primarily in terms of casualties. Its thrust and emphasis dealt with what happened to the people inside the vehicle after a hit. The damage to the vehicle itself was of secondary importance— people first, vehicle second.

The Army's report had a different perspective. Its thrust and emphasis were primarily on what happened to the vehicle, and the people inside came second. The report did not ignore casualties, but the Army's main concern clearly was whether the Bradley could still move and shoot after a hit. The Bradley did a little better than the BMP in this regard, so the Army seized on this factor.

From the same data base, we had two entirely different perspectives on which aspects of the tests were the most important. The Army and I agreed that the vast amount of ammunition stored in the troop compartment was the greatest hazard to the crew. Bradley casualties were two to three times higher when the ammunition was hit than when it was not hit. To me, that was the single most important result, and it should dictate how to modify the Bradley so that it would be a safer vehicle. We obviously needed to separate the troops from the ammunition and fuel in the troop compartment. Clearly, testing in Phase II should employ such concepts as external fuel tanks and ammunition compartments that exploded outward to the atmosphere when hit, thereby not harming the troops inside.

In its report, the Army downplayed the importance of the primary hazard of ammunition and fuel. It claimed that the Bradley's mobility and firepower on the battlefield would prevent the troops inside from being subjected to excessive danger.[6] Eighteen months later, the first real operational test of a Bradley on a battlefield would prove this claim to be false.[7]

I insisted that both the Army's report and mine contain all the pretest predictions of the computer models, so that the predictions could be compared with the actual results. The models were way off in one direction on some tests and way off in another direction on other tests. They completely failed to predict fires and explosions, but, most damaging of all, they simply could not deal with flash blindness, burns, lung collapse due to blast waves, and the terrible effects of noxious gases. Consequently, they could not predict casualties at all for these kinds of injuries. In my view, therefore, the models were worthless because my main concern was casualties.

Yet, the Army claimed that the models did fairly well. It arrived at this conclusion by cleverly averaging the gross errors. This is like holding one hand in scalding hot water, holding the other in ice water, and concluding that, on the average, the water temperature is very comfortable.

The Army report contained a lengthy section in which the models were used to evaluate possible modifications for testing during Phase II. My report stated, as the data in the appendices clearly showed, that "the models were no more accurate than a flip of a coin." The Army, however, used the models to justify modifications to the Bradley that dealt with secondary problems, rather than the primary problem of all that ammunition in the troop compartment. This situation was typical of how computer models are used to justify preconceived notions.

The final topic of major disagreement between the two reports, casualties resulting from toxic gases, fueled the fires of controversy and again catapulted me into the public eye. During the vaporifics tests, I had concluded that no one could stay inside the Bradley and survive the milky white gases that resulted from the vaporifics fireball. We now had two additional sources of noxious gases to consider.

The Bradley's automatic halon fire extinguisher is quite effective at putting out fuel fires, but it has no effect on ammunition fires because ammunition contains its own sources of oxygen in the propellants. Although halon is a nonlethal toxic gas, it can cause irregular heartbeats and leave people who breathe it confused and disoriented.[8] One medical report said, "It has the same effect as two stiff drinks on an empty stomach."

Halon puts out fires through displacement of oxygen, as well as the chemical reaction of halon to fire. I found old test reports where the toxic gas by-products of halon reacting with a fire caused deaths in animals who breathed these gases for only a few minutes.[9]

In addition, burning ammunition produces toxic gases that can be fatal. All of these considerations led me to state in my report that the atmosphere inside the Bradley after a hit was intolerable. In my view, the surviving troops would be driven out, gas masks or no gas masks.

The Army disagreed strongly, but it had no data to refute what I was saying. In an attempt to counter my claims, Lt. Gen. Louis C. Wagner, head of Army research and development, sent a memorandum to the Army Surgeon General. Wagner pleaded, "We need your help. Initially it would be very helpful for you to restate your previous findings in a strong, hard hitting report refuting the potential toxic effects of vaporifics and Halon in the Bradley."[10]

Wagner wanted a report that said the terrible gases in the Bradley were not really so bad. Wagner's memo became known around the Pentagon (and in the press) as the "Auschwitz Memo." An eventual leak of the memo to the press caused the Army all kinds of problems.[11] The Surgeon General could not refute what I was saying, so the Army agreed to a comprehensive series of toxic gas measurement tests in conjunction with Phase II of the Bradley testing in the spring. Those tests would prove my claims absolutely correct.

By the second week of December 1985, the Army's report and my report were finished and ready to be submitted to Congress. We had our differences, and the two reports clearly indicated them. If my interpretation of the test results was correct, the Bradley program could be in serious trouble. The situation was extremely tense. Billions of dollars and possibly thousands of lives were at stake, not to mention a few careers.

Both reports were given to Charlie Watt, who was at the next level above my immediate supervisor, General Jones. Watt still had the word *acting* in front of his title. After 18 months in the job, he had not acquired enough political support in the Pentagon to be designated permanent director of development testing. Above Watt was Under Secretary of Defense Dr. Donald Hicks, a former Northrop executive.

Watt decided that the Army's report would be forwarded to Secretary Weinberger to be transmitted to Congress as the official Department of Defense report. My report went into the files. The Army's report would be delivered to Congress the next morning, 17 December.

On the evening of 16 December, Watt called me at home. He said that Hicks wanted to see me in his office at 0730 the next morning. Apparently, trouble loomed.

Watt accompanied me on my visit to Hicks's office. Hicks was very upset. He had received a call the previous day from Congressman Denny Smith, who had asked for a copy of my independent report. Hicks accused me of going around him and setting up the call from Congressman Smith in order to get my report to Capitol Hill.

I denied this accusation. I had not talked to Smith or any of his staff. Hicks then wanted to know how Smith knew about my report. I informed him that the whole world knew about my report. The Army and the OSD staff had at least a hundred copies, for everyone had critiqued it for me twice. In addition, Beverly Breen of the General Accounting Office (GAO) had been in my office almost every day to ask for a copy. Congress had charged the GAO to investigate the Bradley live-fire tests. General Jones and I had informed Breen that a copy of my report would be available to the GAO when it was finished. If the GAO knew about my report, then the Congress knew. (The GAO is the investigative arm of the Congress.) I had followed the rules to the letter in dealing with the GAO, and General Jones always had been present when I met with its representatives.

The widespread knowledge of my report surprised Dr. Hicks. Still upset, he told me that I was not to write any independent reports about anything. From now on, all I could do was to watch tests, not write about them. As I was leaving the room, he had one last comment, "If I get any more calls from Congress about you, you're fired."

This angered me. I turned around and went back into his office. We had a heated discussion, nose to nose. I resented the charge that I had intentionally gone outside the system. I was living in a fishbowl, and there was nothing I could do about it. The Congress, the GAO, the press, the senior officials in the Army and OSD, and everyone involved in the defense business had been watching the Bradley controversy between the Army and me through a microscope. The controversy was now so large and messy that I could not prevent people from tracking me if I wanted to. Our shouting match was interrupted by Hicks's secretary. He and I glared at each other in anger as he left for another appointment.

Everyone in my office was waiting to hear why Hicks had called me in. I repeated everything that Hicks had said, including the directive that we were not to write any more reports on test results because they caused too much trouble. I also told everyone about the threat of being fired.[12] People just shook their heads in disbelief.

Word of my confrontation with Hicks spread like wildfire throughout the Pentagon. Everyone I ran into in the halls wanted to hear about it. The news also spread to Capitol Hill.

At mid-morning, Watt came into my office and told me to grab my coat. We were going for a ride. As we climbed into a staff car, he told me we were headed for Capitol Hill. A subcommittee of the House Armed Services Committee wanted to meet with me. I was stunned.

The Army report had just been delivered to Congress that morning. Congressman Samuel S. "Sam" Stratton's Procurement and Military Nuclear Systems Subcommittee (hereafter referred to as Procurement Subcommittee) wanted to question me about the report and the test results. This was not a hearing, just a meeting. At least, that is what Watt said. As we walked into a hearing room, it looked like a formal hearing to me. The committee members, sitting up in their high perches, were grilling the Army's General Wagner, who was sitting at the witness table. I was plopped down next to General Wagner.

The congressmen were angry with the Army, in general, and General Wagner, in particular. Wagner had held a press conference on 11 December, six days before the Army's report had been delivered to Congress, and had revealed some of the test results to the press. On top of that, he had given videotape copies of some of the test shots to the media. The tapes had been on the *Today Show* before Congress had a chance to see any data. Of course, the information that Wagner had given the press and the *Today Show* was highly selective and supported the Army's claim that the Bradley came through the tests basically unscathed. It was the typical "everything is beautiful" public relations pitch.

I sat down next to General Wagner. The committee members were furiously questioning him about his 11 December press release. When they recognized me, they dropped the subject and began to ask me questions about the Army's report. Before I could answer, Anthony "Tony" Battista, a staff member of the House Armed Services Committee, came storming into the room. He waved a document in the air and proclaimed, "I've got the real report."

He was holding a copy of my report. To this day, I have no idea how he obtained it. Battista, the most powerful defense staffer on the Hill, had connections at every level inside the Pentagon. Apparently, just before I had arrived, Congressman Stratton had asked Wagner about my independent report. Wagner had responded, "No, no, never heard of it. There's only one report, the Army's and you've got it, sir."[13]

All hell broke loose. Battista immediately started reading my report to the committee. As he read, he emphasized its differences with the Army report.

Battista then turned to me and asked, "Colonel Burton, did you have a meeting this morning with Dr. Hicks?"

My heart jumped into my throat. I responded, "Yes."

"Did Dr. Hicks threaten you about talking to Congress?"

"I prefer not to answer that question."

I saw nothing to be gained by airing our dirty laundry in public. Hicks's threats to me were no big deal in my mind. This sort of thing happened all the time in the Pentagon.

Battista put his hand over the microphone and huddled privately with the committee members. They honored my request to drop the subject, but I was still unnerved. As the meeting continued and questions were fired at me, I did not do a good job of answering. Because I was not mentally or emotionally prepared for this situation, I felt like I was having an out-of-body experience and everything around me was a dream. I was not in control of my faculties and simply could not think straight.

This fog continued as Watt and I went to see Congressmen Denny Smith and Mel Levine after the committee meeting. They too wanted to know about the threat, but I refused to talk about it. Once again, I did a terrible job of explaining the differences between my report and the Army's report.

I was not happy with my performance that day. Also, I was not happy with Congress. The committee members had expected me to rant and rave and create a lot of controversy over the fact that my report had not been forwarded to them. I had not done that. Rather, I had tried to point out that the Army's report contained enough basic raw data for them to make a reasoned judgment on the Bradley. They did not want to dig out the data in the appendices; they wanted me to, but I was not prepared to do it on the spot.

Boyd called me that night and started giving me a hard time about my morning on Capitol Hill—I should have done this, or I should have said that. I was physically and mentally exhausted, and I became very upset with him. For the first time in the eleven years that I had known Boyd, I hung up on him. I drank myself to sleep that night, something that was beginning to happen all too frequently, and it was beginning to worry my wife Nancy. An occasional glass of wine with dinner was too often turning into a bottle.

Congress now knew for certain that I had written a report, and the press would also soon know about it. The very next day, the "Hammer of God" came down hard on the Army. The lead editorial of *The New York Times*, titled "Another Test of Truth for the Army," referred to the unflattering test results that were leaking out.[14] I was again mentioned by name in the *Times* editorial.

A few days later, on the morning of 20 December, Fred Hiatt of *The Washington Post* submitted a press inquiry to Dr. Hicks. Was it true that Colonel Burton had written an independent report? Had Dr. Hicks threatened to fire Colonel Burton for spreading his report around town? Was Colonel Burton being forced to agree with the Army report? Was Colonel Burton being transferred to Alaska again?[15]

I helped the OSD public affairs official, Jan Bodanyi, to prepare a response to the *Post*. It confirmed that I had written an independent report and finessed the question about the threat. Again, I saw no reason to go into that subject and air the Pentagon's dirty linen in public. The public would not understand that this type of threat happened all the time in the Pentagon.

Unbelievably, the written response actually given to the *Post* that afternoon (prepared by Dr. Hicks's military assistant, Army Col. Ken Hollander, after a telephone consultation with Dr. Hicks, who was out of town) denied that I had written an independent report and also denied the threat. Three statements included in the response were: (1) "Colonel Burton had merely prepared a rough draft of his observations"; (2) "Dr. Hicks did not threaten Colonel Burton on this topic"; and (3) "Colonel Burton was not going to Alaska."[16]

A little more than a year later—15 February 1987—after Dr. Hicks had left government service and started his own defense consulting firm, he admitted on camera in an interview with CBS's *60 Minutes* that, in fact, he may have issued the threat:

> Morley Safer: "Did you say to him [Burton] that 'If I get one more call from the Hill about your report, I'll have your ass'?"
> Hicks: "I, uh, was very unhappy and that might have been what I said."

The same day as Hiatt's inquiry, 20 December 1985, Fred Kaplan of the *Boston Globe* ran a lengthy story about my report. Kaplan quoted Army spokesmen and OSD officials as saying that my report did not exist. He then printed various excerpts from my nonexistent report and pointed out the differences between it and the official party line coming from the Army.[17]

On 26 December, *The Washington Post* ran a similar story that made the front page of the Yellow Bird.[18] Fred Hiatt had finally gotten his hands on a copy of the report that Dr. Hicks had told him did not exist.

A few days later, Tim Carrington of *The Wall Street Journal* blasted the Pentagon for covering up the existence of my report.[19] He quoted Army officials, who still contended that my report did not exist. According to Carrington, an Army official said, "There is no second report. There never was a second report . . . only early notes Colonel Burton wrote on the tests months ago."

Carrington then quoted not only from my report but also from its cover letter that stated, "I began this effort when it appeared that the Army's report was going to be incomplete and unacceptable." In addition, Carrington reported that Congressman Sam Stratton was now demanding a copy of my report from the Pentagon. Carrington expressed doubt that Stratton would ever get a copy.

By now, the Pentagon was besieged by Congress for copies of my report, but the party line continued: "There is no Burton report." At Secretary Weinberger's staff meeting, Hicks maintained that I had not written one. Therefore, Weinberger responded to Congress with the same denial. Again, Weinberger was a prisoner of the Pentagon.

Director of Operational Testing John E. "Jack" Krings was now on board as Weinberger's chief tester. He held the position created by Congress in 1983. (This was the position for which I had been twice nominated by the Military Reform Caucus.) Krings attended Weinberger's staff meeting daily because of the reform legislation that had created his job.

Krings knew that Hicks was misleading Weinberger because Krings had copies of my "nonexistent" report. He asked for a private meeting with Weinberger, whereupon he gave the secretary a copy of the "nonexistent Burton report." Krings told me immediately after their meeting that Weinberger's reaction was, "It sure looks like a report to me. It is even thicker than the Army's." Weinberger then proceeded to read my report from cover to cover.

Weinberger was very angry that Hicks had misled him. He instructed Hicks personally to carry an official copy of my report to Capitol Hill and present it to Congressman Stratton of the Procurement Subcommittee. Hicks made the trip to the Hill and took Charlie Watt with him. I was not invited to go.

Before the report was given to Congressman Stratton, my superiors altered the first page. Without my knowledge or agreement, the beginning of the report was changed to eliminate all reference to the fact that it had been prepared as a formal report for the secretary of defense to send to Congress. Words were inserted to support the official party line that I had merely prepared "a rough draft of my observations" for my superiors to use as a guide to assess the validity of the Army report. One of the secretaries who made the alterations felt that I should know what had happened, so she let me see a copy of the altered report after it had gone to Capitol Hill.

On 10 January 1986, Fred Kaplan reported in the *Boston Globe* that Hicks gave a copy of my report to Congressman Stratton.[20] (As chairman of the powerful Procurement Subcommittee, Stratton was well known as a friend to the Army, in general, and to the Bradley, in particular. His subcommittee controlled Bradley production funds.) Kaplan also reported that both Stratton and the Pentagon had refused to give copies of my report to the General Accounting Office, despite its repeated requests. More fuel was thrown on the fire.

I was visiting my sister in North Carolina for the holidays when Peter Jennings reported the controversy of my nonexistent report on the ABC evening news. As we watched Dennis Troute read from a copy of the nonexistent report, I told my family, "Here we go again."[21]

All of this controversy naturally led to congressional hearings. The Research and Development Subcommittee of the House Armed Services Committee scheduled a hearing for 28 January 1986. The subcommittee specifically requested that I appear as the official OSD witness. Gen. Max Thurman, the Army vice chief of staff, was scheduled to represent the Army. Of course, he would take legions of generals and colonels with him, but none of my superiors wanted to go with me. They did not want to be anywhere near the hearing. I was instructed to go alone to defend myself and my views against the Army. That was fine with me. Why should we change things now?

Pierre helped me to get my thoughts together and lay out a prepared statement. The formal statement would be cleared by Security Review, Department of Defense, for release to the public at the beginning of the hearing. It would constitute my opening remarks to the subcommittee in an open hearing attended by the public and the press.

A few days before the hearing, Dr. Hicks asked me to come to his office to discuss my testimony with him and Watt. This was my first meeting with Hicks since our shouting match in December. I was in no mood for a similar experience.

Hicks held up a copy of my proposed statement and said, "I don't like your statement and I want you to change it."

I responded, "I'll be happy to correct any mistakes I have made. If I have said something that is wrong, I'll change it."

"Oh, everything you have said is correct, but I don't like the tone. I don't like your adjectives, change them."

I refused, whereupon he threw his hands up in the air in disgust and dismissed me. We have never met since then.

At 1700 on 27 January, the Army struck again. As I was preparing to go home, the OSD public affairs office informed me of the Army's decision that all of my comments about the Bradley were classified and I could not say them in an open hearing.[22] I was stunned. I knew this was not true because I had been careful to use only unclassified documents as the source for every statement in my testimony. In addition, all of my unclassified sources were Army documents. (Typical of my comments in the prepared statement that the Army claimed were classified was the innocuous sentence on page 4: "Bradley casualties can be significantly reduced." Of course, they can, but the Army did not want me to say this in public.)

General Jones then came into my office and told me that a group of Army generals wanted me to come down to the Army Staff and negotiate with them on what I would be allowed to say at the hearing. I was tired and my patience had run out. "I'm sick and tired of talking to f___ing Army generals. I'm going home."

Jones stepped back about three steps, startled, and said, "Well, what are you going to do tomorrow? What are you going to say at the hearing?"

With total disgust in my voice, I said, "I don't know what I'm going to do tomorrow. I may not even go to the hearing. I may just call up Congress and tell them I'm not coming—I just don't know and I'm too tired to think about it." I left and went home.

I had a late dinner with Nancy, drank too much wine, discussed the day's events with Boyd on the telephone, and, exhausted, finally collapsed into bed. Nancy was beginning to worry about my physical health.

The next morning, I telephoned Army Lt. Col. Raymond "Ray" Kaufman, my Army Staff contact, and told him what I planned to do at the hearing that afternoon.

"Tell your vice chief of staff that if you guys don't reverse your decision about classifying my prepared statement, I intend to stand up in front of the Committee at 1 P.M. and say, 'My testimony today has been censored by the United States Army. I have been forbidden to say what needs to be said in a public hearing. I am prepared to prove that my testimony is unclassified. I am also prepared to prove that certain Army generals who are present in the room have themselves revealed classified information to the press in recent days because it suited their purpose to support the Bradley.' I will then sit down. That will be my testimony today in front of the TV cameras.'"

I could hear Kaufman sucking in wind on the other end of the line. "I'll get back with you," he said.

About an hour before the hearing started, my original prepared statement was formally cleared for public release with no changes and no restrictions.[23] At 1300, I walked into a congressional hearing room packed with the public, the press, television cameras, and congressmen. I was scared to death.

11

Going Public

I clearly recall the tragic day of 28 January 1986. At mid-morning, as I was preparing opening remarks for my announcement of the Army's censorship of my testimony to take place that afternoon, I received word of the space shuttle accident. The thought of the astronauts trapped in the Challenger made my own problems seem insignificant. It also reinforced in my mind how precious human life is. I was about to raise concerns publicly, for the first time, about the lives of many young people who would ride in another vehicle—the Bradley.

The shuttle tragedy dominated the Washington press that day, but the press still gave considerable coverage to the Bradley hearing, in fact, more than the Army wanted. The hearing was the opening round of a serious two-year debate by Congress on the fate of the Bradley Fighting Vehicle. It was exactly the kind of debate the Army had hoped to avoid.

Because the Research and Development Subcommittee did not have jurisdiction over the

Bradley, the hearing was advertised as a hearing on testing, in general, and my Joint Live-Fire Test Program, in particular. Chairman Melvin Price went to great lengths in his opening remarks to announce that the Bradley was being used only as an example for the purposes of discussion on how so many weapons got through the system without adequate testing. In his words, "I would like to emphasize that this is not a hearing to evaluate the Bradley test results or decide the fate of this vehicle."[1] But, of course, it was, and everyone knew it.

Price's Research and Development Subcommittee was very critical of the Bradley. The use of my live-fire test program as the topic for the hearing gave it the opportunity to get at the Bradley. Congressman Stratton's Procurement Subcommittee had jurisdiction over the Bradley, and it was far more friendly toward the Army. The many defense contracts in Stratton's district strengthened the bonds of friendship.

The House Armed Services Committee's chief staffer, Tony Battista, testified as a witness to open the hearing.[2] He presented a long list of questionable programs that had skated through the acquisition process with inadequate testing. The Maverick missile was again used as one of these horrible examples. After a reasonable treatment of other systems, Battista finally got to the Bradley.

Battista traced the history of the Bradley and how its mission changed so many times over its seventeen-year development. He raised the fundamental issues of what the Bradley was supposed to do and how it would be used in combat. How could it be used in conjunction with our M-1 tanks to fight enemy armor forces when it was so vulnerable to antitank weapons of any caliber? This key question was now squarely on the table. The Army would stumble and fumble as it tried to answer.

In the middle of Battista's testimony, Congressman Stratton came into the room and objected to the hearing. Interrupting Battista, he attacked him for his criticism of the Bradley. He claimed that Battista's arguments had no place in this hearing because Stratton's Procurement Subcommittee had jurisdiction over the Bradley and planned its own hearing the following month.

Battista and Stratton got into a heated argument, the kind of thing the press loves. Flashbulbs were popping all over the place. (The press really played up this confrontation. The story in the 23 February issue of *Defense News*, "Stratton Storms In-and-Out over Turf Fight over Bradley," was typical, and it was complete with pictures.) Stratton stormed out of the hearing in the middle of one of Battista's responses to him. I knew that I was going to appear before Stratton at his hearing. It was clear that the environment would be considerably more hostile as a result of Stratton's and Battista's exchanges.

I followed Battista. This time I was prepared mentally and emotionally to face a congressional committee. I explained the entire Joint Live-Fire Test Program, of which the Bradley tests were only a portion. Of course, that was the part that everyone wanted to hear.

My comments on the Bradley tests were short and to the point. The purpose of the tests was to reduce combat casualties in our equipment. I presented the following briefing chart that dealt strictly with the casualty implications of the test results:

> Ammunition in the troop compartment is the major cause of unnecessary casualties:
> —When ammo is hit, Bradley casualties increase by factors of 2 to 3; same for BMP (Soviet Counterpart to Bradley) and M-113.
> Fuel + fire extinguishers in the troop compartment may force troops out of the vehicle almost every time it is hit.
> —The atmosphere inside after a hit is simply intolerable. Bradley casualties can be significantly reduced. Moving ammo, fuel and extinguishers out of troop compartment would provide the greatest combat casualty reductions.
> When ammunition was hit, Bradley casualties were about the same as BMP casualties: the Bradley's ammunition presents about three times as much area to a hit as does the BMP's ammunition. We can therefore expect greater Bradley casualties in combat."[3]

It was on the table—the most important Bradley results and their implications. The microphone would soon pass to the Army. Before that, however, I had to relate an instruction from my superiors. My explanation raised several eyebrows. The final topic in my opening remarks dealt with lessons that had been learned about how to conduct live-fire tests. I pointed out the need for independent on-site observations of the tests, complete access to all data, and finally: "Independent assessments on results in parallel with Service assessment are crucial." In other words, independent reports are necessary to keep the system honest. My superiors had instructed me to explain to the subcommittee that this final point was my own personal opinion and did not reflect their views.[4] They did not believe in independent reports, as their actions over the previous months had clearly demonstrated. The subcommittee found this revelation quite disturbing. A lengthy discussion and a new line of questioning followed. The disclaimer that had been forced on me presented rather sinister implications of senior Pentagon managers opposed to independent views on test results because those views might expose dirty games.

An entirely new subject was now on the table. In my view, this subject needed public airing. The philosophy of intolerance with differing points of view historically dominated Pentagon politics and had particularly marked Dr. Hicks's administration.

(In an interview with *The New York Times* shortly after the hearing, Dr. Hicks openly criticized the fact that my report had caused so much attention on Capitol Hill. He stated: "Call it something else, but it's really anarchy."[5]

This interview was followed by another one with *Science Magazine*, in which Hicks freely admitted that he would award research funds only to scientists who publicly supported the Pentagon's programs. He had made that proclamation during his Senate confirmation hearings, "I am not particularly interested in seeing department money going to someplace where an individual is outspoken of department aims, even for basic research." *Science Magazine* asked him if he really meant that only those who agreed with the Pentagon should receive its funds. "Absolutely," was his response. "Freedom works both ways. They're free to keep their mouths shut . . . [and] I'm also free to not give the money." He added, "I have a tough time with disloyalty."[6]

This kind of philosophy represented an attitude that I abhor. In my view, the notion that there can be only one interpretation or one perspective of an extremely complex issue is very dangerous. Yet, it was the policy of the Pentagon leadership. If Congress permitted this policy to continue, then, as far as I was concerned, it too was part of the problem.)

When I finished my testimony, Army Vice Chief of Staff General Thurman stepped forward. General Thurman was an astute and clever man. He quickly detected an undercurrent of support for me by the majority of the subcommittee. During his testimony, Thurman went out of his way to be respectful and courteous toward me. He did not challenge my testimony, and he admitted that the test results showed the Bradley to be very vulnerable.

Thurman tried to convince the subcommittee that the doctrine and tactics the Army had developed for the Bradley would prevent it from being ravaged on the battlefield. His strategy was to accept the fact that it is vulnerable but, at the same time, to persuade Congress that the Army could use the Bradley on the battlefield in such a way that its vulnerability would not show. To do this, Thurman needed a little help. The following is an excerpt from his testimony:

> I am the Vice Chief of Staff, U.S. Army, and I brought a couple of experts along with me. One is on my right, Lt. Gen. Louis Wagner, the Deputy Chief of Staff for Research, Development,

and Acquisition and a frequent visitor to your committee, and a
Distinguished Service Cross holder, I might add. On my left is
Major General Burba, whose father, as indicated by General
Hollingsworth, was also a distinguished general officer. General
Burba now commands the Infantry Center at Fort Benning, Ga.

On my right, on your left, is Brig. General Ed Leland, who
commands the National Training Center, which is the fulcrum of
simulated combat, or as close as we can get, located at Ft. Irwin in
the California desert.

On my left, your right, is a distinguished young officer who
has just come back from 2 years overseas in Germany. He is Col.
Bob Foley, a Medal of Honor winner, who has commanded both
a battalion of M-113's and a brigade of M-1 tanks and Bradley
Fighting Vehicles.

Not at the table, but available for the committee are three distinguished soldiers sitting to my rear, Captain Derouchey, who
commands a company of Bradleys now; Sergeant First Class
Herrmann, who is a platoon sergeant and master gunner for that
unit; and a Private First Class White, who is the driver of the
Bradley.[7]

Seated behind all those distinguished witnesses was a sea of Army
green uniforms—more experts, staff officers, and aides, who nodded in
unison every time General Thurman spoke.

General Thurman presented the Army's interpretation of the test
results. On a screen, he flashed a briefing chart listing the most important results from the Army's perspective (I have added a few of my own
comments in brackets):

WHAT WE HAVE LEARNED

—Automatic fire suppression system effective in extinguishing
fuel fires [The Army forgot to say that two out of three times it
discharged, there was no fire.]
—Little effect on vehicle or crew due to overpressure and temperature (vaporific effect) [Overpressures were high enough
to rupture eardrums. The Army did not consider eardrum rupture a casualty, but I did.]
—Prevention of penetration and spall will reduce vehicle damage and casualties [Spall fragments are metal slivers of the
vehicle's own armor, slivers that ricochet around inside the
vehicle. This was the first sales pitch for a new high-tech armor
concept, one that future events would show could not prevent
major penetrations.]

—Spall has minimal effect on ammunition due to ammunition packaging [Impacts from small, low-speed fragments did not set off ammo; large, high-speed fragment impacts did.]
—Secondary fires unlikely
—Survivability can be improved [The Army said this, while it was attempting to prevent me from saying, "Bradley casualties could be significantly reduced," because it claimed that my comment was classified.][8]

Even though the Army report previously given to Congress contained the statement: "Direct hits by the primary penetrator on explosive or propellant sections of on-board ammunition pose the most significant hazard to the crew," the Army apparently felt that it was not important enough to share with the subcommittee.[9] The statement was absent from Thurman's "Lessons Learned" remarks. Instead, the Army chose to dwell on secondary and tertiary findings, several of which were totally misleading.

For example, the fire extinguisher did a very good job in putting out fuel fires, as the Army stated, but it had a high false alarm rate. For every time it discharged when it was supposed to, it discharged twice when it was not supposed to, thereby driving the crew out of the vehicle. Of course, the Army did not mention the toxic gas situation that resulted from all those discharges or the more serious toxic gas by-products of the halon reacting with a fire. (A halon–fire reaction produces hydrogen fluoride gases, which cause serious injury to the respiratory tract and sometimes possible death.)

The two briefing charts shown above demonstrate the differences between the Army's perspective and mine. I point out the most important test results and their implications of high, unnecessary casualties caused by all that ammunition stored in the troop compartment. The Army's chart tends to ignore this aspect of the test results.

For several hours, the Army tried to explain to the subcommittee how it would use the Bradley in combat to lessen the chances of troop casualties, but the explanations did not make sense. The subcommittee members became exasperated. Congressman Charles Bennett asked, in the simplest terms, whether the Bradley in combat would be in front of our own tanks, beside them, or behind them. The Army could not answer even that question in a straightforward, understandable fashion. Finally, the subcommittee asked the Army to take its time in preparing a written answer and insert it in the record at a later date. The two-page description of the Bradley battlefield doctrine submitted by Maj. Gen. Edwin H. Burba, Jr., did nothing to cut through the confusion.

The hearing exposed the physical vulnerabilities of the Bradley and the dangers posed to the troops inside. Even more revealing was the fact that the Army did not completely understand how it would use the Bradley in combat to mitigate those vulnerabilities and to keep down casualties. Every attempt to explain the doctrine, tactics, or maneuvers led to more questions, confusion, and skepticism for people both inside and outside the government.

The Army's worst fears were beginning to assume tangible form. The dust had barely started to settle from the DIVAD escapade. Weinberger's cancellation of DIVAD, after tests showed that it did not work, was still sending shock waves through the Army. The public debate over the Bradley was exhibiting DIVAD symptoms. Two major program cancellations would destroy the Army leadership.

On 4 February 1986 in a lead editorial titled "The Folly of Untested Weapons," *The New York Times* again chastised the Army for not testing its weapons properly and thereby endangering the people who use the equipment: "But even though the Army agreed to test its Bradley Fighting Vehicle, it does not seem reconciled to the verdict."[10] The *Times* called on the Army to accept my recommendation to remove the fuel and ammunition from the Bradley troop compartment.

The New York Times was not alone. The same theme appeared throughout the press after the hearing. The Yellow Bird was saturated with stories. Storm clouds were threatening, and the Bradley program could be in serious trouble.

The Army was now compelled to take action to quell the growing concern over the safety of the troops in the Bradley. In early February, Army Chief of Staff Gen. John Wickham announced to Congress and the press that the Army would beef up the Bradley's armor.[11] It would be thicker in some areas; in others, the Army planned to add a new "explosive" armor concept recently developed by BRL. The announcement was crafted to give the impression that the new armor would solve the Bradley's problems and that the troops inside would be safe in combat.

The new armor concept was highly classified at the time, but the Army apparently felt that the growing public concern over the safety of the troops justified a public announcement. Clearly, the Army was getting desperate. This was another example of how information can be classified or declassified at will to suit political needs, rather than to protect national security.

The new armor was called reactive armor. Two steel plates, separated by a layer of an explosive, would be placed inside a metal box about 1 cubic foot in size. Rows of these boxes would be attached at various places on the outside of the Bradley hull. An attacking round would set off the explosive. The explosion would cause the two steel plates to fly in opposite directions, thereby disturbing the attacking round and preventing it from penetrating the hull behind the box, or so the theory went.

The explosion would create a considerable reaction force against the side of the hull, thus the name *reactive* armor. Israel had successfully used this concept on its tanks in the 1982 war. A thick tank hull can withstand such strong reaction forces, but the aluminum Bradley hull is relatively thin and unable to resist these forces.

The larger the attacking round is, the more explosive that is needed to stop the penetration, but this means higher reaction forces. There is a delicate balance between getting enough explosive to prevent an attacking round from penetrating a hull and getting too much explosive, which would cause the hull to cave in on the troops inside.

The Army gave Congress and the public the impression that the balance factor had been worked out and the Bradley troops would be safe. I knew better. The Bradley's hull would withstand reactive forces associated with stopping only small-caliber antitank rounds. BRL's armor would not work against medium- or large-caliber antitank rounds. Antitank missiles or any tank-fired rounds would pass through the BRL reactive armor as if it were not there. We were still left with the same problems: people, fuel, and ammunition all stored together in the troop compartment. Again, the Army and I were engaged in the never-ending battle to keep truth on the table so that people in positions of authority could make decisions based on complete information.

One year later, in the spring of 1987, the first real operational test of Bradleys and M-1 tanks engaged against an opposing force of tanks and BMPs took place. Only 6 percent of the engagements involved small-caliber rounds, the only type for which the new BRL armor offered protection. During those engagements, the Bradley troops were not in the vehicle; they had dismounted. This meant that BRL was developing a new armor that protected an empty vehicle in only 6 percent of its battlefield engagements—hardly the ultimate solution. The same tests showed that when the medium- and large-caliber rounds were fired at a Bradley, with the troops still inside, extremely high casualties resulted. Laser beams were fired instead of real cannon shells and missiles. These results were exactly the opposite of what the Army expected. They strengthened my argument to do something to separate the troops from the fuel and ammunition in the troop compartment because that was the only way to mitigate the effects of medium- and large-caliber rounds.[12] (These test results were remarkably similar to what happened in the Gulf War when the Bradley came under enemy fire.) The day the Army revealed its new armor concept to the public, I met with Gary Holloway at BRL to discuss the plans for Phase II tests scheduled to start in March. The purpose of Phase II was to test various design modifications in order to determine those most effective in reducing casualties. Simply stated, the idea behind the tests was twofold: determine the major sources of casualties (Phase I) and the best solutions for reducing casualties (Phase II). After my meeting with Holloway, however, I was extremely concerned that BRL was structuring the Phase II tests only to make its reactive armor look good.

The aim points, angles, and size of the attacking weapons selected by Holloway all favored a successful test series for the new armor. The armor was extremely sensitive to the angle at which an attacking round struck. Some angles gave optimum armor performance; other angles caused the armor to be totally ineffective, even against small-caliber rounds.

Holloway had planned no tests of any modifications that separated the fuel and ammunition from the troops in the back. BRL wanted no competition to interfere with its testing of the new reactive armor. To me, this was wrong. We had an obligation to the troops in the field to examine every reasonable solution that might save lives in combat. To ignore the most obvious solution indicated to me that the Army had a callous disregard for the lives of the troops. I became very vocal on this point.

BRL had developed the new armor and was naturally anxious to prove to its Army superiors that the new technology would solve everything. Such proof would enhance BRL's image within the Army and preserve its share of the Army's budget.

I strongly believed that having BRL in charge of tests to prove or disprove the validity of its own technical claims was also wrong. This arrangement represented a conflict of interest. In essence, BRL was now in a position to grade its own report card, and we could expect an A+. The stage was now set for the final and most controversial fight between the Army and me. The controversies, confrontations, disagreements, and sordid maneuvers of the Army's past performances would pale in comparison with the events about to unfold.

Upon returning to Washington, I wrote another memorandum for the record documenting my concerns about the direction that the Phase II tests were taking.[13] Within minutes after the memo was completed, the Army had its twenty-one copies. The memo must have struck a nerve. The next day, on 11 February, Army Deputy Under Secretary Walt Hollis responded with a letter to my boss, General Jones. Hollis declared that the senior Army leadership would not approve the test plan (the one I objected to) prepared by Holloway. He further committed the Army to include in the Phase II tests a Bradley configured with fuel and ammunition removed from the troop compartment, as I had asked.[14] We had another hearing coming up in a few days, so I guess the Army preferred to avoid a confrontation on this matter in front of Congress.

The following day, Hollis sent Col. William "Bill" Coomer, the Bradley program manager, and Holloway to see me for details on the modifications that I wanted tested. Coomer and Holloway were not happy troopers. Coomer had been a strong advocate of reactive armor before he became the Bradley program manager. With the Bradley, he saw the opportunity to push the new armor into the inventory, and he did not want any competition.

I explained the modifications and gave Coomer and Holloway a typed list of the features I wanted incorporated on at least one Bradley prototype.[15] Pierre Sprey and I had spent a lot of time in laying out this design with features that, to the best of our knowledge, would reduce casualties. I called this configuration the "Minimum Casualty Baseline Vehicle." Naturally, the Army gave it another name that was a little more colorful. Every Bradley that comes off the production line has the letters "BFV" painted on the side. They stand for Bradley Fighting Vehicle. When the contractor, FMC, finally constructed a prototype Minimum Casualty Baseline Vehicle, FMC engineers told me that the BFV stood for "Burton's F___ing Vehicle." That name stuck and became the unofficial name.

The basic features included storing the cannon shells in ammunition compartments that exploded to the outside atmosphere when hit, storing the TOW missiles on the outside of the Bradley (covered with a thin layer of steel armor to provide protection against small arms), moving the fuel tanks to the outside rear of the vehicle (exactly like the thousands of M-113s being produced at FMC for Israel), and lining the entire troop compartment with a properly spaced Kevlar (a tough plastic) liner. Phase I tests had shown that metal slivers, called spall fragments, had caused three times as many casualties as the penetrating round itself. Tests had proved that this liner could prevent most of the slivers from flying around inside the vehicle.

Even though all of the ammo would be stored outside the troop compartment, the troops would have access to it through sliding panel doors. This feature was standard on the Army's M-1 and M-1A1 tanks. Every time I asked Army officials, at all levels from top to bottom, why this feature was standard on their tanks but never included in the Bradley (which carried more ammo than any tank), I would get blank stares, rolling eyeballs, and the Dickey Bird Shuffle in return.

With the fuel tanks mounted outside, the troublesome automatic fire extinguisher was not needed. It was removed, along with its two sources of toxic gases, halon and the by-products of a combination of halon and a fire.

Bill Coomer said he could have a prototype ready in about six weeks. I had already gone over these features with my technician friends at Aberdeen. They said they could make the vehicle themselves in about four weeks, so I knew that Coomer's estimate wasn't too far off.

Coomer, Holloway, and I agreed that we would proceed with Phase II tests of their reactive armor vehicles. When those tests were done, the Minimum Casualty Baseline Vehicle would be ready and we could test it then. I insisted that no reports go to Congress until both configurations were tested and the results compared. This would become a major sticking point.

On 18 February 1986, General Thurman forwarded to OSD a new test plan for Phase II. This plan was quite different from the one I had been concerned about the week before. In his transmittal letter, General Thurman confirmed the Army's commitment to include the Minimum Casualty Baseline Vehicle in Phase II and asked that I work with the Bradley program manager to make sure that the Army built a vehicle exactly like I wanted.

It was no coincidence that General Thurman's letter arrived on the eighteenth. That was also the date of our second hearing together on Capitol Hill, this time in front of Congressman Stratton's Procurement Subcommittee. By forwarding his new test plan that morning, one that was more acceptable, Thurman could ward off any foot-dragging criticisms at the hearing that afternoon. Once again, I was sent alone to testify. In stark contrast, General Thurman appeared with his legions of Army experts.

This hearing was more contentious than the first. Stratton was a strong Army and Bradley supporter and was not too pleased with the controversy I had caused. I am certain that the Army's large installation, Watervliet Arsenal, in Stratton's district had nothing to do with his pro-Army support.

I used the hearing to announce to Congress and the public that the Army had agreed to include the Minimum Casualty Baseline Vehicle in the Phase II tests.[16] With this fact in the public domain, it would be harder for the Army to wiggle out of its promise to test the vehicle. From my past experience with Army promises I expected it to try to get out of the test, so I used the hearing as a means of locking the Army into its promise. It turned out to be the right thing to do, for the Army eventually did everything in its power to avoid testing this configuration. Congress eventually mandated that the vehicle be tested under threat of closing down the Bradley production line.

Stratton had asked me to explain in my opening remarks the main points of difference between the Army and me. As the following excerpt indicates, my remarks pretty well summed up the situation:

The Army and I agree that the ammunition stowed in the troop compartment is the greatest hazard to the crew and the vehicle. But I go one step farther than the Army and say that must guide the modification packages tested in Phase II this spring. I emphasize that when internal ammunition is hit, the casualties increase by factors of 2–3.

Spall fragments are clearly a major source of casualties. In the 10 Live-Fire shots, spall fragments accounted for 3 times as many casualties as the penetrating (round). The Army downplays the importance of spall as a source of casualties, but is planning to test spall suppression liners in the Phase II tests.

We both agree that the automatic fire suppression system was effective at putting out fuel fires, although it has no effect on ammunition fires. It has a high false alarm rate. For every time it was supposed to discharge, it discharged twice when it was not supposed to.

We disagree on the consequences. All the evidence shows that the troops will be driven out of the vehicle by the contaminated atmosphere inside. This has serious consequences in terms of possibly more casualties and whether or not the vehicle can continue to fight if the troops have evacuated.

From this I conclude that we must arrange things so that the troops do not get driven out. The Army doesn't consider the atmosphere inside a problem, but have agreed to take gas measurements in Phase II to see if the vehicle is habitable.

Now there are two subjects left on disagreements, overall casualty assessments and what we do next in Phase II.

We agree that casualties per hit on ammo would be about the same between the Infantry version of the Bradley and the Soviet BMP. The Army drops the subject there. The critical thing is that the Bradley has far more ammunition stowed inside and therefore we can expect about 2–3 times as many overall casualties in combat—which leads me to the last subject of difference.

If 2–3 times as many casualties are important, then we must test a configuration in Phase II which reduces those casualties as far as possible. The purpose of Phase II tests this spring is to arrive at a modification package which reduces casualties as much as possible—and that really uses what was learned in Phase I last fall.

The initial Army proposal for Phase II was oriented towards one particular approach, one that relies primarily on explosive armor concepts and increased armor thickness, an approach which did not consider removing fuel and ammunition from the troop compartment.

My position was that was fine, and those armor concepts should be tested. But we also have to test a configuration which reduces casualties as far as we know how—and that means one which removes those dangerous materials from the troop compartment and stows them externally. I call this the Minimum Casualty Baseline. I am not trying to tell the Army what the right configuration is, but I am telling them that they won't know until they can compare results from the Minimum Casualty Baseline to the other modification candidates.

I have put my views on this subject in writing and the Army is considering them. They have agreed with me in principle and will test the Minimum Casualty Baseline in Phase II in addition to the modification packages they originally had in mind.

I also asked that no reports be sent to Congress, and no production decisions on configurations be made until the tests on the Minimum Casualty Baseline are complete and the results compared to the other modification packages. We are still negotiating the details of the Phase II tests."[17]

I hope it is clear to the reader that my primary emphasis on the test results and their implications dealt strictly with casualties, and it is in this area that the Army and I had our biggest disagreements. To me, the people came first, the vehicle and its fate came second in priority—people first, vehicle second. I harp on it now because I harped on it then, over and over.

Congress picked up on my proposal for the Minimum Casualty Baseline Vehicle and endorsed my request that no reports be submitted or production decisions made until it was tested and compared with the Army's preferred explosive armor vehicle. Initially, so did Dr. Hicks. On 24 February, Hicks signed a letter to General Thurman that directed the Army to complete Phase II tests on the Minimum Casualty Baseline Vehicle before any report went to Congress.[18] Under pressure from the Army, Hicks would later back off from this directive.

The Army began to drag its feet. Coomer had told me on 12 February that he could have a vehicle ready for testing by 1 May. The Phase II report was due to Congress by 1 June, but we could get an extension if needed. By the second week of March, the Army still had not issued any instructions to FMC to begin preparing a vehicle. Once again, the game was afoot.

12

The Great Memo War

The Army was doing everything possible to delay preparations for the Minimum Casualty Baseline Vehicle tests. This included not passing along the specifications for the vehicle to FMC. Fred Widicus, FMC's Washington representative, approached me privately for a copy of the specifications so that FMC could begin construction. After I gave the copy to Fred, FMC officials invited me to visit their Bradley plant in San Jose, California, to inspect a full-scale wooden mock-up that had been quickly constructed. They wanted to make sure that they understood everything I had asked for in the design. Throughout the entire two-year fight over the Bradley, I had had little contact with FMC. The contractor had remained in the shadows as it worked hand in glove with the Army.

During this visit in March 1986, the FMC engineers revealed the unofficial name that they and the Army had given the Minimum Casualty Baseline Vehicle—"Burton's F___ing Vehicle."

As we toured the plant, I noticed two different

configurations of M-113 personnel carriers lined up in the parking lot. The M-113 was still in production, even though the Bradley was slated to replace it. One of the configurations had the fuel tanks mounted on the outside of the vehicle, external to the troop compartment. The other had the fuel tanks inside the troop compartment. I asked Rex Vaughn, the FMC official in charge of the plant, why there were two versions. I knew the answer, but I wanted him to say it. He replied, "The ones with external fuel tanks are for Israel, the ones with fuel tanks in the troop compartment are for our own Army."

Israel had learned from combat that the M-113 was a "burner" when hit. It wanted fuel fires to occur outside the vehicle, not inside where the troops were. Israel's experience had led me to place the fuel tanks externally in the Minimum Casualty Baseline Vehicle. Burn casualties in the 1973 Middle East war had made a lasting impression on the Israeli military. It appeared that the U.S. Army did not care that much about the fate of its troops when it kept the fuel tank inside the vehicle as a bench for the troops to sit on.

When I asked Vaughn why we didn't configure our vehicles like the Israeli version, he responded with the standard, convenient answer: "I only do what the Army tells me." We argued a lot that day about such items.

FMC and the Army now began their all-out campaign to get OSD (read: Hicks) and me to agree to their going ahead with the BRL armored vehicle test and sending a report to Congress on it alone. FMC went to great lengths to explain how it had to study very carefully all implications of the design features that I had requested, and those studies would take a long time. I did not find FMC's arguments persuasive.

The Army claimed that an entire year would be needed to finish the studies and the actual tests on the Minimum Casualty Baseline Vehicle. After that, it could then send a second report to Congress. Now the game was clear.

If the Army stalled long enough, interest in the whole subject of seriously modifying the Bradley to make it safer would fade. The changes that FMC and the Army wanted to make were relatively cheap and simple from a manufacturing standpoint. In my view, however, they did not make things much safer for the troops inside because they did not separate the troops from the fuel and ammo.

The FMC engineers made it clear that adding the BRL armor would be a minor disruption to the production line. All they had to do was add a few mounting attachments at various places—no big deal. On the other hand, if they had to incorporate many of the features I was asking for, they would have to make significant changes to the design. This would cause a major disruption to the work flow in the plant.

You would think that the lives of the troops who would ride in a Bradley would be more important than the smooth operation of a contractor's production line. Sadly, that was not the case. This whole episode would reveal, once again, the real priorities in the defense business.

By this time, my second-level superior, Charles Watt, had left the government. He had served for almost two years with the word *acting* in front of his title. His replacement, Dr. Joseph Navarro, who was chosen by Dr. Hicks, never had that word associated with his title. Navarro came from a Washington consulting firm. He was an analyst by profession and a "modeler" by perspective. More importantly, he was a team player, and Hicks certainly liked team players.

The Army began to work on both Navarro and Hicks to convince them that it would take another year to build and test the Minimum Casualty Baseline Vehicle and that it should be allowed to go ahead with tests on the BRL vehicle and a separate report to Congress. Navarro and Hicks were caving in from the pressure, no matter how strongly I argued that the Army was intentionally stonewalling. They finally yielded to the Army and agreed to split Phase II into two separate tests and reports. I now believed that "Burton's F___ing Vehicle" would never make it to the test range.

In a memorandum to the Army dated 1 April 1986, Dr. Navarro directed it to use a random shot selection scheme for the forthcoming Phase II tests.[1] There had been considerable criticism in Phase I over the fact that BRL had handpicked the aim points to avoid hitting ammunition. I had argued that a random selection scheme using actual combat data would avoid any real or perceived bias. In my mind, it was the only way to proceed. To Navarro's credit, he agreed and issued the order. Naturally, the Army ignored him and proceeded with shots that were handpicked by BRL.

On 3 April, the Air Force personnel system struck again. I was informed that I had seven days in which to accept a new assignment to Wright Patterson Air Force Base, Ohio, or agree to retire. Word of this leaked to Capitol Hill and the press almost immediately. Another fire storm occurred on Capitol Hill. By 9 April, numerous letters of protest from congressmen and senators once again flooded the Pentagon.

A blistering letter to Dr. Hicks from Congressman John M. Spratt of South Carolina was typical:

> During our joint appearance at the Brookings Institution forum
> two weeks ago, you corrected me and assured the audience that

Colonel James Burton had full, unfettered authority to conduct the Joint Live Fire Testing program. In light of your comments, I was deeply disappointed to learn yesterday that Colonel Burton is being transferred from his post before testing of the Bradley Fighting Vehicle has been completed. . . . If he is transferred as a consequence of his zeal and dedication, DoD will be setting a dangerous precedent. Any other officer who insists on rigorous testing will remember the fate of Colonel Burton, and his zeal will be surely chilled."[2]

House Armed Services Committee Chairman Les Aspin and ranking minority member William Dickinson cosigned one letter, and the four cochairmen of the Military Reform Caucus signed another. Even the House Research and Development Subcommittee sent a letter with every member's signature.[3] (Once again, Senator Kassebaum was conspicuous by her absence.)

Letters poured into Secretary Weinberger's office not only from my congressional supporters but also congressional critics. Congressman Stratton asked Weinberger to keep me in place until the Bradley tests were finished. As Stratton said in his letter, I was not his favorite witness, but he feared that my transfer might rally Bradley critics on the Hill, and they might gather enough strength to cancel the program. "I can guarantee you that if Colonel Burton is transferred, we can kiss the Bradley program goodbye."[4]

FMC officials, of all people, felt the same, and they too lobbied Weinberger to cancel the transfer.

I learned of these letters only by reading the newspapers. They were full of stories about my transfer. *Defense News* quoted excerpts from many letters and claimed that Hicks was behind the transfer: "Hick's office is urging the Air Force to try again to transfer Burton because of his help in designing the 'minimum casualty baseline' configuration of the vehicle."[5]

My superiors did not allow me to see any of these letters or any of their responses to Capitol Hill. As I would learn much later, the responses were not truthful, which is probably why I was intentionally kept in the dark.

Fred Widicus, the FMC Washington representative, came to my office to see how I was holding up under the pressure. Fred was a retired Air Force colonel and an old personal friend of mine—this caused him considerable trouble as he tried to walk the fine line between loyalty to his company and our friendship. He mentioned all of the letters about me and was shocked when I said I had not been allowed to see a single one. He returned to his office, where he had a copy of every letter. He made an extra copy of each one for me and returned. I found this absolutely astounding. FMC had such a terrific spy network that it had copies and I didn't. The copies of these letters that are now in my scrapbook, involving some eighteen senators and members of Congress writing on my behalf, all came from FMC, the Bradley contractor. What a strange world.

10 April was the deadline for my formal decision to accept the transfer or retire. That day, my boss, Army Gen. Donald P. Jones, and Air Force Maj. Gen. Robert "Bob" Oaks, head of Air Force personnel on the Air Staff, were summoned to Capitol Hill to meet with the staff of the House Armed Services Committee. There, they were pressured to cancel my transfer, but they stood firm and insisted that I had to go. At the Armed Services Committee staff's request, General Oaks extended the deadline for my decision another seven days until 17 April.[6] The congressional staff hoped that the extension would allow a little more time to work something out.

The important thing about this meeting between Oaks and Jones and the staff of the Armed Services Committee is something that did not occur. Neither Oaks nor Jones mentioned that if I decided to accept the transfer to Ohio, I could remain in my current job in the Pentagon until the Phase II tests on the BRL vehicle were finished, even if the tests lasted beyond my transfer date. Additionally, they did not tell the congressional staff of the Air Force's agreement to make me available to return to Washington from my new assignment when the time came to monitor the tests on the Minimum Casualty Baseline Vehicle. Oaks and Jones did not explain these details because the arrangement did not exist on 10 April. Yet, Secretary Weinberger, in a letter to Congress, would imply that these arrangements had been agreed to by the Air Force and explained to me on 7 April by Dr. Navarro.[7] There would be more misrepresentations and even bold-faced lies as events became more exciting.

On 10 April, also a big day at Aberdeen, a Phase II test shot against a Bradley equipped with BRL explosive armor caused the biggest explosion yet but one of a different kind. The BRL armor failed to stop the attacking round. The round penetrated the armor and the Bradley hull and struck two 5-gallon water cans that had been intentionally placed directly behind the aim point.

The Bradleys used in the test were new models right off the production line at San Jose. When the test vehicles were delivered by FMC to Aberdeen, two 5-gallon water cans were mounted in the left rear of the troop compartment. The night before the tests began, BRL ordered the technicians to reposition the water cans directly behind the aim point for the 10 April shot. Originally, there had been two boxes of cannon ammunition in that location.

Now, when the attacking round penetrated, water was spewed throughout the troop compartment instead of burning and exploding cannon shells. Consequently, few casualties were recorded because no fire or explosion occurred. This was a blatant act to prevent embarrassing test results.

When it was safe to inspect the vehicle the next morning, I drove to Aberdeen to examine the shattered water cans. While there, I also reexamined all of the aim points that BRL had handpicked for Phase II. Suddenly, I realized that hitting the water cans was not an accident or a coincidence. Eight of the thirty-four planned shots were aimed at the repositioned water cans. There could be no justification for this concentration of test shots in one tightly confined area.

That weekend, I began writing what would become my most famous memo. Using combat data from all of the previous wars, I calculated the probability of the water cans being hit in their original location and compared that with the probability of their being hit in the new location. There was no significant difference, as Figures 1 and 2 clearly show. This meant that switching the water cans would not change the Bradley's vulnerability in combat, but it certainly changed the test results because almost 25 percent of the test shots were aimed at the cans. Obviously, this was an attempt to influence the outcome of the tests in case the BRL reactive armor did not stop the attacking round—and it did not.

On 15 April 1986, I launched "The Water Can Memo"—twenty-one copies to the Army and countless numbers to the rest of the OSD staff:

> Eight of the planned 34 Phase II test shots are aimed at the repositioned water cans. . . . When the round penetrates the explosive armor, it will now strike water cans instead of ammunition.
>
> Since 1984 there has been a pattern of key BRL attempts to reduce the apparent casualties caused by the Bradley during tests, including:
>
> a. Watering the dummy uniforms in 1984.
> b. Selecting the 5-man M-3 configuration to test in 1985 instead of the 9-man M-2.
> c. Using selected instead of random aim points during Phase I.
> d. Switching water cans and ammunition in Phase II.
>
> No one involved in these decisions has been held responsible. In fact, one of the participants has twice been reassigned to positions of higher authority and broader responsibilities. The March

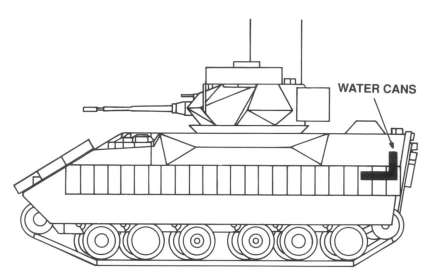

FIGURE 1: *Sketch shows the location of the water cans before the Ballistic Research Laboratory switched them with ammunition boxes. Based on the combat hit distribution, 99.3 percent of the shots would miss the water cans located in this original position. Source: Ballistic Research Laboratory, computer model–generated sketch.*

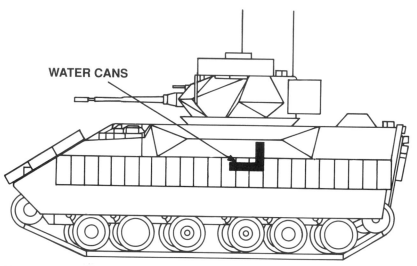

FIGURE 2: *Sketch shows the location of the water cans in the Bradley Fighting Vehicle after the Ballistic Research Laboratory switched them with ammunition boxes that had been in that location previously. Based on the combat hit distribution, 1.3 percent of shots in combat would hit the water cans located in the new location, yet almost 25 percent of test shots were aimed at this location. Figures 1 and 2, taken together, show that switching the water can locations would not have changed combat vulnerability but would have significantly changed the test results. Source: Ballistic Research Laboratory, computer model–generated sketch.*

16 switching of water cans makes it clear that this pattern of changing tests to produce favorable casualty results has not ceased. It appears that by holding no one responsible for these actions, the Army may be tacitly condoning them. If so, it appears prudent to expect a continuation of these patterns in Bradley testing."[8]

Well now, that certainly put the fat in the fire. These were very serious charges, and I expected the Army to come unglued. I was not disappointed. I had challenged its integrity, and the challenge demanded a response. Open warfare followed.

The memo leaked out of the Pentagon almost before the ink was dry. The Army was furious. My superiors were stunned. Everyone knew what was coming. People started diving for the nearest bunker.

The next morning, 16 April, Congressman Charles Bennett called a press conference for 1100. An hour before the press conference, an Army two-star general asked me to come to his office. When I arrived, he requested that I join him in a call to Congressman Bennett to persuade him to call off the press conference. I refused.

The general placed the call anyway, but he could not get through to Bennett. Instead, he talked to one of Bennett's aides and pleaded unsuccessfully to have the press conference canceled. The general said, "Tell Bennett we didn't mean to do it [water can switch]. Tell him the Army isn't devious, we're just dumb."

The aide, who did not know I was in the room and listening on the speaker box, then completely destroyed the general. "Oh by the way, General, we didn't get Burton's memo from Burton. A senior Army officer gave it to us." With this revelation, the general, visibly shaken, slumped in his chair.

Bennett held his press conference and released copies of the water can memo.[9] He called for a formal congressional investigation into the charges I had made. House Armed Services Chairman Les Aspin agreed with his request and appointed an investigating team of four staff aides.

The press had a field day. This episode was linked to all of the previous controversies between the Army and me. The Pentagon had to read the old stories once again—along with a new chapter.

Army Chief of Staff Gen. John Wickham issued a public statement: "I cannot highly regard implications that the United States Army is institutionally dishonest. . . . When the integrity of the Army is called into question, a line is crossed and I cannot maintain polite silence. . . . We stake our lives and the freedom of our country on our sacred honor."[10]

General Wickham then announced that he was suspending indefinitely all Bradley Phase II tests until the controversies, charges, and countercharges were resolved. There was no telling how long that would take. Chaos reigned.

Army spokesman Lt. Col. Craig McNabb began a concentrated press campaign to justify the switching of the water cans and ammunition boxes. In interviews with the *Boston Globe, The Washington Post, The New York Times,* and anyone else who would listen, he claimed that most hits in combat would be concentrated around the center of mass of the Bradley. Therefore, placing the water cans there, instead of ammo boxes, would reduce the Bradley's vulnerability in combat. He admitted in the *Globe,* however, that he had never actually examined the combat data himself.[11] Had he done so, he would have seen that his center of mass claims were false.

My water can memo had Figures 1 and 2 attached to show the probabilities of the water cans being hit in combat at each of their locations, before and after the switch. Based on history, approximately 1 percent of combat hits could be expected to strike the water cans in either location, yet almost 25 percent of all test shots were aimed at the cans in their new location. Clearly, combat hits had never been tightly grouped around the center, so the Army had no justification for its claims. Also, it had no justification for constructing an entire test program with shots grouped tightly around the center of mass.

McNabb and his assistant, Maj. Phillip Soucy, as well as other senior Army officials, would continue to claim that combat hits are tightly grouped around the center of a vehicle and that my claims to the contrary "were made in ignorance."[12] They would come to eat these words, with no sugar and cream to sweeten them, as events revealed that the Army's technical experts were wrong.

The day after the press conference, 17 April 1986, was the deadline for my decision on whether to retire or accept the transfer. At 1530 that afternoon, I walked into the Air Force personnel office on the fourth floor of the Pentagon and signed the necessary papers for my retirement, to be effective 30 June. I wrote across the papers in bold script, "All I wanted to do was see the Bradley tests through to the end. It is clear now that I will not be permitted to do that, so I am retiring. My work is finished." That pretty well said it all.

Twenty minutes after I had signed the formal agreement to retire, General Jones came bursting into the Air Force personnel office. I was sitting at a desk and filling out the mountains of paperwork normally associated with retirement. Jones came up to me, handed me a copy of a letter, and asked me to read it. The letter was one of those that Secretary Weinberger had sent to Congress the previous day. It informed Congress that if I agreed to transfer to Ohio, the Air Force would let me stay in the Pentagon and monitor the Bradley Phase II tests on the BRL vehicles until the tests were finished, even if the tests went beyond the transfer date. The letter went on to say that Weinberger would bring me back to

Washington to participate in the testing of the Minimum Casualty Baseline Vehicle when it was ready to test.

This was the first time that these arrangements had been presented to me by my superiors.* I was furious with General Jones and did not even bother to stand up in his presence, something protocol demanded. I said, "You're too late, General. I have already retired. Why are you showing me this now? Why didn't you tell me about these arrangements before I signed the retirement papers?"

He stepped back and mumbled something about not being sure that Weinberger had agreed to the arrangements himself. This did not make sense; Weinberger had signed the letter the day before. This was a deliberate act of withholding information that might have influenced my decision to retire or accept the transfer. Jones knew exactly what he was doing by hiding this information from me. It made it easier for me to decide to retire, and that is exactly what the Army wanted.

I had been through the agonizing and emotional process of reaching a decision. Now, I did not have it in me to change my mind. Also, I did not believe anyone's promises.

(A few weeks after I retired, I had dinner one night with Gen. Bob Oaks at a gathering of Air Force Academy classmates. Bob and I were personal friends. We had mutually decided not to communicate with each other throughout the controversy that took place in April. We played the personnel game strictly by the rules, so that no one could claim favoritism regardless of the outcome.

During the dinner, Bob explained his shock when he had learned that the transfer arrangements presented to Congress by Weinberger had never been actually offered to me until after I had signed the formal retirement papers. Bob had personally negotiated the agreement with General Jones. He thought that I had known about the arrangements before I retired and had factored them into my decision. As he said, "What was the purpose of making these arrangements if they didn't include you in the negotiations?"

To which I responded, "Now you know what kind of people I was dealing with.")

On 26 June, Jack Krings, Weinberger's director of operational testing, called to tell me of his confrontation that day with Dr. Hicks over the matter of how much information about my transfer had been available to me

---

*Jones later admitted to the congressional investigating team and, in sworn testimony, to the Department of Defense Inspector General that he did not inform me of these agreements with the Air Force until after I had signed my retirement papers, as I described above. See Department of Defense, Office of the Inspector General, Special Inquiries, Report of Investigation, Case no. S860000068, 15 December 1986, 13.

as I was trying to decide my future. Krings said that Hicks was telling Weinberger and everyone else at the top that the Air Force itself had explained the arrangements to me before my decision to retire. I did not know whether Hicks was making this up himself or whether Jones and Navarro had fed him the line. Someone was lying, but by now I was so used to the lies that they did not faze me.

The day after I signed the retirement papers, 18 April, the Army briefed Dr. Navarro and me on how the aim points had been selected and why so many of them were directed at the water cans. This was a key meeting, for here the Army exposed the mathematical blunder it had made in constructing the procedure for selecting the shots. This blunder would reveal the entire scheme for what it was—a contrived ruse.

Most of the prime players were present at the briefing: Walt Hollis; his military assistant, Col. Chaunchy McKearn, who was brought along to document the dialogue; Col. Bill Coomer; Gary Holloway; three Army generals; and Raymond Pollard. Pollard was an analyst who was assisting Holloway throughout the test program and had devised the shot selection scheme.

McKearn kept minutes of the meeting.[13] By now, the Army wrote memos for the record on every meeting it had with me. Of course, I did, too. My wife Nancy called it "The Great Memo War." She asked, "What are you going to do, Jim, keep writing memos until the Army surrenders?" That is basically what I did, for my pencil was my only weapon.

Obviously, this collection of Army officials was very unhappy with me, but everyone kept their tempers and tried to be civil. The room seemed to crackle with electricity. Holloway blurted out that he had not tried to cheat or influence the test results by switching the water can locations. I chose not even to debate that subject. Our purpose here was to learn exactly how Holloway had chosen the aim points.

Pollard explained the procedure since he had been instrumental in devising it. For each type of weapon in the test, he had gathered peacetime accuracy data, both aiming errors and ballistic dispersion errors. From these data, he calculated a one-sigma bivariate normal distribution ellipse, essentially a "bell curve" in two dimensions—up and down, and left and right.

He then placed the ellipse over the center of mass of the Bradley profile, as shown in Figure 3 (an actual chart briefed by Pollard that day). Pollard claimed that "most hits in combat would occur inside the ellipse." I asked him what he meant by "most" and he answered, "62 percent," although I believe that he meant 68 percent. He would later brief 68 percent to the congressional team that was formally investigating the whole water can mess.

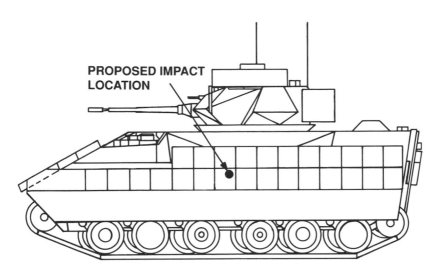

PROPOSED IMPACT LOCATION

FIGURE 3: *Sketch of the Bradley that shows the faulty ellipse overlaid on the center of mass. The entire test program was constructed so that all shots would hit inside the ellipse. The Army claimed that most hits in combat would occur inside the ellipse, so it was justified in selecting all test aim points within this area. Source: Ballistic Research Laboratory, computer model–generated sketch.*

Holloway then selected the specific impact point for each shot somewhere inside the ellipse. Believing that most hits would occur inside this ellipse, he ordered two water cans moved from the lower rear of the vehicle and placed inside the ellipse to replace two ammo boxes originally stored there. The two repositioned ammo boxes were not the only ammo boxes inside the ellipse. In fact, they were two in the middle of a row of eighteen boxes. Why were these two specific ammo boxes replaced with water cans? I would soon learn the answer.

Instinctively, I felt there was something wrong. My examination of the combat data showed that the hits were not as tightly concentrated around the center as this approach indicated. The Army and Dr. Navarro asked me if I could agree to this approach. I said I would agree only if the ellipses were compared with actual combat data to see if they really were an indication of where the hits in combat occurred.[14] The Army would never perform this comparison, but I did later and found that the Army had made a colossal mistake.

That weekend, I called Pierre Sprey and explained Pollard's briefing. Pierre's field was statistics, so he immediately recognized the Army's mistake. "Jim, the 68 percent applies to one-dimensional normal distributions, not bivariate distributions." He got out his statistic textbooks and read to me that Pollard's ellipse represented only 39 percent of the data, not 68 percent. So, instead of most hits occurring inside the ellipse, as the Army was freely telling the press and Congress, most hits had been outside the ellipse. This revelation was a golden nugget.

I trusted Pierre completely, but I never acted on one source of information. The war was so intense now that I could not afford a single mistake. On Monday morning, I called Dr. Lowell Tonnessen of the Institute for Defense Analysis (IDA). Dr. Tonnessen, a mathematician, was under contract to do analytical studies for me. He did a lot of my legwork—gathering data and conducting literature searches—as well as mathematical calculations.

I asked him to give me the percentage of data represented inside a one–standard deviation bivariate normal distribution ellipse. He came back with 39 percent. With that, I knew I had the Army right where I wanted it. I then instructed Dr. Tonnessen to examine the combat data we had gathered and count the number of hits that had actually occurred inside the specific ellipse Pollard had used. The answer was 29 percent.

The Army was telling everyone that because most hits would occur inside the ellipse, it was justified in selecting all test shots inside the ellipse. In theory, however, only 39 percent of hits could fall there, and only 29 percent had fallen inside the ellipse during actual combat. Not only was the Army wrong, but it was not even close to being right. The whole scheme to justify switching the ammo and water cans now appeared to be contrived. How best to deliver the golden nugget?

The following week, on 28 April, the House Armed Services investigating team set up shop in a conference room in the Pentagon and began its inquisition, or so it seemed to me. I spent three straight days in front of this group. We went all the way back to late 1983 and reviewed every controversy and disagreement that had ever occurred between the Army and me, Boyd's advice to keep an audit trail paid off. Feeding the group document after document, I supported my views over a wide range of issues. Paul Bedard wrote in *Defense Week:*

> During the Pentagon interview with Burton, the Air Force colonel turned over several papers which reportedly document Army test abuses in the Bradley program never before made public, sources said. The group was so overwhelmed by the amount of paperwork that they had to recess for a day to study the documents. At that point, the group—which was initially assigned to see why the recent tests were changed and why Burton was told to

move or quit—decided to "go full-bore" with a widespread investigation.[15]

(I learned later from Joseph Cirincione, one of the investigators, that the team told its congressional bosses that it was never able to break any of my arguments. My positions held up, whereas some of the Army's did not.)

The investigating team was composed of four House staffers, Cirincione, Nora Slatkin, Carl Bayer, and William Fleshman. I did not know any of them prior to the investigation, but Pierre's analysis indicated that three out of the four were strong Army supporters. Consequently, we expected a whitewashed report from them.

In my first appearance, I followed Holloway and Pollard. As they came out of the room, I went in. I noticed that someone, probably Pollard, had been lecturing at the blackboard. On the blackboard were several standard bell-shaped curves, with one-sigma lines drawn and the numbers 68 percent written under the curves. Instantly, I knew that I had the Army in a vice and I knew how I would spring the trap. It was clear that Pollard had just been explaining to the investigating team the method—the faulty ellipse—used to select the shots.

During my three days in front of the group, I never mentioned that the Army had made a mistake. Afterward, on 2 May, I wrote a memorandum for the record, which pointed out the Army's mathematical blunders:

> The Army has made public pronouncements that most hits in combat can be expected around the center of mass since that is where gunners are trained to aim. To test this hypothesis, we compared (Pollard's) aiming ellipse for RPG-7's with actual combat data. The first discovery was that a one standard deviation ellipse for a bivariate distribution represents only 39 percent of the data, not the (68) percent briefed by Pollard. Thus an entire test program (20 add on shots) has been based upon an aim point methodology which has been advertised to represent a majority of cases expected in combat, but in reality represents a minority. . . . Actual combat data shows only 29 percent of the combat hits were within the predicted ellipse. . . . The use of the one standard deviation elliptical region overlaid on the center of mass as a basis for selecting the Phase II test shots results in more shots directed at that region than is warranted by combat data.[16]

On Monday, 5 May, I asked Dr. Tonnessen to appear before the congressional team and present a copy of my memo. I let him explain the error the Army had made, as well as show the team all of the combat data supporting my memo. The investigators now had an additional source of information and would not have to rely solely on me.

The congressional team was stunned. The Army had already briefed the team on its elliptical scheme, and most of the team members had accepted the Army's approach as reasonable. They were comfortable with their support for the Army. Now, my memo and Tonnessen's presentation had destroyed not only the Army's case but also its credibility.

The investigators who had supported the Army were embarrassed. Nora Slatkin immediately got Pollard on the phone. She read my memo to him and demanded a response.* There was none. The Army had made a mistake, and it had constructed an entire test program around that mistake.

The congressional team's final report confirmed almost every one of my charges. The team concluded that, among other things, there was no mathematical or historical rationale for switching the water cans: "No shots should have been directed in the vicinity of the water cans, regardless of their location in the vehicle."[17]

The investigators also reported that the decision to make the switch had occurred in a meeting of BRL representatives and several FMC executives at FMC headquarters. The decision had been made after an examination of the aim points that Holloway and Pollard had selected. The congressional inquiry final report stated: "An FMC interoffice memo dated March 10, 1986 documents that 25mm ammunition was stowed 'at the aim point (turret center line)' and suggested that it would be better to move the ammunition and store inert items, including water in this area."[18]

I had expected a whitewash. Instead, I was vindicated. Fred Kaplan of the *Boston Globe* reported that when the team briefed its findings to Stratton's Procurement Subcommittee, most of the members were stunned. They too had expected a different answer. Stratton just hung his head and winced as the team briefed finding after finding that supported my claims.[19]

In mid-May, Dr. Navarro called me into his office and gave me a direct order to stop writing memos—too many of them were causing problems for too many people. Six months earlier, Dr. Hicks had told me that I could no longer write independent reports on test results. Now, I could not even write a memo for the record.

---

*I happened to be in a meeting with Pollard when he was called to the telephone. Standing near him, I could not help but overhear. He was quite shaken by the conversation with Slatkin.

A week later, Dr. Navarro asked me to accompany him to a meeting with the Army. He then asked me to write a memo for the record, in my usual blunt style, attacking the Army. Dr. Navarro would sign the memo, as if he had written it himself. He hoped that it would leak around the Pentagon, as so many of mine did. I wrote the contentious memo for him and then decided to ignore his previous orders to stop writing my own memos. "The Great Memo War" continued.

Just prior to the congressional team's investigation, another august body had gathered to study the differences between the Army and me. Earlier in the spring, the Army had asked a group of distinguished scientists from Los Alamos National Laboratories, chaired by Dr. Perry Studt, to recommend the best way to conduct live-fire tests: by using a random shot selection scheme, as I advocated, or by handpicking specific aim points, as BRL advocated. I spent one day with this group, arguing my case. BRL argued theirs. The group's first report was published on 21 April, right in the middle of all the controversy.[20]

Dr. Studt's report said that if the Army wanted to restore its credibility and to achieve an objective test program free of bias, it should use a random shot selection scheme as I had recommended. The report also recommended that some shots be handpicked—sort of a mixed-bag recommendation—but it went on to state that, by definition, handpicking aim points was biased.

Apparently, the report was not the answer the Army was looking for. It invited a different group of scientists to study the problem, this time, the National Academy of Sciences.[21] The panel of Academy scientists met on 5 and 6 May and listened to BRL present its preferred approach of handpicking aim points to gather specific data that would be used to calibrate its computer models. The models then would assess the vulnerabilities of various vehicles.

In my briefing, I told the group that it would take up to 100,000 shots to validate the computer models and that number was prohibitive. I then showed that 20 to 25 shots, with aim points randomly selected from combat data, would reveal the first, second, third, and fourth sources of casualties with statistical significance (my Alsatian statistician proved this to me first).

The Army must have been confident of the Academy's final report. On 5 June, Army Under Secretary Ambrose and Dr. Hicks cosigned a letter to Congressman Stratton. They announced that the aim points for Phase II, when it resumed, would be selected by this very board of vulnerability experts from the National Academy of Sciences.[22]

On 12 June, the Academy published a draft of its report on the method it would use. It had accepted BRL's philosophy and rejected mine. So, once again, I got out my pencil and wrote a blistering critique of the report, in which I objected to "the unscientific nature of the shot selection scheme" proposed by the Academy:

> Your report has four major faults of purpose:
>
> a. Fails to recognize that the dominant purpose of live fire testing is to reduce casualties. Your report implicitly assumes the primary purpose is to calibrate computer models.
> b. Fails to devise a procedure to find the major sources of casualties.
> c. Fails to even mention that there is a need to develop fixes to reduce those principal casualty sources.
> d. Fails to identify the need to verify that the fixes in fact reduce casualties adequately (i.e., need for retest against a baseline). . . . I cannot even find the word "casualty" in your report. . . . You have adopted a perspective espoused by the computer modelers, namely, a perspective that focuses on vehicle damage, vulnerability assessments and continuous model parameter adjustments. This perspective places higher priority on the vehicle and the models than it does on the troops who will use the vehicle. . . .
>
> If you are going to recommend the use of the BRL computer models, then elementary scientific objectivity requires you to consider whether these models are verified or unverified. If you believe them to be verified, you need to provide the evidence, or references to such evidence. Your report does not provide any such verification and, in fact, questions the accuracy of the model estimates—so how can you rationally recommend their use?[23]

There was much more in my critique. The National Academy of Sciences was shocked by it. I sent a copy to every member of the panel and formally asked them to withdraw the report and redo it. These scientists were not accustomed to such criticism, but I had only a few days left to influence matters and did not want to waste any time in beating around the bush.

Dr. Navarro immediately sent a letter to the panel chairman, Martin Goland, and advised him to ignore my letter because I was speaking only for myself, not OSD. The Academy could not ignore what I had said, however, and the panel members knew it. They went into a huddle and rewrote their report.

To the utter dismay of the Army, the National Academy of Sciences panel revised its decision and chose a random shot selection scheme, as I had asked. In fact, all of the shots for Phase II tests, which resumed several months after I retired, were selected by a random scheme, even the ones against the Minimum Casualty Baseline Vehicle.[24]

"The Great Memo War" was just about over. As my retirement date of 30 June approached, Boyd started working on me to write one last memo. After I had exposed the Army's mathematical blunder about the aiming ellipse, Walt Hollis's military assistant, Chaunchy McKearn, wrote a memo that tried to refute me. It was full of outright falsehoods, and I ignored it. Although I felt that it did not deserve a response, Boyd kept after me. He said, "Jim, you've trumped them on every count so far. The Army is spreading Chaunchy's memo all over Capitol Hill, and some people are giving it credence. You have to tie up this one last loose string."

The day I retired, Nancy and I drove into the Pentagon to have lunch with a group of friends and peers (no superiors) and to pick up my retirement certificate. We had a quiet drive down Shirley Highway for the last time. We did not say much. It was a time for reflection.

Nancy was grateful that the whole mess was coming to an end. It had been harder on her than she had anticipated and harder than I had realized. The tension and pressures had built like rolling thunder and taken a heavy toll on her. I would learn later that she had spent countless hours with professional counselors, friends, and ministers as she tried to find the strength to cope with the problems. She kept this from me because she felt that I had enough to deal with.

She was a kind and loving person who could not stand unpleasantness, yet my daily life at the Pentagon had been full of unpleasantness. As a church choir director for twenty years and a talented musician, Nancy's whole being revolved around creating harmony. My experiences brought disharmony to her life. She was emotionally fragile, which made things doubly difficult for her, but she never complained or asked me to walk away from the battle. Throughout it all, she constantly gave me encouragement and that smile, that wonderful smile. She was a safe haven to come home to at night when I was exhausted, discouraged, and fearful that I might not make it through the next day myself. But now it was ending.

After our luncheon engagement, I sat down at my desk and wrote one last memo for the record.

In a memo to Hollis, Chaunchy had written: "The Army did not claim during the briefing to Dr. Navarro, nor has it ever claimed that most of the hits would fall inside the ellipses."[25] Of course, he was wrong. The

Congressional report had clearly stated on page 8: "The Army witness stated that the majority—68 percent—of the shots in combat would fall in this [ellipse] area." In my memo, I pointed out other falsehoods, errors of logic, and errors of statistics.[26]

Nancy sat quietly as I wrote and waited for the memo to be typed. At 1700, she and I distributed the last shot in "The Great Memo War." We walked the halls of the Pentagon together, as we traced Brudvig's twenty-one-stop Army mail run. Then, holding hands as we had when we were teenagers, we walked out of the Pentagon into retirement. We would have four wonderful years, constantly together, until the good Lord took her.

Case Study

The Navy Runs Aground

The evils of the Pentagon's procurement process, as related in previous chapters, occurred before the mid-1980s and primarily involved the Army and the Air Force. About a year after I retired in 1986, the Pentagon instituted a series of procurement reforms that had been recommended by the Packard Commission, named for its chairman, former Deputy Secretary of Defense David Packard. The reforms, sweeping in nature, were designed to eliminate many of the problems I have discussed in previous chapters. The story here indicates that the evils are still alive and well and that reforms primarily aimed at processes and procedures do not change the Pentagon.

On 7 January 1991, Secretary of Defense Richard Cheney announced that he was canceling the A-12, the Navy's highest-priority aviation program. Cheney's announcement sent shock waves throughout the Pentagon, the Navy, Congress, and the defense industry. Explaining his reason for cancellation of the $57 billion program (the most expensive aviation program in the Navy's his-

213

tory), Cheney stated: "This program cannot be sustained unless I ask Congress for more money and bail the contractors out. But I have made the decision not to do that. No one can tell me exactly how much it will cost to keep this program going. . . . If we cannot spend the taxpayers' money wisely, we will not spend it." [1]

While this appeared to be a sound and convincing reason, one that secretaries of defense should undoubtedly invoke more often, there probably was more to it. I suspect the real reason for his drastic action was that Cheney learned that he had been intentionally misled, from the beginning of the program, by the Navy and his own staff about the costs, schedule, and performance of the new airplane. In turn, he misled his former colleagues on Capitol Hill. When that became apparent to him and everyone else, including the press, he acted. The circumstances leading to this extraordinary decision by Cheney are worth examining in some detail. The behavior of the people involved was scandalous at all levels, and quite possibly criminal, but it was typical of what occurs in most large military programs. This time, however, the boss decided not to put up with the nonsense that his predecessors in the 1980s had accepted as a matter of routine.

The A-12 was born in controversy, so I suppose it is fitting that it died in controversy. To go back to the beginning—on 12 January 1983, Paul Thayer was sworn in as Caspar Weinberger's deputy secretary of defense, the No. 2 civilian position in the Pentagon. Thayer, an ex-Navy fighter pilot, came to the Pentagon from the defense industry, where he had been an executive with LTV Corporation. He was flamboyant and determined to take charge of the Pentagon's business of buying weapons. In World War II, he had shot down six enemy planes, including five Japanese Zeros. [2] He still enjoyed flying everything from the latest military jet fighter to a replica of his World War II Corsair fighter. Thayer knew the aviation business inside out. He had developed and built airplanes and flown the finished products.

Almost from the beginning, Thayer and Navy Secretary John Lehman locked horns in a running battle over the future of naval aviation. It was common knowledge around the Pentagon that Thayer could not stand Lehman. Each had strong wills and different opinions about the best course for the Navy. Their battles became the talk of the building. Lehman was young, cocky, brash, and outspoken. Although many people viewed him as a "young whippersnapper," he would prove to be the most effective Navy secretary of recent times. By effective, I mean that he was able to achieve his agenda better than most of the Pentagon leaders; however, this is not to say that his agenda was necessarily the proper one and that his methods earned everyone's approval. He quickly learned the rules of the Pentagon's games and became one of its better players.

A few months after Thayer came on board, Lehman submitted to Weinberger the Navy's proposed budget for the next five years. Funds to modify two older-model Navy airplanes, the A-6 fighter-bomber and the F-14, were included in the budget. Lehman wanted to increase the life of these planes by adding new equipment. He felt that the Navy could not afford to develop new planes, so the next best thing was to add new equipment to the old ones.

Thayer had other ideas. Besides, here was his chance to take on Lehman. Thayer wanted the Navy to forget about upgrading the aging A-6 and develop a totally new airplane to replace it. He wanted the new plane to be based on the new stealth technology that the Air Force was secretly developing. Naturally, Lehman objected, and they argued. The debate became very heated.[3] As friction mounted between them, Thayer was quoted as saying, "This building isn't big enough for the two of us." He was right.

Bypassing Thayer, Lehman took his case directly to the secretary. Weinberger agreed to allow Lehman the authority to appoint a commission of distinguished outside experts to examine the suitability of stealth technology for the Navy. Lehman, a master at Pentagon bureaucratic battles, then stacked the membership of the board with people who shared his opinion.

The outside commission appointed by Lehman was chaired by Dr. Hans Mark, the deputy director of NASA and a former secretary of the Air Force. He was a strong supporter of stealth technology and had been instrumental in getting the Air Force's B-2 bomber program off the ground. Even so, his commission concluded that the Navy should not pursue a new stealth fighter-bomber, as Thayer wanted, until the Air Force had conclusively demonstrated that stealth technology worked. At this time, stealth was still in its infancy. This was the answer Lehman wanted. Before a rebuttal or minority report could be written by Sol Love and Victor "Vic" Cohen, the two Thayer supporters on the commission, Paul Thayer became a nonplayer in the debate.

The Securities and Exchange Commission (SEC) had been secretly investigating Thayer since the spring of 1982 for possible insider trading violations. The SEC served Thayer with a subpoena two months after he became deputy secretary and interviewed him three times during the next several months as the investigation widened. On 20 December 1983, the commissioners of the SEC authorized their attorneys to file a civil complaint against Thayer for illegal insider trading and to refer the case to the Justice Department for possible criminal charges of fraud, obstruction of justice, and perjury for lying under oath to the SEC.[4]

An unnamed source leaked this information to the press, and stories appeared in the major papers on 29 December.[5] Almost immediately, Thayer submitted his resignation effective 12 January 1984, one year to the day after he had taken office.[6] In the following months, Lehman openly bragged around the Pentagon that he was the one who sent Paul Thayer to jail. I suspect that this was probably just "bar talk," but it certainly added to the lore of the Thayer-Lehman dispute.

The debate over what to do about replacing the A-6 did not disappear when Thayer left. David Chu, head of PA&E and the boss of Tom Christie and the TAC Air Shop, continued to oppose Lehman. Chu argued that it would be cheaper just to buy more F-18s, which were already in production. Lehman did not then, and still does not, like the F-18.[7] Will Taft, Thayer's replacement as deputy secretary of defense, finally settled the argument by imposing a compromise. He directed that the Navy go ahead with upgrading the aging A-6, as Lehman wanted, but he also instructed the Navy to develop a new stealth airplane, as Thayer had wanted. Taft directed that the new plane, which became the A-12, should be developed and produced so that it would be operational by 1994.[8] In a sense, Lehman won, but he also lost.

The Navy immediately put together a team to manage the new program. Because the plane would be based on the fledgling stealth technology, the program immediately went into the "black world," that is, it became classified as Special Access Only. Special Access, or black, programs have flourished in the Pentagon over the past decade or so. They offer the opportunity for severe restriction of the number of people in the Pentagon and Congress who are permitted to know anything about a program, including its very existence. The logic behind black programs is that the technology is so sensitive that security classifications, such as Secret and Top Secret, do not adequately protect them from the enemy. Access to a black program is carefully restricted to a select few, regardless of the level of security clearance other Pentagon officials have. The *real* reason for this designation is to hide what is going on from our own people, not the enemy. The fewer people who know what crimes are being committed behind the green door, the better it is for the perpetrators.

In November 1984, two contractor teams, Northrop/Grumman Aircraft Co. and McDonnell Aircraft Co./General Dynamics (McAir/GD) were selected to develop preliminary concepts of the new airplane. They were each awarded another contract in June 1986 to compete formally for the right to enter full-scale development. At the same time, Navy Capt. Lawrence G. Elberfeld became the program manager.[9]

On paper, Elberfeld was eminently qualified for the job. In reality, his qualifications would turn out to be nothing more than a thin veneer. He was a graduate of the U.S. Naval Academy, with a master's degree in aeronautical engineering from the Naval Post Graduate School and another master's from Massachusetts Institute of Technology. As a pilot, he flew A-4s and A-7s. He understood the weapons system acquisition business. At one time, Elberfeld had been commander of the Navy liaison contingent stationed at the McDonnell Douglas plant in St. Louis, the home plant of one of the A-12 contractors. He was well educated, knew the business, and was considered one of the Navy's rising stars.

Consistent with the Packard Commission reforms, Elberfeld was given what amounts to carte blanche as a program manager and was allowed personally to pick most of his key staff. He was designated to be program manager at least until the A-12 aircraft was built and flown for the first time. His program received full funding from beginning to end, an indication of its high priority, and it was not subject to micro management by OSD or Congress.[10] In short, the A-12 was his baby. He was given all of the money and support he needed, and no one interfered with his operation. Yet, he still managed to blow it.

The contractor team of McAir/GD won the competition for the right to enter full-scale development. The contest was entirely a paper competition. No prototype airplanes were built; no hardware of any kind was built. It was all paper analyses and promises, except for a little wind tunnel work on scale models. I cannot help but compare this situation with the lightweight fighter competition of 1971–1974 that was orchestrated by the Fighter Mafia. Two competing contractors had each built two prototype aircraft apiece and flown head-to-head competition in the same time it took the A-12 competitors to generate paper studies.

The McAir/GD team was awarded the development contract on 13 January 1988. A fixed-price contract for $4.78 billion, it called for first flight in June 1990. The primary difference between the winning McAir/GD proposal and that of Northrop/Grumman was cost. The winner's bid was $1.1 billion less than the loser's.[11] At the time, many insiders believed that the winners were "buying in." This means that a contractor knows full well that its cost will be much higher than the bid but counts on the fact that the Pentagon almost always bails out a contractor when it overruns on a fixed-price contract. When Cheney canceled the program three years later, the cost overrun was estimated at well over $1 billion.

On 26 April 1990, Secretary Cheney testified before Congress that the A-12 program was essentially on track, that there were no signs of trouble, and that he was reaffirming his support for the program. The basis for his testimony was a much ballyhooed three-month exhaustive study of the program just completed by his staff. Five weeks later, on 1 June 1990, the day after the Navy had formally exercised the $1.198 billion contract option to proceed with initial production, the contractor revealed that the development program was at least $1 billion over cost, an overrun that it could not absorb; the schedule had slipped at least eighteen months; and the new airplane would not meet all of the performance specifications of the contract.[12]

News of this megaton bombshell quickly spread out of the "black world" into the sunlight. Again, sunlight proved to be one of the best disinfectants around.

During the next several months, formal investigations by two House committees, the Department of Defense inspector general, and a Navy Board of Administrative Inquiry revealed that senior officials in the Navy and on the staff of the secretary of defense had known all along that the A-12 was in serious trouble and had either ignored that information or suppressed it so that no one else would know. The driving force behind the formal investigations was Andrew "Andy" Ireland, a Republican representative from Florida and member of the House Armed Services Committee. Most of the formal investigations and the myriad of congressional hearings that followed were at Congressman Ireland's specific request.

Ireland's aide, hard-core reformer Charlie Murphy, who had been dubbed "Dr. Root Canal" by his reformer colleagues, had close connections to many sources inside the Pentagon. His sources proved invaluable as these two bulldogs, Ireland and Murphy, launched a campaign to smoke out what happened and to force the system to hold the culprits accountable. By this time, the system, left to its own devices, was well on its way to rewarding many of the culprits with promotions and even cash bonuses, yet simultaneously punishing some of the people who had tried to signal trouble by raising red flags.

The investigative staff of the House Armed Services Committee identified ninety red flags of warning raised by various individuals in the Navy and OSD between January 1988, when the contract was signed, and 26 April 1990, when Cheney testified before the committee that the program was on track. All of the warnings had been ignored or suppressed by people higher up the chain of command.[13]

In his opening remarks at one of several hearings on the sordid mess, Congressman Nicholas Mavroules stated, "It is the thesis of this hearing that these acts of suppression were the key decision points in the A-12 tragedy. The red flags warning that costs were soaring and schedules were slipping were raised by the people paid to look for cost and schedule problems. But their flags were cut down by their immediate supervisors."[14]

Deborah D'Angelo, a GS-13 cost analyst in the Naval Air Systems Command, was tabbed to be Captain Elberfeld's cost analyst for the A-12 in June 1988, six months after the contract had been signed. A competent analyst, D'Angelo had received outstanding performance ratings every year since she had been working for the Navy. Elberfeld described her as "a very nervous and very high-strung individual. She was very timid. She did not like any type of confrontational situation."[15]

In spite of Elberfeld's characterization, if it *was* correct, D'Angelo's actions over the next two years showed tremendous courage. As soon as she came on board, she took one look at the data coming in from the contractor and immediately projected the A-12 to be a budget buster. During the next year and a half, she consistently reported to Elberfeld that the costs were rising out of control and the schedule was slipping. He ignored her. D'Angelo complained to her supervisors as early as February 1989 that Elberfeld and his financial staff were not paying attention to a growing cost problem.[16]

On a regular basis, Elberfeld was required to submit a formal report to OSD, through the Navy chain of command, that documented estimated costs. D'Angelo prepared written estimates for him. She always gave him a range from the lowest possible expected costs to the highest. Her best professional judgment fell in the middle. In seven of the nine official cost estimates that Elberfeld submitted up the chain, he used the lowest possible cost she had given him—the most optimistic picture possible. For the other two reports, her lowest estimates were not low enough to suit him, so he made up his own estimates, each time much lower than her lowest figures.[17]

When Elberfeld was asked by Congress to explain his extremely low estimates, he stated that he did not have an analytical basis. Rather, he alluded to "nonquantifiable variables and other intangibles," including the fact that the two contractors had not reported to the SEC that they were losing money on the program.

Elberfeld stated to the Investigations Subcommittee: "I took into account that corporations have a fiduciary responsibility to report honestly and fairly their projected progress on programs . . . that the corporate chairmen take that responsibility very heavily. And they will not make a SEC report that is misleading."[18] In other words, D'Angelo's estimates must have been wrong because the contractor was not reporting a loss to the SEC. Elberfeld actually expected people to swallow this. There is good reason to believe that his cost estimates were based on political considerations.

The official cost and schedule estimates that Elberfeld submitted up the chain were extremely important because they controlled the flow of money to the contractor. If Elberfeld's estimates were correct, the money would continue to flow. If D'Angelo's best estimates were correct, the contractor would not be legally entitled to the large sums of progress payments it was receiving on a regular basis, for the simple reason that it was not making progress as the contract required. (Guess who was correct. When Cheney canceled the program in January 1991, the contractor had received $1.35 billion in excess progress payments for work not completed.[19] The Pentagon's feeble attempt to retrieve this overpayment is a scandal in itself, as detailed later in this chapter.)

By late summer and early fall 1989, the cost situation was deteriorating rapidly. D'Angelo's reports to Elberfeld demonstrated this dramatically. A second cost analyst now entered the picture and came to the same conclusion, totally independent of D'Angelo's reports.

Every fall, the OSD staff goes through a highly structured budget exercise to prepare the Defense portion of the president's budget that is submitted to Congress in January. As part of this exercise, various elements of the OSD staff prepare budget issues as part of a formal debate. Thomas "Tom" Hafer, a cost analyst working for the OSD comptroller, was cleared into the A-12 program. He was first alerted to cost problems in the program when he met with D'Angelo in August. Visits to the contractor's plants and face-to-face conversations with Elberfeld himself led Hafer to conclude that the development program was running about $500 million over cost and two years behind schedule.[20]

Hafer argued that billions of production dollars could be cut from the budgets for fiscal years 1990 and 1991 because they would not be needed until development was complete. As part of the fall budget exercise, Hafer prepared a draft issue paper to this effect and circulated it to the people cleared into the program throughout OSD and the Navy.[21] The Navy immediately went to red alert. This was the first hint at the OSD level of any trouble in the program.

The Air Force senior leadership, however, knew that the A-12 was in trouble even if OSD did not.[22] In the fall of 1989, Air Force personnel monitoring Air Force programs at the same contractor's plants reported up the chain of command that they estimated the A-12 to be two years behind schedule, just as Hafer had surmised. The Air Force assistant secretary for acquisition was briefed on the estimated two-year schedule slip in November while Hafer was raising the issue around OSD.[23] Why this information never leaked out of the Air Force into OSD is beyond me. Most services jump at the chance of quietly undermining the programs of their sister services by selective leaks of damaging information.

Meanwhile, Elberfeld and the A-12 contractors quickly convinced the Navy chain of command that Hafer was wrong. Navy Secretary Lawrence

Garrett sent a letter of protest to OSD Comptroller Sean O'Keefe that was based on arguments provided by Elberfeld.[24] Garrett asked that Hafer's issue paper be withdrawn from the exercise because Hafer was obviously out of step with everyone else. Cheney's "procurement czar," Under Secretary of Defense for Acquisition John Betti, fired off a similar letter. Faced with this combined opposition, O'Keefe chose not to back his own staff. He withdrew Hafer's issue paper because "no one agreed with us."[25] As a proper reward for causing the controversy, Hafer's annual performance rating was downgraded and he was later reassigned to work on missiles, rather than airplanes.[26]

By the fall of 1989, two cost analysts had independently pointed to trouble, and both had been ignored. A third independent cost analyst would make an assessment identical to Hafer's and D'Angelo's. His message would not be ignored; however, it would be suppressed.

Late in 1989, the circle of people who detected trouble behind the green door continued to widen. (The *green door* is a slang expression for black programs.) Elberfeld himself was now beginning to acknowledge the possibility of a three-month slip in the schedule for the first flight, from June to September 1990. He would make more of these acknowledgments during the next few months, but in such a manner that no one would become overly alarmed. For instance, he might say there was a fifty-fifty chance the first flight might slip six months, but it would not affect the planned operational date or any other important milestone. Program managers learn how to do this subtly; when the roof falls in, they point to a particular briefing or report and say, "See, I warned everyone then."

In mid-December, shortly after the Hafer incident, Secretary Cheney announced that he wanted his staff to conduct a thorough review of the major aircraft programs currently in development and production.[27] The Cold War was winding down, and a declining defense budget was a real prospect on the horizon. Several extremely expensive aircraft programs were under way. Cheney wanted to take a hard look at them to see if their expenses, in the hundreds of billions, were still justified. Specifically, he wanted a thorough scrub of the Air Force's B-2 bomber, C-17 cargo airplane, and Advanced Tactical Fighter and the Navy's A-12. Interestingly, three of these four programs were "stealth" and "black."

Cheney's procurement czar, John Betti, was given the job of chairing this "Major Aircraft Review." Cheney wanted it finished in time for his annual spring trip to Capitol Hill, where he would defend the defense budget in front of his former colleagues.

Betti put together various teams of staff to dig into the four programs. In January, a small group of OSD cost analysts visited the contractors' plants to gather information for the review. Among them was Navy Comdr. Dan Beach.* The visitors expected to observe great activity on the plant floors, such as machines humming and workers assembling the various parts of airplanes. The A-12 contract called for the first flight in June 1990, just a few months away. If the airplane was going to fly then or even three or six months later, as Elberfeld was now saying, the cost analysts should see machine tools on plant floors and various components of an A-12, such as wing sections or landing gear, in the process of assembly.

The visitors were shocked at the first site visited when they found the plant floor empty. One analyst described the floor as "looking like a basketball court, nothing on it except a lot of chalk marks." The chalk marks indicated where various machine tools were supposed to be located. Clearly, something was wrong.

Commander Beach asked a lot of tough questions that January day. He was by far the most critical visitor. As the analysts prepared to leave, the contractor confiscated all of their notes and told them the notes would be returned to them in the Pentagon after they were reviewed for security reasons. Everyone's notes except Commander Beach's were returned. His were mysteriously "lost." After the notes were reported lost, the contractor informed Commander Beach that his notes were not classified after all. Notes (from an unknown source) about Beach's notes were eventually found in government files at the program office.[28] Word of the empty factory floor quickly spread around the Pentagon. The incident caught the attention of Charlie Murphy, Congressman Ireland's aide, and he began to watch the program with a more critical eye from Capitol Hill.

The second visit to an A-12 contractor's plant on 14 March included Cheney and Betti, with their entourage of horse-holders. This time, the factory floor at McDonnell Douglas (McAir) was full of A-12 parts in various stages of assembly. Everything looked normal, and Elberfeld greeted the visitors with his standard "good news" briefing.[29] Cheney left the plant with a warm and fuzzy feeling that the A-12 program was on track. The Navy later revealed that the aircraft parts that Cheney saw had been

*Dan Beach should not be confused with Chester Paul Beach, deputy general counsel of the Navy. Paul Beach's report for the Board of Administrative Inquiry into the A-12 mess was one of the most thorough and candid reports imaginable. It became the source document for numerous other investigations, including those of Congress. The Beach report, as it became known, was well written and documented, even though its conclusions and recommendations appeared to have been written by another author, someone who may not have read the body of the report (too many punches were pulled). Even so, the body of the report is invaluable as an audit trail through the A-12 debacle.

brought into the plant and set up just for his visit. All of the parts were broken or had failed acceptance tests. Workers set up the plant floor to look like everything was progressing normally. Robert Koenig, writing for the contractor's hometown newspaper, the *St. Louis Post-Dispatch*, stated that "McDonnell Douglas Corp. set up a sort of Potemkin village of A-12 Avenger parts." He was referring to the Russian official who had built false house- and storefronts to impress Catherine the Great.[30]

After the visits to the contractors' plants and months of looking at data, Cheney's staff, led by John Betti, was ready to begin a series of briefings to him in late March. Betti instructed his own chief cost analyst, Gary Christle, to take a look at the program on 26 March. This was the first time that Christle had seen the program. He was totally unfamiliar with it and did not have the proper clearance. Later that day, he was cleared and began to look at the cost data. Within twenty-four hours, he completed his analysis and concluded that the program had a $1 billion overrun.[31] The emperor had no clothes, and Gary Christle was not afraid to say so.

Christle's analysis sent shock waves through the A-12 black world. He briefed his results to his superior just one day after he was cleared for the program and one day before Betti and his whole bunch were supposed to begin briefing Cheney on the results of their three-month review of the program.

Betti's first meeting with Cheney the next day elicited only a passing reference (by one of Betti's staff) to the possibility of a cost overrun of a few hundred million dollars. No one got excited, and no one really pressed the issue. Christle's analysis was so far out of line with the story that the Navy and the OSD staff had been touting for so long that no one had the courage on such short notice to engage in any histrionics in front of the secretary.[32] Numerous meetings were held over the next several weeks as the staff scrambled in reaction to Christle's bombshell.

On 29 March, Christle briefed his analysis to Elberfeld and his staff. Christle specifically asked that Elberfeld's cost analyst, Deborah D'Angelo, be present. Elberfeld would not permit her to be in the room. She was instructed to sit in an adjoining room alone and was never allowed to participate in the discussions. Elberfeld claimed that he kept her from the meeting because she was a timid and nervous person who did not like confrontations. Others, according to congressional staff testimony, had said that she was banned from the session for fear she would speak her mind.[33]

According to the Beach report, Elberfeld found Christle's argument "compelling."[34] For the next month or so, Christle briefed most of the important Navy senior people. The day after John Betti was briefed, he called the chief executive officer (CEO) of General Dynamics and the president of McDonnell Douglas. Both claimed that the program was on track and not in financial trouble. The CEO of General Dynamics told Betti that he thought the program's cost would still come within the ceiling, an incredible pronouncement.[35] Betti accepted this reassurance and did not aggressively pursue the ramifications of Christle's analysis. In essence, he discarded Christle as "the new kid on the block." He argued that Christle could not be correct because he had been cleared into the program only a few days earlier. For this, Betti would be severely criticized in the inspector general's final report six months later.

During the next few weeks, Betti and his review team held several more meetings with Cheney. The $1 billion cost overrun, although it had been mentioned previously, was never explored in depth with Cheney. Indeed, it never received much more than a passing comment as the "possibility of a cost risk" or some such nonsense. There was a half-hearted staffwide effort to get at the bottom of the cost overrun picture. David Chu's cost analysts were supposed to have tracked the problem in the past, but they had not done so. They had routinely rubber-stamped and agreed with the cost estimates fed to them by Elberfeld. Chu's analysts quickly huddled together and produced a document that said Gary Christle's $1 billion overrun estimate could be correct, but it went on to say that Elberfeld's estimates were achievable.[36]

Betti was reluctant to place too much weight on Christle's analysis. He preferred to believe his friends in industry who were telling him that everything was under control. On 17 April, he sent a memo to Cheney that hinted at the possibility of a $1 billion overrun, but Betti downplayed it.[37]

After all of the meetings and memos, Cheney was still confidant that the program was on track. On 26 April, he so testified before the House Armed Services Committee. The committee had not yet heard the rumblings of cost and schedule problems, so it accepted Cheney's testimony without question. Later, in referring to Cheney's testimony, Chairman Les Aspin stated, "There was nothing in that testimony to signal serious problems in the A-12 program."[38] Yet, there was obviously serious trouble. Cheney's senior staff and the Navy knew it, but they let Cheney go to Capitol Hill and mislead the Congress.

A week after Cheney's trip to the Hill, the whole program started to unravel. On 4 May 1990, representatives of McDonnell Douglas and General Dynamics met with Elberfeld and informed him that the program, in fact, was $1 billion over cost; the contractors could not absorb the cost overruns; the schedule was eighteen months behind, which meant that the airplane would not be operational in 1994; and the performance of the new plane would not meet contract specifications.[39]

Incredibly, Elberfeld was surprised by these revelations, or so he told Congress and the Navy Board of Administrative Inquiry during their investigations.[40] His own cost analyst had been telling Elberfeld for a year that the program was going to be $1 billion over. Tom Hafer had raised the issue seven months earlier and Gary Christle one month earlier. Yet, Elberfeld was "surprised."

The contractors told Elberfeld that they were going to seek financial help, restructuring of the development contract, and repricing of the early production lots (read: bailout). They were not going to swallow the $1 billion overrun by themselves. Then came the key revelation. Their corporate leaders were planning to visit senior OSD leaders, John Betti, and perhaps even the deputy secretary of defense and directly share this wonderful news with them.

Elberfeld must have gone into shock. As soon as word of this disaster reached the senior levels of the Navy and OSD, all hell would break loose. He had spent the better part of the past year assuring these people that the program was on track and everything was all right. Now, the contractors were going to destroy that image and in the process, probably ruin Elberfeld's credibility and career, as well. It was time for damage control—better that the seniors learn of this disaster from him, not the contractors.

Elberfeld started up the chain of command with the bad news. As soon as his meeting with the contractors was over, he immediately notified his two-star boss, Adm. John F. Calvert, and his civilian contact on the Navy secretariat, Robert H. Thompson. He told both of them the substance of the contractors' message.[41] Now, the real dirty games could begin.

Had the original development contract been on schedule, the contract for the initial production lot would have been signed at the end of May and the first flight would have occurred the next month in June. The Navy needed permission from its civilian acquisition executive, Assistant Secretary of the Navy Gerry Cann, as well as OSD agreement from either John Betti or his deputy, Donald Yockey, to exercise the first production lot option. Signing a production contract is a major milestone and generally guarantees the continuation of a program for many years, no matter what disasters befall it. In theory, if the senior Navy or OSD leaders knew of the A-12 contractors' revelations, they would never agree to signing the first production lot contract. It was time for the cover-up.

Elberfeld began preparing a briefing to take forward to Assistant Secretary Cann. The briefing would put all of the bad news out on the table. He had already informed Cann's staffer, Thompson, so it was reasonable to assume that Cann and Navy Secretary Garrett knew.[42]

A meeting with Cann was scheduled for 21 May. Elberfeld's two Navy bosses, Vice Adm. Richard Gentz and Rear Adm. John Calvert, decided that the May meeting would deal only with securing Cann's permission to exercise the lot No. 1 production contract. Elberfeld was instructed not to mention any of the information the contractors had revealed to him on 4 May because that might jeopardize the chances of getting Cann's approval.[43] In other words, Cann was to be deliberately misled about the status and health of the program so that he would approve a $1 billion lot No. 1 production contract. Elberfeld followed orders.

When Elberfeld was later asked by Congress why he intentionally deceived Cann at the 21 May meeting by not telling him about the contractors' admission on 4 May that the program was in serious trouble, he explained: "After being told six times by a two-star and three times by a three-star [not to tell Cann], I accepted their decision and their judgment. I am an officer and I have been trained to respect the chain of command and to accede to the wishes of my superiors once I have fully informed them of the situation."[44] In the business, this is known as the "Nuremberg excuse."

Cann approved the lot No. 1 decision on the spot. Everyone who was at the 21 May meeting (Cann, Elberfeld, Calvert, and Thompson) claimed that the subject of a $1 billion overrun never came up, yet everyone in the room knew about it. I find it hard to believe that it was not discussed.

Cann's decision meant that the government would obligate over $1 billion of production funds to two contractors who were not able to enter lot No. 1 production, even if they wanted to, because the development process was not ready for production. On 31 May, Elberfeld and his gang briefed Betti's deputy, Donald Yockey, and secured OSD agreement to exercise the lot No. 1 option. Again, no mention was made of the contractors' admission. The deal was done, at least for that day.

The next day, however, a team of executives from McDonnell Douglas and General Dynamics walked into Assistant Secretary Cann's office and revealed everything that they had admitted to Elberfeld on 4 May. The cost was $1 billion over ceiling, and the contractors could not absorb the overrun. They wanted the contract restructured in order to recoup their losses. The first flight had slipped until March 1991, and most production milestones and the operational date of 1994 also had slipped. Finally, the plane would not perform to specifications primarily because of continued weight growth. The contractors wanted to restructure the whole program completely, so that, in essence, the Navy would bail them out.[45] I did not learn of Cann's reaction, but he immediately notified Navy Secretary Garrett and John Betti at OSD of his meeting with the contractors. Cheney was then informed. Word quickly leaked out of the Pentagon, and the press had a field day.

Betti claimed to be surprised by the contractors' revelations. *The Wall Street Journal* reported that Betti was "taken aback by the contractor's admission of problems and questioned why they hadn't surfaced during the Pentagon's major aircraft review which Secretary of Defense delivered to lawmakers in April."[46] Of course, the problems had surfaced then, but Betti had not pursued the matter.

Gerry Cann would claim that he was not surprised by the contractors' revelations in his office because he believed that most of the black programs were in trouble of one kind or another. He maintained, however, that he did not have specific knowledge of the A-12 contractors' situation until their representatives walked into his office on 1 June and told him.[47] This claim has a hollow ring to it.

First, Cann had been informed of Gary Christle's analysis on 28 March, so he was aware of a problem. At that time, Christle's analysis was the hottest topic around the halls of the Pentagon. Second, even though Cann had just recently taken office as assistant secretary on 12 March in the middle of the Major Aircraft Review, his previous position had been vice president of General Dynamics, one of the A-12 contractors.[48] It does not appear reasonable that a vice president would be uninformed about his company's $1 billion cost overrun on a government contract.

The cat was now out of the bag. The time had come for investigations and finger pointing. I am convinced that had it not been for Congressman Andy Ireland, any investigations of this disaster would have turned into whitewashes. On 15 June Ireland summoned Derek Vander Schaaf, Cheney's deputy inspector general, to his office. Vander Schaaf had a fairly good reputation for getting to the bottom of messy situations.

Ireland demanded a full investigation of the A-12 program. How could these events have occurred and who was responsible? For the next year, Ireland's was the strongest voice to call for accountability and to insist that the responsible people be held accountable. The time had passed for blaming things on "the system," which had been the usual case in such matters.

Ireland's request triggered two investigations within the Pentagon and one in Congress. During the next several months, OSD Inspector General Susan Crawford investigated the actions and behavior of the OSD people who had been involved in any way in either the A-12 program or the cover-up. Navy Secretary Garrett appointed Chester Paul Beach, his deputy general counsel, to chair an administrative inquiry into the Navy's conduct. The House Armed Services Committee and the Government Operations Committee held investigative hearings.

In late fall, the results of Crawford's and Beach's investigations were made public. Both investigations documented, with exhaustive details, that just about everyone involved in the process, from top to bottom, knew of the serious problems and the fact that they continued to get worse as time went on, but no one did anything about them until the contractors cried for a bailout. Once that occurred, the mess was on the table for all to see. By then, it was too late.

The people who knew about the A-12 situation were responsible for determining the causes of obvious problems. Their jobs required them to do so. Instead, they consciously ignored signs of trouble and, in some cases, suppressed those signs so that others would do nothing to disturb the program.

Beach called it a "cultural problem." In his report, he stated: "There is no reason to believe that the factors which made these officials choose to respond the way they did are unique to [the Navy]. Indeed, experience suggests that they are not. Unless means can be found to solve this abiding cultural problem, the failures evidenced in this report can be anticipated to occur again in the same or similar form."[49]

The key players were faulted. Inspector General Crawford was extremely critical of Under Secretary of Defense John Betti. In her view, Betti was not vigorous enough at getting to the bottom of the ominous signs of cost overruns that surfaced time and again during the entire episode and especially during the Major Aircraft Review in the spring of 1990. As she testified before Congress on 10 December: "I feel that more vigorous steps could have been taken to at least start the ball rolling so the Secretary could have been alerted to the significance of these cost overrun figures."[50] A few weeks after Crawford's testimony, Betti resigned from government service. His resignation was not officially linked to the A-12 fiasco, but I suspect that it was a key factor in his decision.

Beach was equally critical of Elberfeld, Calvert, and Gentz. Over a period of one year, Elberfeld had systematically converted the pessimistic information that he had received about the contractors' performance into optimistic progress reports regularly sent up the chain of command. When Elberfeld finally attempted to inform the senior leaders of the true state of affairs, only because the contractors said they were going to tell everyone, Calvert and Gentz suppressed the bad news until the production contract was signed.

As result of Beach's report, Navy Secretary Garrett removed Captain Elberfeld as program manager and placed a formal letter of censure in his personnel folder. Garrett also censured Admiral Calvert and transferred him to another job. Admiral Gentz was asked to retire, which he did.[51]

There can be no question that Garrett's actions amounted to little more than slaps on the wrist. *While placing a letter of censure in Elberfeld's file, the Navy, at the same time, promoted him to the rank of admiral.* In addition, the Navy gave him a $2,000 cash bonus for his good performance as a program manager. Only after the A-12 fiasco became public did the Navy ask Elberfeld to return the money; this he did.[52]

As the Navy "punished" Elberfeld, it simultaneously "rewarded" Deborah D'Angelo, Elberfeld's cost analyst, who was consistently correct in her unwavering reports of a growing cost overrun. D'Angelo had received an "outstanding" performance rating every year as she progressed through the Navy civilian ranks from GS-5 through GS-13. In August 1990, after news of the A-12 fiasco became public, she was given a rating one level below outstanding, the kiss of death in the Navy's personnel system. She was informally told that she would never receive another promotion in the Navy Department, so she transferred to another government agency.[53] What a strange system of rewards and punishments!

A week after the Beach report was completed, Secretary Cheney directed the Navy to show cause by 4 January 1991 why he should not cancel the A-12 program, since it was off track and had serious management problems.[54] Donald Yockey, who had been Betti's deputy before Betti retired and was now acting under secretary for acquisitions, and the Navy's Gerry Cann met with General Dynamics and McDonnell Douglas executives. They reported to Cheney that they could not tell him how much it would cost to complete the program. Three days later on 7 January 1991, Cheney canceled the program and stated that he would not bail out the contractors. As he uttered those words, his staff was busy doing just that.

The Beach report confirmed that the contractors had been paid $1.35 billion in excess progress payments, money for work that had not been done. On 5 February 1991, the Pentagon sent a letter to the contractors and instructed them to repay the $1.35 billion. Curiously, the letter went on to say that if the contractors found it too inconvenient to pay the money back, they could request a deferral until some undetermined future date. The contractors naturally jumped on this suggestion and formally requested a deferral. The deferral was *immediately* granted. All three letters—the Navy's letter asking for the money back or a request for a deferral, the contractors' letter asking for a deferral of payment, and the Navy's letter approving the largest deferral in history—by a strange coincidence, were signed on 5 February 1991.[55]

At the same time, the Pentagon arranged for the contractors to receive an expedited $770 million advance progress payment on another contract not related to the A-12.[56] Although, technically, these two actions did not constitute a bailout, they had the same effect. Congress was furious. The House Government Operations Committee summoned Cheney's contracting specialist, Director of Defense Procurement Eleanor Spector, to explain these extraordinary measures.

Spector's reasoning was simple. She had approved the two actions because she was afraid the contractors might go bankrupt without the Pentagon's help. When pressed by Congress to provide the analysis of the contractors' financial conditions that led her to this conclusion, she claimed proprietary information and refused to do so.[57] Continued probing by Congress revealed that her "analysis" was nothing more than a cursory review of information provided by one of the contractors, McDonnell Douglas, without any independent verification of the information.

Herbert Lanese, senior vice president for finance of McDonnell Douglas, and Donald Putnam, corporate director of contracts and technical analysis of General Dynamics, in testifying before the same committee, said that their companies never had any plans to file for bankruptcy, with or without the deferment.[58]

The whole situation had an extraordinary odor about it. The more that Congress looked into the deferment, the stronger the odor became. In fact, the more that anyone looked into any aspect of the A-12 fiasco, the more the odor intensified, especially when one looked at the punishment and reward system in this case.

At the very time when Spector was making decisions that were so generous to the two contractors, she received a $20,000 cash bonus for being an outstanding contract specialist on Cheney's staff.[59] Two other individuals, Frank Kendall and Ken Hinman, each received a $10,000 cash bonus for their work as John Betti's deputies, in managing the Military Aircraft Review. This was the review that had misled Cheney about the A-12 and embarrassed the Defense Department no end. Kendall's and Hinman's superiors had justified the bonuses because of their outstanding contributions to that ill-fated review.[60] Yes, indeed, the Pentagon has a strange sense of punishment and reward.

When Cheney canceled the A-12 program, the Navy started a new program for an airplane called the AX that would replace the A-12. Elberfeld's chief engineer on the A-12, Navy Capt. Jeffrey Cook, was promoted to program manager for the AX project. Cook had been in charge of the engineering aspects of the A-12, the very aspects that had led to the schedule slips and cost overrun. Although he had been unable to control the weight growth in the A-12, the Navy apparently felt that he could handle the whole nine yards on a new plane.

Another Navy captain deeply involved in the A-12 received a somewhat different kind of reward. Capt. Carl P. McCullough was the commander of the Navy's contingent of three hundred personnel stationed at the McDonnell plant in St. Louis. His job was to watch the contractor closely every day and keep the Navy informed of progress and problems. Under McCullough's watchful eye, the contractor was able to keep its problems hidden for more than a year. Four low-ranking civilian Navy employees at the plant were eventually given reprimands for approving work that had not been done. A month after the contractor came clean about the cost overruns in June 1990, McCullough retired from the Navy and went to work for the contractor (all completely legal).[61]

Congressman Ireland was furious when news of Captain Elberfeld's promotion to admiral became public, right about the time the Beach report was published. In Ireland's view, this promotion sent the wrong signal. While Congress and the Defense Department were trying to get to the bottom of one of the most embarrassing chapters in recent Naval history, one of the people most responsible for the mess was being promoted to admiral. It did not make sense to Ireland, and he immediately launched a campaign to overturn the promotion. In separate letters to President Bush, Vice President Quayle, Secretary of Defense Cheney, and Navy Secretary Garrett, Ireland asked that Elberfeld's name be removed from the promotion list.[62]

Everyone deferred to the Navy, and Secretary Garrett remained steadfast in his decision to promote Elberfeld. His reasons were basically that Elberfeld was not the only one responsible for the A-12 debacle, Garrett did not want, unnecessarily, to destroy the morale of the rest of the acquisition community (other program managers), and, in addition, this little indiscretion of Elberfeld's was the only wart on an otherwise distinguished career.[63]

Ireland smelled a payoff. He fired off letter after letter to Garrett, Elberfeld, Gerry Cann, Beach, Susan Crawford, Derek Vander Schaaf, Admirals Gentz and Calvert—everyone involved—to check and crosscheck their versions of what happened. At one point, he had fifteen letters of inquiry in various in-baskets throughout the Pentagon. He simply did not believe many of the answers he was getting, especially about Garrett's and Cann's claims that they did not know about the contractors' problems until after the contractors themselves had confessed. He asked for and received a detailed listing of every meeting and the topics discussed among Elberfeld, Garrett, and Cann. An examination of those responses leaves one with the impression that both Cann and Garrett, the two Navy civilian political appointees, may have known more than they publicly admitted.

Garrett had told Congress: "I was stunned by the [contractors'] revelation." [64] Ireland, in an interview with *The Wall Street Journal*, questioned the truthfulness of Garrett's claims. He said, "I'm convinced that may not be an accurate indication of how much he knew. . . . To take the position that nobody told him anything . . . is an incredible lack of responsibility." [65]

Secretary Garrett stuck to his decision to promote Elberfeld as the feud continued through the spring of 1991. In late July 1991, Deborah D'Angelo gave sworn testimony before Congress. She contradicted Captain Elberfeld's previous sworn testimony concerning the cost estimates and warnings she had given Elberfeld throughout her tour as his cost analyst. Her testimony led House Investigations Subcommittee Chairman Nicholas Mavroules to state, "Somebody's not being honest about this." [66]

A few days before D'Angelo's testimony, Elberfeld decided to retire from the Navy. He asked Secretary Garrett to remove his name from the admiral promotion list.[67] Elberfeld must have known that D'Angelo was going to dispute his previously sworn congressional testimony and that Ireland and his bulldog assistant, Charlie Murphy, would probably pursue him to his grave. In an interview with the *Navy Times*, Elberfeld said that he was resigning "because Congress felt I had not been held properly accountable for the A-12's difficulties." [68]

The A-12 chapter did not completely close with Elberfeld's resignation. Investigations are still being conducted; some deal with possible criminal charges of conspiracy to withhold information from Congress. I suspect, however, that interest in the A-12 will fade rather rapidly. Over $3 billion of the taxpayers' money was completely wasted, with nothing of any value received in return. Without Congressman Ireland's tireless efforts to find out who was responsible and to hold these people accountable, I am convinced that the whole debacle would have been quietly swept under the rug.

The business of buying weapons that takes place in the Pentagon is a corrupt business—ethically and morally corrupt from top to bottom. The process is dominated by advocacy, with few, it any, checks and balances. Most people in power like this system of doing business and do not want it changed.

In previous chapters, I strongly criticize the actions and behavior of civilian and military leaders in my own service, the U.S. Air Force, as well as those in the Army. I was personally involved in the stories told in those chapters. By including the Navy A-12 story in this book, I wish to make the point that the whole business stinks, regardless of the service involved. The sad truth is that no one really gives a damn.

Epilogue

Part I: Before the Gulf War
(January 1991)

The events described in this book are a part of U.S. military history—the history of the Pentagon and the Reform Movement from the late 1970s to the mid-1980s. The era was unique. I have tried to capture the Byzantine politics that dominated the scene. Although some readers may not believe certain events related here, I assure them that all are a matter of record.

When I retired in June 1986, the entire Bradley scene was in total chaos. The live-fire Phase II tests were suspended, the National Academy of Sciences was regrouping to decide how the tests should proceed, the number of Bradley critics on Capitol Hill was growing rapidly, and a lot of philosophical and technical differences of opinion between the Army and me were still floating around somewhat unresolved.

Because of all the controversy, there was a concerted effort in the House of Representatives that summer to cancel the Bradley program. This effort was led by Congressman Mel Levine of California—a gutsy move on his part because the Bradley is produced in California. The Army and FMC quickly joined forces. Working the halls of Congress, they pointed out how many jobs would be lost in each congressman's district if the Bradley were canceled.

In the end, their strategy succeeded. They were able to get enough votes, based on the "jobs" issue rather than the Bradley's merits, to defeat Levine's proposal 223–178.[1] But, it was now clear that changes were in order and that Congress would demand reform in the Bradley program and the way the Pentagon conducted its testing business. Those changes and reforms all came about between June 1986 and December 1987, within eighteen months after I had retired. At the same time, all of the philosophical and technical disputes were resolved, mostly in my favor.

Ten significant events occurred during those eighteen months:

1. The Bradley Phase II tests were completed on two philosophically different Bradley configurations—BRL's reactive armor vehicle and the Minimum Casualty Baseline Vehicle, with its external stowage of fuel and ammunition—not because the Army wanted to, but because Congress forced it to. Congress mandated that these tests be completed and the results reported by December 1987 under threat of closing down the Bradley production line.[2]

2. The aim points for Phase II were selected by the National Academy of Sciences with a random-shot selection scheme as I had advocated.[3]

3. All Phase II tests were against "full-up" vehicles with live ammo and fuel on board. No more tests were made against empty vehicles or those with water in the fuel tanks.[4]

4. BRL was removed from all responsibility in Phase II tests. The tests were conducted by the Army's Test and Evaluation Command, and BRL was relegated to the role of observer.

5. As a result of Phase II tests, the Bradley design was significantly changed to make the vehicle safer in combat. Features from both configurations were put into production. Redesigned Bradleys began coming off the production line in May 1988.[5]

Phase II tests showed the Minimum Casualty Baseline had half as many ammunition-related casualties as the BRL-designed reactive armor vehicle—the kind of casualties that I believed would be seen more often in combat.[6] My original concerns about toxic gases were confirmed beyond any doubt. Toxic gases (from the aluminum vaporific fireball, halon, by-products of halon, and a fire or burning ammunition) turned out to be the single largest source of casualties.[7] To this day, the computer models do not even address casualties from toxic gases. These findings warranted moving the fuel and ammo out of the troop compartment. Unfortunately, the Army did not agree. As part of the redesign, the Army had moved some ammo out of the troop compartment and repositioned the rest. In my view, this was good but not good enough. The design should have gone farther in separating the troops from all those dangerous materials, but, by December 1987, Congress was tired of the subject and not willing to press the issue.

The operational test results from the spring of 1987 showed that enemy aim points on the Bradley were not concentrated around the center of mass but were all over the place. About 30 percent were in the sky above the Bradley or on the ground in front of it. The Army test director sought me out at the 17 December 1987 congressional hearing on the test results to make sure I knew that the "center of mass aim point" theory the Army had espoused in 1986 had been proved totally wrong.

6. The Army's M-1 and M-1A1 main battle tanks went through the same live-fire test series as the Bradley. All forty-eight shots were "full up," and all aim points were selected by a random process, not handpicked.[8] Once again, the Army argued that it did not need to conduct these live-fire tests. It had already conducted over three thousand tests against M-1 components, empty vehicles, and pieces or armor plate, according to the philosophy and procedures preached over the years by BRL. As in the Bradley fight, the Army claimed it "already knew everything." It performed the live-fire tests anyway, rather than go through another Bradley-like fight. Once again, major surprises surfaced. Damage mechanisms occurred that were totally unpredicted, and, once again, the computer models failed miserably. They failed to predict over half of the critical components that were actually damaged. This caused the test director to say to me, "The models still need a little work."[9] Major improvements made in the tanks were based on the test results.

7. Several Soviet armored vehicles went through a live-fire test series. For obvious reasons, I cannot discuss the results or how we obtained those vehicles.

8. Congress passed legislation to require all new weapons systems to go through a live-fire test series before commitment to production.[10] This was one of the most significant events for the Reform Movement. It was a major achievement that the reformers can point to with pride.

9. My job as the first director of the Joint Live-Fire Test Program was converted to a civilian senior executive service position and a small staff was added to supervise all of the live-fire tests going on. (Shortly after I retired, Dr. Navarro, my previous supervisor, called me at home and asked me to apply for the job. Although I knew full well that the leader-

ship would never permit me back in the Pentagon, I submitted my application and résumé anyway just to make them squirm a little. After reviewing the candidates, Dr. Navarro decided someone else was more qualified. He hired James O'Bryon, an Army official from Aberdeen. O'Bryon did a good job in supervising the Bradley Phase II tests when they resumed and reporting the results to Congress in December 1987.)

10. The congressional investigating team reported that the events surrounding my retirement were highly unusual and disturbing. It recommended that the Inspector General of the Department of Defense conduct a formal investigation. After I retired, the Inspector General concluded that all three attempts to remove me from the scene were routine personnel actions and were not related to my criticisms of the Army or the Bradley testing program.

On 17 December 1987, a big day in my life, I once again sat at the witness table in front of Congressman Sam Stratton's Procurement Subcommittee. I had been invited by Stratton to appear as a private citizen.

That day, the Army presented the results of the long-delayed Phase II live-fire tests. As a result of those tests, the Army announced that it was making major modifications to all Bradleys coming off the production line, as well as retrofitting more than 2,000 existing Bradleys. A total of 4,582 Bradleys with survivability improvements resulted from the live-fire testing program.[11]

What a difference two years had made. Every speaker at this hearing—representatives of the Army, OSD, and GAO; congressmen; everyone—emphasized casualties and casualty reduction techniques. The data were plentiful and open for all to examine. Apparently the mind-set of the Army had changed, and it publicly attributed that change to me. Whether the change was genuine or merely a carefully contrived ruse, I simply do not know. The Army may have been throwing me a bone for the benefit of those who were watching. Typical of the comments made that day were Army Lt. Gen. Donald Pihl's opening remarks: "We have learned much from the Live Fire and force on force testing, and much of the credit must go to Colonel (Retired) Jim Burton for pushing us in that direction."[12]

The Army never would have tested the Bradley, never would have changed the design, never would have entirely changed the way it conduct vulnerability tests if we had not had out little "shoving match."

Even though the changes the Army made to the Bradley will result in greatly reduced casualties, moving the TOW missiles out of the troop compartment and putting in externally vented ammo compartments for the cannon shells could save many more lives. The empirical evidence of this was overwhelming in the Phase II test results, yet the Army chose to avoid disrupting the smooth flow of the contractor's production line rather than go the extra step to protect the lives of the troops. I argued this point as strongly as I could that day in 1987 before the Stratton subcommittee, but to no avail. Congress was happy that the Army had made significant changes—and so was I—but it was not willing to push the Army any farther. This was truly unfortunate, for the safety of the troops surfaced again in the fall of 1990.

When war seemed imminent in the Persian Gulf, Congressman Charles Bennett of Florida (a former World War II infantryman) complained to Army Secretary Michael Stone that none of the 615 Bradleys deployed to Saudi Arabia was the redesigned, safer version. Reacting to Bennett's criticism, Stone announced on 5 December that 723 redesigned Bradleys were being immediately deployed.[13] (The redesigned Bradleys did not have BRL's reactive armor; it seems that the reactive armor developed technical problems and never made it to production. All those promises about how it was the answer to the Bradley's vulnerability problems turned out to be nothing but hot air.) Concerns over casualties expressed by the Army's representatives at Stratton's hearing may have been just words, words mouthed so they could get through the hearing with no damage to the Bradley program.

As a final note, it is ironic that the Bradley changes and testing reforms came into being at the very moment the Reform Movement was dying. The reforms associated with live-fire testing were one of the biggest successes of the Reform Movement.

The Reform Movement had caught the public eye in October 1979, when James Fallows published his "Muscle-Bound Super Power" article in *The Atlantic Monthly*. On 11 October 1987, Washington columnist and establishment defender Fred Reed published an article in the Outlook section of *The Washington Post*.[14] Reed criticized the Reform Movement in general and personally attacked three reformers, Pierre Sprey, Dina Rasor, and Bill Lind. Attempts to get the congressional Military Reform Caucus to react and come to their defense were useless. The leaders had abandoned their troops under fire. Those of us who were hard-core reformers realized that the movement was dead. The need for reform had not changed, but the spark and fire were gone. The winds of change were still.

When the Reform Movement had first surfaced as a force to be reckoned with, its center of gravity was in the TAC Air Shop in the Pentagon—in the minds and hearts of a handful of people who cared enough for the troops in the field to fight the system. Eight years later when it died, the movement's center resided on Capitol Hill. It is no coincidence

238   that the movement began to die when it shifted to the Hill. Politics and posturing for publicity replaced commitment. Form replaced substance. The hard-core reformers slowly dispersed and moved on to other things.

Pierre Sprey is busy recording music in his homemade studio in Maryland. John Boyd retired to Florida. Dina Rasor moved to California to raise a family. Bob Dilger is farming in Ohio. Tom Amlie retired for a second time. I retired to a small, rural county in Virginia; I have remarried and spend a lot of my time tweaking the noses of local government officials and politicians. Chuck Spinney and Ernie Fitzgerald are still in the Pentagon and raising hell, but nothing much comes of it anymore. Life moves on.

For eight years, we stood the Pentagon on its head and shook it until its teeth rattled. During that time, Congress passed considerable reform legislation, most of which dealt with weapons testing. Unfortunately, these were temporary reforms. Without constant vigilance, the Pentagon quickly slips back to business as usual. The Navy's conduct in the A-12 fiasco is prime evidence. Even testing is off the scope again. The Pentagon's acquisition executive, claiming live-fire testing is no longer needed, has launched a campaign to repeal all relevant legislation. The Pentagon team appointed to examine the repeal question is headed by a defense contractor—naturally.

All the legislation in the world will not, in itself, reform the Pentagon. Congress cannot legislate integrity, character, and honesty. Yet, these traits must be present in the senior leadership if the Pentagon is ever going to clean up its act for good. The only way to change the system is to find people with these traits and then hold them accountable for their actions. A free, skeptical, and inquiring press, coupled with a watchful Congress, can help keep the games to a minimum. But, in the final analysis, the key to reform lies in the quality of the people who preside over the military and whether or not they permit themselves to become prisoners of the Pentagon. (See Appendix B, "Recommendations for Reform.")

Part II: After the Gulf War
(September 1992)

The moment the Gulf War ended, the time-honored custom of Pentagon political posturing resumed. Various Department of Defense teams were formed to document lessons learned during the war: what happened, which weapons systems and ideas worked, and which ones did not. These efforts quickly turned into "Can you top this?" contests between the revisionists of each service, as they massaged the data and tried to prove that their respective services deserved the lion's share of credit for the victory. With the Cold War ending at about the same time, the military services were facing the real prospect of a shrinking, rather than expanding, Pentagon budget. The service that could claim the greatest contributions to victory would not suffer as much in forthcoming budget reductions. So the posturing began.

"My private conviction is that this is the first time in history that a field army has been defeated by air power." So spoke Air Force Chief of Staff General Merrill McPeak shortly after the war ended.[15] Not to be outdone, the Army responded, by writing in the official history headed for Congress, that the ground forces won the war and that air power cannot defeat an enemy alone: "You must do this the way the Roman legions did, by putting your young men in the mud."[16]

An Air Force briefing chart, labeled "The Value of Stealth," circulated around Capitol Hill. It claimed that eight F-117 Stealth Fighters with two tanker aircraft could have done the same job as seventy-five regular fighters and fighter-bombers during the war.[17] By claiming that stealth aircraft were almost invisible to Iraqi radar, Air Force Secretary Donald Rice hoped to justify more funding for the new B-2 stealth bomber, an airplane with a price tag rapidly approaching $1 billion per plane. The Air Force's claim that Stealth Fighters were invisible and required little support from the other forces was shown to be a gross exaggeration.* The Army quickly pointed out to the press that the Stealth Fighters, by themselves, did not penetrate the Iraqi air defenses undetected in the initial air strike, as claimed by the Air Force. Rather, the F-117s flew through a gaping hole in the Iraqi radar net blasted for them by Army helicopters.[18] When this statement was coupled with the British reports that their destroyers, the *Exeter, Glouster*, and *Cardiff*, routinely detected and tracked the Stealth Fighters at ranges up to 40 miles as they passed to and from the battlefield, the Air Force's credibility suffered greatly.[19]

These are but two examples of exaggerated claims that did the services more harm than good. Many more such claims were initiated by each service. It may be a long time before the exaggerations and overstatements are sorted out and cleaned up, so that the public can learn what actually happened in the war. I offer a few observations based on the limited information available to the public. These observations deal with some of the topics discussed in earlier chapters.

---

*The Air Force has mislabeled the F-117 stealth aircraft. "F" stands for fighter, but the 117's job is to attack ground targets, not to engage enemy fighters in air-to-air combat. The airplane should have been labeled the "A-117."

General McPeak went too far when he claimed that the Air Force won the war all by itself. A more accurate statement would have been that the tremendous pounding from the allied air forces created the environment that led to the collapse of Iraqi forces. I believe this to be a far more defensible claim.

There is no question that the allied air forces inflicted tremendous punishment upon the Iraqi nation, as a whole, and the Iraqi forces, in particular. In a very short war, the U.S. Air Force alone flew approximately 60,000 combat sorties and dropped 84,000 tons of munitions.[20] It was one of the most concentrated and massive bombardments in history. A detailed objective analysis of the effects of that bombardment may never be made, however, because few documented bomb damage assessment data are available. There are mountains of input data in the form of video and film of guided munitions striking targets but little physical evidence of the extent of the damage, or output data.

People will forever debate the value of the massive strategic bombing of Baghdad and other Iraqi targets in the north. An argument can be made that the bombing helped to shorten the war, yet another can be made that it had little or nothing to do with the length of the war. I leave that debate to others.

There can be no question that the massive air attacks against the Iraqi field army contributed directly to its defeat. Thousands of enemy troops were killed or wounded by air attacks, and thousands of tanks, artillery pieces, armored personnel carriers, trucks, and other vehicles were destroyed. Yet, once again it appears that interdiction as a concept failed—failed to prevent the flow of enemy troops and equipment out of the theater of operations. Despite the massive air attacks that led to the gruesome scenes from the "highway of death" leading out of Kuwait to Baghdad, the majority (as many as four and one-half divisions) of the seven elite Republican Guard divisions escaped to Iraq with their equipment.[21] Those units formed the base of Saddam's continued power and were subsequently used to quell uprisings by the Shiites and the Kurds immediately after the war.

Before the hostilities began, the Air Force identified fifty-four rail and highway bridges linking Kuwait to Baghdad and the north. These classic "interdiction choke point" targets needed to be destroyed to isolate the enemy ground forces in a successful interdiction campaign and prevent them from retreating from the Kuwait theater. At the time of the cease-fire, only forty of those bridges were damaged enough to be classified as "inoperable," despite a concentrated effort to destroy them.[22] General Schwarzkopf indicated in a press conference on 30 January 1991, some two weeks into the forty-three day air war, that the allied air forces already

had flown 790 sorties against thirty-three of those bridges.[23] By the end of
the air war, there is no telling how many sorties had been flown against
the bridges. I point this out because it suggests very strongly that the
claims of pinpoint accuracy by laser-guided munitions, claims such as
McPeak's that these so-called "smart munitions" hit their intended target
90 percent of the time, may not have been totally correct.[24] Despite the
nightly television newscasts showing direct hit after direct hit by laser-
guided bombs, the numbers do not add up, and all the bridges did not
fall down.

The purpose of interdiction is basically to isolate the enemy forces in
a particular area—to prevent the flow of supplies and reinforcements
from reaching them and to prevent to them from escaping that area if
they decide to try. It appears that Saddam Hussein himself was more
responsible for isolating his field army than the interdiction efforts of the
air forces.

In an interview with *Air Force Magazine* after the war, Air Force Lt. Gen.
Charles A. "Chuck" Horner confirmed this. Horner, commander of the
air forces in the Gulf War, said: "We did not want the Republican Guards
to run away early in the campaign. We wanted them to stay fixed, so we
could destroy them [where they were]. They obliged, surprisingly. . . .
General Schwarzkopf was very concerned about them decamping and
going back to Baghdad or spreading out. Fortunately, they stayed nicely
grouped up for us."[25]

Because they were "nicely grouped up," the Republican Guards and
the rest of the Iraqi army took a terrible beating from the air. By the time
the ground war started, the air forces had destroyed approximately one-
half of Saddam's tanks, one-half of his artillery, and one-third of his
armored vehicles.[26] To the chagrin of most Air Force leaders, the vast
majority of that damage was caused by the hated brainchild of the
reformers, the A-10 Warthog.*

Recall that the A-10 was the Air Force's first and only combat aircraft
designed specifically to give direct support to the Army's ground forces.
Reformer Pierre Sprey was the architect and prime pusher behind the
A-10. Throughout the 1980s, the senior Air Force leaders did everything
they could to get rid of this inexpensive, simple, slow-flying, ugly but

---

*In addition to the A-10s, much destruction was caused by the Air Force's ageless wonder,
the B-52 strategic bomber. B-52s performed carpet bombing with devastating effects, just as
they had thirty years ago in Vietnam. Whenever the Air Force is asked why the pride and joy
of its bomber fleet, the shiny new B-1, did not participate in the war, it offers the social
excuse of the B-1 having a previous commitment that it simply could not cancel. I suspect
the real reason had more to do with a fear by Air Force leaders that the B-1's performance
would be an embarrassment, so they kept it home.

242   lethal symbol of the Reform Movement. By the Gulf War, many of the A-10s had been prematurely retired to the scrap heap.

As we approached war, Schwarzkopf insisted that the A-10s be sent to the Gulf.[27] He expected a tank war, and the A-10 was the "best tank killer" around. General Horner, Air Force chief of the allied air forces, objected but was overruled by Secretary of Defense Richard Cheney.[28]

In late December 1990, several A-10 units were sent to the Gulf, where they set up shop with 144 aircraft at King Fahd International Air Port, Saudi Arabia. They immediately dubbed themselves "The Fahd Squad."

The A-10s turned out to be one of the true success stories of the war. They represented only 15 percent of the combat aircraft in the war, yet, according to the *Air Force Times*, "flew about a third of the total sorties and were responsible for more than half the confirmed bomb damage" against the enemy.[29] Put another way, the A-10 was responsible for more damage to the enemy than all the other combat aircraft put together[30]— a remarkable feat for an airplane the Air Force never wanted.

Soon after hostilities began and the A-10 started piling up impressive combat results, General Horner told his battle staff, "I take back all the bad things I've said about the A-10s. I love them. They're saving our asses."[31] In view of the *Air Force Times* report, General Horner's comments were correct.

After the war was over, however, the Air Force A-10 lobotomy took effect.

In an interview with *Air Force Magazine*, Horner resumed his prewar criticism of the A-10. He maintained that "the A-10 is vulnerable to hits because its speed is limited. . . . We had a lot of A-10s take a lot of ground fire hits." He went on to say that it was time to replace the A-10 with new versions of the F-16, which could do the same job.

The A-10s, in fact, did take a lot of hits from enemy ground fire. They flew close to the ground in the teeth of the defenses and gave the ground troops the support they needed. The A-10 was the only aircraft permitted to bomb and strafe at these low altitudes because it was designed to take the hits and still get its pilots home.* On the other hand, the F-16 is relatively fragile when hit by ground fire. It was forced to deliver its ordnance

---

*The A-10 units flew daily sorties from their home base in Saudi Arabia to two forward operating locations nearer the battlefield. From there, each A-10 flew numerous combat sorties per day before returning to King Fahd International Air Port at night. During approximately 8,624 combat sorties, only six A-10s were lost. Two of them crashed while landing, which resulted in one of the two pilot fatalities that occurred. In addition to the six losses, four other A-10s received major battle damage; they were all repaired and resumed flying. It seems that Horner's criticisms were unfounded. Source: Fahd Squad Operation Desert Storm Combat Recap Briefing.

from higher altitudes, above 10,000 feet, while flying at speeds too fast for the pilot to sort out friendly ground troops from the enemy when they were in close proximity or intertwined. The F-16 performed admirably in its role of attacking ground targets, but its accomplishments pale in comparison to those of the A-10.

Before the war, General Horner criticized the A-10; during the war, he praised it; and, after the war, he criticized it again. General Horner's views on the A-10 represent the sentiment of most Air Force generals—in peacetime, the A-10 is a terrible airplane; in wartime it's terrific.

Pushing Them Out the Back Door

My final comments on the Gulf War deal with the ground campaign. In chapter 3, I relate the story of how the Army went through a gut-wrenching internal debate in the early 1980s that led to a major change in its war-fighting philosophy. In 1982, the philosophy of the Vietnam-era leaders, one that emphasized force ratios, firepower, attrition, and head-on assaults, was replaced, for the most part, with a philosophy of maneuver and deception as espoused by reformer John Boyd. I use the term, for the most part, because the Army did not get everything quite right.

The Army's new doctrine was called "Air Land Battle" and had four major components: depth, initiative, agility, and synchronization. If its architects had really understood the concepts they were trying to embrace, they would have titled their doctrine "Air Land Operations." Preoccupation with battles was a carryover from the firepower and attrition mind-set of Vietnam. The attrition philosophy has as its precept the notion that you should always race to meet the enemy in a decisive battle. The maneuver philosophy that was adopted in 1982 is based on the Eastern notion of subduing an enemy by avoiding battles. The word battle in the title suggests that the Army did not completely abandon its Vietnam approach.

When the new doctrine was first published, Boyd publicly praised the Army for throwing out most of the firepower and attrition philosophy. He congratulated it on the first three components of the new doctrine: depth of operations, initiative at the lower levels, and agility inherent in fast-moving armored forces; however, he criticized the inclusion of synchronization, which he felt was logically inconsistent with the other three components.

"You synchronize watches, not people," Boyd would say over and over. He argued that if people must synchronize their actions, then their initiative and agility are stifled, which reduces their ability to quickly get deep behind the enemy forces, cut off their retreat, and come at them through the back door. "Synchronized units can only move at the pace of the slowest unit, therefore the initiative and agility of the entire force will suffer," Boyd said. His criticisms fell on deaf ears. What happened in the Gulf War suggests that the Army should have listened.

The plans for the ground war were brilliantly conceived.[32] They were modeled after the old General Patton expression, "Hold them by the nose and kick them in the butt." As the ground war approached, the majority of the allied forces massed in Saudi Arabia directly across the southern border of Kuwait. This gave the impression that the main attack would be a straight-ahead bull rush directly into Kuwait. Meanwhile, a small force of Marines openly rehearsed amphibious operations just off the Kuwait shore to the east in full view of the international press. All of this activity was designed to focus the attention of the Iraqi forces to the south and east.

Early on the morning of 24 February, the allied forces, who were massed on the southern Kuwait border, attacked the Iraqis. These forces were primarily U.S. Marines but also included units from Saudi Arabia, Egypt, Qatar, and Kuwait. A few days before the attack, a large allied armored force hiding behind the Marines raced two hundred miles directly to the west, still behind the allied lines. There, on the second day of the war, the armored force planned to break through a more lightly defended area and race northward through the western desert to circle around behind the Iraqi forces who were concentrating on repelling the Marine attack from the south. The rapidly moving armored force was, in fact, the planned main thrust, neatly disguised so it could get behind the Iraqi army and cut off any retreat to Iraq.

Seven divisions of Iraq's finest forces, the Republican Guard, were held in reserve well north of the Kuwait-Saudi border, while the Iraqis waited to see where the main thrust of the allied attack was centered.[33] As the Marine forces poured across the Kuwait border, the Republican Guard, orienting itself to the south to meet the invaders, either did not notice or ignored the armored force that had moved laterally to the west behind the allied lines.

Two things prevented this excellent plan from being executed flawlessly—jet engines and a large dose of dinosaur blood flowing in the veins of one of the commanders with the western armored force.

The allied force in the west consisted of two U.S. Army corps, augmented with units from Great Britain and France. The two corps were commanded by Lieutenant Generals Gary Luck, and Frederick Franks, Jr. Luck's forces were the farthest to the west and their job was to circle all the way around the Iraqi forces and cut off their escape routes to the north. Luck had the farthest to go but had the least resistance from the enemy. Franks, the commander of the Army's VII Corps, was given the specific job of destroying the Republican Guard.[34]

Franks's objective was made perfectly clear by General Schwarzkopf when he first revealed his plan for the ground war to the generals and admirals under his command on 14 November 1990. He emphasized the importance of destroying the Republican Guard, which he considered the center of gravity of the Iraqi forces: "We need to destroy—not attack, not damage, not surround—I want you to *destroy* the Republican Guard. When you are done with them, I don't want them to be an effective fighting force anymore. I don't want them to exist as a military organization."[35]

His instructions that day to his commanders, in general, and Franks, in particular, left little doubt in anyone's mind that destruction of the Republican Guard was a key military objective. Schwarzkopf would continue to emphasize the destruction of the Republican Guard as a prime objective until 28 February 1991, the day the war ended.

Franks's armored forces were equipped mostly with M-1A1 tanks, the Army's newest version of the M-1, and Bradley Fighting Vehicles. Both the M-1 and M-1A1 tanks are powered by gas turbine engines, similar to aircraft jet engines, not the diesel engines used in previous Army tanks and in the tanks of every other army in the world. The turbine engines permit the M-1 and the M-1A1 to zoom across the countryside at terrific speeds. Unfortunately, they burn a lot of fuel in the process, much more than their diesel counterparts. M-1A1 tanks burn seven gallons of fuel per mile—not miles per gallon, but gallons per mile. Their turbine engines burn about the same amount of fuel when they are idling, which is 70 percent of the time, as when cruising.[36] Consequently, the tanks have to stop very three hours or so to refuel. The diesel-powered Bradleys, traveling with the jet-powered M-1A1 tanks, had no fuel problems. When the tanks stopped to refuel, some as often as every two hours, the Bradleys' fuel tanks were still one-half to three-fourths full.[37]

Because turbine engines require large volumes of clean air for the burning process, the tank crews had to stop, climb outside, and change the air filters, also every three hours. In sandstorms, which were common, the filters clogged every fifteen minutes, thus causing the engines to quit.[38]

Shortly after the Marines crossed the Kuwait border on the morning of 24 February, it became apparent to Schwarzkopf that the entire Iraqi army might flee to Iraq, rather than stay and fight. The Marines were enjoying far more success than anyone had envisioned. They were supposed to be merely a holding force designed to fix the Iraqi forces in place while Luck and Franks circled around behind them. Practicing the maneuver concepts they had adopted in the late 1980s, the Marines feinted left and right, launched multiple thrusts, dashed through openings, sought out areas of least resistance, and slithered through the Iraqi forces in front of them like water flowing downhill. They quickly turned the southern front into a rout. Large numbers of Iraqi soldiers surrendered, and even larger numbers retreated pell-mell to the north.

In one sense this was good; in another it was bad. Time was now of the essence. Gen. Colin Powell, chairman of the Joint Chiefs of Staff, had already gone on television and told the American public that our forces were going to cut off the head of the Iraqi army and kill it. Fearing that most of the Iraqi army, including the ballyhooed Republican Guard, would escape to Iraq before it could be destroyed or captured, Schwarzkopf ordered Luck and Franks to launch their race through the western desert fifteen hours earlier than originally planned.[39] Franks had planned to use those hours to pre-position large caches of fuel deep behind enemy lines in the western desert.[40] That way, his thirsty jet-powered tanks would have fuel out in front of them so that they could travel at their own speed, instead of stopping every few hours to wait for fuel trucks to catch up to them.

On the afternoon of the first day of the ground war, not the morning of the second day as originally planned, Luck and Franks took off through the desert in their attempt to trap the Iraqi army before it escaped. They did not quite make it. The events of the next eighty-nine hours of armored warfare unfolded at a pace and tempo much quicker than anyone anticipated—and much quicker than Franks could handle.

The war was over almost before it started. The cease-fire occurred at 0800 on the morning of 28 February 1991, a mere one hundred hours after the Marines launched their attack into Kuwait.[41] It was one of the swiftest and most decisive victories in history, or so it seemed at the time. During the evening of 27 February, General Schwarzkopf had held his famous spellbinding press conference, during which he revealed the brilliant plan that had guided the actions of his forces. Everything was going better than planned, he said, and the Iraqi army was trapped by our forces, which had circled around them.

> Schwarzkopf: "To date we have destroyed over twenty-nine—destroyed or rendered inoperable; I don't like to say 'destroyed' because that gives you the visions of absolutely killing everyone, and that's not what we are doing—but we have rendered completely ineffective over twenty-nine Iraqi divisions, and the gates are closed. There is no way out of here, and the enemy is fighting us in this location right here."

Epilogue

Reporter: "You said the gate was closed. Have you got ground forces blocking the road to Basra?" [The highway between Basra and Baghdad was the primary escape route for the Republican Guard.]

Schwarzkopf: "No."

Reporter: "Is there any way they can get out that way?"

Schwarzkopf: "No. That's why the gate's closed." [42]

It would be a year later, almost to the day, before the public would learn that the gate was not closed, that all had not gone as well as Schwarzkopf indicated during his press conference, and that most of the Republican Guard actually escaped to Iraq with its equipment.[43] There, it became "The Palace Guard" and provided Saddam Hussein a strong base of power that helped him to remain in office.

On 24 February 1992, Tom Donnelly of the *Army Times* dropped the bombshell. Donnelly reported that even though the war was a short one, in Schwarzkopf's opinion, it could (and should) have been shorter. From Schwarzkopf's vantage point, the enemy began collapsing almost immediately after the Marines launched their attack. He expected his field commanders to pursue the enemy aggressively and take advantage of the rout that was occurring. In his view, unfortunately, some of his commanders were too cautious and missed great opportunities to hasten the collapse. Schwarzkopf became particularly upset with Franks; he even threatened to replace him on the second day of combat.[44]

Schwarzkopf became furious when he awoke on the second morning of the war and saw that Franks's forces had not continued their advance overnight; in fact, they had not moved since Schwarzkopf had gone to bed. Even though Franks had breached the initial enemy lines and was breaking through, he had stopped to wait for daylight before he continued.

Franks gave three reasons for halting his forces until daylight: (1) they had not practiced breaching operations at night (which raises the key question of why); (2) Franks was afraid some of his forces would get too far ahead of the others, and he wanted to keep everyone in formation; and (3) he feared that even small enemy tank units, if bypassed, would wreak havoc on his long lines of fuel trucks that were carrying thousands of tons of fuel behind his thirsty jet-powered tanks.

The next day, after his forces breached the enemy lines, Franks planned to turn them around, backtrack, and attack to the south to clean up any remnants of bypassed enemy units. This further infuriated Schwarzkopf, who told him "For chrissakes, don't turn south! Turn east! Go after 'em!" [Schwarzkopf was referring to the Republican Guard, which was Franks's primary objective and which he had not yet engaged.][45]

This was not the only time Schwarzkopf was impatient with Franks's progress or lack of it. Long before hostilities began, Schwarzkopf became concerned, and very vocal, about Franks's approach to the impending fight with the Republican Guard. Referring to Franks's proposed battle plan two weeks before the ground war started, Schwarzkopf told Lt. Gen. John Yeosok, who was Franks's immediate superior in the chain of command, "I do not want a slow, ponderous, pachyderm mentality. This is not a deliberate attack. I want [Franks] to *slam* into the Republican Guard. The enemy is not worth shit. . . . Go after them with audacity, shock action and surprise. . . . Let me make it clear, John, I do not want a mechanical, grind it out operation."[46] Yet, that is exactly what he got from Franks throughout the entire ground war.

Schwarzkopf was not the only one frustrated with Franks's slow rate of advance. On the second day of the war, an angry chairman of the Joint Chiefs of Staff, Gen. Colin Powell, told Schwarzkopf, "Call General Yeosok. Tell him the chairman is on the ceiling about this matter of VII Corps [Franks]. I want to know why they're not moving and why they can't attack an enemy that has been bombed continually for thirty days. They've been maneuvering for more than two days and still don't even have contact with the enemy. It's very hard to justify VII Corps' actions to anyone in Washington. I know I shouldn't be second-guessing anyone in the field, but we should be fighting the enemy now."[47] That evening, Schwarzkopf further noted his growing frustration as he wrote in his memoirs, "Until we'd destroyed the Republican Guard, our job was only half done, and all of us felt the window of opportunity was rapidly slamming shut."[48]

Schwarzkopf's anger and frustration at Franks's slow progress was exacerbated by the fact that Luck's forces farther to the west were racing through the desert at tremendous speeds. Luck's lead unit, the 24th Mechanized Infantry Division, was commanded by Maj. Gen. Barry McCaffrey, whom Schwarzkopf would later describe in his memoirs as "the most aggressive and successful ground commander of the war."[49] Because of Franks's plodding progress, Schwarzkopf was forced to order McCaffrey to slow down and restrain his rate of advance for two days because he was getting too far out in front of Franks. Frustrated, Schwarzkopf would later write, "I began to feel as if I were trying to drive a wagon pulled by racehorses and mules."[50]

In interviews with the *Army Times* and his hometown newspaper after the war, Franks defended his actions by explaining that he was not being cautious; rather, he had constantly to align his forces in complex maneuvers to keep them "synchronized." (There's the magic word.) "It was a matter of timing and synchronization," the general said.[51]

Later in one interview, Franks added, "Our leaders and soldiers performed a synchronized maneuver to mass against the Republican Guard and defeat them with a three-division fist."[52]

This preoccupation with "synchronizing" the forces so that he could always keep them in formation to hit the Republican Guard with a "three-division first" was also reported by Lt. Col. Peter Kindsvatter, Franks's official historian. Kindsvatter quotes Franks's instructions to his staff on the night of 26 February after a call from Schwarzkopf, who had again urged him to pick up the pace: "We will synchronize our fight as we always have, but we will have to crank up the heat. The way home is through the [Republican Guard]."[53]

Donnelly's description of Franks's synchronizing is graphic: "In directions to his planners, Franks stressed he wanted to synchronize the attacks so his armored divisions would close together in a fist to slam the Iraqi. . . . The corps had gone through extraordinary gyrations to plan its attacks, sequence the order and position of divisions—each a massive formation stretching across 100 kilometers of desert."[54]

On top of all this synchronizing, Kindsvatter, Brian Duffy, and Tom Donnelly all reported that, on the next to the last day of the war, many of Franks's jet-powered tanks ran critically short of fuel. While the enemy was in retreat, one entire division had to stop and get an emergency ration from a sister division to tide it over until the fuel trucks could catch up. Franks confirmed this in his interview with his hometown paper: "Fuel was a challenge but we met it. On the third day, one of our divisions, the 1st armored, ran close, but we refueled them from the 3rd armored and then their supply lines caught up to them."[55]

Schwarzkopf's concerns about the Republican Guard escaping were well founded. Franks never got behind it to cut off its escape. Instead, his carefully synchronized "three-division fist" literally pushed the Republican Guard out of the theater back to Iraq. It is true that he captured thousands of Iraqi soldiers and destroyed tremendous amounts of enemy equipment. But, it also appears that he was so busy refueling and synchronizing that he did not have time to get after the enemy and exploit the breakthroughs that occurred. Slamming someone with a "synchronized fist" sounds more like the philosophy behind the Army's 1976 attrition doctrine than it does the maneuver doctrine adopted in 1982.

Clearly, General Franks's failure to cut off the Republican Guard's escape can be traced to his strict adherence to the synchronization element of the Army's new doctrine. Synchronization slowed his advance; there can be no question about this. It also prevented Gary Luck and his lead commander, Barry McCaffrey, from circling around behind, as planned, and cutting off the escape routes to the north. In the final moments of the war, McCaffrey was attempting either to take the town of Basra from the west or to cut the highway leading north out of Basra toward Baghdad. When the cease-fire sounded at 0800 on 28 February, McCaffrey's division was sitting in an onion field twenty-seven miles west of Basra.[56] It had been there for five and a half hours, having reached Phase Line Victory, its *limit of advance*. Synchronization had slowed down McCaffrey. As a result, the gate to the north was never closed.

A decade ago, John Boyd was absolutely correct. He had argued with the Army then that synchronizing was a dumb idea and that it would slow down the pace of operations, with a detrimental effect on the other three components of the Army's doctrine, initiative, agility, and depth. We now have empirical evidence to confirm that argument. Franks, with his synchronized advance, was able to push the Iraqi army out of the Kuwait theater, but Iraq was a tenth-rate power. I wonder how Franks would have done against a first-rate power?

There is one other aspect of synchronization that must be examined. Although our overall casualties in the Gulf War were extremely low, almost 25 percent resulted from friendly fire; this was the highest percentage of fratricide in U.S. history.[57] Seven out of the nine M-1A1 tanks lost in combat were destroyed by friendly, not enemy, fire.[58] The Bradley Fighting Vehicle suffered even greater losses. Seventeen out of the twenty destroyed Bradleys were hit by friendly fire—85 percent.

Franks's forces suffered the worst incidence of fratricide in the war.[59] All of the M-1A1 tank losses and 75 percent of the Bradley losses occurred in Franks's unit.[60] During the final hours of the war, when the situation was most fluid on the battlefield, Franks's concern over fratricide caused him to exercise even greater caution in permitting his forces to advance. He ordered his troops to cease fire 37 minutes before the official cease-fire time because he was concerned about fratricide in the final frantic race to cut off the escape road to Basra.

When armored units train to stay synchronized—in formation and in their assigned zones, behind their "limits of advance" phase lines—they are not accustomed to operating in a chaotic, free-flowing situation in actual combat where units unknowingly or intentionally get out of formation. If they encounter other units who are out of an assigned zone or beyond a phase line, they will automatically assume those units must be the enemy and therefore subject to attack. The high percentage of casualties from fratricide was a direct result of trying to operate in an ordered, synchronized fashion on a battlefield that, in reality, was characterized by disorder and chaos. If the units do not practice amid chaos, they are less able to handle this situation when they are dumped into it.

Unfortunately, synchronization may become even more deeply entrenched in Army thinking. General Franks was promoted to four stars shortly after the war and placed in command of the Army's Training and Doctrine Command.[61] Under Franks's reign as chief doctrinaire, I suspect we will see a resurgence of the linear theories of ordered warfare that were so prevalent in Army thinking before World War II. Synchronization will probably move beyond the realm of doctrine to that of dogma. The Army's two most celebrated and respected World War II commanders of armored forces, Gen. George Patton and Maj. Gen. John S. Wood, must turn over in their graves every time someone mentions synchronizing armored forces. If they were alive today, one of them would probably shoot the person who coined the phrase "synchronization."

Time and again, Kindsvatter explained how Franks's various units had to stop when they reached the limit of their advance—imaginary stoplights called "phase lines" drawn on the map. Even though the units were advancing faster than expected, they were constantly held up with instructions, such as "Stop at Phase Line Kiwi or Bullet until we all get synchronized." I cannot help but compare this mode of operation to that of General Wood, the Army's top tank commander during World War II. Hanson Baldwin quotes Wood's memoirs in his 1979 book, *Tiger Jack*: "To me, the division was a reservoir of force to be applied in different combinations as circumstances indicated, which could be changed as needed in the course of combat by a commander in close contact with the situation at the front. *There is no place for detailed orders, limiting lines or zones, phase lines, limited objectives or other restraints* [emphasis added] . . . in the extremely fluid operations after the breakthrough, it was up to higher headquarters to find us, and we hoped now and then they would not do so. . . ." In crossing the Saar River, General Wood "took the division outside the sacrosanct corps and army boundaries, but as Wood later wrote, 'Such lines meant little to me. And I went where the going was good.' "[62]

Patton and Wood used tactical airpower to protect Wood's flanks while he went deep behind German lines, roaring through northern France after the breakout from Normandy in July 1944. In contrast, Schwarzkopf kept McCaffrey from getting too far in front of Franks for fear of exposing a flank. Phase lines were merely checkpoints for Wood to report his progress back to Patton; in Schwarzkopf's synchronized modern army, phase lines and even grid lines a few thousand meters apart were used as "limits of advance" to maintain sychronization. Unlike that of McCaffrey or any of Franks's division commanders, Wood's rate of advance in 1944 was limited only by the actions of the enemy, not by his own headquarters. Consequently, Wood's 4th Armored Division traveled farther and faster in its historic drive from Avranches to the Moselle River against the first-rate Wehrmacht than did any of Franks's or Luck's divisions in the Gulf against a tenth-rate Iraqi army.[63]

Tiger Jack would have had a very difficult time with the concept of synchronization. Franks probably would have had to fire him.

Confusion at the End—and Fixing the Blame

It now appears that most of the Republican Guard got away, perhaps as many as four and one-half out of the original seven divisions. Rather than admit that a faulty doctrine may have been the cause, the Army has pulled out and dusted off the tried and true Vietnam excuse—it was the president's fault. And Schwarzkopf is the one pointing the finger.

Let us review the last two days of the war, when confusion reigned. The day before the war ended, Schwarzkopf, in his now famous press conference of 27 February, said that his mission was to destroy the Republican Guard: "If I'm to accomplish the mission that I was given, and that's to make sure that the Republican Guard is rendered incapable of conducting the type of heinous act they've conducted so often in the past, what has to be done is these forces [Franks's forces] continue to attack across here and put the Republican Guard out of business." [64] That seems perfectly clear.

In the same press conference, he said the gate was closed and there was no way out, no way for the Republican Guard to escape. Now the story gets confusing.

President Bush was beginning to come under a lot of pressure, both domestic and international, to end the war. The graphic television scenes of destroyed Iraqi equipment on "the highway of death" was leading to calls to stop the carnage. The rosy picture painted by Schwarzkopf at the press conference suggested, for all practical purposes, that the war was over since the Republican Guard was trapped. A couple of hours after the press conference, General Powell called Schwarzkopf and asked whether or not he had accomplished his mission and whether he, Schwarzkopf, would agree to calling a halt to offensive operations at 0800 the next morning, 28 February. Schwarzkopf initially said no, he wanted to pro-long the operations for another twenty-four hours. [65] Under continued pressure from Powell, Schwarzkopf finally agreed. In his memoirs, Schwarzkopf states that, when he agreed to the cease-fire, he told Powell, "Our objective was the destruction of the enemy forces, and for all intents and purposes we've accomplished that objective." [66] In retrospect, it is difficult to understand how he could say that to Powell because he knew that the Republican Guard had not yet been destroyed. Neverthe-less, the cease-fire went into effect at 0800 local (Iraqi) time on 28 February.

Epilogue

For decades, military forces have operated under Greenwich Mean Time, rather than local time. The cease-fire was scheduled to go into effect at 0500 Greenwich Mean Time (also known as Zulu Time), or 0800 local time. According to Brian Duffy and colleagues of *U.S. News & World Report*, one of Schwarzkopf's senior staff officers refused to operate under Greenwich Mean Time; as a result, the cease-fire time was erroneously transmitted to many field units as 0500 local time.[67] When the mistake was discovered, these units had already stopped operations, but they resumed fighting and then stopped again three hours later. It seems to me that the Army should have spent more time synchronizing its watches and less time synchronizing its tank units.

Schwarzkopf flew into another rage a few hours after the cease-fire went into effect when he learned that Franks's forces had not cut off the Republican Guard's escape route to Basra, as Schwarzkopf had ordered the night before. He had issued that order after he had agreed to the cease-fire and told Powell that he had already accomplished his military objectives. He was furious because he had been told the morning of the cease-fire that Franks owned the highway leading into Basra from the south, but, in fact, Franks did not.[68] Schwarzkopf knew that McCaffrey had not taken Basra or cut the road north out of Basra. All of this meant that the gate was wide open, and much of the Republican Guard escaped with its equipment during the final hours of hostilities. Schwarzkopf believed that he had been lied to.[69] Franks would later say that Schwarzkopf had not been misled, merely misinformed.[70] In any event, Schwarzkopf now had a lot of explaining to do, both to the public and to history.

On 27 March, a month after the war, Schwarzkopf was interviewed on television by David Frost. Schwarzkopf's comments on the cease-fire and Republican Guard's escape are very interesting, coming after a month of reflection on what happened: "Frankly, my recommendation had been, you know, continue the march. I mean we had them in a rout and we could have continued to, you know, wreak great destruction upon them. We could have completely closed the door and made it, in fact, a battle of annihilation. And the President, you know, made the decision that, you know, we should stop at a given time at a given place that did leave some escape routes open to them to get back out and I think it was a very humane decision and a very courageous decision on his part also. . . . It's one of those ones that historians are going to second-guess, you know, forever. Why, you know—'Why didn't we go for one more day?' versus 'Why did we stop when we did, when we had them completely routed?' "[71]

All this appears very confusing to me. First, Schwarzkopf announced that his mission was to destroy the Republican Guard. At the same time, he said the gate was closed so that the Republican Guard could not escape the destruction. Then, he agreed to a cease-fire because, in his words, we had "accomplished our military objectives," which any reasonable person would assume meant that the Republican Guard had been destroyed. Finally, he revealed that the gate was not closed after all; the president had left it open. If Schwarzkopf knew the gate was open, even after telling the public it was closed, why did he agree to a cease-fire when he knew full well that most of the Republican Guard was escaping? Very confusing, indeed.

I can only conclude that the president did not end the war too soon and that Schwarzkopf permitted Franks to act too slowly. And where was the U.S. Air Force in all of this? It too must share in the blame; after all, it had total air supremacy and an arsenal of high-tech sensors (JSTARs and others) and weapons that, according to its claims, permitted the Air Force to attack the enemy's forces any time they tried to move, day or night, good weather or bad.

Franks's cautious approach and his obsession for slamming the enemy with a "synchronized three-division fist" suggest that dinosaur blood runs freely through his veins. There is also an indication that Schwarzkopf himself has a touch of dinosaur blood. During his interview with David Frost, Schwarzkopf expressed outrage at CNN for televising pictures of captured American pilots: "You know, I didn't like the idea that I was seeing it on CNN. I will have to state that openly. I did resent the—you know, CNN aiding and abetting the enemy who was violating the Geneva Convention by putting, you know—and that's a clear violation of the Geneva Convention, yet CNN was broadcasting it to the world."[72]

Schwarzkopf's comments suggest that he does not understand the moral dimension of conflict. Yes, he was angry. So was everyone who saw those pictures. The sight of the pilots being paraded on television made many people in this country so angry at Saddam Hussein that they were ready to go out there and kill him themselves. Those pictures galvanized an entire nation and solidified its support for the war. The pilots made a greater contribution to the war effort through their unwilling television appearance than if they had been free to fly a hundred combat sorties apiece. Schwarzkopf understood the physical dimension of the conflict quite well. It appears that he also had a better understanding of the mental dimension than Franks, for he saw the enemy disintegrating long before Franks did. Like so many of his Vietnam predecessors, however, Schwarzkopf did not have an appreciation of the moral aspect—the aspect that Napoleon claimed was three times more important than the physical aspect.

As reformer John Boyd had preached to the Army more than a decade ago, one of the objectives of maneuver warfare is to come at the enemy through the back door in a moral and mental sense, as well as in the physical sense. The events of Operation Desert Storm indicate that many senior Army leaders have not changed their thinking from the Vietnam era and still prefer to march in synchronized lockstep through the front, or at best the side, door and literally push the enemy out the back door. Schwarzkopf's description of the third day of the war reveals this mindset: "Central Command's Army corps were now moving inexorably east, like the piston in an enormous cider press."[73] In stark contrast, World War II Generals Patton and Wood thought in terms of thrusts, penetrations, and envelopments to get behind the enemy, not pistons pushing the enemy out the back door.

One final comment on the Bradley Fighting Vehicle is in order. The Army has been relatively quiet on the Bradley's performance in the Gulf War. About all it has to say is that the Bradley did what it was designed to do, whatever that means. The General Accounting Office reports that twenty Bradleys were destroyed and another twelve damaged in combat.[74] Sadly, there were several dozen troop fatalities and many, many more wounded.

These figures could have been worse.

The Bradley design changes that were instituted as a result of our live-fire test controversy from 1984 to 1987 saved an untold number of lives. The official Department of Defense report to Congress on the results of the Gulf War clearly pointed this out. The report also suggested that casualties could have been even lower had the Army incorporated all of the design changes that I included in my arguments before Congressman Stratton's Procurement Subcommittee in December 1987. My concerns then were that most Bradley casualties in actual combat would be caused by large-caliber rounds, and the best way to reduce casualties under those circumstances was to incorporate ammunition storage compartments with blow-out panels like those in the M-1 tanks. The Army, however, chose not to accept these design changes for the Bradley.

The final DoD report to Congress on the Gulf War stated: "Most casualties involved crews of armored vehicles struck by high-velocity, non-explosive tank rounds [large caliber] that rely on the force of impact to destroy the target. The number of deaths and injuries from these incidents would have been higher had it not been for the built-in safety and survivability features of the M-1A1 tank and the [Bradley] fighting vehicle, such as fire suppression systems, blow out panels, hardened armor and protective liners."[75]

Blow-out panels are given credit for saving lives in the M-1A1 tanks. They certainly would have saved even more lives during the Gulf War if the Army had incorporated them into the Bradley design, as I had requested in my 1987 congressional testimony. Still, I am grateful for the design changes that were made, even though the Army did not go as far as I had wanted. Army Maj. Gen. Peter McVey, who had been in charge of Bradley production, told a conference of defense vulnerability experts two months after the war, "During Desert Storm, more soldiers' lives were saved as a result of Bradley live-fire testing than we can count."[76]

No more words are necessary.

Appendix A

John Boyd's Source List

The following list of books and articles was required reading for John Boyd's close friends who wished to discuss with him the implications of his *Discourse on Winning and Losing*. This work was more popularly known as the "Green Book."

Boyd's favorite time for talking about the publications in this list, as well as his ideas and theories, was during the middle of the night. In order to delve into this brilliant mind, Boyd's friends had to be willing not only to read all of these books and articles but also require a limited amount of sleep.

Adcock, F. E. *The Greek and Macedonian Art of War.* 1957.
Alger, John I. *The Quest for Victory.* 1982.
Asprey, Robert B. "Guerrilla Warfare." In *Encyclopedia Britannica* (*EB*). 1972.
Asprey, Robert B. "Tactics." In *EB.* 1972.
Asprey, Robert B. *War in the Shadows.* 2 vols. 1975.
Atkins, P. W. *The Second Law.* 1984.
Atkinson, Alexander. *Social Order and the General Theory of Strategy.* 1981.

Appendixes

258 Axelrod, Robert. *The Evolution of Cooperation.* 1984.

Balck, William. *The Development of Tactics.* 1922.

Baldwin, Hanson W. *Tiger Jack.* 1979.

Barnett, Correlli. *Bonaparte.* 1978.

Barron, John. *KGB: The Secret Work of Soviet Secret Agents.* 1974.

Bateson, Gregory. *Mind and Nature.* 1979.

Bayerlein, Fritz. "With the Panzers in Russia 1941 & 43." *Marine Corps Gazette,* December 1954.

BDM. "Generals Balck and Von Mellenthin on Tactics: Implications for Military Doctrine," 19 December 1980.

Beaufre, Andre. *An Introduction to Strategy.* 1965.

Beaufre, Andre. *Strategy of Action.* 1967.

Becker, Ernest. *The Structure of Evil.* 1968.

Beesley, Patrick. *Very Special Intelligence.* 1977.

Beesley, Patrick. *Room 40.* 1982.

Betts, Richard K. *Surprise Attack.* 1982.

Beveridge, W. I. B. *The Art of Scientific Investigation.* 1957.

Bloom, Allan. *The Closing of the American Mind.* 1987.

Blumentritt, G. *Experience Gained from the History of War on the Subject of Command Technique* (pamphlet). January 1947.

Blumentritt, G. *Operations in Darkness and Smoke.* 1952.

Bohm, David, and F. David Peat. *Science, Order and Creativity.* 1987.

Bretnor, Reginald. *Decisive Warfare.* 1969.

Briggs, John, and F. David Peat. *Looking Glass Universe.* 1984.

Briggs, John, and F. David Peat. *Turbulent Mirror.* 1989.

Bronowski, Jacob. *The Identity of Man.* 1971.

Bronowski, Jacob. *The Ascent of Man.* 1973.

Bronowski, Jacob. *A Sense of the Future.* 1977.

Bronowski, Jacob. *The Origins of Knowledge and Imagination.* 1978.

Brown, Anthony Cave. *Bodyguard of Lies.* 1975.

Brown, G. Spencer. *Laws of Form.* 1972.

Brownlow, Donald Grey. *Panzer Baron.* 1975.

Brzezinski, Zbigniew. *Game Plan.* 1986.

Callendar, H. L., and D. H. Andrews. "Heat, Entropy and Information," In *EB.* 1972.

Calvocoressi, Peter. *Top Secret Ultra.* 1980.

Campbell, Jeremy. *Grammatical Man.* 1982.

Capra, Fritjof. *The Tao of Physics.* 1976.

Card, Orson Scott. *Ender's Game.* 1985.

Careri, Giorgio. *Order and Disorder in Matter.* 1984.

Carver, Michael. *The Apostles of Mobility.* 1979.

Chaliand, Gerard, editor. *Guerrilla Strategies.* 1982.

Chambers, James. *The Devil's Horsemen.* 1979.

Chandler, David G. *The Campaigns of Napoleon.* 1966.

Chandler, David G. *Atlas of Military Strategy.* 1980.

Cincinnatus. *Self-Destruction.* 1981.

Clausewitz, Carl von. *Principles of War.* 1812. Translated by Hans W. Gatske, 1942.

Clausewitz, Carl von. *On War.* 1832. Translated by M. Howard and P. Paret, 1976.

Clausewitz, Carl von. *War, Politics and Power.* Translated by Edward M. Collins, 1962.

Cline, Barbara Lovett. *Men Who Made a New Physics*. 1965, 1987.
Cline, Ray S. *Secrets, Spies and Scholars*. 1976.
Clutterbuck, Richard. *Guerrilas and Terrorists*. 1977.
Cole, K. C. *Sympathetic Vibrations*. 1984.
Colin, Jean. *The Transformations of War*. 1912.
Conant, James Bryant. *Two Modes of Thought*. 1970.
Conway, James. "Mr. Secret Weapon." *Washington Post Magazine,* 15 May 1982.
Cooper, Matthew. *The German Army 1933–1945*. 1978.
Corbett, Julian S. *Some Principles of Maritime Strategy*. 1911.
Crease, Robert P., and Charles C. Mann. *The Second Creation*. 1986.
Cruickshank, Charles. *Deception in World War II*. 1979.
Daniel, Donald C., and Katherine L. Herbig. *Strategic Military Deception*. 1982.
Davies, Paul. *The Cosmic Blueprint*. 1988.
Davies, W. J. K. *German Army Handbook 1932–1945*. 1973.
Dawkins, Richard. *The Selfish Gene*. 1976.
Dawkins, Richard. *The Blind Watchmaker*. 1986.
DeBono, Edward. *New Think*. 1971.
DeBono, Edward. *Lateral Thinking: Creativity Step by Step*. 1973.
Deichmann, D. Paul. *German Air Force Operations in Support of the Army*. 1962.
Des Pres, Terrence. *The Survivor*. 1976.
Despres, J., L. Dzirkals, and B. Whaley. *Timely Lessons from History: The Manchurian Model for Soviet Strategy*. (Rand Corporation document, date unknown.)
Doughty, R. A. *The Evolution of U.S. Army Tactical Doctrine, 1946–76*. Leavenworth Papers, No. 1. August 1979.
Downing, David. *The Devil's Virtuosos: German Generals at War 1940–45*. 1977.
Drexler, K. Eric. *Engines of Creation*. 1987.
Dupuy, R. E., and T. N. Dupuy. *Encyclopedia of Military History*. 1977.
Dupuy, T. N. *The Military Life of Genghis, Khan of Khans*. 1969.
Dupuy, T. N. *A Genius for War*. 1977.
Durant, Will, and Ariel Durant. *The Lessons of History*. 1968.
Dyson, Freeman. *Disturbing the Universe*. 1979.
Dzirkals, L. F. "Lightning War in Manchuria: Soviet Military Analysis of the 1945 Far East Campaign." July 1975.
Earle, Edward Mead, et al. *Makers of Modern Strategy*. 1943.
Ekeland, Ivar. *Mathematics and the Unexpected*. 1988.
English, John A. *A Perspective on Infantry*. 1981.
Fall, Barnard B. *Street Without Joy*. 1964.
Fall, Barnard B. *Last Reflections on a War*. 1967.
Falls, Cyril. *The Art of War from the Age of Napoleon to the Present Day*. 1961.
Farago, Ladislas. *The Game of the Foxes*. 1971.
Ferguson, Marilyn. *The Aquarian Conspiracy*. 1980.
Fitzgerald, Frances. *Fire in the Lake*. 1972.
Foster, David. *The Intelligent Universe*. 1975.
Foster, Richard N. *Innovation: The Attacker's Advantage*. 1986.
Freytag-Loringhoven, Hugo von. *The Power of Personality in War*. 1911. Translated by Army War College, 1938.
Fromm, Erich. *The Crisis of Psychoanalysis*. 1971.
Fuller, J. F. C. *Grant and Lee*, 1932, 1957.
Fuller, J. F. C. *The Conduct of War, 1789–1961*, 1961.

260 Gabriel, Richard A., and Reuven Gal. "The IDF Officer: Linchpin in Unit Cohesion." *Army,* January 1984.

Gabriel, Richard A., and Paul L. Savage. *Crisis in Command.* 1978.

Gamow, George. *Thirty Years That Shook Physics.* 1966.

Gardner, Howard. *The Quest for Mind.* 1974.

Gardner, Howard. *The Mind's New Science.* 1985.

Gardner, John W. *Morale.* 1978.

Gardner, Martin. "The Computer as Scientist." *Discover,* June 1983.

Georgescu-Roegen, Nicholas. *The Entropy Law and the Economic Process.* 1971.

German Army Regulation 100/200 "Army Command and Control System," August 1972.

German Army Regulation 100/100 "Command and Control in Battle," September 1973.

Gleick, James. "Exploring the Labyrinth of the Mind." *New York Times Magazine,* 21 August 1983.

Gleick, James. *Chaos.* 1987.

Godel, Kurt. "On Formally Undecidable Propositions of the Principia Mathematica and Related Systems." In *The Undecidable.* 1965:3–38.

Goleman, Daniel. *Vital Lies, Simple Truths.* 1985.

Goodenough, Simon, and Len Deighton. *Tactical Genius in Battle.* 1979.

Gribbin, John. *In Search of Schrodinger's Cat.* 1984.

Griffin, Gary B. "The Directed Telescope: A Traditional Element of Effective Command." Combat Studies Institute, 20 May 1985.

Griffith, Paddy. *Forward into Battle.* 1981.

Grigg, John. *1943 The Victory That Never Was.* 1980.

Guderian, Heinz. *Panzer Leader.* 1952.

Guevara, Che. *Guerrilla Warfare.* 1961.

Hall, Edward T. *Beyond Culture.* 1976.

Handel, Michael I. "The Yom Kippur War and the Inevitability of Surprise." *International Studies Quarterly,* September 1977.

Handel, Michael I. "Clausewitz in the Age of Technology." *Journal of Strategic Studies,* June/September 1986.

Hao Wang. "Metalogic." In *EB.* 1988.

Hawking, Stephen W. *A Brief History of Time.* 1988.

Heider, John. *The Tao of Leadership.* 1985.

Heilbroner, Robert L. *An Inquiry into the Human Prospect.* 1974.

Heilbroner, Robert L. *Marxism: For and Against.* 1980.

Heisenberg, Werner. *Physics and Philosophy.* 1962.

Heisenberg, Werner. *Across the Frontiers.* 1974.

Herbert, Nick. *Quantum Reality.* 1987.

Herrington, Stuart A. *Silence Was a Weapon.* 1982.

Hodges, Andrew. *Alan Turing: The Enigma.* 1983.

Hoffer, Eric. *The True Believer.* 1951.

Holmes, W. J. *Double-Edged Secrets.* 1979.

Howard, Michael. *The Causes of Wars.* 1983.

Hoyle, Fred. *Encounter with the Future.* 1968.

Hoyle, Fred. *The New Face of Science.* 1971.

Hoyt, Edwin P. *Guerilla.* 1981.

Humble, Richard. *Hitler's Generals.* 1974.

Irving, David. *The Trail of the Fox.* 1977.

Isby, David C. "Modern Infantry Tactics, 1914–74." *Strategy and Tactics,* September/October 1974.

Johnson, George. *Machinery of the Mind.* 1986.

Jomini, Henride. *The Art of War.* 1836. Translated by G. H. Mendell and W. P. Craigbill, 1862.

Jomini, Henride. *Summary of the Art of War.* 1838. Edited by J. D. Hittle, 1947.

Jones, R. V. "Intelligence and Deception." Lecture, 29 November 1979.

Jones, Roger S. *Physics as Metaphor.* 1982.

Kahn, David. *The Codebreakers.* 1967.

Kahn, David. *Hitler's Spies.* 1978.

Kaku, Michio, and Jennifer Trainer. *Beyond Einstein.* 1987.

Karnow, Stanley. "In Vietnam, the Enemy Was Right Beside Us." *Washington Star,* 22 March 1981.

Karnow, Stanley. *Vietnam: A History.* 1983.

Keegan, John. *The Face of Battle.* 1977.

Kemeny, John G. "Semantics in Logic." In *EB.* 1972.

Kennedy, Marilyn Moats. *Powerbase: How to Build It; How to Keep It.* 1984.

Kesslering, Albert, et al. *Manual for Command and Combat Employment of Smaller Units.* 1952. (Based on German experiences in World War II.)

Kitson, Frank. *Low Intensity Operations.* 1971.

Kline, Morris. *Mathematics: The Loss of Certainty.* 1980.

Kohn, Hans, and John N. Hazard. "Communism." In *EB.* 1972.

Kramer, Edna E. *The Nature and Growth of Modern Mathematics.* 1974.

Krepinevich, Andrew F., Jr. *The Army and Vietnam.* 1986.

Kuhn, Thomas S. *The Structure of Scientific Revolutions.* 1970.

Lamb, Harold. *Genghis Khan.* 1927.

Landauer, Carl. "Marxism." In *EB.* 1972.

Lanza, Conrad H. *Napoleon and Modern War, His Military Maxims.* 1943.

Laqueur, Walter. *Guerrilla.* 1976.

Laqueur, Walter, editor. *The Guerrilla Reader.* 1977.

Lawrence, T. E. *Seven Pillars of Wisdom.* 1935.

Layzer, David. "The Arrow of Time." *Scientific American,* December 1975.

LeBoeuf, Michael. *GMP* The Greatest Management Principle in the World.* 1985.

Leonard, George. *The Silent Pulse.* 1978.

Levinson, Harry. *The Exceptional Executive.* 1971.

Lewin, Ronald. *Ultra Goes to War.* 1978.

Liddell Hart, B. H. *A Science of Infantry Tactics Simplified.* 1926.

Liddell Hart, B. H. *The Future of Infantry.* 1933.

Liddell Hart, B. H. *The Ghost of Napoleon.* 1934.

Liddell Hart, B. H. *The German Generals Talk.* 1948.

Liddell Hart, B. H. *Strategy.* 1967.

Liddell Hart, B. H. *History of the Second World War.* 2 vols. 1970.

Lorenz, Konrad. *Behind the Mirror.* 1973. Translated by Ronald Taylor, 1977.

Lupfer, Timothy T. *The Dynamics of Doctrine: The Changes in German Tactical Doctrine During the First World War.* Leavenworth Papers, No. 4. July 1981.

Machiavelli, Niccolo. *The Prince.* 1516.

Appendixes

262   Machiavelli, Niccolo. *The Discourses.* 1519.

Macksey, Kenneth. *Panzer Division.* 1968.

Macksey, Kenneth. *Guderian: Creator of the Blitzkrieg.* 1976.

Maltz, Maxwell. *Psycho-Cybernetics.* 1971.

Mann, Charles C. "The Man with All the Answers." *The Atlantic,* January 1990.

Manstein, Erich von. *Lost Victories.* 1958.

Mao Tse-Tung. *On Guerrilla Warfare.* 1937. Translated by S. B. Griffith, 1961.

Mao Tse-Tung. *Basic Tactics.* 1938. Translated by Stuart R. Schram, 1966.

Mao Tse-Tung. *Selected Military Writings.* 1963.

Mao Tse-Tung. *Four Essays on China and World Communism.* 1972.

Marchetti, Victor, and John Marks. *The CIA and the Cult of Intelligence.* 1974, 1980.

Marhsall, S. L. A. *Men Against Fire.* 1947.

Marshall, S. L. A. *The Soldier's Load and the Mobility of a Nation.* 1950.

Martin, David C. *Wilderness of Mirrors.* 1980.

Masterman, John C. *The Double-Cross System.* 1972.

Matloff, Maurice. "Strategy." In *EB.* 1972.

May, Rollo. *The Courage to Create.* 1975, 1976.

McAulifee, Kathleen. "Get Smart: Controlling Chaos." *Omni,* February 1990.

McWhiney, Grady, and Perry D. Jamieson. *Attack and Die.* 1982.

Mellenthin, F. W. von. *Panzer Battles.* 1956.

Mellenthin, F. W. von. *German Generals of World War II.* 1977.

Mellenthin, F. W. von. "Armored Warfare in World War II." Presentation at conference with Military Reformers, Washington, D.C., 10 May 1979.

Mendel, Arthur P., editor. *Essential Works of Marxism.* 1961.

Messenger, Charles. *The Blitzkrieg Story.* 1976.

Mikheyev, Dmitry. "A Model of Soviet Mentality." Presentation to Military Reformers, Washington, D.C., March 1985.

Miksche, F. O. *Blitzkrieg.* 1941.

Miksche, F. O. *Atomic Weapons and Armies.* 1955.

Miller, Russell. *The Commandos.* 1981.

Minsky, Marvin. *The Society of Mind.* 1986.

Montross, Lynn. *War Through the Ages.* 1960.

Morris, E., C. Johnson, C. Chant, and H. P. Wilmott. *Weapons and Warfare of the 20th Century.* 1976.

Musashi, Miyamoto. *The Book of Five Rings.* 1645. Translated by Victor Harris, 1974.

Musashi, Miyamoto. *The Book of Five Rings.* 1645. Translated by Nihon Services, 1982.

Nagel, Ernest, and James R. Newman. *Godel's Proof.* 1958.

National Defense University. *The Art and Practice of Military Strategy.* 1984.

Oman, C. W. C. *The Art of War in the Middle Ages.* 1885. Edited and revised by John H. Beeler, 1953.

ORD/CIA, *Deception Maxims: Fact and Folklore.* April 1980.

Ortega y Gasset, Jose. *The Revolt of the Masses.* 1930. Anonymous translation, 1932.

Osborne, Alex F. *Applied Imagination.* 1963.

Ouchi, William. *Theory Z.* 1981.

Pagels, Heinz R. *The Cosmic Code.* 1982.

Pagels, Heinz R. *Perfect Symmetry.* 1985.

Pagels, Heinz R. *The Dreams of Reason*. 1988.

Palmer, Bruce, Jr. *The 25 Year War*. 1984.

Paret, Peter. *Clausewitz and the State*. 1976.

Pascale, Richard T., and Anthony G. Athos. *The Art of Japanese Management*. 1981.

Patrick, S. B. "Combined Arms Combat Operations in the 20th Century." *Strategy and Tactics*, September/October 1974.

Pauker, Guy J. "Insurgency." In *EB*. 1972.

Pearce, Joseph Chilton. *The Crack in the Cosmic Egg*. 1973.

Pearce, Joseph Chilton. *Exploring the Crack in the Cosmic Egg*. 1975.

Peter, Rozsa. *Playing with Infinity*. 1957.

Peters, Thomas J., and Robert H. Waterman, Jr. *In Search of Excellence*. 1982.

Phillips, T. R., editor. *Roots of Strategy*. 1940, 1985.

Piaget, Jean. *Structuralism*. 1971.

Pike, Douglas. *PAVN: Peoples Army of Vietnam*. 1986.

Pincher, Chapman. *Their Trade Is Treachery*. 1982.

Polanyi, Michael. *The Tacit Dimension*. 1966.

Polanyi, Michael. *Knowing and Being*. 1969.

Polkinghorne, J. C. *The Quantum World*. 1984.

Pomeroy, William J., editor. *Guerrilla Warfare and Marxism*. 1968.

Powers, Thomas. *The Man Who Kept the Secrets*. 1979.

Prigogine, Ilya, and Isabelle Stengers. *Order Out of Chaos*. 1984.

Pustay, John S. *Counterinsurgency Warfare*. 1965.

Rae, Alastair I. M. *Quantum Physics: Illusion or Reality*. 1986.

Reid, T. R. "Birth of a New Idea." *Washington Post Outlook*, 25 July 1982.

Rejai, M. *Mao Tse-Tung On Revolution and War*. 1976.

Restak, Richard M. *The Brain: The Last Frontier*. 1980.

Rifkin, Jeremy, with Ted Howard. *Entropy—A New World View*. 1980.

Rommel, Erwin. *Infantry Attacks*. 1937. Translated by G. E. Kidde, 1944.

Rosen, Ismond. *Genesis*. 1974.

Ross, Steven. "Rethinking Thinking." *Modern Maturity*, February–March 1990.

Rothenberg, Gunther E. *The Art of Warfare in the Age of Napoleon*. 1978.

Rowan, Roy. *The Intuitive Manager*. 1986.

Rucker, Rudy. *Infinity and the Mind*. 1982.

Rucker, Rudy. *Mind Tools*. 1987.

Rushbrooke, George Stanley. "Statistical Mechanics." In *EB*. 1972.

Russell, Francis. *The Secret War*. 1981.

Satter, David. "Soviet Threat Is One of Ideas More Than Arms." *Wall Street Journal*, 23 May 1983.

Savkin, V. YE. *The Basic Principles of Operational Art and Tactics*. 1972. (A Soviet view.)

Sella, Amnon. "Barbarossa: Surprise Attack and Communication." *Journal of Contemporary History*, 1978.

Senger und Etterlin, Frido von. *Neither Fear nor Hope*. 1963.

Shanker, S. G., editor. *Godel's Theorem in Focus*. 1988.

Shannon, Claude E. "Information Theory." In *EB*. 1972.

Sidey, Hugh. "Playing an Assassin Like a Fish." *Washington Star*, 14 June 1981.

Sidorenko, A. A. *The Offensive*. 1970. (A Soviet view.)

Singh, Baljitt, and Ko-Wang Mei. *Modern Guerrilla Warfare*. 1971.

264 Singh, Jagjit. *Great Ideas of Modern Mathematics: Their Nature and Use.* 1959.

Skinner, B. F. *Beyond Freedom and Dignity.* 1972.

Sprey, P. M. "Taped Conversation with General Hermann Balck." Battelle Institute, 12 January and 13 April 1979.

Sprey, P. M. "Taped Conversation with Lt. General Heinz Gaedcke." Battelle Institute, 12 April 1979.

Stevenson, William. *A Man Called Intrepid.* 1976.

Stewart, Ian. *Does God Play Dice.* 1989.

Strausz-Hupe, R., W. R. Kintner, J. E. Dougherty, and A. J. Cottrell. *Protracted Conflict.* 1959, 1963.

Summers, Harry G., Jr. *On Strategy: The Vietnam War in Context.* 1981.

Sun Tzu. *The Art of War.* About 400 B.C. Translated by S. B. Griffith, 1971.

Sun Tzu. *The Art of War.* About 500 B.C. Edited by James Clavell, 1983.

Sun Tzu. *The Art of War.* About 400 B.C. Translated by Thomas Cleary, 1988.

Taber, Robert. *The War of the Flea.* 1965.

Tang Zi-Chang. *Principles of Conflict.* 1969. (Recompilation of Sun Zi's *Art of War.*)

Tao Hanzhang. *Sun Tzu's Art of War.* 1987.

Thayer, Charles W. *Guerrilla.* 1961.

Thompson, R. W. *D-Day.* 1968.

Thompson, William Irwin. *At the Edge of History.* 1972.

Thompson, William Irwin. *Evil and World Order.* 1976.

Thompson, William Irwin. *Darkness and Scattered Light.* 1978.

Toffler, Alvin. *Future Shock.* 1970.

U.S. Army *Field Manual 100-5 "Operations."* July 1976.

U.S. Army *Field Manual 100-5 "Operations."* 20 August 1982.

U.S. Army *Field Manual 100-5 "Operations."* 5 May 1986.

U.S. Army. Pamphlet 20-233. "German Defense Tactics Against Russian Breakthroughs," October 1951.

U.S. Army. Pamphlet 20-269. "Small Unit Actions During the German Campaign in Russia," July 1953.

Van Creveld, Martin. *Supplying War.* 1977.

Van Creveld, Martin. *Fighting Power: German Military Performance, 1914–1945* (report). December 1980.

Van Creveld, Martin. *Command.* 1982.

Vigor, P. H. *Soviet Blitzkrieg Theory.* 1983. (A British view.)

Vo Nguyen Giap. *Peoples War Peoples Army.* 1962.

Vo Nguyen Giap. *How We Won the War.* 1976.

Waismann, Friedrich. *Introduction to Mathematical Thinking.* 1959.

Wallace, Mike. "Inside Yesterday: Target USA." *CBS News,* 21 August 1979.

Watts, Alan. *The Book.* 1972.

Watts, Alan. *Tao: The Watercourse Way.* 1975.

Wernick, Robert. *Blitzkrieg.* 1976.

Westinghouse. *I Am the Punishment of God.* (Westinghouse Integrated Logistic Support No. 5.)

West Point Department of Military Art and Engineering. *Jomini, Clausewitz and Schlieffen.* 1954.

West Point Department of Military Art and Engineering. *Summaries of Selected Military Campaigns.* 1956.

Whiting, Charles. *Patton*. 1970.

Wilczek, Frank, and Betsy Devine. *Longing for the Harmonies*. 1988.

Wilson, Edward O. *On Human Nature*. 1978.

Wing, R. L. *The Art of Strategy*. 1988.

Winterbotham, F. W. *The Ultra Secret*. 1975.

Wintringham, Tom. *The Story of Weapons and Tactics*. 1943.

Wolf, Eric R. *Peasant Wars of the Twentieth Century*. 1969.

Wolf, Fred Alan. *Taking the Quantum Leap*. 1981.

Wylie, J. C. *Military Strategy*. 1967.

Wynne, G. C. *If Germany Attacks*. 1940.

Yukawa, Hideki. *Creativity and Intuition*. 1973.

Zukav, Gary. *The Dancing Wu Li Masters*. 1979.

Appendix B

Recommendations for Reform

I have been extremely critical of the Pentagon procurement process. Although I believe that my criticism is warranted, it cannot be well taken if I have nothing better to offer. As Pierre Sprey constantly reminds me, "Jim, you can't beat something with nothing." In the spirit of making my criticisms constructive, therefore, I recommend certain changes in the process by which the Pentagon develops and buys weapons. These changes are aimed at restoring integrity and honesty to the procurement process by the strengthening of checks and balances.

Many people, both in and out of government, believe that changes in procurement procedures, organizational arrangements, reporting requirements, and the like are sufficient to restore integrity to the business. Those who believe that way are saying, in essence, that the "process" is to blame for the scandalous behavior of Pentagon officials. The process makes people lie about the expected costs of a new weapon; the process makes people concoct phoney intelligence reports to support the need for a new weapon to counter a big bad threat; the process makes people suppress bad news or damaging information about the status of a weapons program; the process makes people slant analyses and interpretations of test results to favor a proposed weapon—"the process made me do it." I do not share that view.

People are what make any process work or not work. If people are inclined to lie, cheat, and steal, they will—no matter what rules and regulations govern a process. Still, certain changes to the process can make it a little more difficult for people to behave like scoundrels, and if they do their behavior and motives will be somewhat more visible. Scoundrels, of course, prefer to sneak around in the dark rather than to operate in the sunlight.

I am indebted to my colleague and fellow reformer, Chuck Spinney, for most of these recommendations. Chuck first published them in the fall of 1990 in a Fund for Constitutional Government report titled "Defense Power Games." I supported the recommendations then; with Chuck's permission, I repeat them now.

Sworn Testimony

Every Department of Defense official who testifies before Congress should be required to give sworn testimony. This will not prevent people from lying to Congress, but it will make it easier to prosecute those who knowingly and willingly commit perjury. Swearing before an Armed Services Committee that the testimony you are about to give is the truth, the whole truth, and nothing but the truth tends to set the proper atmosphere for the dialogue that follows. Currently, sworn testimony is given only on rare occasions. I think it should be the rule, not the exception.

Open Books

The Pentagon prepares a five-year budget each year. Unfortunately, it does not share this budget with Congress. The first year of the five-year program is always submitted to Congress as part of the president's annual budget. Congress receives only an executive summary of the Pentagon's plans for the four-year period beyond the president's current budget submission. The Pentagon has been known to mislead Congress with its executive summary. That is, the Pentagon, from time to time, has submitted an out-year summary that did not match its actual budget plans by

carrying two sets of books, one for Congress and one for itself. This prac- **269**
tice precludes an intelligent debate between the Pentagon and Congress
about the future direction of the Defense establishment. After all, Congress has the constitutional power to raise and equip the armed forces. I
believe that Congress should have the benefit of the Pentagon's full five-
year defense program, which is the most definitive statement of Defense
policy produced by the executive branch.

Congressional Intelligence Estimate

I recommend that every two years Congress pass a joint resolution assessing military threats that face the United States. That assessment should
be performed by the foreign relations committee of each house and
form the basis for the annual Defense debate with the executive branch.
For too long, the executive branch has held a monopoly on the analysis
of military threats, and that monopoly has been abused.

Analyses by the Pentagon prepared to justify the spending of billions
of dollars on new weapons are almost always grossly exaggerated. We had
the "bomber gap" of the 1950s, the "missile gap" of the 1960s, the "window of vulnerability" of the 1970s, and the "spending gap" of the 1980s,
all of which turned out to be pure concoctions. An independent congressional analysis of military threats will certainly keep the Pentagon's
intelligence community on its toes and result in a little more honesty in
its evaluations.

Limit to "Special Access" Programs

"Special Access," or "black," programs have mushroomed during the past
decade. As indicated earlier, these programs are classified Special Access
more to prevent critical review from within the Defense establishment
than to hide secrets from the enemy. There have been many abuses of
this restrictive category. The Pentagon must take steps to reduce such
abuses. In reality, few truly technical secrets require Special Access clearance categories, and only on extremely rare occasions.

I believe that all Special Access clearances should be revoked when a
program reaches a certain spending threshold, such as $100 million.
Adequate security precautions are associated with regular Secret or Top
Secret clearances to protect any program that gets to the serious money-
spending level.

Defense Evaluation Board

A primary theme of this book is the domination of unchecked advocacy in the Pentagon's weapons procurement process. The information that flows from the lower levels of the organizations to the top levels, where the major decisions are made, is shaped to present the best possible image of the status of a program or the best possible estimate of the future capability of a new weapon. Analyses are conducted, briefings prepared, tests constructed, reports written—all with advocacy in mind. The good news is pumped up and the bad news suppressed. If the people at the top of the chain want to determine the true state of affairs, they must develop sources of information outside the normal channels. Many people at the top are not able to do this, and others are reluctant. They may feel that if they knew the true state of affairs, they would be compelled to make unpopular decisions.

One way to counter unchecked advocacy is to establish a formal "devil's advocacy" element in the organization. I believe very strongly in this concept—the formal presentation of opposing point of view that is argued with as much vigor as the "school solution." In 1980, I was able to convince Air Force Assistant Secretary Robert Hermann to establish a "devil's advocacy" group at the Air Force Secretariat level (see chapter 6). That initiative led to honest and objective debates at the senior level during Hermann's tenure because he insisted that the Air Force play by those rules. I believe that overall Pentagon objectivity is attainable by establishing a similar group at the OSD level.

I offer the following recommendation as an effective solution to unchecked advocacy. A Defense Evaluation Board could be established as a separate regulatory agency. Patterned after the Federal Reserve Board, it would consist of five voting members appointed by the president and confirmed by Congress. Board members would serve for ten years. They would be prohibited from accepting any future employment from any firm that does business with the Pentagon—no employment, consulting, or lobbying relationships of any kind with the defense industry, either directly or indirectly. Each board member would retire at full salary after ten years of service.

The Defense Evaluation Board would have a staff of no more than one hundred people and would be physically located inside the Pentagon. Using legal certification procedures, the board would perform three basic functions designed to improve the quality of information flowing to the secretary of defense and to Congress.

First, the board would certify the accuracy of the data included in the Pentagon's five-year budget plan. An annual unclassified report to the secretary and Congress would identify the structural assumptions and policy decisions embodied in the five-year plan, as well as indicate whether sufficient funds were available for the Joint Chiefs of Staff to execute their war plans.

Second, the board would certify that the information used to support decisions to proceed with the development and production of major weapons systems accurately portrays what is known and what is not known at the time of such decisions. The board would certify that the cost estimates were arrived at independently. (Most cost estimates originate in the program manager's office. The developing agency is the prime source of all cost data.) The board would identify the uncertainties in the cost estimates and the implications of those uncertainties. Also, it would certify that the test results used to justify proceeding to the next milestone were accurately and objectively presented. Before a system could proceed into production, the board would certify that the system met or exceeded its specifications, both contractual and operational, in a realistic operational test conducted by uniformed military personnel randomly selected from operational units. *No weapon would enter production until the board certified the operational test and the test results.* The board would have the power to subpoena information from government agencies and private contractors, as well as to take sworn testimony.

Third, the board, upon request, would provide independent views and analyses to the secretary of defense and Congress on major defense policy issues.

There would be no need for a Defense Evaluation Board if key members of the OSD staff did their jobs. Sadly, this has not been the case for the past decade or so. I point particularly to the chief analyst and chief tester, the two most important members of the secretary's staff and the two biggest failures.

At the insistence of the reformers, Congress created the position of chief tester in the hope that testing reform would curtail the steady flow of untested or unproved weapons into the inventory. Unfortunately, the chief testers appointed to date have been industry touts, ineffective in the position, or totally captured by the Pentagon bureaucracy so that they were independent in name only. Nothing really changed. Adequate testing for weapons system after weapons system was waived as they went through the process, with the result that many did not work when they got to the inventory. The Air Force's B-1 bomber and M-X missile are but two examples.

David Chu was the secretary's chief analyst for eleven years. His basic job was to perform the functions that I have outlined for the Defense Evaluation Board, namely, to give the secretary an independent analysis of a weapons system's costs and effectiveness so that the secretary can make an informed decision. Too many times during the past decade, those responsibilities were abrogated in favor of the politically expedient course of action. During the Navy's A-12 debacle, the inspector general was very critical of Chu's so-called independent cost shop because it did not develop cost estimates independently of the Navy, as it should have done. The A-12 situation was not unique, and the same criticism could be leveled at countless programs.

The chief analyst should not be a team player. Rather, that individual should constantly point out situations in which the emperor has "no clothes." The chief tester should not have the attitude that "sometimes we have to buy scarecrows," as stated by Jack Krings, the first chief tester, in an interview with *Discover Magazine*, instead of purchasing real systems that actually work. Hopefully, the Defense Evaluation Board can be established and promulgate formal requirements that are necessary for thorough, objective evaluations and debate. Perhaps then, the Pentagon will be finally forced to clean up its act.

Notes

Prologue

1. *Field Manual 100-5 Operations* (Washington, D.C.: Headquarters U.S. Army, 1976), 3–6.
2. Col. John Boyd, USAF (Ret.), "A Discourse on Winning and Losing," unpublished treatise on the nature of conflict—all conflict, not just war. The latest version of the treatise was printed and distributed by the U.S. Marine Corps, August 1987, and referred to as the Green Book. The treatise has six sections: Abstract, Patterns of Conflict, Organic Design for Command and Control, The Strategic Game of ? and ?, Destruction and Creation, and Revelation. The Green Book is a reprint of Boyd's briefing charts from his 13-hour lecture on conflict. It contains unique theories and insights on the human aspects of conflict.
3. Col. Mike Wyly, USMC, teacher and Vice President, Marine Corps University, Quantico, Va., interview with author, January 1991.
4. John J. Fialka, "A Very Old General May Hit the Beaches with the Marines," *Wall Street Journal*, 9 January 1991, 1.

5. Col. John Boyd, USAF (Ret.), interview with author, March 1991.

6. Wyly, interview.

7. Boyd, interview. See also Peter Cary, "The Fight to Change How America Fights," *U.S. News & World Report*, 6 May 1991, 30; and Fred Kaplan, "The Force Was with Them," *Boston Globe*, 17 March 1991, A21.

8. Chapter 1 provides detailed documentation. One of the better references is Lt. Col. Jerauld Gentry, USAF, "The Evolution of the F-16 Multi-National Fighter Program" (unpublished student research report, no. 163, Industrial College of the Armed Forces, Washington, D.C., 1976).

Chapter 1. The Fighter Mafia

1. "Welcome to the Pentagon," Department of Defense brochure, 30 July 1981.

2. James Fallows, "Muscle-Bound Super Power: The State of America's Defense," *The Atlantic Monthly*, October 1979, 59–78.

3. Col. John Boyd, USAF (Ret.), interview with author, August 1990.

4. Ibid.

5. Maj. Barry Watts, USAF, "Fire, Movement and Tactics," *Top Gun* (Navy Fighter Weapons School Journal), Winter 1979/1980, 9.

6. Thomas P. Christie, interview with author, August 1991.

7. Lt. Col. Jerauld Gentry, USAF, "The Evolution of the F-16 Multi-National Fighter Program (unpublished student research report, no. 163, Industrial College of the Armed Forces, Washington, D.C., 1976).

8. Ibid., 10.

9. Boyd, interview.

10. Gentry, "Evolution of F-16," 11.

11. Pierre M. Sprey, interview with author, 27 August 1991. Also see Gentry, "Evolution of F-16," 16.

12. Gentry, "Evolution of F-16," 20.

13. Sprey, interview.

14. Gentry, "Evolution of F-16," 25.

15. Ibid., 27.

16. Ibid.

17. Ibid.

18. Bill Minutaglio, "Tales of the Fighter Mafia," *Dallas Life Magazine*, 3 May 1987, 14. I have also heard Everest Riccioni tell this tale many times over a glass of cheer at Sprey's house.

19. A. Ernest Fitzgerald, interview with author, December 1990.

20. Sprey, interview.

21. Boyd, interview. The secretary's decision memorandum on this subject is quoted in Gentry, "Evolution of F-16," 46.

22. Boyd, interview.

23. Gentry, "Evolution of F-16," 58. Packard's decision memorandum of 25 August 1971 led to the first flight in January 1974.

24. Sprey, interview. Many years ago, I carried a copy in my briefcase to show disbelievers.

25. Minutaglio, "Tales of the Fighter Mafia," 28.

26. Fred Kaplan, "The Little Airplane That Could Fly, if the Air Force Would Let It," *Boston Globe*, 14 March 1982.

27. I served as military assistant to the first three chairmen of the consortium steering committee, Drs. Jack Martin, Robert Hermann, and Alton Keel, Jr.

28. Col. James G. Burton, USAF, "Letting Combat Results Shape the Next Air-to-Air Missile," 1986 (study of all documented missile firings in every war involving air-to-air combat). The first and only compilation of all known missile combat data, the study was declassified and released to the public by the Department of Defense on 7 January 1987 in response to a Freedom of Information request from author James P. "Jim" Stevenson. At the request of Congressman Charles Bennett (Florida), I briefed this study to the Congressional Military Reform Caucus on 22 June 1987 at its inaugural public forum on selected defense issues.

29. Burton, "Combat Results Shape."

30. Franklin C. Spinney, Department of Defense analyst, interview with author, August 1990, and selected unclassified aircraft production and budget records.

31. Morton Mintz, "The Maverick Missile: If at First You Don't Succeed . . ." in Dina Rasor, editor, *More Bucks, Less Bang: How the Pentagon Buys Ineffective Weapons* (Washington, D.C.: Fund for Constitutional Government, 1983), 135. Mintz's work is an expanded version of a series of articles that he wrote for *The Washington Post*. The first article appeared in the *Post* on 23 February 1982, one week before a panel of senior Department of Defense officials was scheduled to meet for a decision on whether the Maverick would enter production. Preparing for the series, Mintz interviewed four of the six panel members in a joint interview. The four senior officials, known advocates of the Maverick, met thirty minutes before the Mintz interview and agreed to mislead Mintz on certain aspects of the Maverick's test results, cost, and performance. Unknown to the four senior officials, a staff aide accidentally tape recorded their conspiratorial meeting. The aide, following standard procedures, also tape recorded the full interview that followed. At the conclusion of the interview, Mintz noticed the tape recorder and asked for a copy of the tape. Without listening to what was on it, the staff aide gave the tape to Mintz. Armed with evidence of the conspiracy, Mintz wrote a blistering series of articles critical of almost every aspect of the Maverick program. The production decision meeting scheduled for 2 March 1982 was postponed for six months to let the heat subside.

32. Ibid.

33. Hans Ulrich Rudel, *Stuka Pilot*, (New York: Ballantine Books, 1958). Rudel presented further comments on his World War II experiences (translated into English by Pierre Sprey) at the Air Anti-Tank Seminar, Naval Post Graduate School, Monterey, Calif., 16 and 17 March 1977 (transcript), 3.

34. Gary Streets, Air Force aerospace engineer, letters to author, 18 and 26 August 1983, transmitting unclassified data from Air Force Combat Information Center, Wright Patterson Air Force Base, Ohio.

35. Ibid.

36. Frank Greve, "A Career Cut Mission by a Job Well Done," Knight-Ridder Newspapers (wire service), 15 November 1982; "Cost Cutter," *Time Magazine*, 7 March 1983, 27.
37. Ibid.
38. Office of Air Force History, "Aces and Aerial Victories: The United States Air Forces in South East Asia, 1965–1973," in *USAF Historian* (Washington, D.C.: Headquarters U.S. Air Force, 1976), 51–52.
39. Vernon A. Guidry, "Air Force May Restore Zip in 'Improved,' Less Agile F-16," *Baltimore Sun*, 24 July 1987, 3.

Chapter 2. To Be or to Do

1. Franklin C. Spinney, "The Plans/Reality Mismatch and Why We Need Realistic Budgeting," unclassified Department of Defense study of the projected costs of more than 150 weapons systems in the Reagan administration's proposed defense buildup. See also "The Winds of Reform," *Time Magazine*, 7 March 1983, 13.
2. Nick Kotz, *Wild Blue Yonder: Politics and the B-1 Bomber* (New York: Pantheon Books, 1988), 119–121.
3. The Force Structure Committee was one of several standing committees on the Air Staff. Its purpose was to recommend to the chief of staff the proper mix of fighters, bombers, cargo aircraft, missiles, and other weapons that would make up the total number of weapons systems in the force.
4. General Toomay often related this story to his staff. It always brought a chuckle, as well as a few nodding heads.

Chapter 3. Storm Clouds of Reform

1. "The New Defense Posture: Missiles, Missiles, and Missiles," *Business Week*, 11 August 1980, 78.
2. A proposed Air Force antitank missile called WASP was one of the so-called "brilliant missiles," of which Dr. Perry was so enamored. WASP was advertised as a small, inexpensive ($25,000) missile that could be carried in large numbers aboard a fighter-bomber. Swarms of WASPs would be launched all at once toward large enemy tank formations. The electronics in the WASPs were so sophisticated and brilliant that no two WASPs would attack the same tank. In scientific terms, this factor made WASPs very efficient.
   The first flight test of a prototype WASP missile was designed to demonstrate its ability to sort out and attack a specific tank in a group of tanks, thereby demonstrating its brilliance. Six target tanks were arranged in a column on the test range at Eglin Air Force Base, Florida. The WASP missile was programmed to find the column of tanks, fly down the length of the column, and attack the sixth tank, the last one in the column. After a successful launch from an F-4, the WASP, in fact, did locate the column of tanks, flew down its length, and counted each tank that the WASP sensors detected.

Unfortunately, the WASP miscounted; when it came to the end of the column, it had counted only five tanks. Because it was programmed to attack the sixth tank and it had only detected five, the WASP turned and headed for a second group of vehicles that it detected on another section of the test range. Once again, it failed to count to six, so it turned and headed for a column of automobiles traveling along the civilian highway just outside the boundaries of the test range. Fortunately, the missile ran out of fuel and crashed before it could fly off the test range. Otherwise, some unsuspecting civilian motorist sitting sixth in line at the stoplight would have had a terrible day.

WASP was eventually canceled because its costs grew out of sight and it turned out to be not quite as brilliant as its advocates claimed.

3. Henry Eason, "New Theory Shoots Down Old War Ideas," *Atlanta Constitution*, 22 March 1981, 1C.
4. Col. John Boyd, USAF (Ret.), "Discourse on Winning and Losing" (unpublished treatise, also known as the Green Book), August 1987, 132–137.
5. Mike Getler, "Dogfight Tacks Can Win Big Wars, Pushes Pilot Turned Tactician," *The Washington Post*, 4 January 1981, A3.
6. John J. Fialka, "Congressional Military Reform Caucus Lacks Budget, but Has Power to Provoke Pentagon," *The Wall Street Journal*, 13 April 1982, 52.
7. Gen. Bruce Palmer, USA (Ret.), *The 25 Year War* (New York: Simon & Schuster, 1985), 176, 193.
8. Fialka, "Congressional Military Reform Caucus," 52.
9. Ibid.
10. Maj. Paul H. Herbert, USA, *Deciding What Has to Be Done: General William E. DePuy and the 1976 Edition of FM 100-5 Operations*, Leavenworth Papers, no. 16 (Fort Leavenworth, Kans.; Command Studies Institute, 1988, 86–87.
11. Getler, "Dogfight Tacks," A3.
12. *U.S. News & World Report* staff, *Victory Without Triumph* (New York: Times Books, 1992), 159–164. This is an excellent account of Boyd's contribution to the change in the Army's doctrinal thinking, his influence on the Jedi Knights, and their role in the success of the Gulf War. Desert Storm Commander Gen. Norman Schwarzkopf praised the Jedi Knights on his staff for laying out the operational plans for the Gulf War.
13. Col. Mike Wyly, USMC, interview with author, January 1991.

Chapter 4. Meet Me at the Flags

1. A. Ernest Fitzgerald, interview with author, January 1991. Ernie and I have talked about this incident many times over the years.
2. Ibid.
3. Ibid.
4. A. Ernest Fitzgerald, "Overspending to Weakness," in Dina Rasor, editor, *More Bucks, Less Bang: How the Pentagon Buys Ineffective Weapons* (Washington, D.C.: Fund for Constitutional Government, 1983), 299.
5. Franklin C. Spinney, *"Defense Facts of Life"* (Washington, D.C.: Department of Defense, 5 December 1980), 123.

6. Ibid., 35.

7. Ibid., 99.

8. Ibid.

9. Franklin C. Spinney, interview with author, January 1991.

10. Ibid.

11. Ibid.

12. Ibid.

13. Ibid.

14. Ibid.

15. Ibid.

16. Henry E. Cato, Jr., Assistant Secretary of Defense for Public Affairs, Department of Defense news brief transcript, 1130, 7 December 1982.

17. "The Winds of Reform," *Time Magazine*, 7 March 1983, 12–30.

18. Ibid., 13.

19. Ibid., 15.

20. House Committee on the Budget, *Review of Defense Acquisition and Management*, 98th Cong., 1st sess., hearings of 4, 5, 18, 20, and 26 October and 8 November 1983, ser. no. 98–6 (Washington, D.C.: Government Printing Office, 1984), 196.

21. Ibid., 197.

22. Ibid., 198.

23. Robert Croteau, interview with author, January 1991.

Chapter 5. The Wheel of Conspiracy

1. Franklin C. Spinney, *Defense Facts of Life* (Washington, D.C.: Department of Defense, 5 December 1980), 99.

2. Thomas Christie, interview with author, August 1991. The TAC Air Shop was under Christie's supervision at the time.

3. Ibid.

4. Russell Murray, Director, Program Analysis and Evaluation, note to Secretary of Defense Harold Brown, 24 October 1979, with Frank MacDonald's trip report attached.

5. Antonia Cheyes, Under Secretary of the Air Force, letter to Russell Murray, 16 November 1979.

6. Willard Mitchell, Air Force Deputy Secretary for Programs and Budget, letter to Russell Murray, 16 November 1979.

7. Thomas Christie, memorandum to Russell Murray, 30 October 1979, with three attachments, all different versions of F-111D reliability data provided to Christie by the Air Force.

8. Charles Mohr, "Drop in U.S. Arms Spurs Debate on Military Policy," *The New York Times*, 24 October 1982, 1.

9. Christie, interview.

10. Ibid.

11. I have a copy of this sworn affidavit, signed and dated 16 May 1980.

12. John J. Fialka, "Congressional Military Reform Caucus Lacks Budget, but Has Power to Provoke Pentagon," *The Wall Street Journal*, 13 April 1982, 52.

13. Christie, interview.
14. Ibid.

Chapter 6. The Dickey Bird Shuffle

1. Jeffrey G. Barlow, *Critical Issues: Reforming the Military* (Washington, D.C.: The Heritage Foundation, 1981), vii.
2. Charles Mohr, "Drop in U.S. Arms Spurs Debate on Military Policy," *The New York Times*, 24 October 1982.
3. "Cost Cutter," *Time Magazine*, 7 March 1983, 19.
4. Lt. Col. Clinton D. Summerfield, USAF, Chief, Management Division, Assistant for Colonel Assignments, to Office of the Secretary of Defense, Military Personnel Division, 28 May 1982.

Chapter 7. Hollow Victory

1. Col. James G. Burton, USAF, "Test and Evaluation Perspective," unclassified briefing on test results of assorted weapons before the Defense Science Board, April 1985.
2. Ibid. For an excellent history of the troubled Maverick missile, see Morton Mintz's series of articles, "The Maverick Missile: If at First You Don't Succeed . . . A Case Study of a Defense Procurement Problem," *The Washington Post*, beginning 23 February 1982.
3. Senate Committee on Government Affairs, *Acquisition Process in the Department of Defense*, 97th Cong. 1st sess., hearing of 21 October 1981 (Washington, D.C.: Government Printing Office, 1983), 176.
4. Senate Bill S. 3001, 1 October 1982: "To Establish a Director of Operational Testing and Evaluation in the Department of Defense, and for Other Purposes," sponsored by Senators David Pryor, William Roth, and Carl Levin.
5. Col. Richard E. Guild, USAF, "Implications of Legislation Regarding Operational Testing" (unpublished student research report, National War College, May 1984), 53.
6. Senate Bill S. 1170, 28 April 1983: "To Establish a Director of Operational Testing and Evaluation, and Other Purposes," sponsored by Senators David Pryor, William Roth, and thirteen other senators.
7. Gregg Easterbrook, "DIVAD," *The Atlantic Monthly*, October 1982, 29–39.
8. Hedrick Smith, *The Power Game: How Washington Works* (New York: Random House, 1988), 168–173.
9. Dina Rasor, interview with author, September 1989. Although I had heard this story secondhand, I confirmed it with Dina in this interview.
10. Rear Adm. Isham Linder, USN (Ret.), Director, Defense Test and Evaluation, prepared statement at hearing, *Oversight of DoD's Operational Tests and Evaluation Procedures*, before the Senate Government Affairs Committee, 23 June 1983, 1.
11. Richard DeLauer, Under Secretary of Defense, letter to Senator John Tower, Chairman, Senate Armed Services Committee, 27 June 1983.

280

12. Winslow Wheeler, legislative aide to Senator Nancy Kassebaum, interview with author, July 1987.

13. Rear Adm. Isham Linder, USN (Ret.), "Test and Evaluation of SINGARS," memorandum to Secretary of Defense Caspar Weinberger, 8 March 1984.

14. Army Under Secretary James Ambrose, "SINGARS Radio," memorandum to Secretary of Defense Caspar Weinberger, 19 March 1984.

15. Senator Nancy Kassebaum informed me of Weinberger's pledge to her in a meeting several months later when it became apparent that the promise had been broken. The broken promise initially drew the Congressional Military Reform Caucus into the public controversy that raged between the Army and me between October 1984 and June 1986. Throughout the controversy, Senator Kassebaum chose not to get involved.

16. Senator Nancy Kassebaum, letter to Secretary of Defense Caspar Weinberger, 24 April 1984.

Chapter 8. Crossing the Rubicon

1. James M. Gavin, *On to Berlin* (New York: Viking, 1978), 43.

2. R. P. Hunnicut, *Sherman: A History of the American Medium Tank*, Taurus Enterprises, 261–276.

3. "MERKAVA-2," in *Defense Update*, ed. and publ. Lt. Col. D. Eshel (Ret.), Cologne, West Germany (War Data Series, no. 17, 1984), 8. See also Peter Hellman, "Israel's Chariot of Fire," *The Atlantic Magazine*, March 1985, 95.

4. MEXPO is an acronym for Middle East Exploitation. Copies are on file in Defense Technical Information Center, Cameron Station, Va.

5. Frank Greve, "Dream Weapon a Nightmare," Knight-Ridder Newspapers (wire service), 2 May 1982.

6. Ibid. The six competing bazookas were a Viper, Viper variant, Swedish-built AT-4, U.S. LAW-3, LAW-750, and UK LAW 80. Surprisingly, the Swedish-built AT-4 won the competition. Almost everyone in the defense community who was watching this competition expected the Army's Viper to win.

7. Col. James G. Burton, USAF, prepared statement for hearing, *Department of Defense Test Procedures*, before Research and Development Subcommittee, Committee on Armed Forces, House of Representatives, 99th Cong., 2d sess., 28 January 1986, Report No. HASC 99-27, 52.

8. Rear Adm. Isham Linder, USN (Ret.), Director, Defense Test and Evaluation, "Joint Live Fire Test Charter," memorandum to Director, Joint Staff (Office of Joint Chiefs of Staff), Assistant Secretary of U.S. Army (Research, Development, and Acquisition), Assistant Secretary of U.S. Navy (Research, Engineering, and Support), Assistant Secretary of U.S. Air Force (Research, Development, and Logistics), and Joint Logistics Commanders (Department of Defense), 27 March 1984.

9. Anthony Battista, staff member, House Armed Services Committee, testimony at hearing, *Department of Defense Test Procedures*, before the Research and Development Subcommittee of the House Armed Services Committee, 28 January 1986, Report No. HASC 99-27, 21. Battista's characterization of the history of the

Bradley development was corroborated by Army Vice Chief of Staff Gen. Max Thurman at the same hearing, 80.

10. Battista, testimony, *Defense Test Procedures,* 21.
11. Ibid., 25.
12. Ibid., 76.
13. Col. James G. Burton, USAF, testimony at hearing, *Department of Defense Test Procedures,* 28 January 1986, 60.
14. Percy A. Pierre, Assistant Secretary of the Army for Research, Development, and Acquisition, "IFV/CFV [Infantry Fighting Vehicle/Cavalry Fighting Vehicle, the two versions of the Bradley] Survivability Test Plan," memorandum to Under Secretary of Defense for Research and Engineering, 17 March 1980.
15. William Boly, "The $13 Billion Dud," *California Magazine,* February 1983.
16. William Boly, "The Army's $11-Billion Deathtrap," *Reader's Digest,* August 1983, condensed from *California Magazine,* February 1983.
17. F. P. Watkins, Canadian Defense Establishment, "The UK Wound Ballistics Research Programe on Behind Armour Effects," report presented at The Technical Cooperation Program (TTCP), meeting 8 of Sub-Group W, Technical Panel W-1, Terminal Effects, 15–24 October 1980, Valcartier, Quebec, Canada.
18. Ibid., 212–213.
19. Richard Vitali, Chief, Vulnerability/Lethality Division, U.S. Army Ballistic Research Laboratory, "Proposed Investigation of Behind Armor Effects Associated with Aluminum Armors," memorandum to Office of Secretary of Defense, Attn: Col. J. Burton, 31 May 1983.
20. Robert Dilger, memorandum for the record, prepared for House Armed Services Committee Investigating Team that examined author's charges of Army test rigging on Bradley tests, 1 May 1986, 11. (Dilger and I were accidentally informed of small, 73-mm warheads being used, instead of larger, standard warheads, by a technician who told us that he had been directed to use smaller ones.)
21. Ibid., 8.
22. Ibid., 9.
23. U.S. Army Environmental Hygiene Agency, "Evaluation of Toxic Hazards in M-113 Armored Personnel Carriers Resulting from Extinguishing Gasoline Fires with Automated Halon 1301 Extinguishers," Project No. 246, December 1969–October 1971 (test report, Edgewood Arsenal, Md., 23 March 1972), 8.
24. I testified before Congress on 28 January and 18 February 1986 that the atmosphere inside the Bradley after a hit was intolerable and that the vehicle was uninhabitable. My testimony led to a repetition of the toxic gas experiments by the Army in the presence of observers from the General Accounting Office. The Army Surgeon General's report on those findings was presented to the Procurement and Military Nuclear Systems Subcommittee of the House Armed Services Committee in conjunction with its 17 December 1987 hearing on Bradley live-fire test results. The classified report confirmed my original conclusions. Toxic gases turned out to be the single largest source of casualties in the Bradley tests. For unclassified excerpts from the Surgeon General's report, see Tony Capaccio, "Soldiers in Bradleys Face Toxic Gas Risk," *Defense Week,* 21 December 1987. The article stated, "The new medical analysis tends to confirm Burton's original con-

cerns. 'Oxides of nitrogen from ammunition fires pose the greatest hazard to the crew,' the Army wrote."

25. Col. James G. Burton, USAF, "Joint Live-Fire Test Program," memorandum to James P. Wade, Jr., Principal Deputy Under Secretary of Defense for Research and Engineering, 14 June 1984. An attached Appendix A listed eighteen specific actions by BRL that were the basis for the charges in the "Rubicon Memo."

26. Ibid.

27. Richard Vitali, Chief, Vulnerability/Lethality Division, Ballistic Research Laboratory, "Burton/JLF," memorandum for the record, 10 July 1984; Lt. Col. Chaunchy F. McKearn, USA, Executive Officer to Deputy Under Secretary Walt Hollis, "Bradley Fighting Vehicle Vulnerability Testing," memorandum for the record (documenting the instructions to Vitali), 9 July 1984.

28. JTCG/ME [Joint Technical Coordinating Group/Munitions Effectiveness], "Joint Live Fire (JLF) Test, Armor/Anti-Armor Systems" (proposed test plan submitted to Dr. Wade), August 1984, 19.

29. James P. Wade, Jr., Principal Deputy Under Secretary of Defense for Research and Engineering, "Joint Live Fire Test Program," memorandum for Joint Logistics Commanders, 24 August 1984. Paragraph 4 reads, in part: "Relatively few full-up combat configured tests are planned, and none on U.S. equipment until the end of 1986. This approach is not consistent with the purpose of the JLF." The test plan made no commitment to test a fully loaded Bradley at all.

30. "M-2/3 Bradley Vulnerability Tests," cover brief for transmitting proposed letter prepared by author from Dr. Wade to Dr. Jay Sculley, Army Assistant Secretary, 4 September 1984.

31. Col. James G. Burton, USAF, memorandum for the record, 19 September 1984.

32. James P. Wade, Jr., Principal Deputy Under Secretary for Defense for Research and Engineering, "Joint Live Fire Test Anti-Armor Phase," memorandum to Assistant Secretary of the Army (RD&A) [Research, Development, and Acquisition], Joint Logistics Commanders, 28 September 1984.

33. Ibid.

34. Denny Smith and Mel Levine, Members of Congress, Senator David Pryor, and Senator Charles Grassley, letter to Honorable Caspar W. Weinberger, Secretary of Defense, 27 September 1984.

35. Walter Andrews, "Opposition to Rigging of Tests Led to Ouster, DOD Aide Says," *Washington Times,* 1 October 1984, 1A.

36. Michael Gordon, "Tough Pentagon Tester May Soon Move Out," *National Journal,* 16, no. 41 (1984), 1916; Knight-Ridder Newspapers, "Colonel a Casualty of Arms-Test Fight," *Chicago Tribune,* 1 October 1984; Fred Kaplan, "Memos Cite Army Rigging of Tank Tests," *Boston Globe,* 1 October 1984, 1; Carl M. Cannon, "Critic of New Army Vehicle to Lose Position at Pentagon," *Philadelphia Inquirer,* 4 November 1984, 13C; Gerald Seib, "Army Is Faulted on Its Testing of New Vehicle," *The Wall Street Journal,* 1 October 1984, 2.

Chapter 9. Off to Alaska?

1. Editorial, "Tests the Army Should Not Shirk," *The New York Times,* 8 October 1984, A18.

2. William H. Taft IV, Deputy Secretary of Defense, letter to Honorable Denny Smith, House of Representatives, 11 October 1984. Similar letters were sent to the other three cochairmen of the Military Reform Caucus.

3. Ibid.

4. Dennis Bely, William H. Jack, and William W. Thompson, "Detailed Test Plan for the Bradley Fighting Vehicle Survivability Enhancement Program (Phase I)," (U.S. Army Ballistic Research Laboratory, Aberdeen Proving Ground, Md., January 1985), 16.

5. Col. James G. Burton, USAF, memorandum to James P. Wade, Jr., Principal Deputy Under Secretary of Defense for Research and Engineering, to inform Wade of Ambrose's actions, 21 December 1984.

6. Department of the Army, "Bradley Fighting Vehicle (BFVS) Survivability Program," unclassified priority message to Commander Army Material Command, Alexandria, Va., 30 December 1984. Paragraph 1 states: "Per USA (Under Secretary of the Army) direction on Dec 12 84, BFVS vulnerability on current configured vehicles fully loaded with fuel, ammunition and hydraulic fluid will be conducted as outlined in the October 17, 84 draft test plan as amended during the Nov 1 84 meeting at BRL." The 1 November 1984 meeting at BRL is the one during which I agreed to ten shots, with Holloway handpicking the aim points, but if no Bradleys were destroyed as a result, there would be a second series of random shots until at least one Bradley was destroyed.

7. Bely et al., "Detailed Test Plan," 48.

8. Representative Denny Smith, letter to John Herrington, Director, Office of Presidential Personnel, The White House, 4 January 1985.

9. Geraldine Strozier, "Pentagon Mistakes? They Burn Away Fast," *Cleveland Plain Dealer,* 15 March 1985, 3B.

10. I was informed of the Alaskan Air Command's response by Peter Cetrillo of the Office of the Inspector General (IG) of the Department of Defense. Cetrillo was the investigator chosen to examine the circumstances surrounding my retirement in the spring of 1986.

11. M. Sgt. Jodell Hartley, USAF, notification of PCS (Permanent Change of Station) to Elmendorf Air Force Base, Alaska, to Col. James G. Burton, USAF, 11 March 1985.

12. Congressman Mel Levine shared this conversation with me in a meeting in his office after I retired in the summer of 1986.

13. Dr. Wade told me of this conversation with Taft and Orr after the smoke cleared. He reviewed what had happened and laid out specific ground rules for me to follow for the rest of my time in the Pentagon. He asked me to please stay out of the newspapers and try to stay out of any more controversies because he was not sure that he had any green stamps left to bail me out of trouble. I was not to talk to reporters; I was to make no contact with anyone on Capitol Hill; I was to report to my superiors about any contact I received from the Hill. I followed these rules to the letter, but I still got into more trouble.

14. John Heibusch, aide to Congressman Denny Smith, conversation with author, September 1987.

15. See, for example, Howard Kirtz, "Defense Relents on Transfer of Weapon Critic," *The Washington Post,* 15 March 1985, 19; John J. Fialka, "Officer Who Ignited Army Vehicle Flap Won't Go to Alaska," *The Wall Street Journal,* 15 March 1985, 6;

284

Scripps-Howard, "Pressure from Congress Saves Weapon Testor's Job," *Cleveland Plain Dealer,* 15 March 1985, 8A.

16. Andrew Gallagher, UPI wire service, 15 March 1985.

17. Paul Davies, *The Cosmic Blueprint* (New York: Simon & Schuster, 1988), 54.

18. Lt. Col. James Ball, USAF, Executive Director, Defense Test and Evaluation, cover memorandum to James P. Wade, Jr., 5 September 1985. Ball advised Wade that I had been contacted by Nora Slatkin of the House Armed Services Committee staff. Ball had transmitted an information paper to Slatkin, which I had prepared, that outlined all of the Army agreements involved in Phases I and II of the Bradley tests. Slatkin turned this information into an amendment to the Fiscal Year 1986 Defense Authorization Bill, which was passed by both the House of Representatives and the Senate.

Chapter 10. More Dirty Games

1. Steve Vogel, "We Have Met the Enemy, and It Was Us," *The Washington Post,* 9 February 1992, F1.

2. Gen. Max Thurman, USA, Vice Chief of Staff, Department of the Army, testimony at hearing, *Department of Defense Test Procedures,* before the Research and Development Subcommittee of the House Committee on the Armed Services, 99th Cong., 2d sess., 28 January 1986, 89.

3. Col. James G. Burton, testimony at hearing, *Defense Test Procedures,* 28 January 1986, 60.

4. *Bradley Survivability Enhancement Program, Phase I Results,* unclassified Army test report prepared by Ballistic Research Laboratory, Aberdeen Proving Ground, Maryland, January 1986, 14. The data were only for the five-man M-3 Bradley, eleven-man M-113 armored personnel carrier (APC), and the eleven-man Soviet BMP. No data were included for the nine-man M-2 version of the Bradley, which makes up 90 percent of the Bradleys produced.

5. Ibid., 15. The report states: "Allowing for the differences in crew size, the casualties for BMP (Soviet) and Bradley are comparable." Yet, all charts showed a stark difference in casualty results, with the difference in the Bradley's favor.

6. Ibid., 2–3.

7. Mark Gebicke, Associate Director, National Security and International Affairs Division, General Accounting Office, testimony at hearing, *Department of Defense Reports Required by Fiscal Year 1988 Authorization Act on Live-Fire Testing of Bradley Fighting Vehicle,* before the Procurement and Military Nuclear Systems Subcommittee of the House Committee on the Armed Services, 100th Cong., 1st sess., 17 December 1987, 61. Gebicke stated: "The [enemy] tank gun, while engaging the Bradley only 17 percent of the time, accounted for 53 percent of the Bradley losses in the Operational tests."

8. Maj. E. W. Van Stee, USAF, *A Review of the Toxicology of Halogenated Fire Extinguishing Agents* (Aerospace Medical Research Laboratory, Wright Patterson Air Force Base, November 1974).

9. *Evaluation of Toxic Hazards in M-113 Armored Personnel Carriers Resulting from Extinguishing Gasoline Fires Using Automated Halon 1301 Extinguishers,* Dec. 69–Oct. 71

(Edgewood Arsenal, Md.: U.S. Army Environmental Hygiene Agency, 23 March 1972), 8.

10. Lt. Gen. Louis C. Wagner, USA, Deputy Chief of Staff for Research, Development, and Acquisition, Department of the Army, *Vulnerability Testing of the Bradley Fighting Vehicle System (BFVS)*, memorandum for the Surgeon General of the Army, 8 January 1986.

11. Fred Kaplan, "The War Business," *Regardie's*, September 1986, 128.

12. Col. James G. Burton, USAF, memorandum for the record, 22 December 1985. The memorandum documented the meeting with Donald Hicks and reporting of same to my colleagues by name, who were waiting for me after the Hicks meeting.

13. Kaplan, "The War Business," 127.

14. Lead editorial, "Another Test of Truth for the Army," *The New York Times*, 18 December 1985.

15. Directorate for Defense Information, Defense News Branch, answer to query from Fred Hiatt, *The Washington Post*, 20 December 1985. The answer was prepared by Col. Ken Hollander, USA, and Richard Thomas and provided to *The Washington Post* by Jan Bodanyi, public affairs staff official, on the same day.

16. Ibid.

17. Fred Kaplan, "Troop Vehicle at Risk, Data Say," *Boston Globe*, 20 December 1985, 23.

18. Fred Hiatt, "Critics of Bradley Fighting Vehicle Keep the Army on Defensive," *The Washington Post*, 26 December 1985, 9.

19. Tim Carrington, "Pentagon Gives In-House Critic Cold Shoulder for Questioning Tests Done on Bradley Vehicle," *The Wall Street Journal*, 31 December 1985, 28.

20. Fred Kaplan, "Pentagon Withholds Data on Troop Vehicle Trouble," *Boston Globe*, 10 January 1986, 1.

21. ABC-TV, *ABC World News Tonight*, transcript, 10 January 1986, 1.

22. Col. James G. Burton, USAF, statement prepared for a hearing of the Research and Development Subcommittee, House Committee on the Armed Services, 28 January 1986. The prepared statement was cleared for public release by Security Review, Department of Defense, *as amended*, on 27 January 1986.

23. Ibid. The original statement was cleared for public release, without amendment, on 28 January 1986.

Chapter 11. Going Public

1. Representative Melvin Price, Chairman, Research and Development Subcommittee, opening remarks at hearing, *Department of Defense Test Procedures*, Research and Development Subcommittee of the House Committee on the Armed Services, 99th Cong., 2d sess., 28 January 1986, 1.

2. Anthony Battista, testimony at hearing, *Defense Test Procedures*, 2–27.

3. Col. James G. Burton, USAF, testimony at hearing, *Defense Test Procedures*, 28 January 1986, 60.

4. Ibid., 61.

5. Bill Keller, "Working Profile: Don Hicks, Pentagon's New Yes-and-No Man on Weapons," *The New York Times*, 18 February 1986, B8.

6. R. J. S., "Hicks Attacks SDI Critics," *Science Magazine* 232 (April 1986): 444.

7. Gen. Max Thurman, USA, Vice Chief of Staff, Department of the Army, testimony at hearing, *Defense Test Procedures*, 28 January 1986, 79.

8. Ibid., 87.

9. U.S. Army, *Bradley Survivability Enhancement Program, Phase I Results,* January 1986, 11. This unclassified report was submitted to Congress on 14 March 1986, under cover of letter signed by Secretary of Defense Caspar Weinberger. I had a copy in early January (this was unknown to senior Army leaders) and used it to help in preparing my opening remarks for the hearing. I used this document because it was unclassified; the initial Army report sent to Congress on 17 December 1985 was classified "Secret."

10. Lead editorial, "The Folly of Untested Weapons," *The New York Times*, 4 February 1986.

11. Walter Andrews, "New Type of Armor to Protect Bradley," *The Washington Times*, 11 February 1986, 8.

12. Mark Gebicke, Associate Director, National Security and International Affairs Division, General Accounting Office, testimony at hearing, *Department of Defense Reports Required by Fiscal Year 1988 Authorization Act on Live Fire Testing of Bradley Fighting Vehicle*, before the Procurement and Military Nuclear Systems Subcommittee of the House Committee on the Armed Services, 100th Cong., 1st sess., 17 December 1987, 61.

13. Col. James G. Burton, USAF, "Trip Report—Bradley Phase II Test Plan Meeting," memorandum for the record, 10 February 1986.

14. Walter W. Hollis, Deputy Under Secretary of the Army (Operations Research), "Bradley Live Fire Phase II," memorandum for Brig. Gen. Donald W. Jones, 11 February 1986.

15. Col. James G. Burton, USAF, "Minimum Casualty Baseline Vehicle Configuration," memorandum for Gary Holloway, Test Director for Bradley Live-Fire Tests, Ballistic Research Laboratory, and Col. Bill Coomer, Bradley Program Manager, 12 February 1986.

16. Col. James G. Burton, USAF, opening remarks at hearing, *The Army's Bradley Fighting Vehicle*, before the Procurement and Military Nuclear Systems Subcommittee of the House Committee on the Armed Services, 99th Cong., 2d sess., 18 February 1986, 63.

17. Ibid., 61–63.

18. Donald A. Hicks, Under Secretary of Defense for Research and Engineering, "Bradley Phase II Outline Test Plan," memorandum for Vice Chief of Staff, Army, 24 February 1986.

Chapter 12. The Great Memo War

1. Joseph A. Navarro, Deputy Under Secretary of Defense (Test and Evaluation), "Bradley Phase II Outline Test Plan," memorandum for Deputy Under Secretary of the Army (Operations Research), 1 April 1986.

2. John M. Spratt, Jr., Member of Congress, letter to the Honorable Donald A. Hicks, Under Secretary of Defense for Research and Engineering, 9 April 1986.

3. Les Aspin, Chairman, and William L. Dickinson, Ranking Minority Member, House Armed Services Committee, letter to the Honorable Caspar Weinberger, Secretary of Defense, 9 April 1986; David Pryor, U.S. Senate; Chuck Grassley, U.S. Senate; Denny Smith, Member of Congress; and Mel Levine, Member of Congress, letter to the Honorable Caspar Weinberger, Secretary of Defense, 9 April 1986; Mel Price, Charles Bennett, Beverly B. Byron, Frank McCloskey, et al., letter to the Honorable Caspar Weinberger, Secretary of Defense, 9 April 1986.

4. Samuel S. Stratton, Chairman, Subcommittee on Procurement and Military Nuclear Systems, Committee on the Armed Services, House of Representatives, letter to the Honorable Caspar Weinberger, Secretary of Defense, 10 April 1986.

5. Tom Donnelly, "Pentagon, Hill Clash on Fate of Bradley Live-Fire Test Advocate," *Defense News,* 14 April 1986, 3.

6. Department of Defense, Office of the Inspector General, Special Inquiries, report of investigation, Case No. S860000068, 15 December 1986, 8.

7. Caspar Weinberger, Secretary of Defense, letter to the Honorable Denny Smith, House of Representatives, 16 April 1986. The same letter was sent to all senators and members of Congress who had written to Weinberger on my behalf the week earlier. Paragraph 1 of this letter stated: "I expect that this series [Bradley Live-Fire Tests Phase IIA (BRL vehicle)] will be completed in June; however, if there is a delay, the Air Force will allow Colonel Burton to remain with us until that effort is completed and the report is submitted to the Committees as requested. Colonel Burton was advised of this possibility on 7 April 1986."

This statement is partially correct. On 7 April 1986, Dr. Navarro told me that he would try to make such an arrangement. *He never notified me that he was able to get Air Force agreement.*

Paragraph 3 of Weinberger's letter, in reference to testing the Minimum Casualty Baseline Vehicle, stated: ". . . although he will be in his new assignment when the test commences, the Air Force will make him available to us again during this period of testing to assist us in whatever way possible." I was never informed of this arrangement until after I had signed formal papers agreeing to retire on 17 April 1986, one day after Weinberger sent this letter to Congress. General Jones admitted that I was not informed of this in a sworn statement to the Department of Defense Inspector General. See ibid., 13.

8. Col. James G. Burton, USAF, "Bradley Phase II Tests," memorandum for Dr. Joseph Navarro, Deputy Under Secretary of Defense (Test and Evaluation), 15 April 1986.

9. Charles Mohr, "Tests of Bradley Armored Vehicle Criticized," *The New York Times,* 18 April 1986, A20.

10. Fred Kaplan, "Army Manipulated Test, Memo Shows," *Boston Globe,* 17 April 1986, 1.

11. Ibid.

12. Myra MacPherson, "The Man Who Made War on a Weapon," *The Washington Post,* 8 May 1986, C1.

13. Lt. Col. Chaunchy F. McKearn, USA, Military Assistant to Deputy Under Secretary of the Army (Operations Research), "Meeting with Dr. Navarro Concerning

288   Random Aim Points for the BFV Live Fire Tests," memorandum for the record, 18 April 1986.

14. Ibid., 2.

15. Paul Bedard, "Bradley Faces Renewed Scrutiny," *Defense Week*, 28 April 1986, 2.

16. Col. James G. Burton, USAF, "Bradley Phase II Shot Selection Scheme," memorandum for the record, 2 May 1986.

17. Nora Slatkin, Joseph Cirincione, Carl Bayer, and William Fleshman, staff members of House Armed Services Committee, "House Armed Services Committee Inquiry into the Bradley Live Fire Test Program," report to the Committee on Armed Services, House of Representatives, May 1986, vi.

18. Ibid., 5.

19. Fred Kaplan, "War Business," *Regardie's*, September 1986, 242.

20. Dr. Perry Studt, Statistics and Operations Research Group of Los Alamos National Laboratories, "Statistical Aspects of Live Fire Tests." A copy was transmitted to author under memorandum of 21 April 1986 from Hunter Woodall, Jr., Army staff.

21. Walter W. Hollis, Deputy Under Secretary of the Army (Operations Research), letter to Martin Goland, Southwest Research Institute, San Antonio, Tex., 9 April 1986. Goland was chairman of the National Academy of Sciences panel that Hollis had invited to examine the shot selection methodology selected by the Army. This letter advised Goland that he should invite me to address the panel.

22. Donald A. Hicks, Under Secretary of Defense for Research and Engineering, and James R. Ambrose, Under Secretary of the Army, letter to the Honorable Samuel S. Stratton, Chairman, Subcommittee on Procurement and Military Nuclear Systems, Committee on the Armed Services, House of Representatives, 5 June 1986.

23. Col. James G. Burton, USAF, letter to Martin Goland, Chairman, Panel on Vulnerability Analysis, Board of Army Science and Technology, National Research Council [National Academy of Sciences], 12 June 1986.

24. James O'Bryon, Director, Joint Live Fire Test Program, testimony at hearing, *Department of Defense Reports Required by Fiscal Year 1988 Authorization Act on Live Fire Testing of Bradley Fighting Vehicle*, before the Procurement and Military Nuclear Systems Subcommittee, of the House Committee on the Armed Services, 100th Cong., 1st sess., 17 December 1987, 9.

25. Lt. Col. Chaunchy F. McKearn, USA, "Review of Col. Burton's MFR on Bradley Phase II Shot Selection Methodology Dated 2 May 1986," memorandum for Walt Hollis, James Ambrose, Gen. Max Thurman, et al., 13 May 1986.

26. Col. James G. Burton, USAF, "Bradley Phase II Shot Selection Scheme," memorandum for the record, 30 June 1986. This final shot in the "Great Memo War" led to Raymond Pollard sending a letter to Walt Hollis on 5 July 1986, in which he admitted that he had made a mathematical error with the famous ellipse. My respect for Pollard increased several notches when he admitted his mistake.

Case Study—The Navy Runs Aground

1. Molly Moore, "Stealth Jet for Navy Is Cancelled," *The Washington Post*, 8 January 1991, A1.

2. Peter Elkind, "The Double Life of Paul Thayer," *Texas Monthly,* September 1984, **289** 146.
3. Tom Breen, "A Chat with John Lehman," *Inside the Navy,* 18 November 1991, 5.
4. Elkind, "Double Life of Paul Thayer," 252.
5. Kenneth B. Noble, "U.S. Steps Against Thayer Seen," *The New York Times,* 29 December 1983, D1.
6. Elkind, "Double Life of Paul Thayer," 253.
7. Breen, "Chat with John Lehman," 5.
8. Chester Paul Beach, Jr., Principal Deputy General Counsel for the Navy, "A-12 Administrative Inquiry," memorandum for the Secretary of the Navy, 28 November 1990.
9. Ibid., 2.
10. Ibid., 34.
11. H. Lawrence Garrett III, Secretary of the Navy, testimony at joint hearing, *The Navy's A-12 Aircraft Program,* before the Procurement and Military Nuclear Systems Subcommittee, Research and Development Subcommittee, and Investigations Subcommittee of the House Committee on the Armed Services, 101st Cong., 2d sess., 10 December 1990, 76.
12. Beach, "A-12 Administrative Inquiry," 1–30.
13. "Chronology of A-12 Warning Flags," informal report prepared by the staff of the House Armed Services Committee and furnished to all committee members. The undated document is in the form of a desk calendar with a listing of key events in the A-12's history between the dates of 13 January 1988, when the contract was awarded, and 26 April 1990, when Secretary of Defense Richard Cheney testified before the House Armed Services Committee: "The A-12 will have . . . first operational capability in 1994."
14. Congressman Nicholas Mavroules, Chairman, Subcommittee on Investigations, House Committee on the Armed Services, opening remarks (18 April 1991) at subcommittee hearing, "*A-12 Acquisition,*" 102d Cong. 1st sess., 9 and 18 April and 18, 23, and 24 July 1991, 122.
15. Capt. Lawrence Elberfeld, USN, testimony at hearing, *A-12 Acquisition,* 178.
16. Chris D. Aldridge, Professional Staff Member, House Committee on the Armed Services, testimony at hearing, *A-12 Acquisition,* 129–130. Aldridge testified in lieu of Deborah D'Angelo, who was a reluctant witness. Aldridge's comments were based on an extensive interview with D'Angelo.
17. Elberfeld, testimony at hearing, *A-12 Acquisition,* 150.
18. Ibid., 188.
19. Congressman John Conyers, Chairman, Legislation and National Security Subcommittee, House Committee on Government Operations, opening remarks at subcommittee hearing, *Deferment Actions Associated with the A-12 Aircraft,* 102d Cong., 1st sess., 11 April and 24 July 1991, 1.
20. Beach, "A-12 Administrative Inquiry," 21–22.
21. Ibid., 22.
22. Gen. Merrill McPeak, Chief of Staff, U.S. Air Force, letter to Congressman Andrew Ireland, 9 July 1991.
23. Ibid.
24. Garrett, testimony at joint hearing, *Navy's A-12 Aircraft Program,* 79.
25. Beach, "A-12 Administrative Inquiry," 22.

290

26. Congressman Andrew Ireland, letter to Derek Vander Schaaf, Department of Defense Deputy Inspector General, 27 February 1991. Ireland complained of retribution against Hafer and D'Angelo for their roles in the A-12 controversy.

27. Richard Cheney, Secretary of Defense, "Major Aircraft Review," memorandum for Deputy Secretary of Defense, 19 December 1989. Cheney directed the staff to prepare a major review of the Air Force's B-2, C-17, and Advanced Tactical Fighter and the Navy's A-12 programs during the following spring.

28. Charlie Murphy, aide to Congressman Andrew Ireland, "'Lost' CAIG Documents," memorandum for the record, 12 September 1991. Letters were exchanged between Congressman Ireland (17 September 1991) and OSD Inspector General Susan J. Crawford (20 December 1991). Ireland was concerned that Commander Beach's notes were relevant to the many investigations but were conveniently never found in time for consideration. Crawford informed him that they were still trying to find the notes.

29. Beach, "A-12 Administrative Inquiry," 24.

30. Robert L. Koenig, "Navy: McDonnell Faked A-12 Display," *St. Louis Post-Dispatch*, 25 July 1991, 1.

31. Beach, "A-12 Administrative Inquiry," 24.

32. Ibid., 25.

33. Capt. Lawrence Elberfeld, USN, and Congressman Andrew Ireland, dialogue during hearing, *A-12 Acquisition*, 180.

34. Beach, "A-12 Administrative Inquiry," 25.

35. Ibid., 26.

36. Ibid.

37. Ibid., 27.

38. Congressman Les Aspin, opening statement at joint hearing, *Navy's A-12 Aircraft Program*, 1.

39. Beach, "A-12 Administrative Inquiry," 17.

40. Ibid., 17–20. Also, Elberfeld, opening remarks at hearing, *A-12 Acquisition*, 136.

41. Beach, "A-12 Administrative Inquiry," 18.

42. Ibid., 20. Thompson withheld the information for three reasons: he felt that it was not important enough to warrant alarm at the secretariat level; he did not want to jeopardize the trust of the uniformed Navy by "ratting" on them; and he felt that it was the job of Captain Elberfeld and his admiral bosses, not him, to inform the Navy secretariat.

43. Ibid.

44. Elberfeld, testimony at hearing, *A-12 Acquisition*, 173.

45. Beach, "A-12 Administrative Inquiry," 20.

46. Rick Wartzman and David J. Jefferson, "Delays in A-12 Seen Leading to Write-Offs," *The Wall Street Journal*, 11 June 1990, A4.

47. Gerald A. Cann, Assistant Secretary of the Navy for Research, Development, and Acquisition, letter to Congressman Andrew Ireland, 20 March 1991.

48. Gerald A. Cann, letter to Congressman Andrew Ireland, 15 April 1991. Cann was employed by General Dynamics Corporation from 4 January 1988 (one week before the A-12 contract was signed) until he became assistant secretary of the

Navy on 12 March 1990 (two weeks before Gary Christle revealed the $1 billion cost overrun).

49. Beach, "A-12 Administrative Inquiry," 35.

50. Susan J. Crawford, Inspector General, Department of Defense, testimony at joint hearing, *Navy's A-12 Aircraft Program*, 89.

51. Garrett, opening remarks at joint hearing, *Navy's A-12 Aircraft Program*, 56.

52. Derek J. Vander Schaaf, Deputy Inspector General, Department of Defense, letter to Congressman Andrew Ireland, 10 December 1991.

53. Congressman Lawrence J. Hopkins, testimony at hearing, *A-12 Acquisition*, 133.

54. Office of Assistant Secretary of Defense for Public Affairs, "DOD Postpones Collecting Payment For A-12 Contract," news release, 6 February 1991.

55. Frank C. Conahan, Assistant Comptroller General, General Accounting Office, prepared statement at hearing, *Deferment Actions Associated with A-12*, 24 July 1991, 153.

56. Congressman John Conyers, Jr., opening remarks at hearing, *Deferment Actions Associated with A-12*, 145–146.

57. Eleanor Spector, Director of Defense Procurement, opening statement at hearing, *Deferment Actions Associated with A-12*, 51.

58. Hebert Lanese, Senior Vice President for Finance, McDonnell Douglas, and Donald Putnam, Corporate Director of Contracts and Technical Analysis, General Dynamics Corporation, testimony at hearing, *Deferment Actions Associated with A-12*, 11 April 1991, 122, 125.

59. David O. Cook, Director of Administration, Office of the Secretary of Defense, "1990 Senior Executive Service Presidential Awards," memorandum for Chairman, Joint Chiefs of Staff et al., 11 January 1991.

60. Ibid.

61. Adam Goodman, "A-12 Chief Got Job Quickly," *St. Louis Post-Dispatch*, 12 January 1991, 1.

62. Congressman Andrew Ireland, letter to President George Bush, 10 December 1990; letter to Vice President Dan Quayle, 9 July 1991; letter to Richard Cheney, Secretary of Defense, 10 January 1991; and a series of letters to H. Lawrence Garrett III, Secretary of the Navy, beginning 18 January 1991 and continuing through the spring of 1991.

63. H. Lawrence Garrett III, Secretary of the Navy, letter to Congressman Andrew Ireland, 5 February 1991.

64. Andy Pasztor, "Navy Head Reversing Himself, Concedes He Got Early Word on A-12 Cost Overrun," *The Wall Street Journal*, 9 April 1991, A24.

65. Ibid.

66. "Navy Cost Analyst Warned A-12 Program Manager of Cost Overruns," *Aviation Week and Space Technology*, 29 July 1991, 24.

67. David S. Steigman, "Elberfeld Resigns; Blistering Hearings Held on A-12," *The Navy Times*, 29 July 1991, A12. The news of Elberfeld's request to retire and have his name removed from the promotion to admiral list was confirmed in H. Lawrence Garrett III, Secretary of the Navy, letter to Congressman Andrew Ireland, 30 September 1991.

68. Steigman, "Elberfeld Resigns," 24.

Epilogue

1. I watched on C-SPAN as this debate and vote by the House unfolded on 11 August 1986. The arguments for canceling the Bradley were primarily based on its vulnerability in combat. The arguments against canceling it were based on saving jobs at defense plants around the country.

2. The National Defense Authorization Act for Fiscal Year 1987 required the Department of Defense to conduct the Phase II tests on both the BRL-designed vehicle and the Minimum Casualty Baseline Vehicle. Just to make sure the Army got the message, Congressman Charles Bennett of Florida offered an amendment to the National Defense Authorization Act for Fiscal Year 1988, approved by both the House and Senate, which restricted production of the Bradley until the Phase II tests were completed and the results reported to Congress. Production funds would have ceased after December 1987 if the Army had not complied. See U.S. Congress, House of Representatives, 100th Cong. 1st sess., 1987, for the debate on the amendment offered by Bennett.

3. James O'Bryon, assistant deputy director, Defense Research and Engineering (Live-Fire Testing), statement at hearing, *Department of Defense Reports Required by Fiscal Year 1988 Authorization Act on Live-Fire Testing of the Bradley Fighting Vehicle*, before the Procurement and Military Nuclear Systems Subcommittee, Committee of the Armed Services, House of Representatives, 100th Cong. 1st sess., 17 December 1987, 9.

4. Ibid.

5. Lt. Gen. Donald S. Pihl, USA, testimony at hearing, *Defense Reports Required*, 148.

6. Col. James G. Burton, USAF (Ret.), testimony at hearing, *Defense Reports Required*, 73, 99, confirmed by O'Bryon's testimony, same pages. Mr. O'Bryon: "What I am saying, what we have demonstrated is, if you stow the TOWs on the outside [of the Bradley], we can successfully isolate the crew from catastrophic injury."

   Mark Gebicke, testifying for the General Accounting Office, 61–63, agreed with me that the 25-mm ammunition compartments worked and were a good idea to incorporate into the Bradley design. He also stated that, with a little more work, the external stowage of the TOW missiles also could be incorporated.

   The empirical evidence was overwhelming that external stowage of fuel and ammunition saved countless lives, but the Army was not willing to go through the trouble of redesigning the Bradleys to accommodate these features.

7. Conclusions contained in unclassified portions of the Army's report of test results provided to the Procurement and Military Nuclear Systems Subcommittee (Stratton Subcommittee) in support of the 17 December 1987 hearing. See portions quoted in Toni Cappacio, "Soldiers in Bradleys Face Toxic Gas Risk," *Defense Week*, 21 December 1987. James O'Bryon, assistant deputy director, Defense Research and Engineering (Live-Fire Testing) Program, restated this finding in "Model Adequacy in Test and Evaluation," *Army Research, Development and Acquisition Bulletin*, November–December 1990, 31. He pointed out that computer models of vulnerability completely ignore casualties from toxic gases, even though toxic gases were the single largest source of casualties in the Bradley tests.

8. Conversations with O'Bryon, January 1991.

9. Ibid. Also see O'Bryon, "Model Adequacy," 31.

10. National Defense Authorization Act for Fiscal Year 1986, Public Law 99-145, 99 Stat. 583, required all tracked vehicles, tanks, and armored personnel carriers to undergo live-fire testing. National Defense Authorization Act for Fiscal Year 1987, Public Law 99-661, 100 Stat. 3816, expanded the requirement to include all weapons systems.

11. Pihl, testimony at hearing, *Defense Reports Required*, 165.

12. Ibid., 31–32.

13. Sarah A. Christy, "Beefed Up Bradleys Sent to the Gulf," *Defense Week*, 7 January 1991, 1.

14. Fred Reed, "Let's Reform the Military Reformers," *The Washington Post*, Outlook section, 11 October 1987, H1.

15. Barton Gellman, "U.S. Bombs Missed 70% of Time," *The Washington Post*, 16 March 1991, A1.

16. Barton Gellman, "Disputes Delay Gulf War History," *The Washington Post*, 28 January 1991, A14.

17. Barton Gellman, "Air Force Released Misleading Chart to 'Sell' Stealth," *Aerospace Daily*, 13 November 1991, 237.

18. Ibid.

19. Michael White, "Stealth Defence Pierced," *The Guardian*, 25 March 1991, 1.

20. Air Force Chief of Staff Senior Statesmen briefing to retired Air Force generals, 19 March 1991.

21. Brian Duffy, Peter Cary, Bruce Auster, and Joseph L. Galloway, "A Desert Storm Accounting," *U.S. News & World Report*, 16 March 1992. 35.

22. Air Force Senior Statesmen briefing.

23. Rick Atkinson and Barton Gellman, "Schwarzkopf Sees No Evidence Iraqis Are Close to Collapse," *The Washington Post*, 31 January 1991, A21.

24. Gellman, "U.S. Bombs Missed 70%," A1.

25. Richard Mackenzie, "A Conversation with Chuck Horner," *Air Force Magazine*, June 1991, 60.

26. Air Force Senior Statesmen briefing.

27. John J. Fialka, "A-10 'Warthog,' A Gulf Hero, Would Fly to Scrap Heap if Air Force Brass Has Its Way," *The Wall Street Journal*, 29 March 1991, 12.

28. Jack Anderson, "The Hero That Almost Missed the War," *The Washington Post*, 5 March 1991, C9.

29. Joby Warrick, "Air Force Gives Itself an A-Plus on War Role," *Air Force Times*, 13 May 1991, 25.

30. Enemy targets destroyed by the A-10 units—confirmed:

Tanks	987
Artillery	926
Armored personnel carriers	501
Trucks	1,106
Command vehicles	249
Military structures	112
Radars	96
Helicopters (shot down)	2
Bunkers	72
Anti-aircraft artillery (AAA)	50

Command posts	28
SCUD missiles	51
FROG missiles	11
Surface to air missiles (SAMs)	9
Fuel tanks	8
Fighter aircraft (on the ground)	10

Most reformers were surprised to learn that the Maverick anti-tank missile turned out to be a popular weapon that was used by both A-10 and F-16 pilots going after tanks. The reformers were highly critical of the Maverick in the late 1970s and early 1980s. The Air Force reports that most tanks were destroyed by Mavericks. A total of 5,013 Mavericks were launched (at $144,000 each). The number of destroyed tanks listed above suggests that many Mavericks either missed or were unwittingly launched against much softer targets. The 30-mm gun proved to be an extremely lethal weapon against a wide range of targets. Almost one million rounds were fired (at $23 each) and resulted in most of the target damage listed above. Source: Fahd Squad Operation Desert Storm Combat Recap.

31. Battle Staff Directive No. 7, "CENTAF Battle Staff Meeting," 20 January 1991/0500L. Horner's quote was transmitted to A-10 units with message: "Well done Fahd Squad."

32. Reuter News Service, transcript of Gen. Norman Schwarzkopf's press conference of 27 February 1991, *The Washington Post*, 28 February 1991, A35–A36. This is the famous press conference in which Schwarzkopf explained the game plan and how the first three days of the ground war unfolded.

33. Lt. Col. Peter S. Kindsvatter, USA, "VII Corps in the Gulf War," *Military Review*, February 1992, 18. Kindsvatter, a Jedi Knight graduate of the Army's School of Advanced Military Studies, was the official historian of Gen. Frederick Franks's VII Corps during the war.

34. Duffy et al., "Desert Storm Accounting," 36. Interview with General Franks.

35. Gen. H. Norman Schwarzkopf, USA (Ret.), *It Doesn't Take a Hero* (New York: Linda Grey Bantam Books, 1992), 380.

36. Bruce Ingersol and Patrick Oster, "M-1," *Chicago Sun-Times*, 26 April 1981. More than a decade ago, Army officials expressed concern about the M-1's limited mileage—4 gallons per mile. Since 1981, the fuel mileage problem apparently has gotten worse, not better. U.S. General Accounting Office, *Operation Desert Storm: Early Performance Assessment of Bradley and Abrams* [M-1 and M-1A1 tanks], Report B-247224, 10 January 1992, reports that M-1A1s consumed 7 gallons per mile in the Gulf War.

37. General Accounting Office, *Operation Desert Storm*, 18.

38. Ibid., 29.

39. Kindsvatter, "VII Corps in Gulf War," 22; confirmed by Schwarzkopf in his 27 February press conference.

40. Duffy et al., "Desert Storm Accounting," 35.

41. Kindsvatter, "VII Corps in Gulf War," 37.

42. Reuter News Service, transcript of Schwarzkopf's 27 February 1991 press conference, A35–A36.

43. Duffy et al., "Desert Storm Accounting," 36.

44. Tom Donnelly, "Battles," *Army Times*, 24 February 1992, 8.

45. Schwarzkopf, *It Doesn't Take a Hero*, 463.

46. Ibid., 433.

47. Ibid., 463.

48. Ibid., 465.

49. Ibid., caption under picture of Schwarzkopf and McCaffrey between pages 338 and 339.

50. Ibid., 456.

51. Peter L. DeCoursey, "General Blames Threats on Heat of Conflict," *Reading (Pa.) Times,* 1 March 1992, 3.

52. Ibid.

53. Kindsvatter, "VII Corps in Gulf War," 32.

54. Donnelly, "Battles," 16.

55. DeCoursey, "General Blames Threats," 3.

56. Joseph L. Galloway, "The Point of the Spear," *U.S. News & World Report,* 11 March 1991, 32.

57. Steve Vogel, "We Have Met the Enemy. And It Was Us." *The Washington Post,* 9 February 1992, F1.

58. General Accounting Office, *Operation Desert Storm,* 5.

59. Donnelly, "Battles," 18.

60. Kindsvatter, "VII Corps in Gulf War," 17. This information correlates with General Accounting Office, *Operation Desert Storm,* 24.

61. Donnelly, "Battles," 16.

62. Hanson Baldwin, *Tiger Jack* (Fort Collins, Colo.: The Old Army Press, 1979), 156.

63. Maj. Richard J. Bestor, USA, et al., *Armor in Exploitation (The Fourth Armored Division Across France to the Moselle River),* research report, Committee 13, Officers Advanced Course, Armored School, Fort Knox, Ky., May 1949, 34.

64. Reuter News Service, transcript of Schwarzkopf's 27 February 1991 press conference, A36.

65. Schwarzkopf, *It Doesn't Take a Hero,* 468–471.

66. Ibid., 470.

67. Duffy et al., "Desert Storm Accounting," 37. In his memoirs, Schwarzkopf blames the confusion on the White House for changing the cease-fire time. I queried Duffy and colleagues, and they stand by their version. Both may be correct.

68. Schwarzkopf, *It Doesn't Take a Hero,* 475.

69. Ibid. See also DeCoursey, "General Blames Threats," 3, in which Franks claimed that Schwarzkopf was given erroneous information. Franks confirmed that he had been given the task of cutting the retreat highway but failed to get there before the Republican Guard and seven hundred tanks escaped.

70. DeCoursey, "General Blames Threats," 17.

71. Gen. Norman Schwarzkopf, transcript of television interview, WETA-TV, *Talking with David Frost,* 27 March 1991. New York: Journal Graphics Inc., 12.

72. Ibid., 8.

73. Schwarzkopf, *It Doesn't Take a Hero,* 466.

74. General Accounting Office, *Operation Desert Storm,* 16.

75. Department of Defense, *Conduct of the Persian Gulf War: Final Report to Congress,* pursuant to Title V of the Gulf Conflicts Supplemental Authorization and Personnel Benefits Act of 1991, Public Law 102-25, April 1992, M-4.

76. Maj. Gen. Peter McVey, USA, presentation at Combat Vehicle Survivability Conference, Gaithersburg, Md., 15 April 1991, sponsored by American Defense Preparedness Association. This quote was relayed to me by several people who were present at the conference, all of whom wish to remain anonymous.

Index

A-6, 215, 216

A-10: close air support mission of, 22, 26; design and development of, 24–26, 294n.30; and Fighter Mafia, 21–22, 26, 27; in Gulf War, 25–27, 241–43, 293n.30; Sprey as father of, 3, 241; as symbol of Reform Movement, 241–42. *See also* Fighter Mafia

A-12: cancellation of, 47, 213, 229; Cheney and, 222–24; and cost analysts' warnings of trouble, 219–21, 223–24; and cover-up attempt, 225–26, 227; excess progress payments at cancellation of, 217, 220, 229–30; first production lot option approval of, 225–26; hearings on, 218–19, 227, 230, 232; investigations of, 218, 227–29, 230, 232; origins of, 214, 215–17; program difficulties revealed to Navy, 218, 224–25, 226; as subject of 1990 Major Aircraft Review, 221, 222–23, 228. *See also* Elberfeld, Lawrence G.; Navy

Acquisition Review Council, 120, 122, 123–24, 130

Aerial Attack Study, 12

Air Force, U.S.: Air Staff and TAC Air Shop, 88–94, 99–100; and "The Chief's Group," 91–92; close air support mission of, 22–23, 24–26; Coronas, 32; decision-making process of, 29–31; and Gulf War, 21, 23, 239–43, 254; interdiction mission of, 23–24, 84; and Key West Agreement, 22; and "Sleez" affair, 89–91

"Air Land Battle," 51–53, 243

Air National Guard. *See* National Guard

Aldridge, Edward C. (Pete), 26

Allen, Lew, 85–86, 87, 90, 92–93, 107–8

Aluminum vaporifics tests, 137–39, 140, 172, 281n.24

Ambrose, James R., 119, 123–24, 136, 152–53, 209

Armed Services Committee: and A-12

Index

Index

Index

About the Author

James G. Burton retired from the U.S. Air Force as a colonel in 1986. He grew up in Normal, Illinois, and was a member of the first class to graduate from the Air Force Academy in June 1959. He earned an M.B.A. at Auburn University in 1969 and also studied mechanical engineering at the graduate level there. He was the first academy graduate to attend all three military professional schools: Squadron Officers School, the Air Command and Staff College, and the Industrial College of the Armed Forces.

After flying tankers for the Strategic Air Command, Burton specialized in the acquisition and testing of weapons systems. For fourteen years he worked in the Pentagon, becoming aligned with the small group of reformers who sought to ensure that the government got its money's worth from military suppliers and contractors.

In the mid-1980s he clashed with the Army over the vulnerability of the Bradley Fighting Vehicle to antiarmor weapons. The changes made to the design of the vehicle—as a result of the tests Burton supervised— saved many lives during the Gulf War. Colonel Burton now resides with his wife, Lina, in rural Aldie, Virginia.

THE NAVAL INSTITUTE PRESS

THE PENTAGON WARS
Reformers Challenge the Old Guard

Designed by Karen L. White

Set in Baskerville and Placard Condensed Bold
by BG Composition
Baltimore, Maryland

Printed on 50-lb. Glatfelter A-50 Hi Opaque
    smooth antique white
and bound in Holliston Roxite B vellum
by The Maple-Vail Book Manufacturing Group
    York, Pennsylvania